BLUEPRINT TO THE DIGITAL ECONOMY

BLUEPRINT TO THE DIGITAL ECONOMY

CREATING WEALTH IN THE ERA OF E-BUSINESS

EDITED BY

Don Tapscott,
Alex Lowy,
AND David Ticoll

ASSOCIATE EDITOR,
NATALIE KLYM

McGraw-Hill
New York   San Francisco   Washington, D.C.   Auckland   Bogotá
Caracas   Lisbon   London   Madrid   Mexico City   Milan
Montreal   New Delhi   San Juan   Singapore
Sydney   Tokyo   Toronto

Library of Congress Cataloging-in-Publication Data

Blueprint to the digital economy / edited by Don Tapscott, Alex Lowy,
and David Ticoll : associate editor Natalie Klym.
    p.   cm.
    Includes index.
    ISBN 0-07-063349-5 (alk. paper)
    1. Information technology—Economic aspects
    2. Telecommunication—Technological innovations. 3. Electronic
commerce. I. Tapscott, Don, date. II. Lowy, Alex.
III. Ticoll, David. IV. Klym, Natalie.
HC79.I55B57 1998
658.4'038—dc21   98-16041
                                      CIP

McGraw-Hill

A Division of The McGraw-Hill Companies

  2 3 4 5 6 7 8 9 0 DOC/DOC 9 0 3 2 1 0 9 8

ISBN 0-07-063349-5

CONTENTS

PREFACE AND ACKNOWLEDGMENTS

*B*lueprint to the Digital Economy grew out of a two-year, multi-client research and consulting program conducted by the Alliance for Converging Technologies. Launched in 1994, this was the Alliance's first major undertaking. It attracted over 35 corporate and government sponsors. Anticipating the revolutionary impact of the World Wide Web, the program created working models of inter-networked enterprises where rich, multimedia-based exchanges would become commonplace. The research posited a host of provocative "what if?" questions and attempted to forecast the future based on creative interpretations of technology, social, and industry trends.

In April 1994, Netscape launched the Navigator browser, and "out-of-the-box" speculation became reality. The hitherto arcane communications platform of the Internet suddenly became available to all, and, almost overnight, we began to feel the effects of an internetworked world.

The idea of a book on these new realities, written by leaders of some of the world's most influential corporations, seemed a natural next step. The initiatives and insights of these organizations represent in a tangible way the state of progress made thus far, the visions propelling R&D investments around the globe, and their concerns about what is known and what is possible.

You might ask (as some of our contributors did) why we chose to publish these chapters as a book rather than in digital format. Furthermore, why the title *Blueprint*, which connotes a static, inflexible paper document based on pencil drawings?

A book conveys a unique sort of message. Compared with an online forum, for example, the book publishing process provides more time for idea development and reflection. Likewise, readers are expected to invest a little more of themselves to extract value. And while some individual facts may become dated in the near term, the lessons learned and analysis often prove invaluable for a long time to come. Most importantly, a book can permanently document an important moment.

Why call it a *Blueprint*? On the surface it appears antithetical to the just-in-time agility our contributors describe. But we have observed that there is indeed an underlying logic and order to the emerging digital organizational form. This form is network-enabled, interenterprise, and core competency based. Customers are integrated; knowledge is actively and freely created and exchanged. What we are witnessing is the emergence of a new kind of blueprint; perhaps hard to decipher, but no less essential.

MANY THANKS

This book is the product of many peoples' hard work. First and foremost, we are grateful to the 23 contributors whose careful and generous efforts made the book possible. Fourteen hold senior positions in their respective organizations, and already must respond to more than enough demands for their time and attention. During the writing of the book, several contributors were promoted to more senior positions, while two left their companies to start new careers. Of the companies represented, some have faced significant market challenges, while others have risen to new heights. Through all this, the commitment and responsiveness of the authors was tremendous. Not only did they work long and hard to deliver their best thinking, but they willingly endured "enriching" challenges and suggestions from our editorial team.

In addition to the leaders themselves, we are indebted to their organizations for supporting their involvement, and for agreeing to share strategies and lessons. We thank the writing and research teams who worked in support of the contributors, helping to make each chapter as complete and authoritative as possible.

Toward the middle of the project, we realized that a number of vital topics had not been addressed. To fill these gaps, we turned to respected colleagues from around the world to request contributions on subjects we believed they understood better than anyone else. Sometimes under the most intense of conflicting circumstances, they each came through with superb material.

James Moore, author of *The Death of Competition,* and chairman of GeoPartners Research, contributed a creative and clear piece about the emerging organizational design he calls the E-form. Carol Twigg, Vice President of Educom, collaborated with Alliance Partner Michael Miloff to describe the network-enabled future in postsecondary education. Mike Nelson, previously Special Assistant for Information Technology at the White House, and now Director for Technology Policy at the Federal Communications Commission, provided insights regarding electronically enabled government. We are especially appreciative to Mike for staying with the writing through both a job change and the birth of a new baby! Stephen Kobrin from the Wharton School questioned the very meaning of a national economy. Riel Miller of the OECD delivered a conclusive chapter on the future development of the Internet. Ravi Kalakota, Director of the Center for Digital Commerce at Georgia State University, coauthored our chapter describing recent learnings about the e-business community phenomenon. To all of these friends, practitioners, and thinkers, we owe a great deal.

Other Alliance team members contributed in many ways. Chuck Martin, author of *The Digital Estate,* and a senior Alliance Associate, wrote an excellent and visionary essay on the future of publishing. Paul Woolner, Alliance Co-founder and Director, produced an insightful description of the digital enterprise. Phil Hood, Alliance Senior Technology Analyst, assisted throughout with his wisdom and extensive industry knowledge. All the other members of the Alliance consulting team made it possible for us to learn and create a new vocabulary for digital economy strategy. Thanks also to our friend and colleague Rob Howie, Vice President of Marketing at Renaissance Worldwide, for his insightful suggestions and early encouragement to tackle this project.

Our publisher at McGraw-Hill, Phil Ruppel, and our editor, Betsy Brown, and her assistant, Kurt Nelson, have been helpful throughout, and more understanding and flexible than any of us ever imagined might be necessary. (Someone warned us at the outset that collecting final copy from about 20 hyper-busy execs would be harder than herding cats!)

At the center of all this, coordinating and cajoling, shaping and advising, was our associate editor, Natalie Klym. Natalie brought judgment, creativity, and perseverance to the project in more ways than we could ever count. Thank you, Natalie!

Finally, we owe much thanks to each of our respective families for indulging us through this creative venture, and supporting us in pursuing our goals. Thank you, Ana, Nicole, and Alexander; Julia, André, and Benjamin; and Tracey and Amy.

Don Tapscott
Alex Lowy
David Ticoll

CONTRIBUTORS

Vincent P. Barabba is General Manager of Corporate Strategy and Knowledge Development at General Motors. Prior to joining GM in 1985, he was Director, Market Intelligence for Xerox Corporation and Eastman Kodak Company. His public service includes two terms as Director of the Bureau of the Census, U.S. Department of Commerce, U.S. Representative to the Population Commission of the United States, and Chairman of the National Research Council Panel to review the statistical program of the National Center for Education Statistics. Mr. Barabba is the past President and a Fellow of the American Statistical Association and the recipient of the American Marketing Association's Charles Coolidge Parlin Award. Mr. Barabba is author of a number of books, including *Meeting of the Minds* (Harvard Business School Press, 1995), and *Hearing the Voice of the Market* with Gerald Zaltman (Harvard Business School Press, 1991). Mr. Barabba received an M.B.A. in Marketing from UCLA in 1964.

Robba L. Benjamin is a Managing Partner of Benjamin/Nair and advises clients on Internet strategy and market selection and deployment. Prior to August 1997, Benjamin was Senior Vice President of Sprint and Chief of Staff of its Long Distance business. Before assuming this role in March 1997, Benjamin was President of the Sprint Multimedia Group, responsible for Sprint's consumer and business Internet product lines. Previously, Benjamin was President of US WEST's Publishing Divisions and led its yellow pages, printing, and new media business units. Benjamin has also held executive positions in consumer banking and in financial services. She has a B.A. from Occidental College and an M.B.A. from Stanford University.

John Seely Brown is the Chief Scientist at Xerox Corporation and the Director of its Palo Alto Research Center (PARC). At Xerox, Dr. Brown has been deeply involved in the formation of corporate strategy and the company's positioning as The Document Company. He has expanded the role of corporate research to include such topics as organizational learning, ethnographies of the workplace, complex adaptive systems and techniques for unfreezing the corporate mind. Dr. Brown is a co-founder of the Institute for Research on Learning, a nonprofit institute for addressing the problems of lifelong-learning. He is a member of the National Academy of Education and a Fellow of the American Association for Artificial Intelligence. He also serves on numerous advisory boards and boards of directors. He has published over 90 papers in scientific journals and was awarded the *Harvard Business Review*'s 1991 McKinsey Award for his article, "Research that Reinvents the Corporation." More recently he has published, *Seeing Differently: Insights on Innovation* (Harvard Business Review Books, 1997). Brown was an Executive Producer for the award- winning film, *Art • Lunch • Internet • Dinner*, which won a bronze medal at Worldfest '94, the Charleston International Film Festival.

Vinton G. Cerf is Senior Vice President of Internet Architecture and Engineering for MCI Communications Corp. Mr. Cerf is world-renowned as the co-developer of the computer networking protocol, TCP/IP, which has become the language for Internet communications. He served from 1992 to 1995 as the Founding President of the Internet Society. More recently, he was appointed by President Clinton to advise the High Performance Communications Office on plans for the "next generation" Internet. Mr. Cerf first worked with MCI during the early 1980s as Vice President of Digital Information Services. Prior to that he was at the Department of Defense's Advanced Research Projects Agency (ARPA) from 1976 to 1982. Mr. Cerf has received numerous prestigious awards and is currently a Fellow of the Institute of Electrical and Electronic Engineers, the Association for Computing, the American Association for Advancement of Science, and the American Academy of Arts and Sciences. He holds a B.Sc. in Mathematics from Stanford University and an M.Sc. and Ph.D. in Computer Science from UCLA.

Lloyd F. Darlington has served as Chief Technology Officer and General Manager, Emfisys (formerly Operations Group) for Bank of Montreal and its U.S. subsidiary, Harris Bank, since May 1996. He is also Chairman of Symcor Services, one of the largest document processing companies in North America. Since joining Bank of Montreal in 1969 as a Branch Accountant, Mr. Darlington has held a wide variety of senior positions. He joined the executive ranks in 1980 as Vice President, Administration and Control, Domestic Banking. Subsequent posts included Senior Vice President and Corporate Controller, Senior Vice President, Operations and Executive Vice President, Operations. He currently serves as a Director of his organization's electronic commerce solutions provider, Cebra. He is also a Director of the McMichael Foundation and a Member of the Bankers Roundtable. Mr. Darlington received his M.B.A. with honors from Sir George Williams University (now Concordia).

Carl E. Gustin, Jr. is Chief Marketing Officer (CMO) and Senior Vice President at Eastman Kodak Company. Prior to his appointment in October 1995, Mr. Gustin served as Vice President and General Manager of the company's Digital and Applied Imaging Division. During his tenure as CMO, Eastman Kodak has received numerous advertising and marketing awards, including the American Marketing Association's 1997 EFFIE Award. Mr. Gustin was personally honored for his leadership in the field by the Delaney Report which named him Corporate Marketing Executive of the Year in 1996. Prior to joining Eastman Kodak, Mr. Gustin has served in various senior positions within the information technology and communications industries including Digital Equipment Corp., Apple Computer, and Young & Rubicam. He currently serves on the Board of Trustees for the Association of National Advertisers.

J. Bruce Harreld is Senior Vice President, Strategy, at International Business Machines Corporation. Responsible for assisting in the formulation of IBM's overall commercial and technical strategy, Mr. Harreld is a member of IBM's Corporate Executive Committee and Corporate Technology Council. In addition, he is responsible for IBM's internal business transformation and information technology efforts. Prior to joining IBM, Mr. Harreld was President of Boston Chicken, and an Adjunct Professor at Northwestern University's Kellogg Graduate School of Business Administration. Mr. Harreld has also held senior positions at Kraft General Foods. He served as Senior Vice President, Marketing and Information Services, and as the organization's first Chief Information Officer from 1989 to 1993. He remains a member of Boston Chicken's Board of Directors, and, as time permits, teaches courses on the strategic use of information technology and change management. He holds an M.B.A. from Harvard and an engineering degree from Purdue University.

Dennis H. Jones is Executive Vice President of Information and Logistics Services and Chief Information Officer for FDX Corporation. He is a member of the five-person executive committee responsible for planning and executing all service functions. Jones is responsible for all aspects of FDX Corporation's logistics and electronic commerce initiatives, as well as strategic information systems processing, systems engineering, software development and design. He also manages information and telecommunications for FDX's six business units, including Federal Express. Before joining FDX in 1998, Jones was Senior Vice President of Information and Telecommunications, and CIO for Federal Express. Mr. Jones joined Federal Express in 1975 as a Senior Financial Analyst and subsequently held several Managing Director roles in the company's Finance Division.

In 1986 he was promoted to Vice President, Customer Automation and Invoicing. Mr. Jones holds an M.A. in Accounting and Finance from the University of Memphis.

Ravi Kalakota is the Director of the Center for Digital Commerce and Chair Professor of Information Systems at Georgia State University. Ravi was Co-chair and Organizing Committee Chairman of the First International Conference on Electronic Commerce, held in 1995 in Austin, Texas. He is the author of *Frontiers of Electronic Commerce* (Addison-Wesley, 1996), and the recently published *Electronic Commerce: A Manager's Guide* (Addison-Wesley, 1996). He received his Ph.D. in Information Systems from the University of Texas at Austin, M.Sc. in computer science from the University of Hawaii, and Bachelor of Technology in Computer Science from Osmania University, India.

Stephen J. Kobrin is William H. Wurster Professor of Multinational Management at the Wharton School, and Director of the Joseph H. Lauder Institute of Management and International Studies at the University of Pennsylvania. His research focuses on global integration and the relationship between multinational business and international politics. Prior to joining the Wharton School in 1987, he worked as a brand manager for Procter & Gamble in the United States and Venezuela, and taught at MIT's Sloan School of Management and NYU's Graduate School of Business. Professor Kobrin has published extensively, including three books and numerous articles related to geopolitics, economics, and technology. Professor Kobrin has served in leadership roles in various professional associations and on the editorial boards of academic publications. He is currently a Fellow of the World Economic Forum. Professor Kobrin has a Ph.D. in International Business from the University of Michigan, an M.B.A. from the Wharton School, and a B.Mgt.Eng. from the Rensselaer Polytechnic Institute.

Raymond J. Lane is President and Chief Operating Officer of Oracle Corporation. Under Mr. Lane's leadership, Oracle has expanded beyond its core database technology, and has created leadership positions in the fast-growing markets for mission-critical business applications and professional services. Mr. Lane joined the company in 1992 as President of Oracle USA and held the post of President of Worldwide Operations prior to his current position. Before joining Oracle, Mr. Lane was a senior partner with the firm of Booz Allen and Hamilton where he pioneered and led their Information Technology Group. He also served on the firm's Executive Committee and Board of Directors. He has also held management and executive positions with IBM and EDS. Mr. Lane and his wife Stephanie participate in many San Francisco Bay Area civic activities. Besides serving on Oracle's Board of Directors, Mr. Lane serves on the boards of Carnegie Mellon University, Marimba, Novell, and the Special Olympics. He holds a degree in mathematics from West Virginia University where he has been recognized as a Distinguished Alumni, and he holds an honorary Ph.D. from Golden Gate University.

Alex Lowy is Managing Partner and co-founder of the Alliance for Converging Technologies. He is a leading management consultant and educator. In addition to his consulting activities, Mr. Lowy is an active researcher, author, and conference presenter on the subjects of organizational learning, strategy, and high-performing systems. He has a B.A. in Psychology from McGill University, a B.A. in Applied Social Science and Philosophy from Concordia University, and a Master's of Environmental Studies from York University.

John A. MacDonald is President and Chief Operating Officer at Bell Canada. He is also Chairman of Stentor Canadian Network Management. Prior to joining Bell Canada in 1994, Mr. MacDonald was President and Chief Executive Officer at the New Brunswick Telephone Company. During his career at NBTel, Mr. MacDonald held a wide variety of positions including General Manager of Engineering and Information Systems and Vice President of Planning. Currently, he serves as a member of the board of directors of Tele-Direct (Publications), Bell-Northern Research, SRCI, Bell Sygma, CANARIE, and Jones Intercable. He is also a member of the University of New Brunswick Venture Campaign Cabinet. Mr. MacDonald is a graduate of Dalhousie University and the Technical University of Nova Scotia where he received a B.Sc. in electrical engineering in 1977.

Chuck Martin is an Associate of the Alliance for Converging Technologies and President of The Digital Estate Group, LLC. Previously, Martin was Vice President, Publishing and Advertising, at IBM. Martin was also the founding publisher of *Interactive Age*, the publication that helped define the interactive marketplace. Prior to founding *Interactive Age*, Martin was Associate Publisher for *Information Week* and editor-in-chief of *Personal Computing*. He also served as corporate technology editor for *Time*. He is a consultant, lecturer, and author, having written the nationwide bestseller, *The Digital Estate: Strategies for Competing, Surviving, and Thriving in an Internetworked World* (McGraw-Hill, 1997). He is Chairman of the @D:TECH conference and Senior Advisor to the media investment banking firm DeSilva & Philips. He is working on another Internet-related business book to be published in late 1998. (chuckmartin@worldnet.att.net)

Riel Miller works in the International Futures Programme and is a Principal Administrator in the Advisory Unit on Multidisciplinary Issues to the Secretary General of the OECD, Paris. Dr. Miller started his career as a professional economist in the early 1980s at the OECD's Economics and Statistics Directorate. Dr. Miller's recent publications are in the areas of human capital accounting, the knowledge economy, community economic development policies and practices, and the future of the Internet. He holds a Ph.D. in economics from the New School for Social Research, New York; an M.A. in Social and Political Thought from York University, and an Honors B.A. in Economics and Political Science from Carleton University.

Michael Miloff is a Partner with the Alliance for Converging Technologies Corporation. During the past decade, Mr. Miloff has advised senior executives on enterprise restructuring, private-public partnerships and organizational development in construction, law enforcement, health care, publishing, telecommunications, and other sectors. Mr. Miloff is co-owner of Yale Media, which produces Web sites and CD-ROMs for a wide range of private, public, and nonprofit clients. He holds an Honors B.A. in Psychology and a Masters of Environmental Studies.

James F. Moore is the Founder and Chairman of GeoPartners Research, a strategy consulting and investment firm based in Cambridge, Massachusetts. His firm is known internationally for scenario development, corporate strategic planning, and technology assessment in the computer, communications, and media sector. He is author of *The Death of Competition: Leadership and Strategy in the Age of Business Ecosystems* (HarperCollins in the United States, and John Wiley & Sons in the United Kingdom). Dr. Moore's earlier *Harvard Business Review* article, "Predators and Prey: A New Ecology of Competition," won the 1993 McKinsey Award for best article. He authors a regular column in *Upside*, the Silicon Valley tech-exec monthly. A visiting member of the faculty at the University of Virginia Darden Graduate School of Business, he is educated in both strategy and psychology. He received his Ph.D. in Human Development from Harvard University, and conducted research on strategy, organizations, and technology at Stanford and Harvard Business Schools.

William J. Murphy is Director of Internet Marketing at Hewlett-Packard. He is responsible for worldwide marketing of all of Hewlett-Packard's Internet activities. Mr. Murphy joined Hewlett-Packard in 1969 as a service engineer in the San Diego Division after a brief period as an electronics engineer with General Electric. He has held a variety of positions within the firm including Group Marketing Manager of the Peripherals Group and, subsequently, of the Personal Computer Group. In 1989, he was named Director of Marketing for Hewlett-Packard's Computer Systems Organization. In 1991, he was named Director of Global Accounts, with marketing and sales responsibility for Hewlett-Packard's largest worldwide accounts. Mr. Murphy is active in community and national affairs. He has been Chairman of local chapters of the American Red Cross and the Board for the National Information Infrastructure Testbed. He is currently a member of the American Management Association and the Conference Board and serves on the Board of Governors for the Silicon Valley Capital Club and the Board of Trustees for the Montalvo Center for the Arts. Mr. Murphy holds a B.Eng. in electrical engineering from Tufts University and an M.B.A. from San Diego State University.

Michael R. Nelson is Director for Technology Policy in the Office of Plans and Policy at the Federal Communications Commission. In this newly created position, Nelson works on the interface between technology and policy making. Prior to joining the FCC in 1997, Nelson was Special Assistant for Information Technology at the White House Office of Science and Technology Policy (OSTP) where he worked with the President's Science Advisor, Jack Gibbons, and with Vice President Gore on a range of issues relating to the Global Information Infrastructure, including telecommunications policy, information technology, electronic commerce, and information policy. Before joining the OSTP in 1993, Nelson served for 5 years as a professional staff member for the Senate's Subcommittee on Science, Technology, and Space, chaired by then-Senator Gore. He was the lead Senate staffer for the High-Performance Computing Act. Nelson has a B.Sc. in Geology from Caltech, and a Ph.D. in Geophysics from MIT.

John A. Roth is President and Chief Executive Officer of Northern Telecom (Nortel), and a member of the company's Board of Directors. Since joining Nortel in 1969 as a Design Engineer, Mr. Roth has held a wide range of executive positions within the company and its subsidiaries. Notably, he was President of Bell-Northern Research (now Nortel Technology) and also started Nortel's wireless business (which now accounts for 19 percent of revenues). Between 1993 and 1995, he ran Nortel's North American operations, instituting the current lines of business model for the corporation. Mr. Roth has also served on the Canadian Prime Minister's Industry Advisory Board on Science and Technology. He holds a B.Eng. in electrical engineering and an M.Eng. from McGill University.

Don Tapscott is Chairman of the Alliance for Converging Technologies and President of New Paradigm Learning Corporation. He is an internationally sought consultant, speaker, and authority on information technology in business. In Canada, in 1992 he chaired the first information highway advisory council ever established—setting a model emulated by many countries. Mr. Tapscott has authored several books on technology in business including *The Digital Economy: Promise and Peril in the Age of Networked Intelligence* (McGraw-Hill, New York). Mr. Tapscott is also the co-author of *Paradigm Shift: The New Promise of Information Technology*, which is now in its eleventh printing and has been translated into seven languages. He co-authored *Who Knows: Safeguarding Your Privacy in a Networked World* (Random House, Toronto). His most recent book is *Growing up Digital: The Rise of the Net Generation*. Don holds a B.Sc. in Psychology and Statistics and a M.Ed. specializing in Research Methodology.

David Ticoll is President and co-founder of the Alliance for Converging Technologies where he leads the organization's operations, research, consulting, and publishing activities. Mr. Ticoll spent 6 years as Director at DMR Group where he led the ground-breaking global program, *Strategies for Open Systems*, which defined this new environment for users and suppliers of information technology. Before joining DMR, Mr. Ticoll established the Canadian program of Gartner Group in the early 1980s. He has an Honors B.A. from McGill University in Sociology and Political Science, and has pursued graduate work in communications, information systems, and marketing research.

Jim Tobin is Executive Vice President of Bell Canada, and President of Bell Emergis. Mr. Tobin has been involved in moving Bell into the applications and platforms world. He has been one of the principal creators of Stentor's vision to "make Canada the world's first digital economy." Prior to joining Bell, Tobin was a consultant with McKinsey & Company for 7 years. Tobin also managed a laser technology feasibility project as an intern with Xerox (PARC) and worked as a mergers and acquisitions specialist at First Boston where he focused on technology and media. He has co-authored major reports on the outlooks for the U.S. microcomputer industry and Canada's R&D environment. Mr. Tobin has a B.A. in Philosophy from Yale University, and an M.B.A. from the Harvard Business School.

Carol A. Twigg is Vice President of Educom, a nonprofit consortium of 600 colleges and universities dedicated to the transformation of higher education through the application of information technology. Before joining Educom, she served as Associate Vice Chancellor for Learning Technologies for the State University of New York. For 16 years prior to that, she held a number of senior academic administrative positions at SUNY Empire State College. She has taught at SUNY/Buffalo, the State University College at Buffalo and Empire State College. Dr. Twigg has published and given numerous presentations on the impact of information technology on teaching and learning and on institutional restructuring.

She received her B.A. from the College of William and Mary and a Ph.D. in English Literature from the State University of New York at Buffalo.

Mark Weiser is the Chief Technology Officer at the Xerox Palo Alto Research Center (PARC). Dr. Weiser joined Xerox in 1987 as a member of the company's technical staff and later headed the Computer Science Laboratory for 7 years. Dr. Weiser came to Xerox from the University of Maryland where he was Associate Professor and Associate Chair in the Computer Science Department. Throughout his career, he has started three companies and produced over 75 technical publications. His writing has covered a diverse range of subjects including the psychology of programming, program slicing, operating systems, programming environments, garbage collection, and technological ethics. Since 1988, Dr. Weiser's work has been focused on Ubiquitous Computing, a program he initiated that envisions PCs being replaced with invisible computers imbedded in everyday objects. Dr. Weiser is the drummer with the rock band Severe Tire Damage, arguably the first live band on the Internet. Dr. Weiser received a Ph.D. in Computer and Communications Sciences from the University of Michigan in 1979.

Paul Woolner is a Partner and co-founder of the Alliance for Converging Technologies Corporation where he focuses on the design and implementation of high-performance learning organizations. His organizational models are used internationally by practitioners and researchers. He has worked with large enterprises on corporate learning strategies and management development programs. He has also led the organizational strategy design and implementation for many entrepreneurial enterprises. He serves as a Director and Chair on a number of Corporate Boards and plays an advisory role to venture capitalists. Paul holds a Ed.D. in Educational Theory from the University of Toronto where he is an Adjunct Professor.

INTRODUCTION

by Don Tapscott
Alliance for Converging Technologies

Since the publication of *The Digital Economy* less than 3 years ago, the technology industry and the world at large have seen a major shakedown. Old leaders of mainframe, minicomputer, PC, LAN, software, and telephony industries alike have fallen, giving way to the new. At the time of publication, Netscape had just gone public; few had heard of a seemingly irrelevant networking company called WorldCom, and many of today's hottest technology and Net-based companies like Firefly did not even exist.

On the customer side, electronic commerce was used more often as a punch line in jokes and everyone asked, "But can you make money on the Net?" Examples of "inter-networked businesses" were few and far between.

In terms of new business models and new economic forces, little was published, and the *Harvard Business Review* was just beginning to think about what comes after reengineering. A year later, James Moore published the seminal *The Death of Competition*[1] and thereafter a series of interesting books began to appear.

Clearly, the first 40 years of the computing revolution have been preamble. Much greater change lies just ahead. The marriage of computers and communication networks is transforming most aspects of business and consumer activities. Organizations face enormous changes, many occurring simultaneously.

We're all wondering how digital media is changing business. How big will electronic commerce be? When will it take off? What will the new enterprise look like? What will happen to the brand? It's as if we're sitting on a beach wondering what the weather will be

1

like today. But we haven't noticed that just beyond the horizon is a 100-foot-high tsunami, which will not only affect the weather today, but will sweep us all away if we don't get ready.

There *is* a tsunami approaching which few have noticed. This tidal wave results from the intersection of the technology revolution and a demographic revolution which I call the Net Generation, or N-Gen (children aged 2–22 in 1999). This baby boom "echo" is the largest generation we've seen, and because they are the first to come of age in the digital era, they have a different culture, psychology, and approach to learning, consuming, working, and playing than their boomer parents. As these kids enter the workforce, they will blow all our estimates for electronic commerce right out of the water.

Central to the changes afoot are our notions of the firm and competition. New models of the enterprise and of how wealth is created are emerging. They are about as different from the old corporation as it was from the feudal craft shop of the agricultural economy.

As I discussed in *The Digital Economy,* it was over 50 years ago that the famous economist Ronald Coase asked why firms exist. Why are there groups of people working together under one organizational framework? He wondered why there is no market within the firm. Why is it unprofitable to have each step in the production process, each worker, become an independent buyer and seller? Why doesn't the draftsperson auction their services to the engineer? Why is it that the engineer does not sell designs to the highest bidder?

One of the most common answers to these questions has to do with the cost and challenges of managing information. Producing a loaf of bread, assembling a car, or running a hospital emergency ward involves a number of steps where cooperation and common purpose are essential for a useful product. An emergency room where each doctor bids for nursing services in an attempt to get the lowest price, while at the same time determining if the nurse is actually capable of assisting with the operation, might provide an efficient market, but, to a dead patient, this is not a particularly useful service. Similarly, holding an auction before the axle assembler in an automotive manufacturing plant passes along his or her product to the chassis assembler might slow down the line. It would be even less efficient if information on engineering viability and compatibility needed to be purchased on the shop-floor marketplace at every step.

What makes a pure market impractical is the time and cost of acquiring the information needed to undertake complex production processes. What is being sold? What is the quality of the labor? What is the quality of the raw material or intermediate input? What is the price for the final product? How will it be sold? By whom? With what kind of information or marketing? Who will finance the production process and how much will financing cost? The ensemble of functions within a firm consists not only of a series of discrete products but also of the infrastructure of collaboration.

A clear framework and strict regimentation worked on many battlefields and marketplaces of the past. The role of the overarching infrastructure of the firm or army was clear and indivisible. But today, as Alliance collaborator Riel Miller puts it: "The Net changes what is possible. It opens up new horizons for what is economically and practically feasible. The costs of information and coordination are dropping. More than ever we are in a position to create wealth by adding knowledge to each product at each step."

So how are these developments changing the nature of the firm? What are the new concepts to be implemented for success in the new economy? Most important is the concept of community—much touted but little understood. Relationships, both business-to-business and business-to-consumer, are key as firms learn to coevolve in online business communities—dubbed by the Alliance as "e-business communities."[2]

E-business communities are a new form of commercial organization that are enabled by digital technology. Driven by the need to reduce supply chain costs and respond more quickly to end-user demands, communities of companies are using networks to trade with one another and create products or services that draw on the talents of many players. Digitally-savvy firms in every industry are beginning to use this model to establish the conditions for value creation and for dominance.

For example, in the electric power industry, 172 transmission providers are joined in OASIS (open access, same time information system), an e-business community that enables firms to buy and sell electric transmission capacity in an online marketplace. Negotiations that formerly took days are now accomplished in seconds by software, and the cost of doing business has fallen dramatically.

High technology firms such as Nortel and Cisco have created end-to-end digital information systems that tie distributors, component suppliers, and manufacturers in highly efficient cooperative supply networks. By crafting a corporate culture that focuses on core competencies and by using digital technology to share information with supply network partners, these companies have emerged as a time-to-market leader in a field where products have a half-life measured in months.

In Hollywood, the high-speed, high-bandwidth Drums network, established by Sprint, allows movie companies, animators, film editors, and others to work together online in real time. The impacts are impressive: months are shaved off production schedules and firms can work with creative professionals anywhere, as long as they're on the network. Collaboration tools, such as online film editing and video conferencing, enable producers, directors, and editors to quickly solve problems and reach decisions that used to be delayed by the need to meet in person.

In each of these cases internetworked enterprises are creating products and services through collaboration in e-business communities. These new models of wealth creation are at the center of *Blueprint to the Digital Economy*.

The book captures the insights of many of the leaders of the digital revolution. In the following pages, they share their visions about converting digital promise into reality. The authors represent some of the most influential companies in the world and are themselves a good selection of leading thinkers and practitioners of the radical changes occurring today in business and society. The authors are members or collaborators of the Alliance for Converging Technologies or Alliance collaborators.

The editors of this collection have divided the essays into four parts: Part One covers the new rules of competition; Part Two covers the transformation of vertical industries such as banking, automotive, government, logistics; Part Three is a discussion of some key challenges in enabling the internetworked enterprise; and Part Four is centered on the theme of governance in the twenty-first century.

PART ONE. THE NEW RULES OF COMPETITION

Most managers now recognize that digital media and electronic commerce are affecting the rules of competition. Requirements for success are changing, along with business goals. Nothing new there.

But what are some of the new rules and requirements? Two thoughtful pieces from leaders of the Alliance for Converging Technologies explore this question and create the context for the rest of the book.

The first, by David Ticoll, Alex Lowy, and Ravi Kalakota lays down the cornerstone by explaining how Net-based "industry environments" support "e-business communities" (EBCs) which are populated by "internetworked enterprises." Firms that evolve with partners will achieve success in "value creation." An e-business community leader focuses on enhancing the success of its cosuppliers and customers through mutually beneficial long-term relationships and complementary, system-enhancing offerings. By defining the four kinds of e-business communities, the authors provide practical tools for rethinking business strategy.

By recognizing the types of opportunities to create new relationships with business partners on the Net, as well as new channels for reaching customers, new kinds of firms and business models are emerging that create wealth in radically new ways.

But how do we design these new business models and what is the process whereby a new vision can be forged? Vince Barabba of General Motors shares for the first time publicly the invaluable experience of GM with its "envisioning process." The idea is not just to avoid crossing what I have previously referred to as the fine line between vision and hallucination, but to use envisioning for quite practical purposes—as a decision support process. Businesses that want to be successful in the future must begin working today to define what type of companies they want to be. Dealing with tomorrow's uncertainty requires a "learning" rather than "knowing" attitude toward the future.

The envisioning process involves bringing together leading experts from a variety of fields, along with a company's own executives, to develop scenarios—plausible, challenging stories about what might happen in the future—for their industry. These are not predictions, rather they leave the organization with an understanding of *possibilities*. By taking certain actions the desired reality can be achieved.

Barabba's discussion is not abstract, but rather outlines the process GM management went through to envision the future. (I was very fortunate to participate in this process.) Four very stimulating scenarios regarding the future of the transportation industry were developed and presented. You will learn a new approach to systematic thinking about the future, which differs significantly from traditional scenario planning. The approach builds on what is already known (that is still worth knowing), recognizes the uncertainty of what we don't know (but need to know), and attempts to bound that uncertainty by helping us take steps to shape the future. Like many of the essays in the book, this one is worth the price of admission.

IBM strategist Bruce Harreld adds another critical thread in this rich tapestry—the intersection of organizational speed and knowledge. For years leading thinkers and practitioners have been discussing both topics. Immediacy is a driver of the digital economy—commerce is nonstop and real time; products obsolesce more quickly; the first to market are rewarded. Agility and the capacity to shift to ever-changing conditions are basic.

Similarly the recent debates about intellectual capital (for which balance sheet measures will, no doubt, soon be required by the SEC) reflect the growing appreciation that human know-how, intellectual assets, and the management of knowledge is a key requirement for success. It has been estimated that 80 percent of the information that companies need to know about their competitors is already known to their own employees, suppliers, or customers. Businesses today are unable to execute their strategies fast enough. The cause lies in the growing knowledge content of what is fast becoming the digital economy. The fact is, our traditional ways of organizing ourselves as businesses have left us unable to deal with all the knowledge that organizations now accumulate. The capture, dissemination, application, and retention of all these kinds of knowledge are what the learning organization is all about.

But while many organizations are accelerating business processes and building their knowledge resources, few have seized a larger opportunity—to combine speed with knowledge to dramatically affect performance. Harreld sets out to explain how organizations can become smarter faster, and he succeeds. Just as Big Blue got smarter faster than Gary Kasparov, so can your organization.

James Moore approaches the issue of e-business communities from the perspective of strategic partnering. He effectively argues that any truly revolutionary advances in serving customers, in creating and transforming markets, in introducing new products or processes, or in restructuring the enterprise require complementary adaptations—coevolution—on the part of many other organizations. Coevolution is at the heart of e-business communities and wealth creation in the digital economy. Enabled by network technologies, we have entered an age of organizational plasticity where the key to growth is found in building innovative business community relationships and mastering business design. Companies are establishing networks of complementary functions—some provided by themselves, but most contributed by others—that comprise synergistic communities, or "business ecosystems." Accordingly, Moore explains, the focus of competitive strategy is shifting toward the creation of new markets and industries and away from core operations.

Organizational form follows function and as the functionality required for wealth creation changes, so does its form. The old multidivisional firm (M-form organization) is giving away to the E-form (ecosystem form) organization which is focused on markets and potential markets within ecosystems. E-form organizations pull together the functions needed to establish product architectures, end-to-end business processes, organizational networks, and business arrangements essential to ensuring supply. E-form organizations manage the economics of the total business ecosystem to its advantage. Chances are, your company needs to evolve into an E-form organization.

The picture is completed by the Alliance contribution by Paul Woolner, whose special interest is the capital market side. The opportunity for new enterprise in the digital economy has attracted near-frenzy investor interest and produced unprecedented levels of return. In early 1997, Web-based enterprises were still finding valuations that are up to 15 to 20 times greater than projected revenues. But, according to Woolner, there are serious questions as to whether this approach is sustainable. The gold rush may be over, or may end soon, and that will rapidly change the context for what is required to build the successful, entrepreneurial digital enterprise.

PART TWO. INDUSTRY TRANSFORMATIONS

In the old economy there were many different industrial "sectors" such as retail, financial services, manufacturing, and education. But these old sectors break down in the new economy.

Money is numbers, issued by central banks and printed on paper. Soon money will be encrypted numbers issued onto hard drives. What will it mean to be a financial services company when a 14-year-old purchases a hot new song off the Net, transferring digital cash from her hard drive to that of the recording artist? She and the artist are both the "financial services company." There is no bank or credit card company involved.

What does it mean to be a manufacturing company in the new economy? An airplane, as they say, is "a collection of parts flying together in close formation." Now Boeing becomes a design, networking, project management, and marketing company working with suppliers and customers to design aircraft in cyberspace. The specifications are shared on the Net with all relevant parties, and the plane is constructed on a network by knowledge workers in remote locations. If a third of the cost of a 777 is software, then Boeing is in the "software industry" and the new value leaders in the "aircraft industry" can be software companies.

What does it mean to be in the educational sector when work and learning become the same activity? Every company will become an "education" company or it will fail. If your company doesn't have plans to establish its own "college," it is probably in trouble.

Every industry is affected. Who will be the leaders in the "health care industry" when much of health care is delivered on networks? How did it happen that Microsoft became one of the largest "travel agents" in the world with Expedia—$100 million in revenue in the first year? Is not the competition of a newspaper like the *Charlotte Observer*, Charlotte's Web—a community-based Web site which has much of the function of a newspaper and a lot more? What about the photographic and image industries when pictures become bits?

This section of the book shares intimate and thoughtful insights into how important companies see their futures. What are their responses to the forces of change; how are they changing their business strategy to correspond to market and industry upheaval?

The following chapters emerge from the frontlines of some key industry sectors, starting with the financial services industry. One bank best positioned, in our opinion, to avoid disintermediation is the Bank of Montreal. Walter Wriston, former chairman of Citibank, shocked his company and the world years ago by posing the question "who will create the financial services market? Something called a bank?" Personally he is skeptical, thinking companies like GE (with massive cash flows) and 7-Eleven, with access to a high-transaction customer base, were both well positioned.[3] The Bank of Montreal is working hard to reintermediate— to create new value between customers and suppliers based on the digital media.

Lloyd Darlington of Bank of Montreal explains that for the first time in 300 years, the very nature of banking has changed. The banking industry—or, more accurately, a significant number of individual financial institutions—has had to confront three new facts of business. First, banks are now competing in a customer's market. Second, customers can access this market from anywhere in the world, at any time. Third, the competition for these customers is coming from very powerful nonbank players and from outside national borders. Using a delightfully polemical style, he counterposes his company's views on the reinvention of financial services and the survivability of the banks. You'll enjoy and learn from this chapter, not just as a business strategist but as a consumer of financial services.

According to Chuck Martin, author of the *The Digital Estate,* and a leading thinker about the digital revolution, publishing is one of the industries most threatened by the digital economy, but at the same time it is offered the greatest opportunity to redefine itself. For traditional publishers, the dictum is e-publish or perish. But this involves more than just delivering the same information online. An entirely new business model is required. As the potential for interactivity and commerce increases, the entire publishing space is transformed. Traditional publishers are threatened by new entrants, eroding advertising revenue streams, and declining levels of literacy. To compete in this new environment, publishers must move from static, content-focused publications to online services. This involves developing customized content, new community aggregation models, and other value-added services, as well as creating new revenue methods that exploit core editorial competencies while opening the way to new partnerships.

Linked to publishing, the photographic and image industries are also in upheaval. I got a taste of this last year when, 2 hours after my niece Marisa was born in Denver, members of my family in several cities thousands of miles apart were all looking at pictures of her, in turn looking at the world for the first time. The convulsions in the image industry became clear to millions in a cover story in *Business Week* that discussed Hewlett-Packard's plans to take over the photography business.[4] "An HP moment? I don't think so!" responded Kodak CEO, George Fisher.

In a jarring discussion of photos in the digital economy, Kodak's Carl Gustin presents views which suggest that Kodak may be an exception to the old rule of paradigm shifts—leaders of the old are often the last to embrace the new. In the twenty-first century, photographs, he says, will serve as information tools beyond what the early photographers ever dreamed about. They will link people and ideas over time and distance, using developments in digital technology that are just beginning to take shape. The capabilities of "industrial-strength" imaging tools are finding their way to desktops in organizations of all sizes. But to Gustin, that's just the beginning; it's what people do with the picture once it's digital that's important.

But, writes Gustin, while digital technology is good and getting better, a low-cost point-and-shoot camera with traditional film can still record a scene in much greater detail than all but the most expensive digital cameras, and this will remain the case in the foreseeable future. When quality of the image is paramount, conventional film is still the technology of choice. It is after the original image is recorded that digital technology revolutionizes the craft. Because the two technologies can happily coexist and complement each other, he sees the growth of the global photographic industry proceeding down two almost parallel tracks. I personally learned a lot about an important technology and industry reading this chapter.

At the center of these changes is learning and education. Peter Drucker shocked many in 1997 when he declared that in 30 years the universities of America would be barren wastelands.[5] The implication of his statement was that education, particularly the postsecondary variety, came out of an old economy where learning happened for a certain period of one's life and could only occur at a specified location. With the rise of life-long learning and networked-based learning, both assumptions are obviated. Many would hope that Drucker is wrong, arguing that surely there is a role for a campus experience in a young person's life. Nevertheless, many of our colleges and universities clearly have their heads in the sand.

Carol Twigg is, in my opinion, one of the leading thinkers in the reinvention of learning for a digital economy. She and Alliance principal Michael Miloff discuss how the digital media is making it possible for us to think about new ways of responding to new demands for learning. During the past two decades, major shifts in who is learning—when and where—have resulted in a mismatch between the role of the traditional campus and the needs of students. In addition, the knowledge explosion is calling into question long-held beliefs about what students need to learn during their undergraduate years, while newly emerging tools for accessing, creating, displaying, and assessing information are transforming the nature of the learning process.

In particular, they discuss a watershed initiative that will soon affect each of us—the Global Learning Infrastructure (GLI) which is currently being constructed to meet the learning needs of the twenty-first century. The GLI enables us to move beyond campus-centric models of the university, engage diverse learning styles, embrace life-long learning, and meet the demands of both an increasingly heterogeneous student population and a new economy. The university will increasingly function as an internetworked enterprise, leading to the emergence of new e-business communities including media organizations, publishers, content specialists, and technology companies.

There has been much talk of the customer over the last decade, of being customer-focused and customer-intimate, etc. John MacDonald and Jim Tobin of Bell Canada breathe new life into this issue (and this coming from two senior executives in what was once "the phone company"—the archetypal basis for Scott Adams' book *The Dilbert Principle*.)[6]

For MacDonald and Tobin, new technologies equip the hunted with better camouflage, or perhaps it turns the tables completely, and the hunted becomes the hunter. They imagine a future where people deal not with computer operating systems but rather personal operating systems. People will be able to establish a personal electronic space, creating a number of "persona," each with a specific profile and customized interface to communities of interest. Electronic agents would become a key part of this scenario, searching the network, completing transactions, and negotiating with other agents. Rather than the vague and vacuous talk about customer empowerment, MacDonald and Tobin show how the new marketplace is shifting real power to customers, with huge implications for industry strategy, marketing, and technology infrastructure.

As firms become internetworked in function and form and as information flows become digital, there is still a need to move physical goods around, especially from suppliers and to customers. Logistics become more, not less, important. The pressure is on logistics companies to provide services that keep up with this metamorphosis by offering comprehensive state-of-the-art solutions for supply-chain management and by allowing retailers to furnish products more quickly and more cheaply to a more demanding marketplace. In the spirit of e-business communities, it increasingly makes sense to partner for logistics rather than home growing the function. Federal Express has been the world's leader in rethinking logistics and Dennis Jones is one of its leading thinkers and executives. The FedEx story he tells is rich with lessons.

PART THREE. ENABLING THE INTERNETWORKED ENTERPRISE

This section looks at the point of intersection of IT and business strategy, that is, how businesses actually operate in the new electronic space. Together infrastructure, enabling technologies, and applications deliver a company's business solutions.

When it comes to internal IT architecture, the big innovation, anticipated in *The Digital Economy*, and catching on like a prairie fire, has been the intranet. Hewlett-Packard, as much as any company, has been a leader on this issue, boasting, among other things, the world's largest intranet. In a stimulating and somewhat shocking essay, HP's Bill Murphy now argues that the same challenges that encouraged businesses to make intranets a strategic imperative are now making today's intranets obsolete. Companies must leverage Internet and existing IT investments to internetwork the enterprise beyond the corporate firewall. By extending the intranet to customers, suppliers, channel partners, distributors, and remote workers, new types of firms can create a secure, robust, high-function, and reliable base for a new era of e-business, and an e-world.

Oracle Corporation has been surprising the world for several years now—not only with its spectacular growth but also with its unanticipated new directions into new technologies such as video servers and the NC (network computer). Ray Lane has strong views on the technology infrastructure which is required for the digital economy. He argues that we will not have an information age until everyone can participate, and that won't happen until the cost and complexity of computing is substantially reduced. This will only happen through a standard, low-cost device that provides universal access. He imagines computers integrated with our telephone, faxes, and televisions for a few hundred dollars. With complexity moved to the network, and low cost and simplicity moved to the end user, the delivery model and distribution economics of telephony and broadcast television will be replicated in computing.

One of the ways I judge an executive, firm, or national culture is the level of personal use of the Net. Personal use is one of the best predictors of individual, corporate, or national success, not just because it measures openness and curiosity but because, through personal use we learn about new possibilities. Nortel's John Roth presents a lucid discussion of how the shift from dial tone to webtone is changing business. His views are based not only on his experience as CEO of one of the most successful companies in the world, but also from his own personal experience using the Net. An ancillary benefit for you as reader is that it makes for very personal, enjoyable, and accessible prose.

Roth argues that business today depends on information networks the way the human body relies on circulatory and nervous systems. In a striking indication of the extent of Net adoption, Roth points out that only a few years ago the bulk of traffic on the telephone network was voice. Today, more than 50 percent is teledata, and it is growing. New high-speed, high-capacity fiber-optic transmission technologies (capable of terabit speeds of more than 2 trillion bits per second, which could deliver the entire contents of the Library of Congress in 20 seconds) are shrinking the cost of long-distance services to 1/128th of what it was 20 years ago. What we are witnessing is a new phenomenon: the death of distance. For years we've been saying the network is the computer. It's now time to understand that the network is your business.

Since Howard Reingold's seminal work *Virtual Communities,* there has been much discussion of the human dimension of networking.[7] If you read the flood of antitechnology books over the last couple of years, you heard a pretty bleak story, especially when pundits discussed technology and children. Apparently there is a new generation of "screenagers," lifelessly glued to their keyboards, Net-addicted, having lost the capacity for human communication. Robba Benjamin begs to differ. Taking on the cybercritics, she presents an enthusiastic view of virtual communities. The real secret, she says, to making cyberspace a humane environment for communication lies not as much in the paradigm of technology as it does in the construct of community. What we've been doing up till now, namely, building infrastructure, gaining access, and publishing information, is only the first phase of the communications revolution. The true challenge will be to build online communities that are actually "better than being there."

Ending this section is one of the most unique pieces in the book, an essay by Xerox PARC's John Seely Brown and Mark Weiser. The authors get right down to the actual experience of using digital technology, and reveal how far we have yet to go in developing user interfaces and implementation models. While many of us take for granted that "being digital" means typing on a keyboard and looking into a screen all day, these top technology researchers force us to think otherwise. They liken the effect of current digital communication systems to "going through your day with two toilet paper tubes taped to your eyes." All peripheral perception is gone, either stripped out entirely or "flattened" as it is channeled through the narrow tubes of current digital technology. They argue that successful companies in the digital age will be those that learn to balance the center and the periphery.

PART FOUR. GOVERNANCE IN THE TWENTY-FIRST CENTURY

This section addresses two themes—the future of government and the overall governance of the Internet. The digital economy will change the environment in which governments operate and the expectations of their citizens, leading to fundamental changes in the structure and function of government. Additionally, there are big issues regarding the evolution of the Net and regulation on topics surrounding it. What are and will be the forces guiding the development of the Internet? What will be the role of politics and economic policy? What are some of the sociological trends that will require special Internet policies and laws or technological solutions such as cryptography, or moral codes of behavior?

Mike Nelson, formerly a key advisor to President Clinton and Vice President Gore on science and technology and now with the Federal Communications Commission, notes that while a great deal of attention has been given to government's role in promoting the development of the information infrastructure, much less attention has been given to how networking will change the way government carries out its functions. Even less attention has been given to how those functions will change. What does it mean to have governance in an age of networked intelligence?

Stephen Kobrin, of the Wharton School, takes this issue further. In the new digital economy, transactions take place in cyberspace rather than geographic space. Cyberspace is intangible rather than physical: the "where" question simply is not relevant. As a result, the emergence of an electronically integrated digital economy renders geographical jurisdiction and territorial sovereignty problematic. Kobrin explains how this basic disconnect between geographic space and cyberspace raises fundamental questions about national economic control and, indeed, the very meaning of a national economy. He explores three emerging digital markets: electronic cash, software services, and Web-based music delivery. Each poses new questions for national economic governance; questions that must be asked but are difficult to answer.

Each of us has to answer another question of personal governance on a daily basis as we move around cyberspace. What is real and what is truth? Vinton Cerf, who many credit with having created the Internet, discusses the implications of computer power and networking on the capacity to alter all types of information. As communications and information technologies meld into ever more powerful forms, we are going to be subject to increasingly clever and insidious types of digital fraud and deception. Even without fraudulent intent, one can be misled by misinformation propagated by internauts who are misinformed. For Cerf, fraud and deception on the Internet are stranger than truth and fiction.

There is little doubt that within 20 years the Internet will become as ubiquitous and invisible as today's phone or electrical networks. Alliance collaborator and OECD researcher Riel Miller notes that, remarkably, this new frontier is rising up—"not out of the sea like a continent from the earth's crust—but from our collective imagination and technological capability." Haphazard or unruly discovery, however, will not provide a blueprint for the future of cyberspace. There are two extreme possibilities: cyberspace could turn into a place where people set up shop, build communities, share ideas, and shape the future on the basis of democratic choices. Or, it could continue to hurtle along as a Wild West type outpost where anonymity, lack of privacy, and unsecured communications keep outlaws and high risk takers happy.

Miller explains that which of these very different trajectories is taken will largely be a question of what kind of infrastructure develops. Cyberspace will be shaped by the physical, economic, legal, institutional, social, political, and cultural structures that emerge to create frameworks for commerce and community building. But when it comes to infrastructure on this scale it will not, nor has it ever been, just a question of building something like the railroads and then waiting for prosperity. Argentina, Russia, and Canada all built railways, but the results were hardly the same. Wealth creation and well-being both inside and out of virtual reality will depend on what kinds of infrastructure develop. Cyberspace is there to be developed, the question is how. His answers are provocative.

We hope you enjoy and prosper from this book. To learn more about the Alliance, join us at *www.actnet.com*.

Read on.

NOTES

1. James Moore, *The Death of Competition: Leadership and Strategy in the Age of Business Ecosystems* (New York: Harper Business), 1996.

2. The Alliance has coined the term "e-business community," to extend the concept of "e-business" which was trademarked and popularized by IBM.

3. Bass, Thomas A., "The Future of Money," *Wired*, Issue 4.10, October 1996.

4. Burrows, Peter, "HP Pictures the Future," *Business Week*, 7/7/97, p. 100.

5. Drucker, Peter, *Fortune*, 1997.

6. Adams, Scott, *The Dilbert Principle: A Cubicle's-Eye View of Bosses, Meetings, Management Fads, and Other Workplace Afflictions* (New York: Harper Business), 1997. Adams worked for Pacific Bell and derived his ideas from his experience in a traditional bureaucracy.

7. Reingold, Howard, *Virtual Communities: Homesteading on the Electronic Frontier* (New York: Harper Perennial), 1993.

PART ONE

THE NEW RULES OF COMPETITION

The book opens with a look at the competitive environment of the digital economy, and the implications for strategy. Major themes include the rapid pace of growth and change, the redefinition of value, the growing importance of knowledge and knowledge management, and new organizational forms. Each of these areas is crucial to understanding the emerging rules of competition and how to win in the new world of e-business communities. The underlying message is that traditional business models are dead.

JOINED AT THE BIT

THE EMERGENCE OF THE
E-BUSINESS COMMUNITY

by David Ticoll and Alex Lowy
Alliance for Converging Technologies

Ravi Kalakota
Georgia State University

Throughout history, new information technologies have enabled and stimulated new organizational forms. With the emergence of the World Wide Web, a totally new business environment is emerging.

As competition intensifies, innovation cannot be attained solely within the integrated industrial enterprise, or even the so-called virtual corporation. Rather, companies must work together to create online networks of customers, suppliers, and value-added processes. The result is what we call the e-business community, or EBC.[1]

We define EBCs as networks of suppliers, distributors, commerce providers, and customers that use the Internet and other electronic media as platforms for collaboration and competition.

The question is not whether e-business communities are upon us, but how to develop strategies that capitalize on this new formation. EBCs are transforming the rules of competition, inventing new value propositions, and mobilizing people and resources to unprecedented levels of performance. Firms must learn to co-evolve with partners to create favorable conditions for all players. The new game is about leading a community for mutually beneficial long-term relationships with cosuppliers and customers.

To achieve these goals, a whole new way of thinking is required:

- It makes more sense to view a company within its e-business community than in competition with firms that have traditionally been considered part of the same "industry."
- Competitive advantage no longer necessarily accrues from economies of scale and scope. Smaller is often better.
- But not always. Net-enabled scale contributes to historically unprecedented levels of "superaggregation."
- Mass customization is no longer enough—the next step is significant service-based value-added.

Only through understanding such new principles of industry design can businesses begin to develop strategies for success. In this chapter, we develop a model for understanding the new rules of competition. More specifically, we look at the four EBC types and their strategic implications. Our premise is that e-business communities are emerging as both the new organizational form and competitive space.

Before examining the new competitive environment, it is important to understand the larger forces of the digital revolution that are driving the e-business community. These are:

- *The redefinition of value.* As wealth creation, communications, commerce, and distribution converge on common digital, networked platforms, industry boundaries blur, causing providers to rethink the basis of value creation. Car manufacturers, for example, are reinventing their offering as a service-enhanced electronics package that also provides mobility. To compete with Net-based periodicals, traditional print publishers have begun delivering customized content in real time while offering value-added services. As broadband data services replace the old voice telephone system, telecommunications companies are moving up the food chain into value-added applications like online shopping and video-on-demand.
- *Digital knowledge economics are fundamentally different and poorly understood.* Hoarding knowledge (as opposed to land, goods, or capital) is typically counterproductive and nearly impossible; in the digital economy, knowledge *must* be shared.

  Knowledge-based products (like software applications or marketing research questionnaires) often obey a law of *increasing*, rather than diminishing returns: the more widely they are used, the greater their value. Consequently, early market entry can yield long-term competitive advantages that far exceed those enjoyed by industrial age innovators.

Measurement is a major issue: we have no commonly accepted "units" of knowledge, and no public markets that meaningfully set its value. "Return on knowledge," as Peter Drucker has suggested, is nearly impossible to measure rigorously.[2] From boardrooms to the Securities Exchange Commission, organizations are trying to figure out how to capitalize these intangible assets.[3]

- *Accelerating technology-driven pace of growth and change.* Information technology is driving change everywhere. Every executive—in every industry—must embrace the pace and dynamics of the information technology industry. Agility, immediacy, and techno-savvy innovation will distinguish the winners.

- *Friction-free electronic business economics mean disintermediation, reintermediation, and customer empowerment.* Moving business processes from physical to digital networks eliminates transactional friction, dramatically reducing costs, time, and opportunities for error. Jobs, business processes, companies— indeed, entire industries—face elimination or digital transformation. Meanwhile, customers gain both tangible (cost, quality) and intangible (information, control, relationships) benefits while they contribute ever more value to the system.

- *The digital implosion drives disaggregation and specialization, undermining the economic rationality of the vertically or horizontally integrated firm.* Digital knowledge reduces the time and financial costs of information and coordination. It is now economically feasible for large and diverse sets of people to have the information they need to make safe decisions in near real time. Consequently, we can increase wealth by adding knowledge value to a product—through innovation, enhancement, cost reduction, or customization—at each step in its life cycle. Often, specialists do a better value-adding job than vertically integrated firms. In the digital economy, the notion of a separate (electronically) negotiated deal at each step of the value cycle becomes a reasonable, indeed, attractive, proposition.[4]

A business strategist must address every one of these forces. Each on its own is tremendously powerful. Together, they have the potential to transform or destroy entire industries.

But it is the disaggregation of the traditional industrial enterprise that is at the heart of the transition to the e-business community. The core customer value proposition is broken down—disaggregated—into its atomic elements and reaggregated to create an entirely new value proposition. The dream (or nightmare) behind Coase's question is now being realized, thanks to the forms of coordination and knowledge deployment which are made possible by the Internet.

E-BUSINESS COMMUNITIES: THE NEW COMPETITIVE SPACE

As illustrated in Fig. 1-1, the first stage of the enterprise was the vertically integrated *industrial age corporation*. With stable industry processes and technologies, its internal structure was hierarchical and labor was organized for mass production. It was supply-driven and employed lengthy planning cycles.

The *virtual corporation* was an important transitional form in the evolution toward a "postmodern" business environment. As described by William Davidow and Michael Malone, the virtual corporation operates "on an integrated network that includes not only

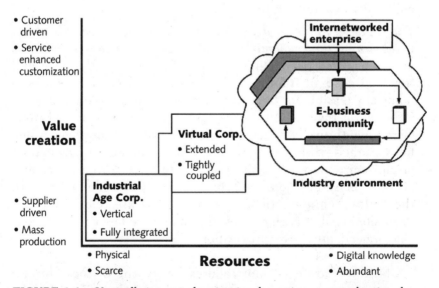

FIGURE 1-1. Vertically integrated enterprises have given way to the virtual corporation and are now moving to the e-business community.

highly skilled employees of the company but also suppliers, distributors, retailers, and even consumers."[5]

The core network technologies of the virtual corporation are EDI (electronic data interchange) and client/server computing, technologies that drive "hub-and-spoke" models of organization. The hub controls interactions and value-creation processes.

Chrysler Corporation, a pioneer in virtual enterprise competitive strategy, worked diligently to bring its suppliers into design, production, and logistics processes but continued to specify the details of parts design. Only recently have Chrysler's suppliers of car interiors begun to conduct their own customer market research. They are starting to gain some freedom to create their own integrated designs, rather than only build to the specs of Chrysler engineers. (But suppliers like Lear and Magna still dream of independently branding their seats and interiors.)

Such changes are happening faster in service industries like banking and health care. As we approach the twenty-first century, the outlines of the postmodern model are becoming sharper, with the emergence of the *internetworked enterprise* in the *e-business community*.[6] The new enabling technology is the Internet, a web of connections where nodes of power and coordination stand out, but with no pure hubs comparable to those of the EDI era.

We define three layers in this new digital economy enterprise model.

1. The *internetworked enterprise* is the basic functional unit of an industry environment. It relies on internetworked, knowledge-based systems to enhance its capacity to learn, be agile, and respond quickly to customer requirements. It collaborates and competes in industry environments and e-business communities—often in several EBCs at once. It embraces digital strategies for developing products and services and for renewing relationships with customers and suppliers.

2. An *e-business community* is a specific set of players with shared interests, who, together, seek market dominance within the industry environment. In the software industry, the leading EBCs are Wintel (led by Microsoft and Intel) and Java (led by Sun, IBM, Oracle, and Netscape). Often, a single company is a member of two or more competing EBCs; Microsoft and Intel, for better or worse, are involved in the Java community. Meanwhile, IBM, Oracle, and Netscape are active players in the Wintel EBC. The term "coopetition" best describes these dynamics.

3. The *industry environment* is the overall context in which businesses operate (for example, the software industry). An industry environment consists of multiple e-business communities, each of which is competing to dominate and control the overall environment.

As noted earlier, it is the coordination of business practices and the deployment of knowledge as enabled by the Internet that distinguishes the new environment. In the EBC, the concept of partnership is not merely a vendor's euphemism for a conventional sales relationship; it takes on real meaning.

- *End customers are genuine "prosumers."* Customers no longer merely tailor products to their own needs (for example, the Levi's jeans kiosk); they gain much more control over every aspect of the value creation experience. They also contribute, adding genuine value to the entire system. At America Online, customers provide over half the content: e-mail, chats, forums, stadium events, etc. In the Java software development community, thousands of individual and corporate customers discuss standards and contribute bits of "code" to a shared resource pool. With collaborative filtering technologies like Firefly, consumers share musical preferences to help the system make recommendations to users who share their tastes.
- *Value network partners share risks and rewards, are encouraged to take initiative, and are expected to understand (often to deal directly with) the end customer.* E*Trade aggregates dozens of content and service providers in its Internet brokerage. Many of these providers deal directly with the consumer once a connection is made through the E*Trade channel. Cisco links its supply chain members directly to its $2 billion sales per year (and growing) Web site, enabling them to sense and respond to changing customer needs in near real time. Microsoft may be a ruthless competitor in many respects, but thousands of software developers (including arch-rivals like Netscape and IBM) contribute independently to the ultimate Windows value proposition.

FOUR TYPES OF EBC

Are all EBCs the same? Much of the writing on the future of "Internet communities" or "value webs" recalls the blind man and the elephant syndrome; an entire scenario for Internet commerce is built on the assumption that the whole world will do business like Microsoft, Netscape, America Online, or whichever company's perspective the author is writing from.

In our work at the Alliance for Converging Technologies, we identified over 170 candidate EBCs, and examined 32 in detail. This analysis helped us to understand that there are a number of fundamental types of EBC. We also learned that an EBC's "type strategy" (whether conscious or implicit) is central to its success or failure.

As Fig. 1-2 illustrates, EBCs differentiate along two primary dimensions: economic control (self-organizing or hierarchical) and value integration (low to high).

Economic control. Only some EBCs are hierarchical in the sense that they have a boss who controls the nature of value and the flow of transactions. Integrated supply networks designed and

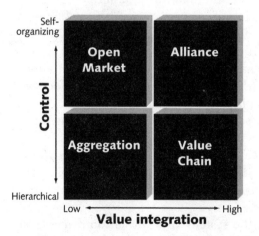

FIGURE 1-2. E-business communities differentiate on axes of economic control and value integration. ©1998 Alliance for Converging Technologies.

managed by a major customer (like General Motors) to produce preconceived products (for example, a Cadillac Catera), are clearly hierarchical. On the other hand, stock exchanges and other types of auctions are self-organizing. No single entity or class of entity drives the content of transactions or the economic outcomes. One day it's the Asian markets crashing, the next day it's the Fed's increasing interest rates, and on the third it's a stampeding group of institutional investors unloading their shares in a panic. (On the other hand, nearly all EBCs have a leader who sets the rules and standards of conduct and interchange. Exceptions include structured democracies or those with distributed rule-making leadership, like Visa and the OASIS network in the electric power industry.)

Value integration. Some EBCs focus on high value integration: facilitating the creation and delivery of specific product/service offerings that integrate components from multiple sources (like cars). Others, which provide low value integration (like supermarkets), focus on facilitating trade in a diverse basket of goods and services.

These two parameters—economic control and value integration—help us understand the fundamental characteristics of the four types of EBC: Open Market, Aggregation, Value Chain, and Alliance. The types are guidelines; in the real world, most situations will blend the features of multiple types. However, the core organizing principle of every EBC can be described by one of these types.

An *Open Market*—like the stock exchange—is the electronic version of the primitive, traditional *agora*, or town market. Anyone can be a buyer or a seller (see Fig. 1-3). Some sellers hawk their own products, while others rely on intermediaries.

Value integration is relatively low, and no single entity is in control. People generally play by the rules, however, in the ebb and flow of commerce, different players and coalitions drive events from moment to moment.

Trust is not inherent in the system, and the maxim *caveat emptor* (buyer beware) is a useful guide to action. Leadership depends on timing and market intelligence (a critical form of knowledge); it's all a matter of being in the right place, at the right time, with the right solution for the right price. In many respects, the Internet as a whole is one big open market. These characteristics help explain why the Net poses a challenge and threat to buyers and sellers who

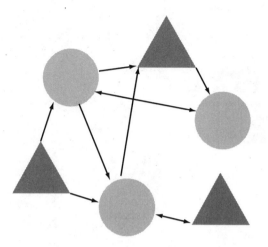

Buyers and Sellers

FIGURE 1-3.   Open Market EBC. ©1998 Alliance for Converging Technologies.

are more accustomed to the Aggregation marketplace model described here.

Examples of an Open Market include eBay, an Internet-based electronic flea-market for consumers and small businesses founded in 1995 with expected 1998 transaction volumes of over $200 million; and OASIS, a $25+ billion emerging Open Market for electrical transmission capacity.

In an *Aggregation* EBC, one company usually leads in hierarchical fashion, positioning itself as an intermediary between producers and customers (see Fig. 1-4). Wal-Mart is the master example of an Aggregation EBC leader, keeping its product suppliers under tight reign. With the emergence of Internet technologies, control and management of the supply chain becomes even more effective and cost efficient. As in many cases, the Net levels the playing field, enabling just about anyone to become an aggregator.

As in the Open Market, value integration is low. America Online, the world's largest proprietary and Web-based online service provider, aggregates 19,000 chat sites and more than 325 retailers. E*Trade, the largest all-electronic brokerage service, brings together more than two dozen strategic partners.

In a *Value Chain* EBC (see Fig. 1-5), the focus is on process optimization. Similar to an Aggregation EBC, a primary company leads in

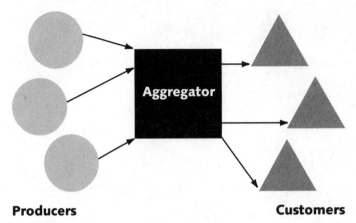

Producers   **Customers**

FIGURE 1-4.   An Aggregation EBC.

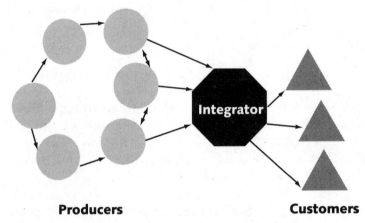

Producers   **Customers**

FIGURE 1-5.   Value Chain EBC. ©1998 Alliance for Converging Technologies.

a more or less hierarchical fashion, but unlike an aggregator, the objective is maximizing value integration through operational effectiveness. Cisco Systems, the leading internetworking technologies company, leverages its supply network to achieve $585,000 in revenues per employee. Firefly Network engages consumers in virtual value networks wherein they share their preferences via collaborative filtering technology.

The *Alliance* EBC is the most "virtual" of the EBCs, aiming to achieve high value integration in the absence of hierarchical con-

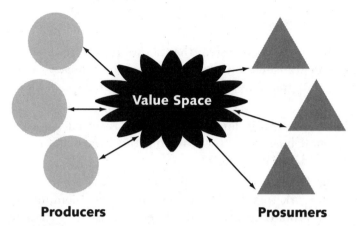

Producers   **Prosumers**

FIGURE 1-6.   Alliance EBC. ©1998 Alliance for Converging Technologies.

trol. An Alliance EBC may have one or more leaders—but the leaders cannot exercise control, and are continually subject to challenges.

A healthy Alliance EBC protects its participants and customers from the Wild West hazards of the Open Market EBC. An Alliance EBC is engineered to enhance a "value space"—an idea, or a vision, of how to meet customer requirements in a specific domain (see Fig. 1-6). Producers comply with standards that result in a "plug-and-play" full-solution environment. Customers have a wide range of choices, with the ability to tailor and integrate their own solutions.

Visa International is an example of a successful Alliance EBC. It has brought together hundreds of competitors, each of whom contributes to a global brand based on shared standards and business practices. In the Java Alliance, Sun, IBM, Oracle, and Netscape are working to mobilize an entire industry behind a new computing platform and engage in competition with the Microsoft-led Wintel Alliance.

STRATEGIC IMPLICATIONS

Strategy depends a lot on EBC type. Digital economy strategies often involve shifting from one type to another. Leaders should consider whether they need to change their EBC type—and the implications of the shift for business strategy and process management.

For example:

- OASIS is an Internet-based system that allows for the reservation of electric power transmission. It is a result of the industry's shift from vertically integrated monopolies toward a deregulated Open Market.
- eBay facilitates electronic auctions over the Internet for consumers and small businesses by providing the infrastructure to enable Open Market transactions.
- Members of the *Java Alliance* (Sun, IBM, Oracle, and others) tried once before to work together in support of "open" computing, when they were promoting Unix and related standards in the late 1980s. This effort failed, in no small measure because each company was jockeying for position in its own self-interest. Meanwhile, Microsoft was harnessing the creativity of hundreds of companies and individual developers through its version of an Alliance value creation model. In their second effort, Java Alliance members are now working much harder to subordinate their individual interests to their broader goals. In essence, they are shifting from a Value Chain to an Alliance orientation.

LEADERSHIP AND GOVERNANCE

Community leadership and management policies are critical. Leading an EBC is not the same as leading in the relatively private and controlled environment of the single enterprise. In theory at least, everyone within the enterprise shares a set of accountabilities; in an EBC, divergence of interests is fundamental to the system. Given this basic tension, the more each and every contributor participates in value processes that focus on the end customer, the more effective the system will be in achieving its strategic objectives.

Shared customer focus depends on some very human "community" practices: high collaboration, mutual respect, trust, information sharing, and—often—joint branding. Successful EBCs, like Cisco and E*Trade, exemplify these traits. Other EBCs—like Wintel and AOL—face challenges precisely because their leaders are viewed as being less than "community friendly."

Governance is not a side issue in e-business communities. It is central to every EBC's mission. The right governance strategy—effectively executed—will contribute to the success and sustainability of the EBC in very tangible ways. The wrong strategy could be disastrous. Because the EBC is by definition a multienterprise endeavor, the standards for rule making and enforcement must be known to all, and therefore should be clearly thought out.

Governance will have a direct impact on the leader's ability to ensure that their strategic objectives are achieved in key areas such as:

- Standardization and market penetration of product/service definitions and technologies
- Ability to attract, retain, and motivate suppliers, partners, channels, and customers
- Market profile and brand image
- Efficiency and effectiveness of business processes, from product/service innovation to customer service
- Effective knowledge creation and deployment

RULE MAKING

Rule making can be highly autocratic (controlled by a single company), highly participative, or—most likely—somewhere in between. Also, rule-making processes may vary from one type of rule to the next. EBC leaders need to decide what types of rules will be critical to their objectives for the EBC initiative, and what are the strategic business issues associated with these rules. For each of these types of rules, they need to think about:

- Which classes of EBC players (for example, Value Chain suppliers, innovation partners, distribution channels, customers) are stakeholders for each type of rule?
- How much control is appropriate to share in order to gain informed, active buy-in? Sometimes it's more effective to leave most of the decisions to the leader; other times, it can be a big mistake.
- How should the rules be made—formal versus informal processes? Part of the trick is to get rule making done in a way that ensures the desired level of participation, but doesn't get bogged down in bureaucracy.

A systematic analysis of a range of successful EBC cases indicates no direct, predictable relationship between EBC type and approach to rule making. However, we have found some important linkages between EBC type and the variables of rule *compliance*.

RULE COMPLIANCE

Rule compliance can be mandatory or voluntary. When compliance is mandatory, the "authorities" of the EBC have the power to enforce compliance and to penalize noncompliance, in some cases, through legal means. People who break the rules in some types of Open Market EBCs—like the New York Stock Exchange—can end up going to jail. At the other extreme, Alliances (like Java and Wintel) depend mainly on participants' voluntary compliance. This can only work over the long run on the basis of self-interest, fear—or some combination thereof. EBC leaders need to determine, again, for each class of rules:

- How "mandatory" or "voluntary" is compliance likely to be?
- What will motivate compliance? What will be the penalties of noncompliance?
- How will compliance and noncompliance be identified and measured—and by whom?
- What formal/informal processes will be put in place to support compliance monitoring and enforcement?
- What are the competitive implications of the EBC's approach to rule making and enforcement?
- What are the legal issues, if any?

CONCLUSION

E-business communities are still in their early, formative days. There is much to learn from pioneers like Cisco, E*Trade, and eBay. Is the e-business community just a transitory consultant's fiction? We don't think so. The evidence suggests that the EBC is a genuinely new business form, with many robust features. It is modular in structure and highly malleable in design. It is capable of rapid innovation and response to customers, technological change, and competitive threats. It is a living system where Darwinian survival of the fittest behavior coexists with social safety nets. It maps well to the increasingly fluid infostructure of the global digital economy. As you explore this book, you can expect to discover many key themes and new rules of competition for the emerging world of e-business communities.

NOTES

1. The key insights presented in this chapter are based on a multiclient research project conducted by the Alliance for Converging Technologies, June 1997–June 1998. The project, called Winning in the Digital Economy, was supported by Andersen Consulting, Bank of Montreal, Bell Atlantic, Bell Canada, Federal Express, Fujitsu, General Motors, GTE, Hewlett-Packard, IBM, McGraw-Hill, Nortel, Oracle, Procter & Gamble, Revenue Canada, and Star Data.

   The Alliance for Converging Technologies has coined the term "e-business communities" to extend the new concept of "e-business," which was trademarked and popularized by IBM.

2. Drucker, Peter, *Post-Capitalist Society* (New York: Harper Business), 1993, p. 189.

3. For a more detailed discussion on knowledge and knowledge management, see Chap. 3, "Building Smarter, Faster Organizations."

4. Alliance for Converging Technologies, Interactive Multimedia in the High Performance Organization: Wealth Creation in the Digital Economy, *Report on State of the Art*, 1995, pp. 1.124–1.126.

5. It is amusing to think of tailor-made clothing as a modern breakthrough, when, in fact, it is actually "off-the-rack" that is new in human sartorial history.

6. This view builds on the concept of the business ecosystem developed by James Moore in *The Death of Competition: Leadership and Strategy in the Age of Business Ecosystems* (New York: Harper Business), 1996. For a more detailed discussion on business ecosystems, see Chap. 4, "The New Corporate Form."

REVISITING PLATO'S CAVE

BUSINESS DESIGN IN AN AGE OF UNCERTAINTY

by Vincent P. Barabba
General Motors

While the emergence of the digital economy is creating new and exciting vistas of opportunity, the upheaval associated with it is producing profound change and discontinuity. The comfortable assumptions that business strategists have become accustomed to no longer apply: it is becoming much more difficult to forecast what customers, community, and competition will be like in the future. At companies like General Motors, whose market has, until recently, been relatively easy to predict, the digital economy is necessitating a new way of thinking and new approaches to business planning and design.

In the automotive industry, the rise of the smart car concept is forcing automakers to consider unfamiliar new features and services—such as entertainment and telecommunications—as carefully as traditional customer considerations. On a much larger scale, transportation needs in general are shifting as our networked—and traffic-congested—society is reshaped by technology-driven trends like telework, virtual communities, and alternative energy sources. One thing, however, is certain: when you're not sure what the future holds, the best approach is to become an agile enterprise that can change course quickly.

This chapter presents a framework that helps business leaders think about what kind of companies they want to become in the face of uncertainty. This kind of strategic thinking is crucial to helping an enterprise find ways to get from where it is now, to where it wants to be in the future. It also requires the business planner to take into consideration changes in the broader societal environment, including customer needs, political realities, economics, and many other factors. On a more practical level, I will demonstrate how to choose between two alternative prototypical business designs, using four alternative future transportation and technology scenarios as a decision support tool.

WHAT IS BUSINESS DESIGN?

In his book *Value Migration*, Adrian J. Slywotzky defines business design as

> the totality of how a company selects its customers, defines and differentiates its offerings (or responses), defines the tasks it will perform itself and those it will outsource, configures its resources, goes to market, creates utility for customers and captures profits. *It is the entire system for delivering utility to customers and earning a profit from that activity* (emphasis added). Companies may offer products, they may offer technology, but that offering is embedded in a comprehensive system of activities and relationships that represents the company's business design.[1]

Slywotzky emphasizes activities and relationships, both of which we can expect to change dramatically in the coming years. The basic question is, how and why will they change?

First, we must consider customer needs, which change rapidly and are difficult to predict. The digital economy's primary effect has not been change itself, but an increase in the rate of change. Just as an organization begins to understand customer wants and needs, those wants and needs change, in both subtle and dramatic ways.

Second, as computing and communication technologies improve—along with our understanding of their applications—they will enable businesses to acquire deep and broad external knowledge of current and potential markets, thus allowing us to better sense changes in customer requirements. These technologies will also help us reconfigure and make better use of internal knowledge of our own company's capabilities as an extended enterprise, allowing us to innovatively serve those markets. This knowledge, in the context of a shared corporate business design, can enable a company's decision makers to decide how to "deliver utility to customers and earn a profit from that activity," as Slywotzky suggests.

Finally, technology is redefining the nature of competition. Businesses are expanding their radar screens, realizing that the Internet and other nontraditional technologies present a type and scope of competition that is unfamiliar to most traditional enterprises.

All of this leads to a playing field that is changing faster than our ability to respond using traditional methods. And that is why we must learn to approach change in a different way. As Albert Einstein pointed out: "Without changing our patterns of thought, we will not be able to solve the problems we created with our current patterns of thought."

Lacking a crystal ball, we can only assume that the future will be different from the present. How different remains to be seen. It should be clear by now that we must learn how to design our businesses to deal with this uncertainty. With few exceptions, it is futile to attempt to predict a certain, single future by listing precise preconditions—such as point estimates of the growth of the GNP, price indices, population growth, competitive actions, cost of raw materials, etc.

The futility lies in the fact that the more point estimates one lists, the higher the probability that one or more of those assumptions will be wrong. Yet in spite of such faulty logic, this is the approach that underlies most businesses' long-range plans and thinking.

A more sensible approach would be to develop a business design that meets the organization's needs, and then to determine how robust that design is over a range of alternative scenarios. Challenging existing business designs can help us challenge our patterns of thought, as we attempt to improve our methods of serving our customers and increasing our market value.

WHAT ARE THE ALTERNATIVE BUSINESS DESIGNS?[2]

A business interacts with its customers in at least two ways: it makes offers to them, and responds to requests from them. All businesses do some of both, but each type of behavior calls for a different organizing principle.

Two prototypical business designs address these roles. The first, which Stephan Haeckel of the IBM Advanced Business Institute calls "make-and-sell," is the underlying paradigm of the industrial age, and, as such, is the most common in today's business environment. A make-and-sell organization does just that: predicts what the market will demand, makes a product, then goes out and sells it. The make-and-sell enterprise views itself as an efficient mechanism for making offers, relying primarily on interchangeable parts and economies of scale. It depends on learning curves and interchangeable people—people who execute defined procedures in accordance with a prescribed business plan.

Haeckel describes the "sense-and-respond" organization, on the other hand, as one that says to customers, "help me to identify your needs and let's work together to satisfy them." A sense-and-respond organization sees itself as an adaptive system for responding to unpredictable requests. It is built around dynamically linked subprocesses and relies on economies of scope rather than economies of scale. The people in a sense-and-respond environment are empowered and accountable, and spend their time producing customized outcomes in accordance with an adaptive business design. Table 2-1 explores the differences between make-and-sell and sense-and-respond in greater detail.

HYBRID MODELS

A quick look at this table could lead one to conclude that the sense-and-respond model is superior, because it demands that we respond to what customers want, and relies on empowered workers—both good things in our increasingly service-oriented economy. But it would be foolish to assume that one model is inherently better than the other. As will be demonstrated later in this chapter, what we'll most likely see in the digital economy is a hybrid model of make-and-sell and sense-and-respond.

TABLE 2-1. Characteristics of Make-and-Sell and Sense-and-Respond Organizations

CHARACTERISTIC	MAKE AND SELL	SENSE AND RESPOND
Mindset behind strategic intent	Business as an *efficient* mechanism for making and selling offers to well-defined market segments with predictable needs.	Business as an *adaptive system* for responding to unanticipated requests in unpredictable environments.
Basic metaphor	A *fixed-rail system* efficiently *scheduling* vehicles to stop at predetermined places along preplanned routes, based on predictions about where most people will want to go.	A *taxi company* dynamically *dispatching vehicles* to pick up individual customers and take them where they want to go at this time. Allows drivers the flexibility to position themselves where people may want them.
Know-how	*Embedded in products.* The expertise of designers, engineers, or actuaries is captured as a new braking system, style innovation, insurance policy, etc., is incorporated in an offer.	*Embedded in people and processes.* Expertise is codified in processes and identified by individuals. It is applied on demand to respond to a customer request.
Process	*Mass production.* Emphasis on repeatable procedures, replaceable parts, and standard job definitions to efficiently make a lot of the products *defined by the company.*	*Mass customization.* Modular products and services, produced by modular processes that are linked to create customized responses to requests *defined by customers.*
Organization, priority	*Efficiency and predictability.* Control company's destiny by accurately forecasting changes in market demand, and *scheduling* the production of offers at low cost.	*Flexibility and responsiveness.* Manage change, rather than try to predict it. Invest in capabilities and a system for rapidly and dynamically *dispatching* them into the processes required to respond to an individual customer request.

Profit focus	*Profit margins on products and economies of scale.* Make and sell as much of the same thing as possible to reduce the fixed cost per unit of production.	*Returns on investments and economies of scope.* Reduce cost of customized responses by reusing modular assets over a wide range of product components and customers.
Operational concept and governance mechanism	*Functional and sequential activity.* Centralize planning and followup by a specialized planning staff. Cascade orders down the chain of command in accordance with a predefined value chain.	*Networked and parallel activity.* Dynamically formed teams making decentralized decisions within a shared enterprise context. Common commitment management protocol used to coordinate the production of customized outcomes in accordance with the business design.
Information architecture	*Functionally managed,* for use by people in the function. Each function creates its own view of "what's going on out there" and has its own processes for "how we do things around here." Focus on providing the information needed to execute the business plan.	*Enterprise management* of essential information to create a unified view of environment and key processes. Support decentralized decision making. Focus on providing the information needed to determine what the business plan should be for a specific request.
IT architecture	*Host-centric.* Shadowing the hierarchical top-down command and control management system.	*Network-centric.* Shadowing the dynamic network of people and teams.
Market leader criterion	*Share of offering market.* Share of midsized vehicles sold, personal computers sold, full-life policy premiums, etc.	*Share of customer spending* on a class of needs. Share of spending on personal transportation, information and knowledge management, financial security, etc.
Articulation of strategy	*Strategy as plan* to aim defined products and services at defined markets.	*Strategy as adaptive business design* to sense earlier and respond faster to unpredictable change.

Most large industrial corporations, including General Motors and IBM, grew successfully by using customer research to efficiently predict, then make-and-sell products in cadence with changes in customer needs. In many cases, they even defined those needs by creating innovative products, then communicating the benefits of those products to prospective customers. In those instances when the enterprise didn't get it right, the discrepancies were generally resolved by adjusting prices. Our brand new widget isn't exactly what the customer wanted? We'll "deal" with that discrepancy by marking its price down—until someone buys it.

On the other hand, today's winning companies, including systems integrators like Bechtel, Fluor, EDS, and IBM's Global Services organization, have grown successfully because they organized themselves to respond flexibly and economically to individual customer requests in the required time frame.

In times of discontinuous change, customers themselves are sometimes unable to know and articulate what they will want, leading to "requests" that are often tacit and implicit. An important attribute of sense-and-respond organizations, therefore, is an ability to capture and interpret clues about emerging customer needs as soon as possible. However, some elements of customer demand will remain predictable. An issue for many businesses, then, is how to accommodate increasingly discontinuous change in their customers' range of needs without totally overthrowing their make-and-sell business design. Given that most businesses cannot afford to offer custom products to every customer, we must build flexibility into our processes, while still relying on a certain amount of standardization.

THINKING STRATEGICALLY

Dealing with uncertainty requires that we adopt a "learning" rather than a "knowing" attitude toward the future. Stephan Haeckel and Richard Nolan remind us that, "To be useful in today's dynamic business environment, an enterprise model must do more than represent a static version of 'what's going on out there' and 'how we do things around here.' It must also include the capacity to adapt systematically and rapidly."[3] In other words, it is no longer valuable for a manager to seek only the "right" decision. Rather, decision-making processes should aim to increase the chances of making the best choice among the alternatives.

Nonetheless, successful companies are notorious for believing that they know what's best, regardless of how the world is changing around them. Central planning staffs and long-range business plans based on a long list of single-point assumptions have traditionally been the norm.

However, discontinuous change has made long-term plans untenable. Hence, a framework for strategic thinking is more important than ever to help us approach our options with intelligence and insight. But instead of expressing the results as a plan, we must, instead, consider a set of possibilities linked to a set of possible responses. Strategic thinking, in comparison to traditional planning, can only operate within a business design that is market-based and adaptive to unpredictable change, then uses that capacity in either make-and-sell or sense-and-respond applications.

ENVISIONING AS A DECISION-MAKING SUPPORT TOOL

Haeckel and Nolan use a generic adaptive loop to illustrate this process of choosing among alternative plans or ideas. The loop consists of four steps: sense, interpret, decide, and act. This model is continuous, and emphasizes that the environment may have changed since the last cycle and that, in acting, we alter the original environment, and thus need to begin sensing again (Fig. 2-1).

To work successfully in the face of longer-term and less predictable change, the model must also help us determine how robust a decision would be in an uncertain future. This is no small challenge. While everyone agrees the digital economy will definitely influence the transportation infrastructure of the future, there is little agreement on precisely how or when it will happen. Dealing with this uncertainty requires an envisioning process that senses and interprets a broad expanse of technological, societal, and demographic trends in order to gain an understanding about what could occur in the future.

Peter Drucker, in *Managing in a Time of Great Change*, points out that "One cannot make decisions for the future. Decisions are commitments to action. And actions are always in the present, and in the present only. But actions in the present are also the one and only way to make the future."

The value of the envisioning process, as a decision support tool,

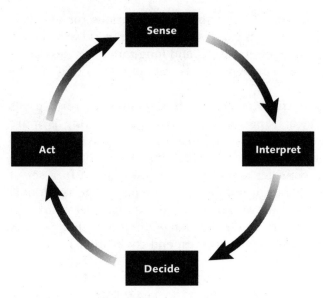

FIGURE 2-1.   Adaptive loop.[4]

is to improve the probability that the actions we take today will lead to the future to which we aspire. The envisioning process enables better interpretations of our future business environment, especially in areas over which we have only some, or very little control, but which still impact—and are impacted by—the decisions we make.

Note, however, that we are not limited to taking action based on the precise scenarios that emerge from the envisioning process. Instead, it is the process of developing and struggling to define these scenarios that can help us create the future. Envisioning is but one of many decision-making tools characteristic of a learning organization. It is by no means the only tool, and must be used in the context of other decision-making and planning approaches—as a process to support the development of strategies that will carry an enterprise into the future.

At GM, for example, we try to involve those who will implement an idea or plan in a dialogue process that leads to the decision they will carry out. The envisioning process acts as a support tool in that dialogue. Envisioning helps to surface the implicit assumptions that decision makers often keep to themselves. By bringing these assumptions to the surface, we are able to address them in the context of possible, but uncertain, conditions—conditions that are neither easily seen nor easily considered.

The envisioning process begins by gathering together experts from a variety of key fields. Together, with our own managers and executives from around the world, we provide foresight to develop a set of scenarios—plausible, challenging stories about what might happen in the future. These are not forecasts. They do not predict by extrapolation. Instead, these scenarios leave us in a state of understanding possibilities, but not knowing exactly what the future might hold.

The state of "not knowing" versus "knowing," or of differentiating reality from its manifestations has puzzled thinkers throughout time. In *Republic*, Plato offers the allegory of the cave, in which human knowledge is likened to the shadows (reflections of reality) that play on the walls of the cave as people and objects pass between the walls and the light. As Plato tells us through Socrates, "The forms which these people draw or make...are converted by them into images. But they are really seeking to behold the things themselves, which can only be seen with the eye of the mind."

Many business decision makers like to simplify things by getting to know "the things themselves." But approaching a problem as an object of their experience or what they believe they know can be damaging. As Russ Ackoff points out: "Problems are abstractions extracted from experience by analysis. They are related to experience as atoms are to tables. Tables are experienced, not atoms. Managers are not confronted with separate problems, but with situations that consist of complex systems of strongly interacting problems."[5]

As we try to move closer to "reality," we must keep in mind that our knowledge is based on images and reflections of our personal and organizational experiences. These images, like those on Plato's cave walls, provide no more than a reflection of market reality. Decision makers need a system that allows us to get closer to reality, but in the context of the broader system which contains the situation we are dealing with.

What follows is an approach that attempts to maintain as much of reality's complexity as possible, while allowing us to make decisions in the context of an uncertain future. The scenarios that emerge from the envisioning process, combined with the appropriate decision process, help us to prepare for discontinuities and sudden change, and help us to recognize and interpret important events and new developments as they occur. We have found that the envisioning process, and the subsequent analysis of scenarios, challenges the mental maps of individuals, which in turn affects the decisions we make and the opportunities the company pursues.

TRANSPORTATION AND TECHNOLOGY SCENARIO DEVELOPMENT

At GM, there is an obvious need to try to envision how the transportation industry is likely to evolve in the future. Like many industries, the evolution of transportation is being shaped by a wide range of societal forces, including technology, politics, economics, human conflict, and international relations. Understanding how those forces are likely to shape the world and society in the coming years can lead to a greater understanding of the future challenges and opportunities facing a particular industry.

In order to try to map out several possible world scenarios and how they would affect the transportation industry in the next few decades, GM recently decided to conduct an envisioning session that would bring together a diverse range of experts and decision makers from the fields of information technology, publishing, politics, culture, and business. Joining them were managers from GM and systems integrator Electronic Data Systems (EDS). Participants agreed that, while technology and other factors will definitely influence the transportation infrastructure of the future, no one knew precisely how. The group's goal was to work together to envision a number of possibilities.

What emerged, after a series of presentations, guided discussions, and small interactive exercises, were four widely divergent scenarios, each of them painting a detailed picture of a future world and its politics, human condition, technology, and commerce. Each of these scenarios also described how transportation might function in such a society—the way we travel, how we use leisure time, and what we expect from our vehicles.

The following section includes simplified, modified versions of these scenarios in some detail, and offers a taste of the envisioning process at work. A matrix identifying key dimensions of the scenarios is often used to ensure that the scenarios cover a wide range of possibilities. The four scenarios developed as a result of this particular session can be placed into the two-dimensional framework

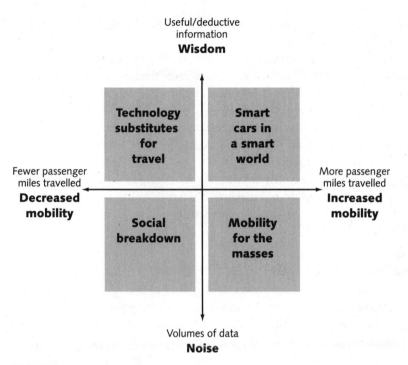

FIGURE 2-2.   Scenario matrix.

illustrated in Fig. 2-2. The horizontal axis reflects the potential for increased or decreased mobility in the future, while the vertical axis reflects the development of technology as either a source of information relevant to specific problems (knowledge), or simply a source of more and more information for its own sake (noise).

It is important to note that other dimensions could have been developed in addition to or in place of those illustrated here. These are by no means the definitive dimensions for considering the interactions of transportation and technology. Rather, they developed as a result of discussions between particular individuals in this particular session, and should be considered as such. The important point is that developing scenarios is a process that causes us to think about the unthinkable and to do so in the context of the broader system in which we must make decisions.

People sometimes find scenarios too "far out" to be of practical value. The extent to which the scenarios create a sense of discomfort is an indication that the developers have done a pretty good job of getting "out of the box" in their thinking. On the other hand, what appears outlandish today might be more likely than we would expect. The "smart cars in a smart world" scenario, for example, suggests a time when smart highways carry passengers to their destinations automatically. In fact, a specially designed Buick LeSabre can do just that today on the "smart highway" currently being tested in San Diego, California.

It is worth considering the scenarios as end-points, and to consider what steps exist between today's reality and the proposed future state. This approach often tempers the tendency to believe that the scenarios are unrealistic. As Microsoft's Bill Gates is fond of saying, "Most people overestimate what is going to happen in the next two or three years and underestimate what is going to happen in the next decade."

Scenario 1: Smart Cars in a Smart World

In this scenario, features and service rule the day. While personal vehicles are still the primary source of daily transportation, information-rich smart cars also provide entertainment and data to both passengers and drivers. Technological advances such as route guidance, auto-piloting, and high-speed, safe superexpressways have made travel so fast and efficient that traveling by car is as quick, cost-effective, and convenient as air travel.

Greater environmental awareness has contributed to a cleaner world, primarily through better traffic management, fuel management, and the use of alternative fuel vehicles. The entire transportation system is more efficient and environmentally friendly. There is some electric transportation, and high-speed intermodal transportation is also available. Improvements in mass transit have led to increased acceptance and use. Airplanes and other vehicles have also benefited from advances in information technology and the demand for customization. Computers, video games, gambling, telephones, fax machines, and other equipment are available at every seat.

Transportation of goods has changed as well. Postal and trucking companies have converged, and companies such as FedEx and UPS have become the carriers of choice. Information technology plays an increasingly greater role in this industry. Instead of the bar codes of the past, every product contains an identity chip.

Mobility and Information Infrastructures.   Highway companies own most vehicles and charge drivers by the mile. On-board concierge services also provide information regarding lodging, restaurants, and traffic. Systems in the car and the transportation infrastructure are so well integrated that features and functions can be upgraded with ease. The smart highway delivers the driver directly to his or her destination, thereby eliminating the need for road signs. Auto pilot has made driver's licenses obsolete, and children use vehicles on their own. Parents can control routes and vehicle functions from home or any remote location.

Auto companies still sell vehicles, but they are primarily in the business of linking information and mobility. They compete to control the access of information to the vehicle, by bridging the two vast infrastructures with newer and better services. The manufacturer who can offer the most and highest quality information attracts and keeps its customers. While customers still appreciate styling and engine performance, these attributes have become less important for some customers. Instead, the service itself is most crucial.

This highly integrated information and transportation system is part of an increasingly information- and culture-rich world. Time is tremendously valuable, and vast improvements in worker productivity allow people to enjoy arts and leisure to an extent unheard of 30 years ago. People also spend their free time learning. In more mature countries, education has become the basis for competition in society. Virtual universities, which students can access and attend from anywhere in the world, are as common as the traditional campus-based colleges of the past. People also travel more. Nations which have not been able to afford the cost of change, and therefore have not seen such dramatic technological advances, are particularly popular destinations.

Politics and Economics.   Technology has become an integral part of democracy. At first, politicians were slow to embrace advances in information technology because such changes were perceived as leading to a loss of control. Eventually though, the political system caught up with the rest of society. In the United States, Congress meets virtually, allowing political leaders to live and work in the states they represent. In this environment, dictatorships and communist governments cannot survive. Information is too readily available to accommodate such centralized and complete control over citizens.

SCENARIO 2: TECHNOLOGY SUBSTITUTES FOR TRAVEL

In this scenario, information technology has grown by leaps and bounds. Business, work, learning, and play have been transformed by the deep, rich infrastructure, which delivers a vast array of information and services in interactive multimedia form to every home, community, and institution. Work, learning, health care, entertainment, shopping, and social interactions—which were largely displaced from the home during the industrial economy— are increasingly reverting back to the home, and the extended family has been resurrected as the central social structure in most people's lives. Individuals interact with the rest of the world but in a much more limited fashion. (Kinesthetic feedback has not yet developed to the point where a cyberhug is equivalent to the real thing.) The world is full of highly personalized products and services, and people and organizations can establish a virtual presence in any environment.

Children, because they do not view technology as a foreign concept, or as a barrier to learning, seeing, or experiencing what they want, continue to be the most active and informed users. Since children are so involved with cybercommunications, and because customization is a given in every aspect of life, families and individuals rely on customized rating services, intelligent agents, and filters to ensure that everyone has an electronic experience that corresponds to their values and interests. Personally owned vehicles are used primarily for recreation and other specialized purposes. Since everything else is delivered in a highly entertaining and information-rich manner, customers demand similar capabilities from their vehicles.

Mobility and Information Infrastructures.   Overall, technology has substituted for travel. Traditional highway, air, and rail systems are primarily used for commercial purposes, and communities have developed alternative transportation modes and distribution channels to deliver goods for both consumption and construction. In most cases, people rely on virtual travel as a means to see and experience other locations and cultures.

At the same time, the information infrastructure is stronger and more diverse than ever. A broadband system has developed in which computing is as natural as any other daily activity. Services, access, and bandwidth are virtually unlimited. This infrastructure is funded in different ways by different countries, but various mechanisms have been developed to ensure widespread access. Still, some people have much greater access than others, and, as a result, societies are divided into dramatically unequal groups of technology "haves" and "have-nots."

Politics and Economics.   New forms of direct or semidirect democracy have emerged in which citizens participate heavily in political life by directly influencing public officials. Much of this interaction occurs online, through virtual brainstorming sessions and cyberspace interest groups. People belong to two types of communities: one is physical and the other computer-based. Individuals interact on a regular basis with those in their immediate physical community, but they are also members of constantly changing, geographically independent communities on the Internet.

Unfortunately, those who aren't plugged in can't communicate as well with the rest of the world. Their interactions are purely local, thus limiting their economic independence, social access, and political influence.

Advertising is everywhere, though consumers are also better able to avoid it by zapping past it on their computers. Because advertising is so common, messages are more entertaining and richer in content.

SCENARIO 3: SOCIAL BREAKDOWN

This scenario assumes that either terrorism, miniplagues, economic breakdown, or political inability to deal with worldwide unemployment or new technology causes people to revert to insular, close-knit communities. People develop small businesses close to their homes and rarely venture beyond their immediate surroundings. Individuals travel very little, and when they do, they only go short distances. Suburbs have collapsed and cities have broken into small compounds, where daily commutes are quite short. Regional wars, rampant terrorism, and severe outbreaks of communicable diseases discourage travel as well. Commercial air travel is a vague memory. If people must travel by air, they do so via private jet.

Mobility and Information Infrastructures.   Fanatical concerns over privacy dominate the development of information technology, to the point that encryption inhibits the free flow of information. The vast capabilities of information technology have emerged, though slowly. The Internet also continues to develop, but its high price makes it accessible almost exclusively to businesses, not to individuals. As information flow has been stunted, IBM and other IT companies have cut back.

Information management has become, in great part, the management of misinformation. Radio is more local, and 50,000-watt stations have been taken over by governments. A previously well-informed public has reverted to the days before CNN and other news services brought world events into every living room and office suite.

In the transportation arena, information technology is used to manage logistics, primarily to get heavily armored trucks from one community to another. There has been an increase in the use of fossil fuels, and an increase in vehicle emissions. People use their personal vehicles for local travel. For trips between communities, they rely almost entirely on heavily armored trucks equipped with state-of-the-art electronic communications systems. Criminal organizations and police forces, on the other hand, demand special-ordered luxury vehicles, complete with armor and electronics.

Politics and Economics. Internationalism is dead. The United Nations has lost all power, and major governments are unable to revive once thriving economies. Nationalized industries have replaced global operations. Most dramatically, the "emerging markets" of the late twentieth century never emerged. All over the world, people live more insular, fearful lives. Partly, this is because of unexpected breakdowns of presumably stable nuclear power plants (similar to the Chernobyl disaster), civil wars that closed Russian and Gulf oil fields, and increasingly unreliable energy grids. In addition, deteriorating dams and pipelines caused local battles over water.

No one trusts anyone outside their immediate boundaries. Local private police forces continue to gain power as communities prepare for the worst. Economies of scale and scope are a thing of the past, and the variety of consumer goods is severely limited. People buy what they can find. Local markets dominate the commercial landscape, and black markets thrive. Emerging markets have deteriorated to the point that they resemble medieval multiwarlord states, in many cases dominated by religion.

SCENARIO 4: MOBILITY FOR THE MASSES

In this scenario, the term "third world" no longer refers to geographic locations. Instead, it has become an economic statement. Third world conditions are evident in both developed and underdeveloped countries, and citizens of these countries live either "developed" or "underdeveloped" economic lives. People either have vast resources or they have almost none. Since the majority have almost none, most consumer behavior is driven by consumers' desire to secure the most basic daily requirements. Under these conditions, firms are able to predict consumer behavior with high certainty.

In all cities, congestion is a serious problem, and economy of movement is critical. At the same time, people desire freedom and mobility, and long for independence.

Mobility and Information Infrastructures.   As with most products in most industries, vehicles, except those available to the "haves," are inexpensive, durable, and simple to fix. They also have extended range and extra fuel capacity. The information infrastructure, on the other hand, is more sophisticated than the mobility infrastructure. Unfortunately, the interaction between the two depends on geography, and is patchy.

Politics and Economics.   Most nations operate as market economies. But because of a shrinking middle class, the "have nots" continue to grow and the threat of unrest looms large. Automakers, like manufacturers in other industries, offer products that appeal to consumers in all markets. Products are able to serve different geographic segments—a small car in the United States might be considered a medium car in another country. Structurally, industries are based on public and private alliances.

PUTTING THE SCENARIOS TO GOOD USE

The real benefit of envisioning such scenarios is that it allows decision makers to think about how they would respond in a number of different eventualities. It also alerts us to signs, or "indicators of change," that some of these scenarios are actually turning into reality. By tracking the assumptions underlying each scenario, decision makers can determine which parts of the scenarios are coming true and are better prepared to respond (see Table 2-2).

The scenarios, in conjunction with many other decision-making tools and criteria, play a significant role in helping GM determine what its future might look like. We can ask how we should consider our future as a make-and-sell or a sense-and-respond company.

For a more in-depth discussion of decision-making tools, see Chap. 3 in the book *Meeting of the Minds.*[6]

TABLE 2-2. **Scenario Table**

SCENARIO	MOBILITY INFRASTRUCTURE	INFORMATION INFRASTRUCTURE	POLITICAL ENVIRONMENT	SOCIAL AND ECONOMIC ENVIRONMENT
Smart cars in a smart world	Smart highways eliminate transportation's most perplexing problems.	Significant worker productivity allows more free time.	Technology becomes an integral part of democracy. Central governments lose control to local citizen groups.	People spend newly acquired free time learning. Virtual campuses make education more available.
Technology substitutes for travel	Highways are primarily used to convey goods. People rely on virtual travel to see and experience other locations.	Computing is as natural as any other daily activity. The infrastructure is stronger and more diverse.	New forms of direct or semidirect democracy emerge in which citizens participate heavily in political life by directly influencing public officials.	The "physical" community is joined by the "computer-based" community. Society is divided into technologically advantaged "haves" and disadvantaged "have-nots."
Social breakdown	Information technology is used to manage logistics, primarily to get heavily armored trucks from one community to another.	Concerns over privacy have led to extensive encryption, inhibiting the free flow of information.	Internationalism is dead. Nationalized industries have replaced global enterprises.	People live more insular, fearful lives. No one trusts anyone outside their immediate boundaries. The variety of consumer goods is severely limited.
Mobility for the masses	Vehicles are inexpensive, durable, and simple to fix. They have extended range through greater fuel capacity.	The information infrastructure is more sophisticated than the mobility infrastructure. The interaction between the two depends on local leadership and is patchy at best.	Most nations operate as market economies. However, because of a shrinking middle class, the "have-nots" continue to grow, and the threat of unrest looms large.	The term "third world" no longer refers to geographic locations. People either have vast resources or they have almost none. Manufacturers produce global products that appeal to consumers in all markets.

DECISION MAKING TODAY FOR AN UNCERTAIN FUTURE

Now that we have envisioned in detail several possible future scenarios, it is useful to consider how our choice of business design fits in with those scenarios. In order to appreciate the risks and rewards associated with each of the alternative business designs, we must understand the outcomes of each design over the range of possible future business environments. We can map these possible outcomes in a decision-tree format, as seen in Fig. 2-3. For the purposes of this chapter, we will consider our choice of business design under only two of the four scenarios—smart cars in a smart world and mobility for the masses. Note that the decision tree reflects one interpretation of make-and-sell or sense-and-respond under each scenario. If the tree were completed by others, the interpretation of the expected results might be different. The value of the process is in defining our terms and speaking the same language as we approach an uncertain future.

For this hypothetical analysis, assume that our objective is to choose between the make-and-sell and sense-and-respond business designs. Our criteria for selection will be limited to two items: (1) which design will increase the number of customers with whom we will have a long-term relationship; and (2) which business design will increase the "share of their wallet" that those customers spend with us. If we choose the make-and-sell business design, we could expect the following to occur:

Under the smart cars in a smart world scenario, we are likely to end up with fewer customers, because it will be difficult to predict their future needs. As new competitors enter the market, customers will have far greater choice. They will also have much more time to devote to the choices available to them. As companies try to predict needs, then make and sell products, those who respond most quickly to customer requests will gain a share of the customers' expenditures, and our average share of the wallet will decrease.

Under the mobility for the masses scenario, we can expect to significantly increase the number of customers we serve, because customers within geographic areas will have similar basic requirements they need satisfied. This makes it easy to predict not only

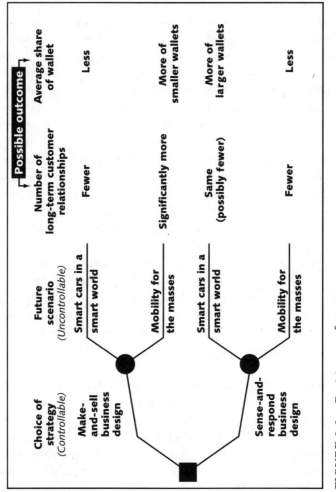

FIGURE 2-3. Decision-tree format.

what is needed, but the quantity that will be required. This similarity and the fact that what we sell meets basic requirements will allow us to more efficiently communicate with our customers. This will allow us to take advantage of economies of scale. As the have-nots occupy a greater proportion of the market, our share of the wallet will remain about the same. However, the total wallet will decrease in size.

If we choose the sense-and-respond business design, we could expect the following to occur:

Under the smart cars in a smart world scenario, we could either end up with approximately the same number of customers, if, in our sense-and-respond business design, we chose to respond with relevant product concepts to each existing customers' requirements, or we could end up with fewer customers if we chose to target only the more profitable customers with the objective of establishing a significantly longer and more profitable relationship with them. Since predicting customers' future needs will be extremely difficult for everyone in our industry, we would experience a competitive advantage if we were able to move to sense-and-respond before major competitors, thus allowing us to gain more understanding about each customer's unique profile of preferences, and the value that they associate with each.

To ensure we capture sufficient profits to justify the costs of developing the ability to respond to customer needs better than anyone else, we must also develop the competency to sense earlier than others (perhaps even earlier than the customers themselves), changing usage patterns that signal a tacit change in preferences. This would result in an increase in our share of these new expenditures, thus significantly increasing both our average share of the wallet and the average profitability of that share.

Under the mobility for the masses scenario, we would probably lose some customers, since the flexibility we have built into our response capability has raised our cost structure to the point that we could not meet the price point of those price conscious customers who cannot afford customized product or service offerings. We would attempt to make up for this loss of customers by seeking economies of scope through sharing those modular capabilities that satisfy customer needs that cross market segments. The degree to which we would be successful in achieving these economies of scope would determine whether we would be able to maintain the same share of a shrinking wallet.

Limiting ourselves to the expected outcomes of this hypothetical analysis, the decision surrounding which business design to choose is affected by which scenario we expect to emerge.

Decision makers under these circumstances are left with several choices: (1) Do what they want to do and hope the future environment goes their way; (2) see what they can do to encourage the desired future environment, or (3) try to develop a business design that is robust for both scenarios.

If the decision makers choose the latter approach, they might take two important steps. First, look to the advantages of economies of scale inherent in make-and-sell business designs in building the more predictable basic components of the product. This approach leads to the significant gains in the number of customers in the mobility for the masses scenario.

Second, given the accelerated pace of change in the digital economy, the decision makers should consider integrating electronic enabling capabilities into the product that allow the enterprise to adapt the basic product to changing customer requests. These changes are inherent in the sense-and-respond business design, which leads to the significant increase in share of wallet in the smart cars in a smart world scenario.

At GM, we have found that when we review alternative strategies for addressing a problem in this manner, a hybrid strategy generally emerges which is superior to the initial strategies used in conducting the analysis. In this case, one might choose to create a make-and-sell organization with sense-and-respond characteristics, or vice versa. In the future it will not be wise to strictly choose one over the other. There is great value in developing a business design that avoids the tyranny of "either/or," and takes advantage of the opportunity presented by "and."

General Motors' introduction of the OnStar mobile communication system in 1996–1997 is a case in point. If the automobile is the epitome of the make-and-sell offering, how does an auto company create a customized sense-and-respond value proposition for the customer? Faced with this question, General Motors created OnStar—an onboard computer connected via cellular phone to a satellite system and a central customer service center. Vehicle owners who purchase OnStar receive the ultimate sense-and-respond add-on to their vehicle. OnStar customers can call for directions, information, or personalized music. An OnStar service representative can unlock a car door via phone, order flowers, or dispatch emergency help in the event that the airbag deploys.

The sense-and-respond aspects of OnStar work because the basic vehicle was specifically designed to satisfy individuals clustered in a customer segment—the best of the make-and-sell model. Rather than attempting to make the basic vehicle, which would be so costly as to take it beyond the reach of most customers, GM designed an electronic infrastructure into the vehicle that allows the customer to switch on and pay for only those features he or she wants.

There are, of course, other avenues open to satisfy customer requirements. For example, customers have a number of options for how they want to receive product information and acquire the vehicle of their choice. They can also select the manner in which their vehicle is serviced.

Recent experience has shown that regardless of how much analysis we conduct, we still can't predict which future will emerge. It could be one of the scenarios we have envisioned, or another, entirely unexpected alternative. However, if we know what conditions could occur, we are faced with at least two options: We can determine how robust we want our plans to be across the range of scenarios, or take action to allocate resources to try to bring about the scenario that offers the best competitive position.

CONCLUSION

All this strategic thinking is well and good, but it is insufficient without the proper tools for implementation. As enterprises choose their strategic business design, we will have to develop and implement several key competencies.

First, we will need improved sensing mechanisms to alert us as early as possible if one or the other alternative futures is actually developing as expected. These sensing mechanisms will also need to anticipate changes in customer requirements. In this way, we would be prepared to adapt as quickly as possible to changing customer needs and the broader environment.

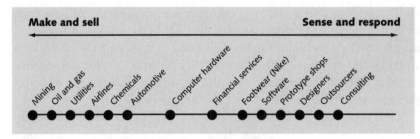

FIGURE 2-4. The current state of American industry.

In the present state, we can envision numerous familiar industries along a continuum, with make-and-sell at one end and sense-and-respond at the other (Fig. 2-4). Many industries have a long way to go on the road to embracing sense-and-respond as all or part of their business design. At the present time, industries such as mining, oil and gas, and utilities are most entrenched in the make-and-sell business design.

But, given the potential of the digital economy to cause discontinuous change, none of us should be fooled into looking at our competitors (either within our own industries or outside) solely on the basis of where their industry stands on this continuum. Figure 2-5 illustrates that some firms are adjusting to find the right spot on the continuum. Some enterprises, like USAA, have built their entire business design on sense-and-respond concepts. Others, like GM with OnStar, and IBM with SystemCare—a concept that gives cus-

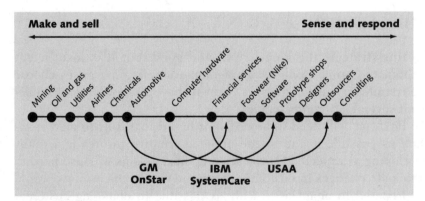

FIGURE 2-5. Adjusting along the continuum.

tomers the ability to acquire, manage, and exchange their PCs and other information technology assets through resellers for a single monthly payment—have taken their basic make-and-sell products and found ways to provide them to their customers with more sense-and-respond concepts.

"Actions in the present are the one and only way to make the future," Peter Drucker has said. We may not be able to predict the future, but we can help make it happen. To do so, we must have a rough idea in mind of what the future could be like, along with an understanding of the assumptions that underlie all the alternatives. The approach discussed in the chapter is designed to help us decide between alternative approaches to solving a problem, by making our assumptions about the future explicit, and by testing our ideas with external sources of expertise.

This systematic way of approaching the future builds on what we already know (that is still worth knowing), recognizes the uncertainty of what we don't know (but need to know), and, perhaps, most significantly, attempts to bound that uncertainty by helping us make our best assessment, thus preparing us to understand the possibilities before we decide, then act.

NOTES

1. Slywotzky, Adrian J., *Value Migration* (Cambridge: Harvard Business School Press), 1991, p. 4.
2. Portions of the discussion on sense-and-respond were developed in collaboration with Stephan H. Haeckel. See his article "Adaptive Enterprise Design: The Sense-and-Respond Model," *Planning Review* (Chicago: The Planning Forum), May/June 1995.
3. Haeckel, Stephan H., and Richard L. Nolan, "Managing by Wire," *Harvard Business Review*, September–October 1993, p. 128.
4. Haeckel, Stephan H., "Adaptive Enterprise Design: The Sense-and-Response Model," *Planning Review* (Chicago: The Planning Forum, May/June 1995), p. 12.
5. Ackoff, Russ, *The Democratic Corporation: A Radical Prescription for Recreating Corporate America and Rediscovering Success* (New York: Oxford University Press), 1994, p. 211.
6. Barabba, Vincent P., *Meeting of the Minds* (Cambridge: Harvard Business School Press), 1995.

BUILDING SMARTER, FASTER ORGANIZATIONS

by J. Bruce Harreld
IBM Corporation

In 1968, senior executives at AT&T commissioned Alvin Toffler to peer into the future and advise them how advancing technologies and shifts in government policy might require them to change the way AT&T approached its business. Toffler responded with a treatise that was decades ahead of its time. "Change" was too mild a word to describe what he saw coming; "upheaval" was more like it.

Toffler argued that a new economic era was emerging, a postindustrial age built on the convergence of information and communications technologies. He didn't predict network computing or electronic commerce, of course. Yet with remarkable prescience, he envisioned the transformations that converging technologies would induce—corporate hierarchies breaking down into "ad-hocracies" of internal units and external partners; production processes shifting from mass standardization to mass customization; rigid lines of authority dissolving into looser, team-based frameworks. This new economic age didn't arrive abruptly; its predicted transformations advanced steadily for decades. Still, when the transformations reached a crescendo in the 1990s, many organizations were caught unprepared.

Perhaps no corporation entered the postindustrial age with

greater agony or greater notoriety than IBM. Beginning in the 1980s, the dominant player in enterprise computing was rocked by the rise of personal computing and client/server technology. The corporation soon started losing ground to younger, smaller, more agile competitors. By the 1990s, IBM's stock looked to be in a death spiral. The company's management reevaluated many of IBM's long-standing practices and recognized that chain-of-command management, drawn-out product-development cycles, and other systems that had served them so well in decades past just weren't working anymore. Broadscale change would be required to stabilize the corporation and restore its competitive strength.

IBM was hardly alone. Burdened with uncompetitive and unsustainable cost structures, virtually all corporations that came of age in the industrial era eventually were compelled to downsize, reengineer, or generally rethink their ways of doing business. Like IBM, many turned around their fortunes by reducing costs, accelerating technology innovation and time to market, and refocusing on customers. But the transition is far from complete. Network computing—the defining technology of the new economic age—continues to overturn conventional business models, forcing enterprises of all kinds to reexamine how they compete and deliver value. As the networked era unfolds, most organizations are just beginning to contend with two of the most profound transformations that Toffler forecast decades ago.

The first is speed. In the networked economy, commerce is non-stop; new technologies obsolesce in a matter of months; products that once took years to develop now hit the market in a fraction of that time. But faster production cycles are only part of the challenge. The new economy also rewards those who are quickest to sense change and first to capitalize on new opportunities. In this environment, even the largest organizations must be nimble, and ready to shift direction as market conditions fluctuate.

The second is the increasing power of knowledge. Although we live in the so-called information age, knowledge is the true asset. Information we have in abundance, piling up in databases and streaming to our desktops over broadband networks. Knowledge, on the other hand, is information that has been "edited," put into context and analyzed in a way that makes it meaningful, and therefore valuable to an organization. It is the brain power behind patented technologies, successful products, and effective strategies.

The collective knowledge of an organization—the cumulative experience and expertise of its employees, partners, and suppliers—is its *intellectual capital*. And this, more than physical capital, is the principal driver of market value in the networked economy.

Many organizations are accelerating business processes and building their knowledge resources. But few, if any, have seized the larger opportunity: to *combine speed with knowledge* to improve performance. When that happens, the organization will be able to absorb new information more readily and translate its learning into sounder strategies and wiser actions. When it senses change in the marketplace, the organization will be agile enough to reallocate resources and redirect its market activities. Speed and knowledge will work together so that decision making is swift, but not hasty; thoughtful, but not ponderous. In short, the organization will get *smarter faster*, and will use this capability to increase its market value.

The advent of a new economic model premised on network computing makes it imperative that organizations master the speed-with-knowledge combination. Network computing delivers powerful new tools for capturing knowledge and disseminating it instantaneously. Organizations that capitalize on networking technology to develop a rapid-learning capability will exercise a decided advantage over those that do not.

As part of our continuing transition to the networked economy, IBM is deploying new tools and processes designed to make us a smarter, faster organization. We are also engaged with a number of customers in applying networking technologies to support a variety of knowledge-based initiatives. This chapter is based on our experience in developing systems for managing intellectual resources and preparing individuals to perform effectively in a networked environment. It is not a road map; IBM, like many other organizations, is still exploring the role that such academic-sounding concepts as "knowledge management" and "organizational learning" will play in the new economy. No one—not even Toffler—has all the answers. But we have journeyed far enough to see the road that lies ahead.

NEW MANAGEMENT FOR A NEW ERA

A century ago, when industrialism came of age, the new economy required new approaches to management. Frederick Winslow Taylor pioneered work processes that squeezed more productivity from factory laborers. Accountants developed standard procedures for managing financial capital. Supply chains, warehouses, and distribution systems were put in place to manage physical inventories. Now, at the dawn of the networked age, the new economy again demands new management methods—this time for managing knowledge workers, intellectual capital, and knowledge inventories in times of continuous change.

MANAGING INFORMATION FLOW

The forward march of information technology has steadily eroded communication boundaries and unleashed a torrent of information into the workplace. During the era of mainframe computing in the 1960s and 1970s, mission-critical information was centralized and closely held. Information flowed vertically, often sluggishly, through the corporate hierarchy. But by the 1980s, personal computing and client/server technology made it possible to deliver information from the back-office database to the desktop. By dispersing information more widely within the organization, client/server technology contributed to the breakdown of traditional hierarchies. But the technology had its limits.

It's now clear that client/server technology never delivered on its promise of seamless, "any client to any server" computing. The reason: While client/server enabled organizations to automate key departmental functions, from order entry to accounts payable to customer service, it didn't allow for information sharing across departmental lines. Departments typically automated their own processes and managed their own data without regard to enterprisewide integration. As a result, islands of automation arose, each fully tooled to process customer data, but none equipped to communicate electronically with one another. When organizations began reengineering—analyzing business processes end-to-end—these "information silos" were immediately branded as too costly and inefficient to maintain. Cross-functional business processes required systems that could move information horizontally, across departmental lines.

Network computing, enabled by the mass adoption of standard communication protocols, bridges the islands and fosters information sharing on an unprecedented scale. In networked organizations, information not only moves across departmental lines, but beyond corporate walls and geographic boundaries as well. Corporations working with outside consultants, outsourcing firms, joint-venture partners, and independent distributors can link these external partners to their information network as well.

If there's a downside to all this connectivity, it's overload. People already have access to more information than they can digest. But is it the *right* information? Is it the *best* information? Analysts in IBM's software group estimate that businesses use only 7 percent of the information that's available to them. The other 93 percent may contain valuable knowledge, too, but few of us have time to wade through the stream to find the nuggets of gold.

The challenge for knowledge managers is twofold: to implement systems that will coordinate the information flows, so that employees gain access to the specific knowledge that's important to their jobs; and to create processes that will enable individuals from different business functions, perhaps different parts of the world, to share knowledge and put it to effective use. The point of all this information sharing is to ensure that the organization makes the best use of the knowledge resources at its command.

Managing Intellectual Inventories

As the term implies, an *intellectual inventory* is the storehouse of an organization's intellectual capital. Much of the inventory already is in place; organizations already maintain databases of customer information, employee records, competitive intelligence, patent libraries, and other obvious forms of intellectual capital. But these databases exclude a wealth of hidden assets that lie deep within most organizations.

For instance, knowledge experts talk about "tacit knowledge" to refer to the valuable things people know from experience, intuition, or study. Organizations routinely make multimillion-dollar decisions based heavily on the tacit knowledge of key individuals. Yet few organizations make much attempt to manage this valuable resource. Typically, tacit knowledge is so widely dispersed and so closely held that most organizations don't realize the breadth of their collective intelligence, much less how to capitalize on it. Tacit knowledge isn't written down or recorded for others to use. It's stored only in individual memory. When experienced people are "downsized," retire, or take jobs elsewhere, their knowledge is lost to the organization.

Meanwhile, people are learning more every day—in research labs, during customer engagements, on project teams, and so forth.

Yet the internal machinery running most organizations wasn't built to capture new knowledge and move it around. Patented technologies find their way to product development teams all right, but what about, say, the experience of a marketing team in Japan? Is that learning immediately available to another marketing team in Germany? If organizations are going to fully capitalize on their intellectual capital, they must devise systems for retaining tacit knowledge, building intellectual inventories as individuals continue to learn, and making these assets instantly available to the people who need them.

MANAGING CONTINUOUS LEARNING

Given the value of knowledge in the networked economy, organizations must reassess their ability to build their knowledge resources—to learn, in other words. The recent acceleration of product-development processes offers a good metaphor for what organizational learning can become.

In the industrial economy, the process of making and selling products was slower and more deliberate than it is today. Learning, equally so. *Consider:* In the 1970s and 1980s, IBM often took as long as seven years to develop a new mainframe. The company concentrated on improving its technology and assessing long-term market trends. It conducted extensive customer surveys to determine their future technology requirements. Then it parlayed all of this knowledge back into product development, and eventually introduced a new-and-improved mainframe. This was the "make-and-sell" model that most companies followed: study, plan, manufacture, sell. Learning typically came at the end of the line—after the product was released to the market and customers had their first opportunity to sample it and respond.

No more. Linear processes take too long in an economy that demands speed. Organizations now must be able to learn, adapt, and respond to the market in a rapid and continuous cycle. Stephan Haeckel at the IBM Advanced Business Institute refers to it as the "sense-and-respond" model. Lotus Development Corporation took this approach when it created Domino, the Web server for its Lotus Notes groupware product. The Domino team made working versions of the software available on the Internet so that end users could experiment and offer suggestions: *sense*. Then, virtually overnight, the team integrated customer feedback into an updated version: *respond*. The process repeated itself many times before the first version of Domino was delivered, and it's still going on. Domino hit the market years ahead of the competition, and continual refinement has enabled Lotus to maintain its technological edge.

More than a product-development model, sense-and-respond also suggests a learning process that can enable organizations to continuously improve their decisions and strategies. Instead of investing years in exhaustive market studies or strategic plans (which often are outdated as soon as they're completed), a sense-and-respond organization will ship a prototype or implement a strategy early. It will test the market, sense the reaction, and interpret what it learns. Then it will respond—quickly—capitalizing on its new knowledge to upgrade the product or rethink the strategy. Such a process requires systems for collecting market information, disseminating it, interpreting results, and feeding new knowledge back into the decision cycle. With these systems in motion, decision makers get smarter with every rotation. Speed and knowledge work together to improve organizational performance.

"To win using the sense-and-respond approach," Haeckel says, "corporations must become constantly adapting organisms."[1] The operative word is "constantly." Organizations no longer have the luxury of learning and adapting at a gradual pace. In the networked age, "adapting organisms" must evolve rapidly and methodically. Technology delivers that capability.

WHAT TECHNOLOGY CAN DO

In May 1997, IBM's chess-playing computer, Deep Blue, astonished everyone with its victory over the world's champion, Gary Kasparov. To a large extent, the media played up the event as a contest of "man versus machine." But that portrayal missed the point. The match wasn't man versus machine, but man versus man-and-machine. Deep Blue's success demonstrated, in a dramatic way, what human beings can accomplish with the latest computing technologies at their disposal. It also provided an instructive metaphor for visualizing what organizations can achieve when they apply technology to become faster and smarter.

On the surface, Deep Blue seemed to be a thinking machine, capable of anticipating its opponent's moves, plotting a strategy, and responding to the action on the board. The computer seemed to learn as the match progressed, revising its strategy on the fly to keep a step ahead of Kasparov. Deep Blue didn't have a brain, of course; it had a database, loaded with millions of possible chess moves and algorithms that captured the competitive strategies of multiple grand masters of the game. It also had 512 microprocessors calculating 200 million moves per second and evaluating various courses of action. The computer matched board positions with historic patterns to determine the best sequence of moves. Deep Blue didn't "think" or even attempt to mimic thought. Rather, it was able to capitalize on a database of human knowledge and experience to magnify and extend human brain power.

C. J. Tan, the Deep Blue project manager at IBM, commented after the match that "the computer played grand master chess using both knowledge and speed."[2] What if organizations could compete in the same way? Imagine if a corporation could draw on the combined knowledge of its employees and business partners before making a strategic move—just as Deep Blue drew upon the expertise of all those grand masters whose strategies were stored in its memory. Imagine if a corporation could read the market as astutely as Deep Blue read the chess board—and respond as rapidly and flexibly to new knowledge.

That's what organizations in the age of network computing must aspire to. Deep Blue demonstrated how technology, *combined with human judgment*, can accelerate and improve an organization's strategic capabilities. Consider just a few examples of what technology can do to amplify the power of knowledge:

MEDIA MINING

Every day, organizations generate and record thousands of pieces of data regarding point-of-sale transactions, customer needs, and other aspects of their operations. Data mining—which uses advanced software to explore voluminous databases—can extract valuable insights from mountains of seemingly random detail. Data mining can identify patterns in customer purchasing, expose unnecessary costs, and use historical data to predict customer behavior. For instance, publishers, cellular phone companies, and subscriber-based services can extrapolate spending patterns to predict which customers are likely to let their subscriptions lapse (and then devise strategies to keep them). Decision makers can query a database for evidence to substantiate (or refute) a hypothesis, then use this knowledge to make smarter decisions. Used in this way, data mining can eliminate strategies and actions based on intuition, hunches, and guesswork.

Because 80 percent of the world's electronic data is stored in words, not numbers, organizations also require tools for mining text. Search engines can locate specific content, of course, but newer technology is emerging that can harvest new intelligence from an abundance of words. Organizations might employ text mining to analyze the mass of customer feedback they collect through customer surveys, call center operations, sales calls, and other interactions. The technology is particularly suited to capitalizing on the wealth of words available on the Internet. *One example:* IBM recently worked with an electrical utility company in France to measure public perceptions of electric-powered cars as a future mode of transportation. The project team downloaded tens of thousands of press clips from the Net, then used a text mining application to sort the information into thematic groups, analyze them to derive predominant messages, and track trends in popular opinion.

KNOWLEDGE REPOSITORIES

Unlike traditional databases, which are mostly huge collections of facts and figures, knowledge repositories contain tacit knowledge that has been rendered explicitly. In other words, people have written down or otherwise recorded what they know. Capturing this knowledge in context preserves its meaning and makes it of greater value to future decision makers. A knowledge repository might house transcripts or audio tapes from strategic planning sessions, consultants' reports in text or multimedia formats, videotaped presentations, market trend analyses, and any number of information-rich resources. Knowledge stored in digitized form can be processed, indexed, searched, sorted, converted, retrieved, and transmitted relatively easily and cost effectively. Using contextual search engines, multimedia mining (which searches by image patterns as well as key words), and other "pull" technologies, executives can draw upon relevant knowledge that will inform their decisions.

COLLABORATIVE TOOLS

The Internet has spawned several tools that allow people to exchange information—e-mail, intranets, news groups, discussion forums, and so forth. While information sharing is important, the more effective use of online communication is structured collaboration. Groupware applications such as Lotus Notes, for instance, allow individuals to convene online in virtual "team rooms" where they can divide responsibilities, share their learning, and track progress on a specific project. With collaborative technologies, organizations can harness more of their dispersed knowledge resources and focus their collective brain power on a given problem or opportunity. A good case study is Chase Manhattan, which has developed an innovative system that gives account managers and senior executives a comprehensive view of the bank's largest customer portfolios. The system extracts real-time account information from various legacy databases, using Lotus Notes as the common interface. Managers and executives share an overall view of each account and can work together to build the customer relationship.[3]

IBM integrated a host of collaborative technologies into its new global headquarters, which opened in 1997. The building houses 28 conference rooms equipped with video/audio conferencing, electronic whiteboards, multimedia devices, and Lotus Notes-based computers. From these facilities, we can conduct interactive meetings with customers, business partners, and IBM business units anywhere in the world, passing information across time zones as easily as we pass it across the table. Beyond our New York headquarters, IBM is deploying a global intranet using Lotus Notes to cultivate a collaborative workplace among our 240,000 employees. We are also linking up with our subsidiaries, customers, and suppliers. With this infrastructure in place, we can quickly implement new processes across our extended enterprise.

The most extensive knowledge-sharing system currently in operation at IBM is the Intellectual Capital Management (ICM) system, created by our Global Services business unit. IBM's service consultants help customers with systems integration, network services, electronic commerce, and other challenges of the networked age. Because knowledge is their core competence, IBM consultants routinely share ideas and solutions with one another through their own networks of professional contacts. But with thousands of consultants deployed across the globe, these informal networks can't possibly embrace the breadth of the organization's expertise. Technology can. ICM's electronic network is designed to leverage the individual expertise of IBM consultants in more than 100 countries in order to improve the collective performance of the Global Services organization.

The ICM system maintains more than 30 knowledge repositories that correspond to the various specialized services that IBM's consultants provide. Each repository contains intellectual capital—

project proposals and work papers, engagement summaries, presentations and reports, process maps, software solutions, and so forth. Consultants pursuing a new business opportunity anywhere in the world can search ICM's central repositories for relevant information to help them develop stronger proposals. Practitioners engaged in a client project can mine them for solutions to specific problems. In addition to the knowledge repositories, consultants can ask for advice and share ideas through online discussion forums and collaborate on projects using virtual team rooms. Consultants also can query a repository of professional resumes to identify colleagues with specialized knowledge or experience and contact those individuals directly.

By leveraging the knowledge of their peers, IBM consultants don't spend time relearning what's already known somewhere in the organization. With ICM, the Global Services organization *knows what it knows*—and reaps the rewards of that knowledge. Individuals work faster and smarter, contributing to stronger results for the organization overall. Consulting communities within Global Services report that ICM has helped reduce time spent preparing proposals by as much as two-thirds, shortened the development of client deliverables by as much as 60 percent, and enabled IBM to win a greater share of competitive engagements.

The Global Services unit has extended ICM beyond its own professional community to include colleagues in IBM's research, marketing, product development, and other divisions as well. As it grows, ICM will interconnect resources around the world and create the kind of "knowledge commerce" that will enable IBM to capitalize more quickly and more fruitfully on its intellectual capital.

Although ICM relies heavily on collaborative tools and global networks, it's important to keep in mind that the technology can't succeed on its own. Knowledge repositories can be vital business tools—or they can become information graveyards. Data mining can yield valuable new information as well as meaningless correlations. Collaborative tools can either promote shared learning or degenerate into chat rooms. People determine the difference. The question is whether individuals in the organization have the skills, incentives—and the right attitude—to work knowledge management technologies to their full potential.

CREATING A KNOWLEDGE-SHARING ENTERPRISE

Not long ago I took part in an education and training conference in Atlanta. Two other speakers on the agenda were Nicholas Negroponte, director of the MIT Media Lab, and the cartoonist Scott Adams, creator of *Dilbert*. For me, the unlikely juxtaposition of the prophet of digitization and the satirist of corporate America perfectly captured this historic period of transition. This is a time when organizations are struggling to adapt to the digital economy that Negroponte and other futurists have foretold. This sometimes-awkward passage—marked by downsizing, reengineering, and attempts to "reinvent" the corporation—provides plenty of fodder for Adams' satire. As he wrote in *The Dilbert Principle*, "No matter how absurd I try to make the comic strip I can't stay ahead of what people are experiencing in their own workplaces."[4]

As Adams understands, managing change in the workplace is no simple task. If an organization introduces new technologies and work processes, people must be willing and prepared to use them. Otherwise, the investment is lost. Consider the varying results that corporations have achieved with intranet technology. In 1997, the Meta Group reported that 32 of 41 organizations surveyed had measured substantial returns (38 percent on average) on their investments in intranets, and two companies were close to breaking even. Among the seven corporations where intranets were *not* delivering value, the survey revealed that the work environment was a major inhibiting factor. "The organizational culture placed a high value on information possession and control," the report said. "These organizations found the basic nature of an intranet (as a network for information access and distribution via a universal client) in direct conflict with their basic business."[5]

The lesson: You can't impose new technologies and management processes on a culture that's not prepared to embrace them. And the fact is, knowledge management asks people to behave in some fairly countercultural ways. Imagine how Dilbert would respond to a management initiative that encouraged him to:

- *Share his know-how with everyone else.* Sounds wholesome enough, but unfortunately, the most knowledgeable people may be the most reluctant to open up. Individuals with specialized expertise have been conditioned to believe that their compensation, job security, and status depend on hoarding knowledge, not sharing it.

- *Make his mistakes public.*   Mistakes are learning opportunities. If a project fails, team members can assess what they did wrong and make better decisions the next time. Mistakes ought to be brought to light and celebrated for the insights they can provide. Yet few of us work in organizations where making mistakes earns gold stars. ("Is it likely that your manager will begin rewarding people who have failed," Adams asks. "Or is it more likely that people who fail will be assigned to Quality Teams...?")[6]

- *Spend a lot of time exchanging information.*   Individuals with full plates can hardly be expected to welcome any initiative that demands more of their time. In a 1996 survey by IBM and the Economist Intelligence Unit, six of 10 organizations rated lack of time as the greatest barrier to sharing information and building knowledge resources.[7]

For a knowledge-management initiative to take hold, the organization must create a climate that values these behaviors. The question is how. Simply providing a powerful new desktop tool won't transform the way people work together. Nor will an "awareness" program or a directive from the human resources department deliver a lasting impact on behavior. Creating change throughout an enterprise requires a comprehensive solution that addresses the full fabric of organizational culture. The immediate and most critical needs are the following:

THE NEED FOR LEADERSHIP

Managers who want to create a free exchange of knowledge must do more than encourage everyone to start sharing. In the IBM/ Economist Intelligence Unit survey, 60 percent of organizations that had introduced knowledge management processes cited "top management leadership by example" as the most critical success factor.[8] A senior executive who takes an active interest in cultivating a knowledge repository or contributing to a discussion forum will soon attract plenty of followers. At Chase Manhattan, the executive vice president in charge of middle-market banking periodically reviews customer accounts through the bank's relationship-management system. Because a question from the executive vice president may come at any time, managers down the line make sure they know the system as well.[9] We all take cues from the people in power; that may be a cultural artifact from the industrial age, but it's a certain holdover to the new age at hand.

THE NEED FOR PROCESS

Once the technologies for knowledge sharing are in place, people must be shown how to use them. User training is the obvious starting point; but to ensure that the new tools are used consistently and effectively, the organization must define a process that integrates technology with day-to-day work activity. At IBM, the ICM system incorporates procedures that encourage consultants to contribute to and draw from the knowledge repositories during every client engagement. For example, the standardized format for new project plans requires consultants to indicate how they intend to reuse intellectual capital to execute an assignment. Afterward, consultants must specify in standard summary reports how they deployed existing knowledge resources to serve the customer and what new intellectual capital they have contributed to the repository. These kinds of procedures enforce a discipline that, over time, changes work habits and gets people using the ICM system as a matter of course.

THE NEED FOR OPERATING STANDARDS

Just as any two people must speak the same language to communicate, individuals across an enterprise must follow common standards for sharing knowledge. If a business unit in Paris wants to learn about improving customer satisfaction from a business unit in London, for instance, it must be certain that the British define and measure satisfaction the same way the French do. Standard terminology is particularly critical when communicating across functional lines; project teams get nowhere when the marketing experts speak their own jargon, the techies theirs, and so forth. One of the benefits of technology is that it imposes a common vocabulary, common definitions, and common procedures on everyone who uses it.

THE NEED FOR QUALITY CONTROL

If an organization expects individuals to dedicate time to knowledge sharing and learning, it must ensure that their time is well spent. That means providing technologies that are easy to navigate and resources that deliver real value. At IBM, teams of consultants called competency network core teams devote about 15 percent of their time to maintaining the quality of ICM knowledge repositories. These core teams (there is one for each of the 30 communities currently engaged in ICM) are responsible for evaluating new contributions. Is the knowledge new? Is it different? Is it valuable? Then they draft an abstract of the new material, index it, and publish it so that other consultants can readily locate it. These procedures help to build confidence in the integrity of the knowledge repositories, which encourages consultants to use them.

THE NEED FOR MEASURES

Measuring the effectiveness of a knowledge-management program serves two purposes: it motivates individuals to keep using it, and it persuades managers to keep funding it. IBM has created a scorecard that combines quantitative measures with qualitative assessments of ICM's return on investment. The scorecard measures how much time consultants save when they use ICM to develop proposals and complete customer engagements, the impact on win/loss ratios, and how consultants rate the ICM system's quality and ease of use.

THE NEED FOR INCENTIVES

Executive leadership is a persuasive means of getting people involved in knowledge sharing and learning. But there are other methods as well. In IBM Global Services, participation in the ICM system is written into consultants' job descriptions and included in their performance evaluations. Because these evaluations bear directly on compensation, consultants have a financial stake in their use of intellectual capital as well. Recognition programs are another avenue. The criteria for IBM's Engagement Excellence Awards—the highest award our consultants can receive—now require recipients to demonstrate leadership in managing intellectual capital (in addition to satisfying customers and generating revenue). This combination of incentives, integrated throughout the organization's management, pay, and recognition procedures, packs more persuasive power than any single incentive by itself could deliver.

THE THREAT OF EXTINCTION (OR WHAT HAPPENS TO SLOW LEARNERS)

When Alvin Toffler eventually published his report to AT&T, he titled the book *The Adaptive Corporation*. In his prologue, he warned organizations to prepare for the new economic age. "The message of change is perfectly plain," he wrote. "Companies will ruthlessly review their basic premises—and stand ready to jettison them—or they will become exhibits in the Museum of Corporate Dinosaurs."[10]

In the early 1990s, IBM was being called a dinosaur. The company was accused of being rigid, bureaucratic, and too slow to respond to the changes swirling about it. It is not too far of a stretch to say that the corporation faced extinction. Some saw breaking up the corporation as the only hope for survival. Instead, IBM sought a middle ground—a solution that maintained the breadth of our technologies, skills, and services, but at the same time instituted a culture based on speed of execution and a maniacal focus on the marketplace. What kept IBM from going the way of the dinosaurs was its ability to adapt, and fast.

Now that the threat of extinction has faded, how does IBM, or any organization, manage to survive and prosper in the networked era? In a knowledge-based economy, successful organizations will figure out how to use knowledge more quickly and effectively than their competitors. IBM's strategy involves finding ways to capitalize on the inordinate brain power that exists within the company; implementing technologies that enable people to share what they know; and creating processes to help us build knowledge and speed into everything we do.

What's taking place at IBM reflects an emerging trend. The Meta Group recently estimated that the nascent market for knowledge-management solutions will balloon to $50 billion by the year 2000 as more organizations attempt to exploit their intellectual assets for strategic advantage.[11] The demand for knowledge management and its enabling technologies will come from virtually every industry—from professional services firms, whose people require continuous training and knowledge sharing to retain their competitive edge; from pharmaceutical companies, technology businesses, and other organizations where success depends on product innovation and speed to market; and from automakers, manufacturers, packaged goods companies, and other businesses where smarter, faster processes can reduce costs and boost profits.

But, like IBM in the early 1990s, organizations looking to adapt to the new economic environment must adhere to the middle ground. Clearly, outmoded bureaucracies, processes, and technologies that obstruct knowledge sharing and burden decision makers must be overthrown. But we must be careful not to go to the other extreme. Releasing the flood gates and subjecting people to an information free-for-all will create chaos—the alternate road to extinction. An environment that combines speed with knowledge still requires structure—systems and processes that will guide people toward a productive use of their intellectual resources, and enable them to translate better knowledge into smarter actions.

Speed and knowledge, working in balance, will deliver the competitive advantage that ensures not only survival, but success, in the networked world.

NOTES

1. Haeckel, Stephan H. "Adaptive Enterprise Design: The Sense-and-Respond Model," *Planning Review,* Vol. 23, No. 3, May/June 1995, p. 14.

2. Quoted in McFadden, Robert D., "Inscrutable Conqueror," *The New York Times,* May 12, 1997, p. A1.

3. Waite & Company, *Beyond Expectations: How Leading Companies Are Using Lotus Notes to Jump-Start the I-Net Revolution* (Cambridge: Lotus Development Corporation), 1997, pp. 14–20.

4. Adams, Scott, *The Dilbert Principle* (New York: Harper Business), 1996, p. 1.

5. Meta Group Consulting, *Intranet Business Value: Return on Investment Analysis* (Stamford: Meta Group, Inc.), 1997, p. 8.

6. Adams, p. 57.

7. The Economist Intelligence Unit and the IBM Consulting Group, *The Learning Organization: Managing Knowledge for Business Success* (New York: The Economist Intelligence Unit), 1996, p. 2.

8. Ibid., p. 3.

9. Waite & Company, p. 18.

10. Toffler, Alvin, *The Adaptive Corporation* (New York: McGraw-Hill), 1985, p. 19.

11. Meta Group, *Advanced Information Management Strategies* (Stamford: Meta Group, Inc.), September 25, 1996.

THE NEW CORPORATE FORM

by James F. Moore
GeoPartners Research

There is much talk in executive suites these days about alliances and virtual organizations, technical standards, and the evolution of business communities. More and more, companies are realizing that they cannot innovate alone. Any truly revolutionary advances in serving customers, in creating and transforming markets, in introducing new products or processes, or in restructuring the enterprise requires complementary adaptations—"coevolution"—on the part of many other organizations.

For this system to work, business models must encompass not only the organization itself, but also what Andy Grove of Intel calls its "fellow travelers." Enabled by network technologies, we have entered an age of organizational plasticity where the key to growth is found in the forging of business community relationships and the mastery of business design.

Networks of complementary functions—some provided by companies themselves, but most contributed by others—are being established. These networks comprise synergistic communities, or what I call "business ecosystems." While business ecosystems themselves are not new, the degree of integration and the opportunity for new organizational forms is enabling the creation of communities never before possible.

In this new environment, rather than focusing on core operations, the new corporation must be centrally engaged in market and industry creation, whether to extend or to replace its existing enterprises. This shift in competitive strategy has given rise to new forms of corporate leadership and structure.

This chapter will examine the new competitive environment and the rise of the E-form organization in detail. Two stories around the development of Java will be told to illustrate how the E-form organization functions in, and exploits, the Net environment.

LEADERSHIP AND COEVOLUTION

Whether they are extending their capabilities or developing new markets, companies must join with other firms to create value for their customers. Growth-oriented synergistic communities—or "business ecosystems"—are made up of customers, suppliers, lead producers, and other stakeholders—even competitors—interacting with one another to produce complementary goods and services in a particular market segment space. These ecosystems form around early species of products, technologies, and business models. In the best situations they flourish and spread across broad market territories.

Like biological ecosystems, business communities develop over time, evolving in a partially intentional—sometimes accidental—but highly self-organizing manner. Members coevolve their capabilities, providing contributions that extend and complement those of the others. That is, each member improves and transforms him- or herself while paying attention to, and actively engaged with, other members—who are doing the same.

Thus, leadership in innovation has come to depend on two types of competencies. First, companies must pay attention to their core businesses and make sure that they aggressively improve performance. Second, companies must systematically form alliances with others to make sure that the required complementary contributions are available.

To grasp the importance of complementary contributions, consider Intel's success. Intel releases new generations of faster and better microprocessors regularly, while cutting prices on previous versions—and ultimately cannibalizing them. The amount of market and industry creation that goes into each new generation of chips is enormous. Market creation focuses on customers and market-making institutions, i.e., "channels," including wholesale distributors, retailers, value-added resellers, and so on. Intel spends tens of millions of dollars each year to encourage customers to embrace computer activities that stress leading edge applications such as video and audio processing, for example, in order to create a consumer desire for ever faster chips.

In addition to educating customers and nurturing the marketing channels, companies must also work together to accelerate the establishment and expansion of new business ecosystems and market segments. By using investment and partnering activities, leading companies ensure that the benefits created by their investment in core contributions are supported by others in the ecosystem.

In the case of Intel, the company works with other technological companies who provide complementary products and services, from software to hardware components to complete systems. Intel makes supply agreements, provides engineering and other technical support, and often makes direct investments in companies with important contributions to the ecosystem. With each new generation, the capabilities of literally thousands of other companies must coevolve with Intel's.

FROM M-FORM TO E-FORM

The centrality of market creation and coevolution in the global economy requires a new corporate form. The traditional corporate form is the so-called M-form organization—the "multidivisional firm" made famous by General Motors. The M-form organization is what most major enterprises use today. It is made up of one or more operating business units, each reporting to a central corporate headquarters. The goal of the traditional corporation is to manage these operations so that they grow revenues and profits, and so that they live long. This form of organization rivets managers' attention on two things: their core markets and their core operations.

The problem with this model is that it creates in managers a corresponding blindness to developments occurring *outside* their core. That is, the "white space" between existing markets and operations is left, to a large extent, unattended. Yet in a global economy with ample free capital, management talent, and technological inventiveness, much of the opportunity facing businesses originates in the white space. This is true whether one is seeking to extend one's existing business—or develop new ones. The growth in Intel's core business is driven largely from the white space—in terms of new media applications, and in terms of new markets in emerging economies. Concurrently, new Intel businesses, in networking and the Internet, for example, have their centers outside core operations and existing market segments.

As business ecosystems emerge, the introverted M-form organization is giving way to the ecosystem form, or, the "E-form" organization.[1,2] Form, after all, follows function. E-form organizations are focused on markets and potential markets. They are able to manage the various elements of market development—ranging from customer selection, design, and testing of value propositions, to putting together the market relationships and complementary business models required to establish effective channels of sales and support.

In parallel, the E-form organization pulls together the functions needed to establish product architectures, end-to-end business processes, and the organizational networks and business arrangements essential to ensuring supply.

An E-form organization must manage the economics of the *total* ecosystem to its advantage—and keep other important players reasonably well satisfied. Intel is probably the best example of an E-form enterprise, whose success comes from focusing multiple functions on one particular ecosystem, in this case, a personal computer-centered ecosystem. At the center, of course, is the microprocessor business, with its torrid requirements for capital, design, and manufacturing process innovation. Fortunately, Intel sells very high volumes of microprocessors, and has high gross margins which more than cover its investments. Feeding this core is the computer systems business, that sells chip sets and boards, up to full computers, mainly in order to bring advanced Intel technology rapidly to market. And concentric to both the systems and processor businesses, Intel has the myriad of activities described previously—delivered by Intel-owned units and other companies but with Intel investments. In these cases the key to Intel's success is that it, in turn, supports the growth and primacy of the Intel architecture and processors.

INTEGRATING FUNCTIONS

A major distinction of an E-form organization is its ability to integrate the functions of business development—writ broadly—from across the corporation. In Table 4-1 we list the major dimensions of strategic action that an E-form organization must integrate, together with some of the strategic questions that must be dealt with as

TABLE **4-1.** Questions Addressed by the E-Form Organization

DIMENSIONS OF STRATEGY	QUESTIONS ADDRESSED BY THE E-FORM ORGANIZATION
Customers	Who are the customers for this ecosystem? What do they value? How do we engage them?
Markets	What is the market for this ecosystem? What are its natural boundaries, who are its gatekeepers and leaders, how do we engage with the important market makers?
Products	What is the product and service architecture that will best serve this ecosystem? Which functions should be provided in integrated bundles with others—and which functions should be joined by open interfaces that encourage alternative sources and solutions?
Processes	What business processes and technical inputs are required? What sorts of performance improvement trajectories can be achieved in the most important processes and technologies? Given an anticipation of these trajectories, how can the process architecture of the ecosystem as a whole be organized to encourage such innovation?
Organizations	What are the organizational structures and relationships that will work best? Which processes and technologies will be supplied by whom? What companies will own and sponsor what organizations? How will the overall community of organizations govern itself? How will intellectual property and other assets be owned or shared?
Stakeholders and financing	How is this ecosystem financed? What are the financial relationships among the participating organizations? How might these change over time? What stakeholders are involved—including both financial and nonfinancial types?
Social values and government policy	What are the social policy and value issues faced in this ecosystem? How might the leaders of this ecosystem establish a constructive, mutually beneficial social contract with the societies and governments that will potentially be affected by this business ecosystem?

the ecosystem forms and matures. An E-form organization finds ways to charter cross-functional teams including sales and marketing, technology and manufacturing, organization and finance, and even government relations. The E-form organization gives the team authority and responsibility to work together closely and quickly to nurture, shape, and *lead* the ecosystem as a whole.

The functions of the E-form organizations themselves are not new. What is new is their integration. Moreover, E-form managers find creative ways to operate much more aggressively and intelligently using fewer human resources, and with whom they share an understanding of the task at hand.

DRAWING RESOURCES FROM THE ENVIRONMENT

Another major point of distinction in the E-form organization is the degree to which resources are seen to lie outside of the normal bounds of the parent units and firm. The task of ecosystem development requires identifying the other power players who have an interest—or might have an interest—in the specific market space. Ecosystem development entails polling those power players to assess the degree to which various interests can be aligned, and working to create consensus and coordinated, mutually beneficial action.

One of the most crucial indicators of the success of an E-form initiative is that there are no important power players left out of consideration—and that, if feasible, all major players are given some stake in the success of the strategy.

A critical part of the challenge, however, involves more than simply identifying and considering potential players. An E-form organization must then capture the imagination of these other power players—including consumers—so that they will want to join them to create, and be a part of, their particular vision for the future of the community—and not a competing vision.

In the old world, an M-form company could use its own invested capital to align interests and build businesses. In today's world of business ecosystems, the aim is to galvanize attention, so that others use their capital to invest in business elements that they believe to be complementary to yours. There is vast free capital and free talent available in the world economy today, coupled with a desire to leave the past behind and secure a beachhead in the future. The consequence is a near frenzy to invest in ventures.

Sophisticated E-form companies learn to direct this energy in order to aggregate free resources in support of their vision. In addition, E-form companies sometimes intervene to try to stop or slow the flow of free resources that support conflicting visions promoted by their E-form competitors. The "standards wars" that have become so much a part of the high technology landscape are a direct manifestation of struggles between E-form competitors. In a manner analogous to a marsh encroaching on a hardwood forest, business ecosystems compete for the same resources to achieve dominance and territory.

What is at stake in these conflicts is the establishment of alternative ecosystems, sometimes with distinct products or processes— but more significantly made up of different companies vying for position as leader. Leadership is becoming the most hotly contested dimension of business in the most fast-moving sectors. As one high technology executive puts it, in many cases the choice is "either win for 10 years, or lose forever."

THE MORE THE MERRIER

Moreover, the control that an E-form manager assumes is of a different nature than that sought in a traditional M-form company. In an M-form company, managers seek as near as possible to absolute control and 100 percent ownership of critical functions. In the E-form organization managers learn that it is often an advantage not to exert complete control over others. In many cases it makes sense to have multiple sources of important contributions and not to devote either attention or investment or working capital to achieve control. The E-form manager is most concerned that whatever investments are made in the sector are intended to support aims consistent with his or her vision for the ecosystem—and not those of competing visions. As long as this is the case, the E-form manager often thinks "the more the merrier."

MANAGING MULTIPLE ECOSYSTEMS

One last distinction I'd like to address is that the E-form organization is adept at managing multiple ecosystems—some established or even declining and others just emerging. One of the best examples of learning to lead in multiple ecosystems in various stages of maturity is Microsoft. Microsoft's main ecosystem is of course the desktop personal computer community in which it has long held primacy. But Microsoft is also making significant investments in other ecosystems, for example in enterprise systems with NT, and in consumer broadband services with WebTV and its alliances and investments in cable television companies. In each of these ecosystems Microsoft is attempting to lead the community and find contributions from which it can make substantial financial returns. Moreover, there are shared, cross-ecosystem resources that Microsoft can use to gain even stronger financial efficiencies and returns, including its brand, talent, influence over distribution channels, and its technology.

E-FORM VERSUS M-FORM, FUTURE VERSUS PAST

The contrasts that I have drawn between the traditional M-form organization and the E-form are summarized in Table 4-2. Note that the E-form organization differs mainly in its orientation to the future, rather than the present, and in its attention to resources and opportunities outside of the traditional organization and its established markets.

While any single difference might not be significant, together they result in an organization that operates with profoundly different priorities and with a dramatically broader and deeper worldview than the M-form. I also wish to emphasize that a successful E-form organization must still achieve excellent management of existing businesses. The E-form capabilities are perhaps most accurately seen as in-addition-to M-form virtues, rather than as substitutes.

E-FORM ORGANIZATIONS AND THE NET

Convergence provides both special opportunities—and special resources—for E-form companies. First, most of the suppliers to the convergence revolution are engaged in intensive ecosystem creation and E-form competition to bring allies together around alternative visions and standards. The hottest sector of ecosystem creation and conflict is network computing technologies—and (as this chapter is written) is focused on Java.

Second, E-form companies can use the Net—with its vast ability to facilitate communication—to share and promote their visions, to find allies, and to bring together new ecosystems.

Third, the transformative power of the Net to enable new business designs means that convergence itself has become a significant factor in new business ecosystems. Thus E-form companies must put the Net at the center of their deliberations as they consider how

TABLE 4-2. Comparison of M-Form and E-Form Organizations

	M-FORM (TRADITIONAL MULTIDIVISIONAL FIRM)	E-FORM (INNOVATIVE ECOSYSTEM-CREATING FIRM)
Organizational priorities	Maintain multiple divisions or operating units	Establish new communities of complementers, that is, new business ecosystems
Market priorities	Retain existing market segment shares	Create and establish new markets
Definition of leadership	Triumph over direct competitors	Lead the coevolution of important parties
Relationship to the noncore "white space" markets and companies	Blindness to the white space issues and opportunities	Focus on white space issues and opportunities
Approach to customer selection and segmentation, market development, process and technology investments, organizational relationships, external stakeholders and financing, and government relations	Isolated into functional silos, not empowered to take integrated action	Integrated around market and ecosystem-creation opportunities, empowered to take action

TABLE 4-2. Comparison of M-Form and E-Form Organizations (*Continued*)

	M-FORM (TRADITIONAL MULTIDIVISIONAL FIRM)	E-FORM (INNOVATIVE ECOSYSTEM-CREATING FIRM)
Financial operating policy	Each business unit is expected to make market returns	Able to optimize the company's total returns from the ecosystem, even if this means taking returns from one unit and investing in another
Types of resources that are considered central to strategy making	Mainly those resources that exist within the firm or organization under the direct control of the person making strategy	All of the resources that can address the market and ecosystem at hand, especially those controlled by other powerful players
Degree of control assumed by managers	Direct control of business activities and investment priorities	Indirect influence over business activities and investment priorities
Span of activities	Multiple existing market segments, addressed by multiple operating companies and assets	Multiple market spaces, as well as market segments, served by ecosystems of varying levels of maturity, with diverse challenges and issues
Promotion, branding, and public relations	Seeks to capture the traditional imagination of the customer, through conventional promotional activities centered around products or the firm's image	Captures the imagination of existing and potential contributors to the ecosystem, knows that perception helps to create reality, mobilizes "swarms"

their currently established businesses are likely to be threatened or augmented—and as they examine opportunities for new market and ecosystem creation based on newly emerging business ideas.

On the following pages I would like to share two stories of how a company is conducting E-form activities. I switch to anecdotes throughout because—as applied to the Net—we are at an early stage in our collective experience of how enterprises, business models, and cooperation, competition, and coevolution will be conducted. In times like these, it is often best to get close to the ground—near to the seeds—and simply observe and try to make sense of what is happening.

ERIC SCHMIDT AND JAVA

Deep in the Silicon Valley, on a geological plain close to San Francisco Bay, is the main campus of Sun Microsystems. The numbered buildings, set in curving drives, are almost indistinguishable in their low-rise, earthquake-resistant simplicity of toned concrete and tinted glass.

Eric Schmidt was Sun's chief technologist until 1997. A software engineer by education, Schmidt first made his mark as a member of Xerox's prestigious Palo Alto Research Center (PARC). By the mid-1980s Schmidt had moved to the hyperactive beehive that was Sun. During the great Unix wars of the late 1980s, Schmidt was in charge of software development. By 1995, he was Chief Technologist, with a portfolio of advanced research activities—and a charter to lead the company into new territories.

One of Schmidt's research programs was a software architecture and language that became known as Java. Java was originally intended for interactive television. It was designed to operate in a hardware environment that combined a broadband network—such as cable companies might provide—with an inexpensive user device, such as a television or set-top box. Such an environment stood the conventions of the personal computer and workstation world on their heads. PCs and workstations were expensive, powerful devices, usually tied together by comparatively narrow bandwidth networks.

Although the Java software architecture and language was technically very interesting, and the team talented, the project seemed to hold little commercial promise. In 1995, the cable companies were retrenching, moving away from interactive television. However, as spring turned into summer, Netscape and other browsers took off, and the Internet bloomed. To any visionary—and Schmidt was one—it began to look like the Internet would become a ubiquitous broadband network. Moreover, one could imagine that the right software architecture could make use of such a network to enable simple, low-cost computers to provide high levels of performance when supported by high-powered network servers.

Schmidt and others within Sun became increasingly convinced that Java held important keys to enabling the Internet to go to the next level of functionality from that provided by browsers. Moreover, the potential benefits to Sun seemed enormous. First, popularizing such an architecture would cement Sun in the minds of customers as the leader of the Internet explosion. Second, the promulgation of the language would provide an alternative to the continuing expansion of Microsoft's architectural hegemony. Third, the Java architecture would play into Sun's expertise in network servers, thus helping to promote its strengths. Conversely, the Java architecture could be made to render high-powered end-user PCs unnecessary. This had the potential to harm Intel, Microsoft, and Compaq, the aristocracy of the traditional personal computer.

At first Schmidt pushed the development team to finish the product and make Java available for general consumption. Unfortunately, the software was more a research prototype than a full offering, and needed substantial development. But, by early 1996 Schmidt saw the light: "I don't need a finished product. What I need is a social movement. I need to build a community of players who will help develop the offer, who will refine the language, who will join together to make this happen."

With this revelation, Schmidt began investing heavily in alliances and relationships. Sun established a licensing program to involve others. Sun began to tout Java not as a finished product of the present, but as the key software technology for the future of convergence. The result was almost unprecedented market and industry development.

MAKING THE SHIFT FROM M-FORM TO E-FORM LEADERSHIP

What we find in this story is the essence of E-form activities. Schmidt realized that the opportunity was there to put together a community of contributors who would create a new set of economic relationships, who would coevolve their capabilities, and who would need leadership. Sun could be that leader. Schmidt—and the rest of Sun management—saw great benefit in this. They would no longer stand alone, but would be supported in their powerful vision by numerous allies. His move from an inward focus on product development to a vision of Java's development as a "social movement" was decisive in his success.

SWARMS AND SWARM MANAGEMENT

In my own work I often use a metaphor that is even more dynamic than ecosystems. For me, much strategic action today has the character of leading and managing "swarms." Especially within the Internet environment, business formation happens with dazzling speed. Moreover, the Internet business community is not comprised of a few megacompanies; rather, it is a loose collaboration of millions of free-spirited individuals and thousands of interpenetrating businesses whose disparate members behave like swarms of bees or flocks of birds; aligning with one another and flying in formation for a while, then disrupting their course and exploding into momentary confusion. A moment later—just as suddenly—they reconfigure around a new course with a new destination. For Sun and others involved in the Internet, to influence such swarms is to benefit from the combined resources of a vast, self-organizing community. One gains "strategic allies for free" as the community rises up to support a particular vision of the future.

The more I delve into the nature of business in and around the Net, the more I am becoming fascinated with the "play within a play" nature of what is going on. The way I see it, the Net is fast becoming a fundamental information and community-building infrastructure that enables the even more rapid coming together of new swarms. These new swarms, in turn, become integrated into the foundation of the core community—and enable new and even more potent community building. Mosaic enabled a swarm that defined the World Wide Web. Netscape used the Web to establish the browser as the most interesting application of the 1990s, and to point to the possibility of the browser as central to an emerging architecture for networked computing. Microsoft, in turn, took the browser and integrated it deeply into its own Windows architecture, and used a combination of conventional distribution and Web-based proliferation to establish its vision—which has subsequently set the stage for further escalations.

If we look more deeply into the story of Java's introduction, we can get a rich sense of this double potential of Web-based "swarm leadership," which not only enshrines certain companies as leaders, but also extends the general foundation for further community building. In the following story we get a sense not only of the importance of galvanizing a community, but the vital role that the Net can play in doing so.

JOHN HERR AND JAVAONE

The time was February 1996. The company was SOFTBANK Forums, a leading marketing services company producing educational events and trade shows for the computer networking business, and hosting a variety of events including Networld + Interop, the industry's annual gathering. John Herr was Vice President of Marketing for SOFTBANK Forums at the time. His task: to promote a new software language called Java.

In some ways Herr typified the new breed of young, classically trained but Net-aware executives. Educated at Harvard Business School, mentored in business strategy at consultants Bain & Company and consumer marketing at Johnson & Johnson, he embodied conventional marketing wisdom. On the other hand, he had dedicated himself completely to the Net as a business environment, and as a master platform for branding and community building.

This story begins in Herr's Silicon Valley office, where, upon receiving his mission, he urgently gathered his colleagues. Pitched into chairs at odd angles in the conference room, his team consisted of an eclectic mix of marketers, public relations strategists, technologists, and "business guys."

The overt task facing the group was the promotion of Java, but the real mission was to nurture the formation of a community of software developers, application consultants, and "raging enthusiasts" who would evangelize the new language to the wider business world.

Herr's Java challenge was not unlike that of a political campaign manager—create a fever for your candidate—in this case a technology—and forge a coherent social movement from a diverse population of potential supporters. His team had some of the frenetic energy reminiscent of the "war room" crowd made famous during Bill Clinton's first run for the U.S. presidency. Like the Clinton campaign, the major challenges facing the team would be lack of time and the inevitability of a massively overloaded organization.

Sun Microsystems was, of course, the immediate client, and Eric Schmidt the sponsor. Sun and Schmidt wanted an event of historic proportions, hosting thousands of people, joining electrifying keynote addresses to meaty educational sessions. Sun was in a race with Microsoft, competing for the hearts and minds of the computer world. Success, in Sun's mind, required working within a short time window and reaching many thousands of potential attendees. Sun wanted the promotion to go from a dead stop to full bore in about 12 weeks. Herr and his group concluded that if they used conventional marketing techniques there was little possibility that 12 weeks would be sufficient. Marketing in the traditional manner, combining magazine ads, direct mail, and phone calls would have a far too superficial impact in the time allotted.

So Herr and the team turned to the Net itself for help, creating a branding and community-organizing campaign almost entirely within cyberspace. First, they approached Netscape, IBM, and other interested companies to become cosponsors of JavaOne. The price of cosponsorship was copromotion via the Web. Each firm put notices on its own Web sites. More important, each agreed to send promotional e-mail alerts to thousands of employees, suppliers, and customers. Second, Herr and his campaigners turned to the heavily trafficked search engine sites on the Web. Yahoo!, the most popular search engine, agreed to sponsor JavaOne, boosting the software to its millions of daily visitors. Third, the campaign established its own JavaOne Web site to provide follow-up information, answer frequently asked questions, and accomplish online registration. Finally, Herr stirred up interest among the Internet press and pundits, who by now saw that JavaOne was likely to become a phenomenon— and, in turn, contributed to the hype, thereby helping to create JavaOne's historic stature as a self-fulfilling prophesy.

A SWARM COMES TOGETHER

The results of this campaign were almost implausible from a conventional marketing point of view. Over the course of about 12 weeks, JavaOne registrations shot to over 6000. Over 5000 of these paid the full registration fee of $1000 per person. Five thousand people paid to become evangelists—to be at the heart of a revolution. Grass roots associations of software developers—often the most resistant to conventional corporate hype—signed on to support the event.

One hundred and sixty companies bought exhibition space in the Java Pavilion to introduce products. They handed out hats and T-shirts—flying flags and banners from their booths, and at home at their own headquarters.

Less tangibly, but perhaps as important, JavaOne made history. The community came together as one, the community could see and behold itself face-to-face—and the community realized that it was formidable. Java was truly on the way to becoming a successful social movement in addition to a technology.

Ultimate success was confirmed a year later, in April 1997, with the second annual JavaOne, now host to over 10,000 communards. A brand had been created, a community formed, and an institution established. And all this was accomplished in true Internet time—with a decisive initial success that required weeks rather than the more traditional months or years. In a bow to JavaOne's significance, Bill Gates of Microsoft—who was not scheduled to speak at JavaOne—was astute enough to book a speaking slot at a nearby event, in order to join the action. The resulting battle of words with Sun's boisterous CEO Scott McNealy was gleefully covered by the press and television.

INCREASING RETURNS AND THE VALUE OF SWARMS

What made this all possible was the communication foundation—the platform—created by the Net. Because the foundation was in place, the incremental cost of each unit of communication was almost zero. Potential members of the community had browsers, participated regularly in Net-based communication, and were receptive to the Net as an interactive medium. Physical reception of the messages was almost assured.

While the incremental cost was low—to SOFTBANK and to the individual members of the community—the value of being in a community—on the Net—was high. Moreover, as the conference and the community grew, the ability to share learning, to make connections, to work together, to promote and explore ideas became higher and higher. Over 70 percent of the attendees visited the JavaOne Web site before the meeting, and many made repeated visits. A JavaOne-centered dynamic of ever-increasing returns to the community was established. The more members that joined, the more value there was in joining.

Herr and his team were able to focus on what really mattered, which was the substantive and emotional content of the campaign. Their message was, "One, information from the source—that is, from Sun and other experts; One, Java is the number one way to develop software; and One, this is the first and preeminent venue for the community." The critical success factor became a question of attitude rather than technology. In this sense it was traditional marketing principles, applied in the new medium, that carried the day. But these principles simply could not have been applied in the time allowed, had the Net and its members not existed as a system.

On the platform side, readily available Net-centric tools and techniques made it easy to produce Net-based promotions, and relatively simple to deal with electronic inquiries and sign-ups. This ease of production applied to JavaOne and SOFTBANK Forums, as well as the cosponsors. Because the incremental cost to the sponsors was minimal and the time-to-message interval was very short, it was easy for the JavaOne team to quickly sign up large numbers of cosponsors. Essentially, it was easy for *everyone* to play. The convergence of computers and communications into the Net makes possible a global marketplace of ideas, and allows for the almost instantaneous formation of communities of even more far-flung members.

THE FUTURE OF BUSINESS DESIGN

One of the most important consequences of convergence is that the rules of organization design—indeed of business ecosystem design—have changed fundamentally. It used to be that one designed an organization or a business with mainly administrative control in mind. The whole of modern business history has been about the struggle to coordinate enterprises. Economies of scale, of scope, and of focus could often be envisioned, but never realized in practice—because of the limits of our administrative capabilities. Sometimes our organizations stayed smaller than was optimal, and in other instances organizations have remained larger.

In the old world, what limited our administrative capabilities was our ability to handle complexity—to analyze—and our ability to communicate among ourselves—that is, to interact effectively. As the tools of convergence enhance our abilities to analyze and interact, a new world is being born. In the new world, administrative limits are falling fast, freeing businesses to reconfigure themselves along theoretically ideal designs. Business ecosystems that could only be dreamed of in the past can now be achieved.

The Netscape-led swarm, for example, that was so fundamental to establishing the Internet as we know it could not possibly have been accomplished without the Web itself. Netscape's fundamental strategic concept was to organize the unorganized—the end users and independent software developers and related professionals. Or more properly, Netscape's strategy was to give the unorganized users of the Web a way to bring themselves together into communities. This would not have been a feasible strategy had the incremental cost not been almost zero for establishing membership for each individual—that is, for providing each person with a browser and a way of accessing Netscape's servers.

SHARING THE FUTURE

Today's world is far too complex, and the permutations too many, for any single company to envision future scenarios. This fact—the unknowable nature of the future—requires a new logic for strategy. On the analytical side, strategy must address how to make these new worlds succeed operationally and financially. On the activist side, strategy must turn these scenarios into programs and plans for achieving a foothold from which the future can then be approached.

One of the most interesting scenario-building programs is Hewlett-Packard's "Creating the Future" workshops. For several years now, HP has convened executives and other key decision makers from a particular sector of the economy. Included are representatives from major companies and other institutions, as well as people representing the customers' perspective. These representatives are then provided with a structure for sharing ideal futures.

From this richness and diversity of visions, the group explores shared goals, as well as potential conflicts, in order to find ways to help each other shape the future. What ultimately emerges are ideas for new business ecosystems, generated by many of the most important potential players themselves.

CONCLUSION

No E-form company is a perfect or complete model. Nonetheless, one can begin to abstract the knowledge, roles, processes, systems, and skills that contribute to the new corporate form's success. Success involves expanding the participation of line managers, business development professionals, and senior management.

Knowledge is key. Members of E-form companies must learn to scan the environment for new species of business activities. They must develop the insight required to combine these into systems of complementary relationships. And the new corporate managers must assess the health and well-being of the various economic ecosystems in which their firm participates, in order to use its resources to effectively foster innovation and growth.

There are rich opportunities available to firms who learn— ahead of others—how to function in the new mode. The world economy has never been more receptive to entrepreneurial activity of the highest level. It is E-form companies that are moving into this unprecedented global opportunity and shaping the future—with themselves at the center.

NOTES

1. Moore, James F., "Predators and Prey: A New Ecology of Competition," *Harvard Business Review,* May/June, 1993.
2. Moore, James F., *The Death of Competition: Leadership and Strategy in the Age of Business Ecosystems* (New York: Harper Business), 1996.

DESIGNING THE NEW DIGITAL ENTERPRISE

by Paul Woolner

Alliance for Converging Technologies

New enterprise in the digital economy has garnered investor interest—at times bordering on frenzy. As a result, many digital start-up ventures have enjoyed high market valuation and easy access to capital. Paradoxically, these favorable conditions may have worked against the development of the organizational processes and systems required to move these businesses beyond their formative stage, and put their futures at risk.

The influx of new money in equity markets has created an over-supply of capital available to new digital enterprises.[1] While this has buffered many businesses in their early stages, providing too much capital, too soon, has often created a false sense of accomplishment and a belief in the inevitability of success—a kind of Midas formula. This does not force a more critical, disciplined management of organizational processes or an understanding of how they add value. It may also de-emphasize the importance of responding to customer preferences in the development of products and services. In the long run, having more capital than capacity to actually use it will hinder building a resilient, sustainable enterprise.

This chapter offers practical lessons from the front lines of an entrepreneurial digitally-based business. The focus is on building new digital enterprises—companies whose products and services are based on interactive and network technologies or who are providers of the technologies supporting digitally-based businesses.

More specifically, the emphasis is on creating sustainable business models, and on the organizational structure and human resources management that foster growth. Because of the frenzied speed of change, these two strategic elements are frequently bumped to the bottom of the list of priorities—often to the demise of the company.

This chapter takes a detailed look at the critical transition point for new digital enterprises as they cross the chasm from being an informal start-up venture to becoming a more complex and successful organization. For the purposes of this chapter, success is considered in terms of increasing the long-term share value for an organization.[2]

THE EMERGING ENVIRONMENT AND IMPLICATIONS FOR NEW DIGITAL ENTERPRISE STRATEGY

The driving forces and dynamics of digital enterprise are at once familiar and significantly novel compared with those of more traditional businesses. Like the first prospectors in the gold and silver rushes of the old West, early entrepreneurs of the Web amassed considerable wealth.

But also like the days of the gold rush, only a few of the earliest Web-based entrepreneurial ventures actually struck it rich; for many who have followed, there has been a lot of hard work with more modest returns, or none at all. Some observers, such as the *Wall Street Journal,* are declaring the Internet a "bust from a commercial perspective." But perhaps the key issue is not whether the Web is a bust—it's whether the expectations of both the markets and the entrepreneurs were unrealistic. Those expectations were based on a context similar to that of a gold rush, in which the value of goods and services goes awry. Everything, from gold itself to food and supplies, becomes wildly overvalued.

By 1997, there were indications that investor interest in the electronic frontier was subsiding. Wired Ventures' public offering collapsed and was withdrawn, and there was a downturn in such initially high-growth businesses as Infoseek and Cybercash. Not that the gold rush was completely over; Web-based enterprises such as

Amazon.com were still seeking high valuations that exceeded their projected revenues by 15 to 20 times. Commentators were mixed on whether or not the gold rush was ending, but there was no doubt it had slowed down. This decline changed the context and the requirements for building sustainable entrepreneurial digital enterprise.[3]

Overall, new digital enterprises initially achieved success by concentrating on the speed to market of new products and services. Much less emphasis was placed on developing a sustainable organization strategy. This is always difficult in entrepreneurial settings, and it seems to be even more so—or at least it has been to date—in Net-based companies.

Consider the case of XLNT Designs, a small California-based engineering firm that designs and manufactures technology upgrade solutions for installed networks. It was initially focused on supplying network builders such as Cisco and Bay Networks. As an OEM provider, XLNT concentrated on speed of product innovation while relying on the large providers to sense and respond to end customer needs.

But XLNT found that being removed from end users meant that knowledge of their needs was being filtered through the other larger organizations, which had their own agenda. Therefore, customer needs regarding XLNT's specialized niche products were not being as sharply identified. There were also production overruns, because it was hard to accurately predict the quantity of product required. XLNT therefore changed its marketing focus, and began selling direct to both network builders *and* users, a strategy that brought them much closer to their customers.

Having achieved a measure of success as a small product-centered business supplying a few clients, XLNT thus faced the challenge of becoming a larger enterprise with new capabilities. Rather than simply selling products to a few large network providers, it had to establish its own brand and sell to a much larger base of customers, which now included the end users.

This involved creating an awareness for its products, and developing a marketing and sales strategy. XLNT had to build quickly upon its engineering and product focus by adding new organizational functions in end-user marketing, sales, and services. It had to recruit new marketing and sales professionals, it had to establish reward systems for a different kind of marketing effort, and it had to develop the processes to support marketing and sales efforts as well as service to users.

To remain competitive, XLNT had to significantly reorganize, but most important, it required the agility to do so quickly and efficiently—while maintaining its product and service quality. As the president of another new digital enterprise once said, "it's like driving a car down the highway at 70 mph, and trying to patch the body and paint it at the same time."

GENETIC CODING FOR GROWTH

In financial markets, there has been increasing expectation that revenues and profitability will be higher—and produced sooner—so that a company can be sustainable based on its operating performance. While many new digital enterprises will continue to be acquisition targets for large enterprises, the timing for such an opportunity is unpredictable. By building organizational capabilities, a company can endure until the right strategic investor appears—and it can also make itself a more attractive, higher-valued investment. But new digital enterprises cannot grow using the free-form organizational model. To satisfy market demands, they must intentionally develop a more formal organization design that captures both the spirit and the characteristics that fostered the success of the entrepreneurial start-up. These must then be embedded in a structural "genetic coding" that can support high growth.

In *Crossing the Chasm*,[4] Geoffrey Moore identifies a critical challenge for enterprises selling high-tech products: to move beyond the ability to market to early adopters and provide whole product solutions to mainstream customers. Many promising firms prove unsuccessful in the long run because their initial achievement depends on a small market of early adopters and they are unable to reach a larger market. To be successful, a company has to cross this market chasm.

Similarly, the new digital enterprise must cross an *organizational* chasm: it must move from being a Stage I forming organization to a Stage II developing organization.[5] Companies that show promise in their start-up phase risk their future unless they can make the transition to a more planned, intentional enterprise design. This is not the only significant organizational chasm they will need to cross. Others will appear at later stages of growth. But the first chasm offers the greatest opportunity to shape the performance and scalability of the company over the short and long term.

Three factors affect the process of crossing the first chasm:

1. Knowledge as a key to competitive advantage
2. Organizational agility
3. Pace of change

These three factors recur throughout the following discussion of the stages of growth and the transitions from one stage to the next.

SEIZING THE DESIGNABLE MOMENT

The transition to a more designed, differentiated organization can positively or negatively affect an enterprise's growth and sustainability—and even its survival. Time is the scarce resource of the 1990s; given intense competing demands for the time and attention of people in a small business, the critical question facing a new enterprise is: When is the right time to invest in organization strategy? Investing too early in organization development can cause an enterprise to fail because attention is diverted from product delivery and revenue-generating activities. But investing too late can hurt, too, because lack of effective organization results in confusion and suboptimal performance.

In models of human learning, the "teachable moment" is defined as a situation in which an individual feels the readiness, need, and openness to acquire new knowledge or adopt a change in attitude. Learning takes place more rapidly and effectively at these moments, and its lasting impact is much greater. Similarly, the entrepreneurial organization has a "designable moment."

The leader of a new digital enterprise who seizes this moment can establish the organizational genetic coding for sustained high growth. Missing the designable moment can hamper performance in ways that may not be immediately evident, but will become so over time as an increasing number of organizational problems arise.

Even worse is a partial crossing. Getting caught in the middle of the organizational chasm can be disastrous; if enterprise members are unsure of the ground rules and *modus operandi*, company performance risks being seriously jeopardized and valuable time is lost. For example, after showing early promise with rapid, profitable growth and the ability to attract capital, one new digital enterprise stalled part way in its transition. The founding partners could not develop a shared vision or agree on the scope and focus of the business. Too many opportunities were pursued without the operational capacity to deliver and without sound financial analysis. New organizational systems and programs were planned and launched, but follow-through and implementation were sporadic at best. Business growth slowed. In a more moderately paced competitive environment these factors might not become critical so quickly. But they adversely affected this enterprise's performance and limited its potential for future growth; as new competitors arrived and it lost its "early-in" advantage.

Seven Leverage Points for Crossing the Organizational Chasm

There are seven critical leverage points in setting the organization strategy for the new digital enterprise. Attention to these levers will optimize the designable moment and enable the crossing of the organizational chasm. It will also set the stage for future transition points, which will vary in scale and complexity. With appropriate resource allocations, the new digital enterprise can improve its overall organizational capabilities and achieve a "smart" context for growth and decisive moves. Not all of the seven leverage points are new, but their integrated development creates the conditions to transform the new digital enterprise.

Leverage Point 1. Vision-Driven, Value-Based Enterprise. The vision and values of the new digital enterprise are especially important when market conditions are volatile and opportunities abound. They provide the directional compass for a host of pressing business decisions. In cyberspace environments, where "the only constant is change," an organization lacking a clear vision will simply drift from opportunity to opportunity. It will lack the fundamental metrics for making decisions and establishing focus.

Values are central to vision: they provide a benchmark for guiding and assessing both team and individual behavior, as well as the ethical standards of the enterprise as a whole. The most powerful visions provide a rich, detailed portrait of the enterprise's desired future, including statements of purpose, business definition, performance, customer and stakeholder relations, company culture, and even the nature, look, and feel of the work environment.

It is important that developing the vision be an inclusive process. Knowledge-based product quality depends on optimizing the collective intelligence of an enterprise. Similarly, involving all levels of the new digital enterprise in setting the larger context for organization strategy yields a higher-quality design and delivery.

Leverage Point 2. Rapid Organization Prototyping. The nature of the technology environment enables speedy construction and testing of products, as well as scalability to new and larger markets. A new digital enterprise must develop similar organizational capabilities. Developing a capacity for rapid organization prototyping is both a reaction to, and a driver of, high growth. Without it, the enterprise will not adequately meet the demands for performance, people, expertise, management, and leadership.

Crossing the organizational chasm is not a one-time event. Because of shifts in scale and strategy, continuous changes to the organizational systems are necessary. For example, the enterprise must have a process for the review and modification of organizational form. An individual or team must be responsible for the architecture and design of organizational systems to identify the need for redesign and respond accordingly. In the industrial age enterprise, organizational forms were expected to be more enduring. Today's digital enterprise, however, must cultivate the mindset that continual organizational change is the norm. The individual's role will be highly changeable as the business shifts from project to project.

The uncertainties of the business environment—where the basis for competing and value-adding is being continually redefined—also necessitate rapid organization prototyping. A new digital enterprise must be able to shift to new organizational forms to accommodate and respond to new external factors. Having a core set of organizational systems enables both rapid organization prototyping and scalability (see Fig. 5-1).

Continually and quickly redesigning the organization stresses people's capacity to live with changing roles and responsibilities. This is especially the case among key leaders and contributors. In the industrial age business, the common complaint was one of tedium: work was stable but repetitive. In many new digital enterprises the challenge is just the opposite: team members look for more stability. Recently, one principal expressed frustration to his Board at having held six positions/assignments in less than three years. He saw it as the result of poor planning, at least in part. But at the

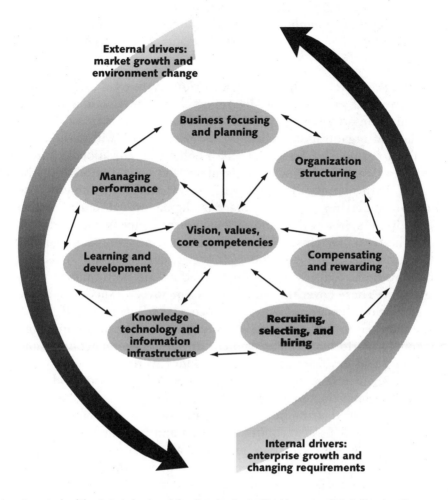

An example of the strategic framework for aligned systems utilized by a new digital enterprise. Change is driven by external and internal factors. The core systemic elements remain constant while rapid redesign and prototyping takes place at the programatic and tool levels of each system. Alignment is achieved through ensuring that all core systems are directed by shared strategic intent captured in the vision, values and core competencies.

FIGURE 5-1. Aligned systemic elements.

executive level, such change was seen as necessary to accommodate a rapidly growing business.

In this environment of rapid change, the source of stability is the enterprise's overall vision rather than defined roles, making vision all the more crucial. It is also important to have a reward system which, through employee equity participation, aligns the interest of the team members with the vision of the company and its shareholders. This provides a critical balance to the stress of organization flux.

Leverage Point 3. Aligned Organization Systems.   The systemic framework of an enterprise determines how effective it is at rapid organization prototyping. At the point of moving from an informal to a planned organization, an opportunity arises that will never come again: To establish a framework for a holistic organizational strategy in which each of the systems is identified and aligned with the vision, with one another, and with the external environment. The central leadership task at this stage is alignment; without it, system effectiveness drops and organizational performance is impaired.

The term "systems" refers to the core elements of the organization's infrastructure. It includes strategies, programs, and tools that the enterprise will use for culture creation and performance management. These cover the whole of any employee's experience of the organization, beginning with the process of being recruited, hired, and oriented to the enterprise. It continues with business and work planning, performance management, rewards and recognition, and learning and development. It also includes working within a technology environment to facilitate work-related processes and, ultimately, organization and work design.

Because of their interdependence, the systems are complex; considerable resources are required to design and implement them. It is unlikely that a new digital enterprise will have the resources to develop all necessary systems and programs when crossing the chasm. Success depends on establishing the enterprise's systems model and the strategic intent of each of its systems. They can then be built on a priority basis, depending on the needs of the business. The systems model provides a planning and management framework to house the knowledge, processes, and tools that will bring each of the systems to life.

Many new digital enterprises do not grasp the opportunity to build aligned organizational systems. Instead, the development of organizational systems is ad hoc. For example, an enterprise vision statement may speak of the importance of teamwork. Perhaps learning opportunities are provided to improve team effectiveness. But what if the compensation system only recognizes individual performance and the organization design emphasizes traditional command and control structures? There is a misalignment of systems that causes confusion among team members as to the underlying intent of the organization and the behavior expected of them. Aligned systems send a clearer message; the result is a stronger, more resilient organizational culture. This type of organizational structure allows individuals, teams, and larger work units to be more self-regulating, and so are much easier to scale to a larger size. In contrast, misaligned systems cause people to become increasingly dysfunctional as an enterprise grows.

At the enterprise level, the ongoing management and alignment of organizational systems beyond the first transition is a key strategic learning capability. The redesign and redeployment of systems becomes a key lever for managing the evolution and growth of the enterprise. For example, at IMG it became apparent that the emphasis on teamwork meant that individual accountability and a performance orientation were being neglected. These factors are extremely important in a rapidly maturing market, and so a number of the organizational systems were altered. New structures created single points of accountability, and there were changes to the performance management program and reward systems. A perfect balance among systems can never be achieved, but speed and agility are crucial when new digital enterprises are adopting systemic elements as levers for achieving new strategy. This is the essence of a learning organization.

Leverage Point 4. Knowledge, Information, and Technology Infrastructure.   During the formative stage of the new digital enterprise, the knowledge base of the organization is embodied in its initial products and service offerings. Because of the informal and almost completely fluid nature of the organization, knowledge creation and dissemination are embedded in the enterprise activities. Knowledge is central to both the products and services and the organizational processes themselves; thus, the ability to embody and embed knowledge and learning must be at the heart of organizational strategy. In industrial age enterprises, human capital was often only a small component of capital resources and assets. But for the new digital enterprise it is the principal basis for competitive advantage. Industrial age enterprise could survive without being a learning organization or could evolve into it more slowly. This is not an option in the digital economy. The new digital enterprise's organizational infrastructure must be driven by the need to optimize its knowledge and learning to achieve high performance.

Table 5-1 lists some of the key characteristics of knowledge and learning deployment required by the new digital enterprise in crossing the organizational chasm. They are illustrated at the individual, team, and enterprise levels.[6] The information infrastructure of the enterprise enables all levels of knowledge deployment and learning. Establishing the enterprise's intranet and extranet platforms—as part of this infrastructure—is also crucial to the successful transition from a Stage I to a Stage II enterprise. Yet even while exploiting leading-edge technology for their products and services, new digital enterprises often will not invest in technological support for its organizational strategy.

The transition to the developing organization provides an opportunity to create, capture, and communicate the core organizational systems. Technological infrastructure is a key enabler of this process; through it, the knowledge and processes contained within these systems can be continuously refined and reinvented. The advantages—in scalability, speed, and effective management of transitions to larger and more complex organizational forms—cannot be overemphasized. IMG learned a painful lesson in this respect: because the information technology strategy was not implemented early enough, work was lost whenever there was a turnover of key team members. This resulted in costly redesign of organizational systems and programs, and difficulty in keeping pace with a rapidly growing workforce. Indeed, it put the organizational culture at risk because so much of it was encoded in the systems and the knowledge they contained. Without an adequate technology infrastructure, it was difficult to communicate IMG's culture and organizational processes to new enterprise members.

Leverage Point 5. Extended Enterprise Mapping.   Many digital start-ups develop their capabilities in the context of numerous extended partnerships and alliances. Considerable competitive advantage can be gained through early and clear delineation of what the new digital enterprise will manage internally and what aspects will be developed through external relations. For example, Cisco grew rapidly through an explicit strategy of working with an extended network of e-business partners. In some instances, these relations can be so complex that a new digital enterprise might be collaborating in one area and competing in another with the same partner.

The extended enterprise strategy has major implications for the company's overall organizational strategy. The forming organization

TABLE 5-1. Knowledge and Learning Development across Three Levels of the Enterprise

INDIVIDUAL	TEAM	ENTERPRISE
Learning needs linked to strategic business issues	Teams recognized as primary means of continuous improvement	Continuous and open monitoring of external environment
Individual competencies linked to key capabilities	Teams also focus on their own performance and development	Opportunity for many people to contribute to business strategy, especially regarding implementation
Learning integrated with day-to-day activities	Team's collective learning generates new business understandings	Business strategy development as part of continuous organizational learning
Individual responsibility taken for learning	Teams surface and reframe underlying assumptions of business	Experimentation and risk taking at all levels
Formal systems and rewards for motivating and supporting continuous learning		

faces the key dilemma of deciding how dependent it wants to be on others for key elements of its value-add. Decisiveness is required to optimally design the enterprise for its next growth stage. The transition from the Forming to Developing organization provides an opportunity to refine an extended enterprise strategy and map out these relations.

Leverage Point 6. Leadership by Reflective Practitioners. The new digital enterprises require leaders who are able to function well in environments that are ambiguous. They must demonstrate effective team-based competencies, provide a charismatic voice to the enterprise vision, and establish and maintain effective relationships characterized by emotional intelligence. In addition, leaders must be able to provide leadership across significantly different scales of the organization during its growth.

In the early start-up, prerevenue stages, the organizational and decision-making processes are significantly different from those required as the organization grows exponentially in revenues and number of employees. For example, the new digital enterprise leader must be able to recognize if and when the requirements of the business outstrip the leader's own competencies and management abilities. To act on this self-awareness and bring in new leaders demands a high degree of personal courage and integrity.

The learning orientation of the leader reflects on the enterprise culture as a whole, determining how knowledge creation and deployment are promoted. It is almost impossible for any one individual to be adept in all of the areas required for effective leadership. As a result, what becomes critical to successful leadership is a metacharacteristic: to be a reflective practitioner. The reflective practitioner is a role model who demonstrates a number of characteristics, including continuous acquisition and renewal of knowledge; flexibility of approaches; the ability to incorporate complex and incomplete sets of information into decision making; and a willingness to learn, to change, and to do things differently. These are also key success factors for the new digital enterprise, and they will not be realized in the enterprise unless they are present in a critical mass of leadership.

For the enterprise crossing the organizational chasm, there is probably no factor more inhibiting than a key leader who does not lead by example and work within the processes and systems designed to move it to the next stage. In these situations, the enterprise will stall part way across the chasm. Having grown too complex to remain in its formative stage, but with no clear leadership for the crossing, the enterprise will seem unable to grow. To succeed, the leader's priority must be organizational benefit, not personal satisfaction: the "organization as hero" rather than "the individual leader as hero." Leadership thus requires great depth of personal objectivity and flexibility.

A significant factor that works against reflective leadership is the speed of the digital economy. The leader, like the enterprise itself, is driven to value action much more than reflection, which is often seen as nonproductive downtime. And yet reflection is a key element in the creation and renewal of knowledge. Indeed, many leading digital enterprises, such as Microsoft and Netscape, had their genesis when their founders were in university—a setting that places a high value on reflective activity. Lessons can be quickly extracted from experience to reshape and improve future action. Even designing the organizational strategy of the new digital enterprise is an essentially reflective activity, but one which swiftly leads to implementation, rapid prototyping, then back to reflection—a continuous cycle of adaptation based on mindful action.

Leverage Point 7. Innovative Organizational Form. The way in which we portray the organization (for example, the organizational chart) and the language that is developed to describe it are both key levers. More traditional language in the organizational form creates a more traditional, bureaucratic mindset. New organizational forms and language have often been used to develop strong high-performance cultures in "green field" sites.

The new digital enterprise can utilize new organizational models and language to better reflect the knowledge- and project-based nature of the work environment. For example, some enterprises substitute new models for the box and wire pyramids of traditional charts. At IMG the challenge when designing the organization was to avoid defaulting to more traditional command and control structures. Instead, IMG wanted to capture the organizational practices and values which had led to success in the forming stage. These were embodied in a more team-based, circular structure. New language was developed to emphasize a team-based and contribution orientation rather than a status orientation. Limiting the use of traditional titles may seem trivial, but it is not. Language and icons are critical elements of building any culture. In the new digital enterprise, organizational nomenclature is an important tool in consciously shaping corporate culture.

AFTER THE GOLD RUSH

Each economic age has its optimal organizational form—a structure that is most aligned with the means of wealth creation, dominant technologies, and social context. The industrial age was epitomized by the command and control bureaucratic organization which, in manufacturing, evolved into the assembly line. With work broken into small component tasks, the underlying principle of human relationship for the industrial age was independence.

In the digital economy, with its basis of wealth creation rooted in knowledge, a new human relationship is required. The underlying principle for the creation of knowledge-based products is interdependence—collective networked intelligence applied to innovation and problem solving. The organization form that is best aligned with the need for interdependent action is characterized by flexibility, distributed decision making, multifunctional teams, and learning. New digital enterprises are challenged to instill these characteristics in their organizations and through this, build the bridges to cross their organizational chasms.

NOTES

1. Perkins, Anthony B., "Have the Rules Really Changed?" *Red Herring,* October 1997. Clinton Wilder, *Gold Rush Is Over,* CMP Publications, 1997.
2. The concepts presented here are based on my work and research with a number of new digital enterprises. They draw especially on my experience leading the organizational strategy for Interactive Media Group (IMG), whose revenues grew from $2 million in 1991 to more than $70 million in 1997. Founded in Toronto, the company now generates most of its revenue in the United States and is expanding across the globe.
3. Perkins, Anthony B., op. cit.
4. Moore, Geoffrey A., *Crossing the Chasm: Marketing and Selling High-Tech Products to Mainstream Customers,* (New York: Harper Business), October 1995.
5. Woolner, Lowy & Associates, *The Learning Organization 5 Stage Diagnostic Survey.*
6. Woolner, Paul, *A Developmental Model of the Learning Organization White Paper,* Institute for Strategic Learning.

PART TWO

INDUSTRY
TRANSFORMATIONS

This section delivers first-hand accounts of digital economy
strategy from six major industries including banking,
publishing, imaging, education, telecommunications, and
logistics. In each case, we get an inside look at the threats and
opportunities facing individual companies and their strategic
responses in the face of gut-wrenching change.

BANKING WITHOUT BOUNDARIES

How The Banking Industry Is Transforming Itself For The Digital Age

by Lloyd Darlington
Bank of Montreal Group of Companies[1]

We need to face as squarely as we can the new realities that are transforming banking so swiftly that to analyze them is like trying to map the clouds. Globalization, changing demographics and exploding information and communication technology have already brought about massive changes in the way you bank. Yet I am as certain as I can be of anything that we are only standing at the threshold of a new world. It is as if we had just invented printing or the steam engine.

MATTHEW W. BARRETT, CHAIRMAN & CEO
BANK OF MONTREAL GROUP OF COMPANIES

It has been 300 years since banking underwent a change of this magnitude. William of Orange was King of England, Louis XIV was King of France, and the two countries were in the midst of one of their many interminable and largely indistinguishable wars. In fact, it can be argued, it was *only* what happened to banking that set the 1689–1697 war apart from the rest.

This singular event, which would determine the course of banking as we've known it for the past three centuries, was the founding, in 1694, of the Bank of England. Seeking an alternative means of financing the war—which had been precipitated by France's efforts to restore the deposed Catholic King James II to the English throne—King William created a bank that would borrow money from the public (as opposed to, say, London's rich usurious gold-smiths) in order to make loans to the government.

Not only did the Bank of England serve its short-term pur-pose—the war *was* "won on England's credit," as historian Sir Roy Strong notes—it also gave England an insurmountable lead in the so-called commercial revolution that spanned the seventeenth and eighteenth centuries in Western Europe. "As the 17th century drew to a close," Sir Roy observes in *The Story of Britain*, "no other coun-try in western Europe could rival England in terms of capital resources and potential investment."

The advantages became even more important, as well as appar-ent, a generation later, when the English led the world into the industrial age. In fact, Alvin Toffler pinpoints the founding of the Bank of England as "the very dawn" of the industrial age. It became "a template for similar centralist institutions in all Second Wave countries," the noted futurist observes in *The Third Wave*.[2] "No country could compete in its Second Wave phase," which he also refers to as *industrial civilization*, "without constructing its own equivalent of this machine for the central control of money and credit."

The *next* time something of this magnitude happened in bank-ing is, of course, this very moment—the dawn of the digital age. To borrow one last turn of phrase from Toffler's 1980 prophecy, the banking industry finds itself at an "explosive moment."

The force of the explosion is so great that many observers—Don Tapscott among them—are already predicting that banking itself will be blown right away. If they are talking about traditional bank-ing, then it is hard to disagree. But if they are speaking of banking as we know it at Bank of Montreal today, then we have a fundamen-tal difference of opinion.

Propelled by the newfound powers of choice that technology has conferred upon the financial services customer, banking is transforming itself at a pace and on a scale that has no historical precedent. In predictable Darwinian fashion, those banks that refuse to adapt will very likely die. But, as I will demonstrate in this chapter, when the dust finally settles, the survivors among the tradi-tional banks will have reinvented themselves into organizations that, among other things, conduct business equally effectively in cyber-space and on Main Street.

QUANTUM LEAP FOR QUANTUM LEAP

Banking entered the 1990s doing, for the most part, what it had always done, albeit with increasing degrees of complexity. Banks, by their very nature, were in the transaction business—taking deposits, cashing checks, making loans. Along with keeping customers' money safe (and earning decent interest), this was roughly the extent of what banks did for a living, and what banking customers expected. Then, suddenly, propelled by the confluence of forces that has redefined the world economy, customers' expectations took one of those quantum leaps. And, consequently, banking had to take a quantum leap of its own.

With this leap, the industry—or, more accurately, some of its members—acknowledged three new and immutable facts, all of them the result of pervasive technologies that erased the old lines between banking delivery channels, between industries and, indeed, between nations. First, we are now competing in a customer's market and, it seems certain, we always will. Second, this market is global. Third, the competition for these customers and their money is no longer confined to the banking *industry*, never mind national economies. In the new world of banking without boundaries, this confluence of forces represents a severe and potentially fatal loss of competitive advantage.

For the first time in 300 years, the very *nature* of banking has changed. We still handle money, but information, not money, is now the lifeblood of our industry. From what was essentially a transaction-based business, where customers came to you (or didn't), banking has to make the leap into what is essentially a sales-and-marketing culture. In the new culture, a bank is defined almost solely by its ability to add value to the customer relationship, which breaks down into the acquiring, analyzing, integrating, and leveraging of information about, from, and *for the benefit of* each individual customer.

The last (but obviously not the least) of our fundamental changes goes to the very heart of *how* banking is done. What used to happen only in branches (and only during "banker's hours") can now happen not just *anywhere* in the world at *any time* of the day or night, but also through just about any delivery channel a customer cares to select—the automated banking machine, the telephone, the personal computer, even the television set.

How significant is the migration to digital channels? Very. According to a 1996 report by Ernst & Young only 56 percent of American retail bank transactions were handled in branches in 1995, and that number was expected to drop to 41 percent in 1998. The Canadian numbers are even more dramatic: only 38 percent of transactions were done in-branch in 1995, and by 1998 that number will have shrunk to 21 percent.[3] So, even without factoring in any of the other life-threatening influences described in this chapter, the numbers alone demand that we ensure that customers receive high levels of service *across* delivery channels; that we offer customized financial solutions; and substantially more convenience.

CASTING A NEW AND WIDER NET

We have come to terms with the fact that the next battle for the hearts and minds of financial services customers will be—and to a certain degree, already is being—waged in cyberspace. And that, for a great many financial institutions, this battle could be their last. While there will be many healthy survivors, there is no question the threats we face are very real, very large, and very immediate.

And, in some ways, very paradoxical. As is so often the case in this digital age, the serious threats that banking faces in cyberspace are accompanied by equally serious attractions. For one thing, start-up costs for a virtual bank are significantly less than those for a traditional bricks-and-mortar retail bank. At the beginning of 1997 the cost of setting up a fully functioning Web site for a full-service retail bank was about the same as the cost of opening a new branch (less real estate costs)—roughly $1 million. However, the Web site would be accessible to an estimated 10 million North American households today, and to an anticipated 16 million households by the end of 2000. In order to reach that same customer base in 1997, the average full-service bank would have to spend in excess of $900 *million* on branches. Even allowing for other substantial costs incurred in creating a virtual bank from scratch, the cost differential continues to be enormous.

To add to the attractions of the Internet, those 16 million households, while representing only 16 percent of banking customers, are expected to generate about 30 percent of retail bank profits. They fit the customer profile so prized by retailers everywhere: they're younger, more affluent, and better educated than the average customer; they maintain a much higher bank balance; they produce a much higher demand for financial products and services; and they are more receptive to cross-selling.

But as attractive as these customers are to banks, we are not setting our focus upon this minority to the exclusion of the majority who do not now and may not ever want to bank in cyberspace. Similarly, we have to guard against tendencies to allow cost and profitability projections to become the be-all and the end-all of our planning for the future. What we are doing in my organization is never taking our eyes off the customer—understanding that customers couldn't care less which delivery channel is more or less profitable to the bank. They will choose the channel that suits *them* best.

IN BANKS WE TRUST

What we are seeing is that banking customers who use either automated banking machines, telephones, or personal computers, tend to use a combination of delivery channels, often including the good old branch on the corner. This situation affords a good example of how the "threat-of-the-Net" can be turned to our advantage. It allows us to ask pointed and rhetorical questions, such as, "Can a faceless—and placeless—Internet provider ever hope to meet the *nonroutine* banking needs of an equally faceless Internet customer in a time of crisis?" And, "In a time of crisis, will their customers be able to get through *to* and get the same kind of help they'd get *from* a full-service *multichannel* banking institution?" Speaking for such an institution, I would have to say that we multichannel banks have entered the digital age much better positioned than our strictly virtual competitors to make the most of brand loyalties.

However, this advantage isn't one to be taken for granted. In cyberspace (at least so far) there is no "best corner in town," and as a result, old brand loyalties don't automatically count for much—this is especially true when it comes to impressing the digital banking crowd. As our research reveals, they are *much* more likely to switch financial institutions—or to give it serious thought—than the average customer. Furthermore, Internet customers have instant access to literally hundreds of reputable financial institutions from all around the world, each of them making offers they hope competitors' customers can't refuse. It would be imprudent (to say the least) to assume that any customer will stick with us for old time's sake. What we do have to assume is that, from the customer's point of view, our venerable old bank really *is* only as good as our last transaction.

INVASION OF THE CHERRY PICKERS

If the threats and advantages associated with brand loyalty are not lost on the traditional banking industry, neither are they lost on a rising tide of "cherry pickers" who are also setting up shop on the Net and attempting to pick off the most lucrative parts of our business. The cherry pickers pose a threat to banks of *all* sizes for the very simple reason that, unlike traditional full-service banks, they do not have to be all things to all people. They do not have to offer a standard package of products and services, and they do not have to maintain a very costly bricks-and-mortar branch system. All they *do* have to do is set up a Web site and begin to peddle their wares—or, as in many cases, their *ware*.

Now cherry-picking is not exactly new in the North American banking industry. The Big 3 auto makers, for example—General Motors, Ford, and Chrysler—have operated their own acceptance corporations for decades, competing very successfully for the lucrative car- and truck-loan business. And in the credit card business, six of the top 10 card issuers in North America are nonfinancial firms known as monoline or single-focus product providers. In the mutual fund market, traditional banks of all sizes are competing with the likes of Charles Schwab & Co., whose $300 billion in customer assets in mid-1997 makes it the largest discount brokerage firm in the United States. Able to offer a no-fee mutual fund supermarket called One Source, Schwab has been very successful in drawing off bank customers and now has more than 850,000 online customers.

Looking back, the writing has been on the wall for a long time. Banks used to have 70 percent of the world's assets, but that figure has been dropping by about 2 percent a year for two decades and now hovers around 30 percent. To put this in perspective, consider that, in North America today, 72 percent of household assets are not in bank accounts, term deposits, and the like but rather are invested in the capital markets. Furthermore, it is likely that the percentage of assets traditionally held by banks will further decline to below 20 percent, meaning that, to survive and prosper, banks must continue to increase the percentage of revenues acquired through fees and nontraditional businesses.

In Canada, even as these words are written, we traditional full-service banks are being challenged by new competitors of all stripes and sizes, coming at us from all directions. Out of the west comes the Vancouver City Credit Union's new branchless bank, the Citizens Bank of Canada. Out of the south, the gigantic Citicorp sends us Citibank Canada and its joint venture with the major Canadian mutual fund manager, AGF Management, to set up a virtual trust company to sell full-service banking packages to AGF's estimable customer base. Also from the south comes Wells Fargo & Company, which is putting on a considerable push to sell instant Internet loans to Canadian small businesses from its U.S. base.

From across the Atlantic comes another gigantic competitor, the Dutch ING Groep NV, an insurance and financial services operation with 1996 assets of $278 billion. (By comparison, the Bank of Montreal Group of Companies had average assets of $134 billion in March 1997.) ING is setting up a virtual trust subsidiary which will market a selection of products electronically and, it has announced, will be competing on "several fronts" (presumably only those fronts that cost little and yield much).

THE "DEATH SPIRAL" SCENARIO

If the cherry pickers like ING and Citicorp and Citizens Bank are successful in luring away large numbers of Internet customers with higher interest rates on deposits and lower interest rates on loans and much-reduced or waived user fees—none of which is impossible—then the landscape for traditional banks will become an increasingly bleak one. In a scenario sketched out by Booz Allen & Hamilton in a 1996 report on Internet banking, there can come a point where a "death spiral" kicks in.

With its high-profit customers lost to cherry pickers, the traditional bank is still faced with supporting an infrastructure, and with the fact that most of the customers who remain will be the heaviest users of the most expensive distribution channel, that is, the branches. And then, if the bank tries to raise its fees or reduce its services, more customers will leave and the cost of providing service will rise once again. Once the death spiral is entered, our consultants noted, it is "extremely difficult to exit."

Short of the worst-case scenario—extinction—the traditional bank may find itself reduced to supplier status on the Internet, which is already seeing the rise of a new breed of "intelligent agent" software that will shop thousands of Web sites to pick off the best deals for what have effectively become *their* customers. Such agents already exist on the Internet—to, for example, fulfill your request for the lowest 5-year mortgage rate available—and they are already actively seeking customers.

We are also seeing the rise of "integrators" who take over management of customers' finances and help them consolidate their financial relationships. What happens here is that the integrator ends up replacing the bank as the customer's primary financial institution and, again, the bank is reduced to a mere supplier. Integrators are already working the Net as well, among them Intuit's Quicken Financial Network. Put agents and integrators together and what you've got is a serious competitor who knows a customer's complete financial picture, and is in charge of where that customer's money is spent. In this scenario, banks would almost inevitably end up paying commissions.

Finally, no discussion about death spirals—or the future of cyberspace banking generally—could be complete without considering what Bill Gates is up to these days. Having dismissed traditional banks as "dinosaurs," the richest man in the world is now going ahead with plans to create his own virtual bank. And this could arguably represent the greatest threat so far to the established North American financial services industry. Unlike software-computer company alliances which require customers to use the Internet or a private value-added network to link their personal computers with their banks, Microsoft can provide access through its privately owned Microsoft Network—which is now linked up with the Internet. And unlike the other value-added networks, Microsoft also combines a dominant presence on personal computers with the capacity to offer a myriad of services.

With exclusive control of its own network, Microsoft could also potentially take control of customer access and software applications as well as pricing and payment. This means that once its network has become a core financial-services customer-access channel, Microsoft could both dictate pricing and heavily influence customer purchasing patterns and financial relationships. Over time, banks, retailers, and other providers could be charged in addition to the customer. Ultimately, Gates could acquire a banking charter himself, become a merchant provider, and compete with the traditional banks on *all* fronts.

WHAT'S IN A NAME?

As threatening as these developments may be, it is important to keep them in perspective. The enormous advantage conferred by brand loyalties has already been discussed, but it is not possible to speak of survival strategies, much less counteroffensives, without returning briefly to the advantage of having "a name you can trust." In the long run, we figure that while some people might be happy to accept a cheap loan from an unfamiliar provider on a Web site, few would be willing to hand over their life savings to such a provider. Would their money be safe and secure? Could they really count on privacy and confidentiality?

The issue of security, privacy, and confidentiality will be with us as long as hackers continue to hack, which is to say forever. On the other hand, banks have been locked in quiet battles with fraud artists and other crooks for centuries, and we have become very proficient in these matters. We have the experience, the mind-set, the state-of-the-art security measures, the long-standing antifraud processes, and consumer safeguards (deposit insurance, for example) to provide customers with by far the highest level of confidence in the safety of their investments. Likewise, we have a long-standing tradition of safeguarding the privacy of sensitive customer information, which positions us to adapt rapidly as the information era forces nearly every organization to develop a more complex understanding of privacy of information.

LEVELING THE PLAYING FIELD

With the increasing number of unregulated nonbank companies providing financial services, serious questions also need to be addressed about the impact of technology on legal and regulatory issues. While there is not exactly a consensus on how to level the playing field for traditional banks, more and more observers believe that a fresh approach to regulation is needed.

For example, as Italian economist Mauro Cipparone notes, the Payment Task Force of the European Union has expressed the opinion that central banks could play a role in leveling the playing field for banks and their unregulated competitors. "[It] is foreseeable that the regulations applied to banks will be extended to all the companies who wish to operate in the payment industry," he writes. "This would avoid [both] unfair competition (if non-banks are not subject to the same rules as banks they have an unfair advantage) and instability."

Others have proposed a more subtle form of compliance, such as a central bank "seal of approval" for nonbank providers of fair and stable banking services. I should say here that if some form of regulation is introduced, we traditional banks will be pleased. But to put it bluntly, we won't be staking our futures on it.

STRANGE BEDFELLOWS

What we are staking our futures on is the development of as many competitive advantages as are or may be available to us, starting with the much improved economies of scale created through mergers and acquisitions. Highlighted by the 1995 merger of Chase Manhattan and Chemical Bank, a union producing a total of $300 billion in assets, the trend toward bigness has seen the number of banks and trusts in the United States plummet from about 14,000 in the mid-1980s to about 9000 in 1996.

There is no such trend in Canada, where mergers have been effectively prevented by the policy of successive federal governments, but there is a growing industry feeling that this regulation should be rescinded. Three of the so-called Big Five banks, including Bank of Montreal, have taken that position, arguing that size really can confer an important competitive advantage internationally, and therefore we need to be free to merge and acquire, as necessary, to maintain a healthy Canadian banking industry. The other two Big Five banks, however, argue for keeping the status quo; they say that the big national banks already have the critical mass needed to compete effectively.

In recent times, however, banks (and many other organizations, to be sure) have begun to explore and develop a third way of improving economies of scale, beyond acquisitions and mergers. The thinking has shifted toward strategic alliances, including alliances with major banking competitors and with outside organizations—computer and telecommunications companies, for example—whose interests converge with ours. In addition to helping banks achieve scale, strategic alliances are also increasingly popular as a defense against the Net-based intelligent agents and integrators mentioned earlier. (Such alliances, it should be noted in passing, represent a radical break for traditional banks, which have always taken special pride in doing *everything* for themselves.)

One trend, involving strategic alliances with financial software companies, allows banks to offer customers a much-expanded range of value-added financial management options. Thanks to an alliance with Intuit Canada, for example, Bank of Montreal customers can seamlessly access bank account information and instantly update their financial records while using their copy of Intuit's Quicken personal finance software. It may be of interest that this particular alliance only became acceptable to us when Intuit moved from a proprietary, closed system to a new open standard that made the *bank* both agent and integrator.

EVEN STRANGER BEDFELLOWS

The pursuit of cross-industry alliances with software companies and other information technology suppliers may seem somewhat strange for an industry that is itself the second-largest producer of information technology—more than $25 billion in North America alone in 1996. But that isn't the half of it.

Achieving overall cost-effectiveness is, of course, the other side of the survival equation for traditional banks. Even if the virtual banks we set up do manage to compete on price with the international megabankers and the cherry pickers on the Internet, we are still left with a massive physical and technological infrastructure to maintain. This is where the *stranger* bedfellows come in. Consider, for instance, that by the mid-1990s, each of Canada's Big Five banks was attempting to come to terms with the fact that when it came to check and document processing, the volumes were going down but the costs were not. Technological solutions—imaging systems—were available, but in the face of declining demand and competing priorities, they turned out to be too expensive to justify.

Despite a history of considerable competition reaching back many decades, our document processing realities forced each of the Big Five banks to go into business with at least one of the others. The second- and fourth-largest banks, Canadian Imperial Bank of

Commerce and ScotiaBank, joined forces in a hookup with one of the big American check and document processors that have sprung to prominence over the past decade or so, and whose success is based on volume and economies of scale. The other three, Bank of Montreal, Royal Bank of Canada, and Toronto-Dominion Bank, decided to go for an all-Canadian solution: in a very short time with an absolute minimum of fuss, we created a new, independent, jointly owned cosourcing company called Symcor Services to handle large-volume item processing for all three banks.

When the transfer of functions is complete in 1999, Symcor will be processing more than two billion checks alone each year, just under half of all checks issued in Canada. Meaning that from the moment it swings into action, Symcor will be *the* largest document processor in the country, with economies of scale to match those of any of the big American processors.

We are also taking steps to ensure that we continue to hold onto another of our core competencies, the credit card issuing business, which also is being taken over by big, aggressive, focused providers in a rapidly consolidating market. In September 1997, Bank of Montreal and our U.S. subsidiary, Chicago-based Harris Bank,[4] announced plans to launch a new credit card company in the United States with two partners: BankBoston, a major banking holding company, and First Annapolis, a consulting firm with substantial expertise in credit cards. The new company will itself be a big, aggressive, focused provider—the plan is to be among the top 15 issuers by the year 2000, in large part by forging more creative alliances with financial institutions.

LIFE IN THE OLD BRANCH YET

But traditional banks are not counting solely on improvements, however massive, in our cost-effectiveness to see us through the digital age. We know cost-effectiveness won't mean very much if we can't attract and please customers. And in North America, as countless surveys show, what financial services customers want, *far* above all else, is convenience. Other things such as price, security, reliability, and expertise being more or less equal, customers will select the bank (or other provider) that operates the most conveniently located service.

The customer surveys also confirm our day-to-day experience

that people who like to bank in person—or to do at least some of their banking in person—still represent a very sizable majority of the people on this continent. No strategy for mainstream banking success can be complete unless it provides for the maintenance of a vibrant retail distribution network. In Canada, in particular, the size and strength of our national branch system, with its powerful, people-focused presence at the community level, does give potential competitors pause. For example, seeking to penetrate the Canadian market, but with only a handful of offices in the country, Citibank entered into a joint venture to sell its products through the huge mutual funds company, AGF Management Ltd., which has many offices coast to coast and a large network of financial planners. "The affiliation approach has a far greater chance than going at it cold," Vice-President Charles Stuart told *The Financial Post*. "It's important to have someone who can go face-to-face with customers."

As the digital age advances, many of these face-to-face connections with financial services customers will undoubtedly be made through video technology linked to the phone, the computer, or the television set. That acknowledged, it is clear that banking habits built up over centuries are not likely to disappear overnight. For evidence, one need look no farther than the "imminent" demise of the check. That was supposed to have happened, also overnight, some three decades ago, but instead it is only recently that the annual *growth* in check volumes has begun to slow down. This is another way of saying that most banks are not impressed by dire predictions of the death of the branch. On the contrary, we believe that the branch will always be with us. And, in accordance with that belief, we will continue to devote a significant portion of our efforts, human *and* technological, to keeping our branches open and viable.

The branches we are talking about here will not necessarily resemble—and, for that matter, are not even *likely* to resemble—branches as North Americans have known them. When we speak of branches these days, we could be referring to anything from a one-stop-shopping financial services emporium to a minibank tucked into the corner of a grocery store or post office, or a kiosk featuring an enhanced automated banking machine and a direct phone link to a customer service representative. To add to the scope of the definition, some branches are becoming little more than pit stops for mobile sales forces that go out to do business with customers in their homes and offices, and at their convenience.

A QUESTION OF TIME AND (CYBER)SPACE

As the focus shifts from physical resources to technological resources, the strategy retains much of that same cover-all-the-angles quality. We have learned, in other words, not to put all our eggs in the same electronic basket. As history has taught us, it is difficult to predict the degree to which consumers will embrace any given technology at any given time. For every case in which the famous inventor has underestimated the appeal of his invention (Edison and his phonograph), there are offsetting cases in which an invention's appeal was vastly overestimated (as in flying cars and CB radios). Then there are the technologies that achieve incredible reach but only very limited utility and importance: although VCRs are in 96 percent of North American homes, most people only use them to play rented videos; and while 95 percent of North American homes have microwave ovens, most people only use them to make popcorn and reheat last night's pasta.

Applying these observations to the technologies that may or may not have profound effects on banking, we arrive at the simple truth that no one knows for sure how quickly technology will improve or how customer banking preferences will evolve. It took 38 years for the radio to reach 50 million U.S. households but only 13 years for television to reach the same mass audience and only 10 years for cable TV. So even as Internet banking emerges as a fact of life, the rate of growth of the Web continues to be anybody's guess. In 1996, the growth of the Internet slowed its rapid pace, at least temporarily, and according to revised projections, only 200 million computers, as opposed to the predicted 300 million, will be connected by the turn of the century. About 10 percent of American and 5 percent of Canadian households went online to access financial services information in 1996, but only 2 percent of American households and 3 to 4 percent of Canadian households actually banked online. At Bank of Montreal, we expect that about 20 percent of Canadian households and 16 percent of American households will be banking online by the year 2000.

It is also important to remember that, in the near term, the personal computer and associated paraphernalia are still relatively expensive and complicated to use—limiting the PC as an accessible banking channel to the technologically literate and those who can afford the high cost of purchasing and maintaining a computer, modem, browsing software, and an Internet service provider.

Admittedly, this limitation may soon disappear as the technology becomes more and more user friendly and as both the Canadian and American governments increase their efforts to make the Internet an information resource that is within the reach of every citizen.

None of this matters, it ought to be emphasized, to the people who want to bank on the Net, and who the banks *want* to bank on the Net—the time-starved professional, for example, with above-average assets to invest in banking products and services; and the equally time-starved entrepreneurs in the booming small-office/home-office (SOHO) market. But it does suggest that our electronic enthusiasms, however understandable, need to be subjected to an ongoing reality check.

THE LURE OF ELECTRONIC BANKING

As noted earlier, one thing we don't have to speculate about any longer is whether or not customers will accept doing business with an automated banking machine. Another, more recent, success is telephone banking, which in 1996 alone accounted for 8.8 billion retail banking transactions across North America. And it is estimated that by the year 2001, more than 11 billion retail banking transactions will be handled by phone across North America. The fact is that aside from transactions involving cash—which should diminish in any case with the popularization of smart cards (discussed in a later section in this chapter)—there is now very little everyday banking that can't be accomplished on the keypad of a standard touch-tone phone.

Consistent with customer profiles for all the other forms of electronic banking, people who telebank tend to be next-generation: more than half of those under 35 bank by phone, as opposed to only 10 percent of those over 65. Also consistent with those other forms, telebanking has turned out to be highly cost-effective—a per-transaction cost, according to the U.S. experience, that is one-third the cost of the same transaction in a branch ($0.35 versus $1.07). The cost of an automated banking machine transaction, interestingly, costs $0.27, while a debit card transaction costs $0.10. On the Internet, transaction costs approach absolute zero.

As impressive as the savings may be, these figures are misleading, since they don't take into account the hundreds of millions of dollars of technology costs in creating the new digital delivery channels and training bank employees.[5] Nor do they take into account all the costs that are as yet unknown. For example, we banks may very well find ourselves spending a lot of time and money providing computer-related support to customers frustrated with the current state of technology. Indeed, some virtual banks have already found that they are dealing with as many technology-related queries ("My modem isn't responding!") as banking transactions.

THE NEXT HOUSEHOLD APPLIANCE

Another technological alternative banks have begun exploring, by way of pilot studies, is the delivery of financial services via high-speed telecommunications channels—meaning fully integrated voice, data, and images that enable customers to do banking transactions while interacting directly with bank representatives via network computers. A network computer (NC) acquires its information from the Internet or an intranet and stores its information there, meaning it does not need its own memory or disk drives. Potentially, this will make the NC much easier to use than the PC—just turn it on and (like the TV set today) the NC will be ready to do business.

What's more, this new technology is expected to be much more affordable than the PC. The cost of an NC will likely drop from about $1000 today to just a few hundred dollars in the very near future. The NC may one day become as affordable—and as pervasive—as the telephone. We will likely deploy it internally at Bank of Montreal to substantially decrease costs and increase productivity. And if it turns out that there are customers out there who want to do their banking via their home NC, we will be among the first to provide them with the opportunity.

Nevertheless, many years could pass before the Internet matches the 49 percent of U.S. homes reached by premium cable television—at least not without major technical enhancements that make it literally as easy to use as a phone or a TV set, and turn it into another basic household appliance. Even if the network computer *does* prove so simple and useful that electronic commerce starts to give retail commerce some serious competition, it is our informed guess that for the next decade at least, customers who are so inclined will continue to do their banking and other electronic commerce through increasingly sophisticated telephone systems and smart cards, modestly interactive TV, and storefront banking kiosks.

THE FUTURE IS IN THE CARDS

Despite the predictions of a number of observers both outside and inside the industry—notably Walter Wriston, the former chairman and CEO of Citibank/Citicorp—few bankers are expecting the so-called cashless society to emerge in either the short *or* the long term. What Wriston told *Wired* magazine was this: "We've used wampum, beads, silver and gold, and now we use paper and call it money. The next transition will be to smart cards."

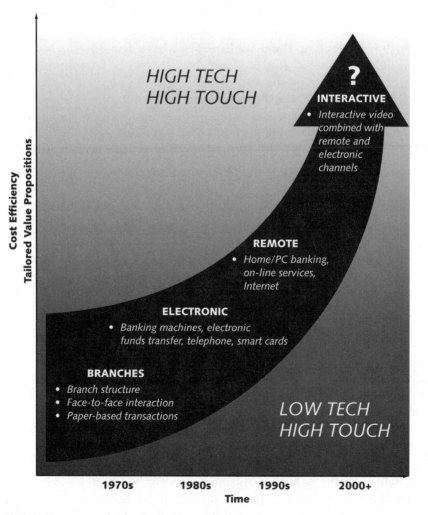

FIGURE 6-1. Multiple channels = multiple options.

While begging to disagree with the sweep of that statement for reasons outlined here, traditional banks have already acknowledged the power of cards. (Credit and debit cards have a magnetic strip which contains limited information about the customer, while smart cards are equipped with a microchip or minicomputer with all the memory and processing functions the name implies.) Certainly, banks have already acknowledged that some customers will prefer to carry their money around in "electronic wallets" instead of cash. As this chapter is written, all five of Canada's major banks, along with the country's largest trust company, are conducting studies into the feasibility of a stored-value smart card, and a slightly less intense level of activity is also under way in the United States. There are more than 50 million smart cards in circulation in the world, more than 95 percent of them in Europe, where the smart card has proved to be one of those overnight successes. That number is expected to double by the end of 1997, with 95 percent of the new cards also being generated in Europe.

The popularity of smart cards in Europe, however, has in part been explained by the relative inefficiency of *credit* card verification, a problem bypassed by the instant transfer of electronic cash from the customer's electronic wallet to the shopkeeper's electronic till. The relative *non*popularity (so far) of smart cards in North America is likewise explained in part by a credit card verification system that is already extremely efficient and growing more so all the time. According to Ed Jensen, President and CEO of Visa, a system will soon be available that will allow customers to make purchases over the Internet—a major *raison d'être* for stored-value cards and the electronic money (e-money, digi-cash) they can store and send.

In North America, smart cards also face a competing payment system—the debit card—that has also turned out to be an overnight success, certainly in Canada where transactions have grown by 35 percent per year since point-of-purchase debit cards were introduced in 1990, and where, in 1996 alone, the system accounted for close to 680 million transactions. It is entirely possible that, as debit card usage proliferates and the transaction price is reduced to that of a cleared check or less, the debit card will have a more profound impact on banking in the near future than smart cards and other innovations. On the one hand, it will reduce credit card profits substantially; on the other, it will open the way for branded banks to learn more about our customers and form retail alliances that will strengthen our position considerably.

In response, there is the case put forward by many observers that "convenient, anonymous cash" will retain its enduring advantages for many customers. While cards have clear advantages in a number of areas, from telephones to vending machines, pocket change is still more convenient for incidental payments to everyone from children and friends to restaurant servers and street vendors. And there are some purchases that some people—even law-abiding ones—will still prefer to make anonymously rather than have them recorded in someone's database. There is also the fact that cash itself has become almost instantly available, with automated banking machines installed in just about every convenience store.

TAKING NO CHANCES

It might appear, in other words, that expensive stored-value cards are a bit of a gamble for North American banks in the immediate future—and even more of a gamble when myriad other concerns are factored in. "There are at present no regulatory or currency controls in the movement of [electronic] money," Professor Stephen Kobrin of the University of Pennsylvania told a session of the World Economic Forum at Davos, Switzerland in February of 1997. "There are taxation implications, money supply implications for central banks, and illegal money laundering and other problems."

While acknowledging and respecting the arguments against investing heavily in smart cards and electronic cash, survival-minded bankers are investing in them anyway. Included in this group of bankers are those who agree with Tapscott's prediction, also voiced at Davos, that electronic money will become transcendent, and who take to heart his conclusion that a majority of today's banks will not survive the transition. Also among them are bankers who disagree, but who know that if *they* don't offer customers a smart-card option, somebody else will, and yes, that *could* put their survival at stake. As the industry discovered with the beyond-all-expectations success of the debit card in Canada, when it comes to customers and technology, no prediction is safe. We have to be ready for all eventualities.

One of those eventualities might very well be the use of bank-supplied and administered smart cards as a convenient and much more cost-effective option for distributing regular government social assistance and pension checks. When "pay day" rolls around each month, recipients "cash their check" by reloading their smart cards at an automated banking machine or some other access device.

Another one of those eventualities might be a role for banks in providing smart cards that carry financial information along with e-cash, becoming a customer's personal access "key" to all forms of electronic banking. Pilot projects are already under way that equip public and private telephones, personal computers, network computers, and television sets with their own smart card point-of-access terminals. Given sufficient demand, this eventuality would enable consumers to replace the confusing array of debit and credit cards they carry in their wallets—each with its own personal identification number—with one all-purpose smart card equipped with a state-of-the-industry security and authentication mechanism. Another potential major benefit would be the card's capacity to provide an integrated and up-to-the-moment record of all of a card holder's financial transactions.

Finally, the one-card-does-all scenario opens up the possibility for banks to add even more value for the customer while offsetting the high unit cost to banks of smart cards (currently about $10) by "renting out" some of the valuable plastic "real estate" on the smart card to other suppliers such as the travel industry. This could be attractive to the frequent traveler (for example) who is looking for vastly simplified mobile electronic access to banking and other services such as hotel and airline information, bookings, ticket purchase, and payment. To cite just one more of the possibilities—one that is already a reality in Europe—the smart card could be used to enable cellular phone users to switch seamlessly from one service provider to another during their travels.

MONEY IN THE BANX

As quaint as it sounds in the digital age, one of the core strategies we have adopted against our nonbank competitors is to fight fire with fire. In fact in some cases we're being pre-emptive, forcing the interlopers to fight *our* fire. By the turn of the century, at least 2000 North American banks will be offering some products on a Web site, and at least 500 of us will be offering a full range of products and services. All the major players in Canada offer (or soon will offer) a full spectrum of virtual banking options that are accessible to customers 24 hours a day, 365 days a year: toll-free phone and fax, an ever-more sophisticated automated banking machine, and the personal computer, via a proprietary connection and/or the public Internet. From a bottom-line perspective, the attraction of virtual banking is, as noted, its impressive cost-effectiveness. The more customers bank through electronic channels—especially the Net— the more cost-effective those customers become.

The lure of cyberspace is offset by the fact that however well informed we bankers have become about the implications of the digital age, we know we still have a lot to learn about how to establish and maintain long-term customer relationships in cyberspace. But, as with smart cards, we bankers are not in a position of being able to wait and see. At the speed with which the industry is undergoing technology-driven change, to fall behind in such technological applications right now is to risk never catching up.

This was some of the thinking that convinced the Bank of Montreal Group of Companies to launch mbanx, the first North American virtual banking unit, in Canada in October of 1996 and the United States in mid-1997. Each launch was followed in quick succession by a steady stream of innovations, such as the almost instant adjudication of loan applications online. For this and a full plate of other good reasons, we anticipate that more than 1 million people will have mbanx accounts within 5 years. Many of them (we hope) will be enticed away from competitors, but if some of our regular Bank of Montreal customers in Canada and Harris Bank customers in the United States decide to switch over to mbanx, we won't exactly be unhappy. If it's a virtual bank they want, we would prefer to keep them in the family.

"VIRTUAL" REALITIES

Strategically, mbanx was designed to be a whole lot more than a logical extension of previous trends in banking. That's because all previous trends in banking have hit the wall of the digital age: their influence ends where the virtual bank begins—at least where *our* virtual bank begins. With mbanx, we found ourselves with what seemed to be a once-in-a-lifetime opportunity to lead the way in redefining banking itself: a whole new kind of bank for a whole new kind of customer—the one who is as pressed for time as she is financially active and who travels frequently (and well). It is for this rapidly growing market segment—which, as previously noted, is expected to generate 30 percent of retail banking profits just a few short years from now—that we created a bank that removes all the limitations and constraints once placed by time and space.

From a different angle, one peculiar to my organization's stated ambition to become the first bank with conventional and virtual retail distribution networks in all three NAFTA countries, mbanx presents us with a perfect opportunity to fly our best colors continent deep.

In Canada, with an mbanx logo that uses the same color blue and the same bar under the "m" as our long-established Bank of Montreal logo, we have been able to leverage and enhance our bank's 180-year-old good name. In the United States, where Bank of Montreal has enjoyed rather low brand recognition to date, mbanx is an opportunity to reposition ourselves. And in Mexico, where we have an equity position and alliance with Grupo Financiero Bancomer, the leading Mexican financial institution, we are looking to mbanx to establish our good name and credentials. As of this writing, the Canadian launch has been under way for 18 months and, as we had hoped, brand recognition has been quickly and indelibly established.

As with all foundings of any importance, mbanx also came with a founding philosophy—a response to both the need and the opportunity to get it right from the start. While discussions of underlying values can often be perceived as cynical and self-serving, I feel that, in this particular case, the values we have attached to mbanx define it just as surely as its logo, or the special and sometimes unique services that it provides. What's more, these are not values that one reflexively associates with a bank.

We are committed, for example, to the notion that change is good, that customers can only be attracted—and well served—if we are constantly challenging our own and everybody else's assumptions of what banking is all about. We are also committed to continuous learning, both to improve the quality of clients' financial lives and to improve the ability of employees to develop professionally as they wish; and to stating our commitments to *all* concerned, clearly and up-front, and to making sure we live by these commitments; and (shades of the Golden Rule) to treating our customers the way we ourselves would like to be treated. For mbanx and any bank that's planning to survive in the digital age, these values are more than nice ideas; they are rules to live by.

In its creation, we also ensured that mbanx would begin life with its own distinct identity and personality—a route not taken by our Canadian competitors, who are "adding on" their virtual banking options. What mbanx affords us here is yet another perfect opportunity to distinguish ourselves from the financial services pack, which has been an integral part of our strategic efforts for close to a decade now.

You could say, in other words, that mbanx is our answer to the death spiral scenario. It is proof positive that a bank *can* change, that a bank *can* redefine the banking relationship, that a bank *can* create and implement a dramatically new and different vision for banking in the digital age, a vision in which our human advantage becomes our competitive advantage, and a vision that applies not just to mbanx and virtual banking, but across our whole Group of Companies, and to banking in all its forms.

ALL ROADS LEAD TO THE CUSTOMER

If the foregoing contains one unified message, it is that the success—and in all probability the survival—of the traditional bank in the digital age has come to rest squarely on how much value bank employees, enabled by technology, can bring to their relationships with customers.

We know that no matter what other strategic measures we adopt and deploy, the one sure way to keep our new and old competitors away from our customers and potential customers is to pre-empt them with our own, irresistible, value-added relationships. Once created, all of our experience shows, value-added relationships are difficult to break up.

So, one way or another, banks are directing just about all their resources, human and technological, toward attracting customers and keeping them happy. We are going on the Internet because, quite simply, increasing numbers of customers want to do their banking that way. We are putting ourselves through wholesale restructuring so that we can improve our expense-to-revenue ratios and, in turn, charge prices that customers are willing to pay. We are sinking serious research and development money into things like smart cards because that smart card could turn out to be a valuable point of contact, possibly the beginning of a mutually profitable life-long relationship. Or it could be yet another good reason for staying in an *existing* relationship.

And all that, in a sentence, is why relationship-building technologies continue to spread so rapidly across the industry, allowing us to develop integrated and highly detailed profiles of each individual customer, profiles that will enable us to understand and then meet the full range of their financial services needs, and then some. This no longer simply involves the cross-selling of other financial products and services; it now involves the tools of the direct marketer, including the creative use of nonfinancial products and services to add value and build brand loyalty.

Indeed, one of a bank's best weapons against single-focus competitors (in particular) is likely to be its ability to provide customers with the convenience and appeal of a whole range of services gathered together in one convenient, credible, secure, and instantly accessible place. This speaks to the yet-to-be-realized potential of a concept called "service aggregation" which is starting to be more broadly interpreted as yet another effective way of adding value to a relationship. To cite a hypothetical example, one day a first-time home buyer who has just taken out a mortgage with mbanx might log on to our Web site to find the perfect proposal for a home-security system customized to his income, neighborhood, and temperament—fulfilling a need the customer hadn't even identified yet.

The potential for service aggregation is expected to grow exponentially as our technologies (and our imaginations) allow us to become ever more adept at another new concept known as microsegmentation—a highly sophisticated profitability breakdown by *customer segment*. Unlike the standard old demographics, microsegmentation (as the name implies) breaks the customer base down into much smaller segments of customers who share very similar profiles and very similar banking needs. Along with the potential for adding even more value to the customer relationship, microsegmentation is also expected to provide a powerful boost to a bank's capacity to develop more creative, cost-effective marketing strategies and delivery systems for all its products and services. After all, the real power of technology lies in information that builds to knowledge that builds to insight.

DANCE OF THE DINOSAURS

Which brings this discussion of the survival of the traditional full-service bank back close to where it started, to the observation that information, not money, is the industry's lifeblood these days. Banking is about collecting, storing, analyzing, packaging, and distributing information about customers and *for* customers. It is only by gathering pertinent, accurate information about the financial lives of our customers—their financial goals and philosophies, their tolerance for risk, the other interests in their lives—that traditional banks (and, let me stress this, any other would-be providers) are able to design customized financial solutions and other high-value services in a world where each customer rightly expects to be treated as a market segment of one.

As we become more and more proficient in identifying which customer will want what product or service and when she or he will want it, the next logical and *strategic* step is to figure out *why*. This is where we venture into the yet-unmined realm of customers' values and their true priorities. And, in a world where providers are many and choices close to endless, this may well emerge as the edge we need to number ourselves among the survivors of the digital revolution in banking. In the long run, it could turn out to be as important to our survival as forming strategic alliances and setting up our own virtual banks. So we make the assumption that successfully managing information to add unparalleled value *will* be our edge, and we govern ourselves accordingly.

And that, in a few close-to-final words, explains why the doomsayers are mistaken when they write the established banks out of their future banking scenarios. What they didn't figure on was how adaptable we have turned out to be—how quickly we'd see what we needed to do to stay and prosper in business, and how quickly we'd get around to doing it. They didn't figure on *dinosaurs* learning new tricks. But, as I hope this chapter confirms, we have learned a lot of them. And we eagerly look forward to learning a whole lot more.

NOTES

1. Bank of Montreal, Canada's first bank, is a highly diversified financial services organization whose 34,000 employees served 7 million customers through 1250 locations in 1997. Bank of Montreal Group of Companies includes Nesbitt Burns, one of Canada's largest full-service investment firms, Chicago-based Harris Bank, and mbanx, the first North America-wide virtual bank. Bank of Montreal also has an equity position in and an alliance with Grupo Financiero Bancomer, Mexico's largest retail bank.

   On January 28, 1998, Bank of Montreal and Royal Bank of Canada, Canada's largest bank, announced a definitive agreement, subject to regulatory and share-holder approval, to merge both banking groups into a new bank as equal part-ners. If the merger is approved, the new bank will rank as one of the top 10 in North America and the top 25 in the world for market capitalization ($26.6 bil-lion as of January 16, 1998).

2. Toffler, Alvin, *The Third Wave* (New York: Bantam Books), 1980, p. 59.

3. Ernst & Young LLP's Financial Services Consulting Practice, *Fifth Annual Special Report on Technology in Banking—Creating the Value Network 1996* (Ernst & Young), 1996.

4. Chicago-based Harris Bank, a major U.S. midwestern financial institution, is one of the Bank of Montreal Group of Companies.

5. In 1996, the Bank of Montreal Group of Companies alone spent $62 million on employee education.

THE NINE DYNAMICS OF FUTURE PUBLISHING

by Chuck Martin
Alliance for Converging Technologies

The publishing industry is one of the most threatened by the digital economy, but at the same time, it is offered the greatest opportunity to redefine itself. Not only are publishers established experts at communications, but their most basic product—information—has conveniently been produced in digital form for decades. As the two primary functions traditionally performed by publishers—gathering and providing information and organizing audiences—are being radically altered by the new interactive and internetworked environment, the challenge for publishers is to develop strategies that capitalize on their existing advantages, while understanding the new dynamics of the Internet, and leveraging its capabilities.

Basically, the traditional "media industry," or what has been termed the Fourth Estate, is giving way to the new Digital Estate. An estate can be thought of as an organized group defined by common economic or philosophical interests. The concept derives from the social and political organization of the Estates-Général in France. The first three estates comprised the clergy, the nobles, and the peasant/merchant class, which eventually clashed and resulted in the French Revolution.[1] When the Fourth Estate subsequently emerged, it represented a new kind of social power based not on class but on literacy and access to information.

The Digital Estate is the result of a more recent communications revolution. The way in which information is produced and distributed has been radically altered, and reflects a shift away from the mediated information of the Fourth Estate to the Digital Estate's instant, direct access via the Internet. With the interactive generation fully tuned to gathering its own information, publishers will be threatened as the prime intermediary. However, they will be in a position to transform their function in myriad ways.

It has taken a few years for publishers, and other companies, to go beyond simply using the Net as an additional distribution medium. In fact, it was the publishing industry that led the trend toward brochureware—less affectionately known as shovelware—where companies repurposed whatever existing material they could get their hands on. This version of electronic publishing characterized what I have identified as the first wave of the Net. The second wave involved the creation of new content, mostly by new media companies, and in the third wave, the Internet went companywide as organizations around the world deployed corporate intranets.

But early publishing efforts missed the full power of the Net's interactive and networking potential. In the emerging Digital Estate, publishers have begun to actually transform their businesses to accommodate the wired consumer. While many publishers ponder the prospects of attracting some of the $7.7 billion in advertising which is projected before the year 2002, others realize that bringing consumers closer to the point of sale could be of higher value. This new view means not only a change in the nature of content but in the entire business model for publishers.

Traditionally, publishers have been in the business of organizing an audience and providing them with suitable and relevant information. They then sell advertising based on how broad and large the audience is, and how frequently they reach its members. Advertising over the decades has been modeled around "reach" and "frequency," which helps determine CPM (cost per thousand people reached), upon which advertising rates are based.

But not all audiences are alike. While a newspaper reaches a geographically organized audience each day or week, a monthly magazine reaches an audience with a specific interest only once a month. However, the magazine might argue that the people they reach are more valuable, since they are specifically interested in the subject matter offered, making them better targets for advertisers.

In the Digital Estate, advertising dollars will become clearly

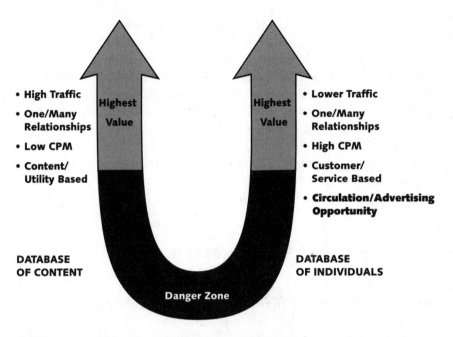

• High Traffic

• One/Many
  Relationships

• Low CPM

• Content/
  Utility Based

Highest
Value

Highest
Value

• Lower Traffic

• One/Many
  Relationships

• High CPM

• Customer/
  Service Based

• **Circulation/Advertising
  Opportunity**

DATABASE
OF CONTENT

DATABASE
OF INDIVIDUALS

Danger Zone

FIGURE 7-1.   The Digital Estate U. ©1998, The Digital Estate Group, LLC.

divided into two value camps. Not only will publishers function in ways they never have before, but new players, who have never "published" before, will enter the game. All will be competing for prime position at the top of what I call "the Digital Estate U" (see Fig. 7-1).

In the new, internetworked environment, the two top parts of the U are the highest value points. The left side of the U involves high traffic—a one-to-many publishing environment with a relatively low CPM. Companies found here are of high value to large numbers of consumers, either because they provide highly valued content (*Time,* CNN, *Wall Street Journal*) or high utility (Netscape, Yahoo, AltaVista).

The right side of the U involves relatively low traffic, more of a one-to-one relationship, and a high CPM for advertising, since those people reached are less of the "masses" and more of the targeted individuals. This is closer to the traditional business-to-business or trade publishing model, where publishers create publications for groups of people based on the particular industry or profession they are in.

On the left side of the U, *content* is of highest value. On the right side of the U, audiences—or *consumers*—are of the highest value.

As the masses become networked, much of the advertising industry will "follow the eyeballs" and move dollars to the left side of the U. Meanwhile, many of the direct-marketing dollars will flow to the right side in pursuit of the more defined and higher-valued networked consumer.

Publishing models for the future must therefore address how people receive, consume, and act on information. In this chapter, I outline the nine primary dynamics that come into play in the transformation of the publishing industry.

SERVICE VERSUS INFORMATION

Traditionally, the CPM economic model has been based on the delivery of information. In the new economy, publishers will have to focus more on providing valuable (and chargeable) services. For example, in addition to providing news and information, *USA Today* allows consumers to download free software or children's games. This transforms *USA Today* into an information *and* service provider.

But this is only part of the story. While publishing companies are busy attempting to create service offerings for their customers, new players are jumping into the field with their own models that are seriously competing for the advertising dollars traditionally belonging to the publishing industry. For example, several companies are offering free e-mail service in exchange for recipients' agreement to receive text-based advertising messages. In each case, the users of the e-mail service supply detailed information about themselves, creating the opportunity for highly targeted advertising messages. So, when HotMail registers 3 million free accounts, for example, and Juno Online registers 2 million members, the advertising base of the publishing industry is tapped.

Even advertisers themselves are getting into the act and creating content or providing services directly to consumers, bypassing publishers altogether. Levi-Strauss' Dockers site, for example, with a budget of $2 million, provides fashion tips and a 24-hour, online customer support network. Procter & Gamble created the Pampers Parenting Institute with service-oriented information for parents of infants up to 3 years old. The content for the site was not created by a publishing company, but rather by an advertising agency. The focus is on valuable service to the consumer.

CONSUMER-CENTRIC VERSUS PUBLISHER-CENTRIC

In the traditional publishing world, information is collected, packaged, and distributed to consumers. The editor of the publication has already made the choices of what content to include and exclude, leaving the consumer to sift through information deemed "fit to print" by someone else.

In the new economy, the editorial process starts with the consumer. What is considered "front page news" may be different for each consumer. What is he or she interested in today? At this very moment? When a person hears a siren down the street, they might want to know what is going on, right then and there. They might want to listen to the election results in a small foreign country. They may want to know details of their favorite Formula One driver's performance in the Brazil Grand Prix the same weekend, or see what the weather is like overseas, where their sister lives. An online newspaper could customize and deliver specific information to that one particular person on demand.

In this consumer-centric environment, the individual drives the content. And in an age of information overload, each need will be different. Readers of the future will only be interested in matters that are most relevant to them at any given moment. Each request for information will be unique, creating the ultimate need for one-to-one information.

The challenge for publishers is to develop a model that matches the right information with the right person at the right time. Traditionally, pursuing this goal has involved distributing printed publications to the consumer through various outlets. Other than inserting specific, predefined content for certain individuals, the most "direct" it ever got was delivering subscriptions to one's doorstep.

When the Internet emerged, some viewed it as an enhanced broadcast medium. Content was delivered directly to individuals via the Web and onto their desktops, sometimes as a screensaver. Others viewed the Net as a narrowcast medium because of its ability to reach very small audiences with specific, targeted messages. Both models form the basis of "push" technology.

But in both broadcast and narrowcast models, there is no guarantee the online viewer will be there to receive the information, or be directed toward a specific message at a given moment. In this sense, the desktop delivery models are only a slight improvement over doorstep delivery. What neither model takes into account is the unique ability of the online consumer to control and even create the programming of information. I call this approach "pullcasting."

Pullcasting may at first suggest to publishers that they "pull" customers in after "casting" their nets—a strategy similar to broad- and narrowcasting models. But leaders in the Digital Estate must recognize that the power to access and control the flow of information is now equally and readily in the hands of consumers. From this perspective, the model is turned inside out and it is the *consumer* who does the pulling and the casting. In this scenario, companies must provide incentives that attract consumers who are seeking information. A well-designed message, delivered at the right time and in the right circumstances, can entice consumers to pull it in of their own free will.

By approaching the Net from the inside out and by using resources such as smart agents so that marketers can better serve the consumer-centric environment, publishers are learning to confront four fundamental challenges in advertising:

- *Targeting/market segmentation:* reaching only the target audience, with the ability to customize messages
- *Reach:* getting to more members of the target audience
- *Frequency and duplication:* eliminating under- or overexposure
- *Measurability:* determining what works in a timely manner

Changes in customer needs and the capabilities provided by an interactive, networked world will fundamentally change the role of publishers. Magazines will be able to act as newspapers and newspapers will be able to act as magazines, cannibalizing advertising revenue from the other. For example, an online magazine can supply relevant classified ads for local areas, cannibalizing business from newspapers. At the same time, newspapers can easily "distribute" outside their geographic areas and cover special events that would have more likely been covered by a special-interest magazine. On the Net, all opportunities are created equally.

DYNAMIC VERSUS PERIODICAL

In the new economy, the electronic publication will render the monthly magazine—even the daily newspaper—out of date as soon as it is printed. This is not to say that printed matter has no future, but rather that publishers will find themselves pressured to create news and information turbines that continually feed their consumers electronically, while gathering and repackaging that same material for their printed counterparts. All publishers will become interactive publishers producing dynamic, living services and online supplements to print properties, and vice versa.

With consumers saying that news is their number one content preference, traditional publishers have a distinct advantage in the real-time, all-the-time world. They already understand the high cost of gathering, sorting, and packaging information, and have such costs covered by their traditional print economics.

One of the more forward thinking publishers is O Estado de Sao Paulo, a 125-year-old family-owned newspaper. The Brazilian newspaper has a daily circulation of 380,000 copies, 640,000 on Sundays. Currently, the company is grappling with the real-time world. Here's the view of O Estado vice president, Roberto Meschita:

> The company focused on newspapers until 1987, when we diversified into telephone book publishing. At that same time, we looked at the impact of IT on our traditional newspaper business. We realized that the technology would allow us to produce information in different ways. Compared to what is gathered, we actually deliver a small amount of information.
>
> The basic strategy was to try different things, keeping in mind that what we do best is provide information. We began by forming a business unit to repackage information, adding real-time information on top of a price-quote service. We also bought a broadcast company, and published information electronically— as we gathered it. That was in 1992. Then we started distributing fax papers, the delivery of specific news by fax, offering information to specialized market segments.
>
> With the Net, we have a new distribution medium, but it requires a different business model. We are looking at how the paper can add value to the Web site, and how the Web site can add value to the paper. We tried to make our newsroom guys do

things in real time, and it was very difficult. But it's time for a big change. We don't know exactly what kind of risks we are facing, but we have to experiment. We have to be very open-minded. The newspaper business is built on habits that are difficult to break. If readership changes, it's from one generation to another, not just overnight. The question is, how well can we serve our readers? This requires a new culture that accommodates the new technology.

As newspaper, magazine, and book publishers enter the new millennium, like O Estado, they will find themselves holders of vast amounts of real-time information, with greater financial pressures to leverage their massive information-gathering infrastructures. The question is whether, and how quickly and efficiently, they can convert their serial production process into an all-the-time publishing model.

CONTEXT VERSUS CONTENT

In an internetworked environment, there is no real advantage to simply providing the electronic version of printed material. In most cases, readers prefer the original print format. For many, the Net still can't compete with the overall experience of reading a glossy magazine on the beach, for example, or the Sunday *Times* in a cafe.

One of the most important qualities that draws consumers to the Net is the capacity to engage more fully with not only the content through interactive searches but also the contextual elements of a networked publication.

The contextual elements in a digital publication differ from print, and they play a different role. In a printed magazine, the associations surrounding the text and images of an article communicate, for example, the level of seriousness or give special status to the author or subject matter. This is communicated through elements such as the positioning of an article, design, advertising, letters to the editor, etc. Further resources or relevant services may be listed at the end of the article, or at the back of the magazine.

In a digital publication, the "context" goes far beyond such two-dimensional elements. Not only might the words and images be moving or continuously "refreshed," but as a networked, interactive medium, users are hyperlinked to other content, both within and outside the publication. For example, a travel publication setting up shop on the Net will not only be expected to provide stories about specific travel destinations, but also the full-service capability to book the trip online. An online health magazine may one day take your pulse, or prescribe a personalized diet after accessing your medical records. Newspapers might be expected to supplement the general news with services such as online discussions about specific news stories of the day. A community can organize around the content, and provide larger context for the event itself. "Letters to the Editor" could take the form of online debates, where the discussions themselves, in turn, serve as new content. And because context is fluid, malleable, responsive, and interactive on the Net, time and place become important contextual elements, in addition to related content.

In the Digital Estate, *context* is king because it fully engages a surrounding network of content through interactivity. In this way, interactivity is more than just a user service; it becomes part of a business plan to outsource content creation. In effect, *any* data potentially becomes content once it is digitized and moved onto the Net. This makes almost any company doing business in the digital world a publisher, while possibly serving as context for another publisher at the same time.

DATABASE OF PEOPLE VERSUS DATABASE OF CONTENT

After decades of gathering, packaging, and distributing content, publishers have accumulated massive databases of this content, ranging from 100 years of book reviews by *The New York Times* to massive archives of photos from *Time* and *Life* magazines. In editorial departments, the database of content has been its most important asset for a long time.

However, in the interactive world, publishers will have to partly shift their focus from gathering information *for* the consumer, to gathering information *about* the consumer. Who are they? Where are they? What do they want? When do they want it?

Because the online consumer makes his or her changing needs directly available, publishers are able to accumulate a detailed database of consumers that enables them to tailor their products and target their users with greater accuracy and precision. And as consumers carry out more of their life functions on the Net, such as online banking and shopping, publishers as well as marketers will be further challenged with tracking these needs on a real-time basis.

The publisher, then, effectively gathers a finely tuned database of consumers, continuously acquiring more information about more people, and generating content in the process. For example, the Internet startup iVillage organizes people with similar interests such as health, parenting, work, lifestyle, and women's issues, around specific community sites dedicated to these interests.[2] The Better Health and Medical Network, for example, draws a predefined consumer, in this case, someone who is particularly interested in health matters. Through online discussions, not only does iVillage generate content for its site, but it also gathers even more specific information about the user's interests, be it a preference for homeopathic medicine, an interest in vitamin supplements, or a request for information regarding the latest in AIDS research. iVillage provides this information, but more significantly, it identifies and makes accessible the most highly prized defined consumer so attractive to direct marketers.

COMMUNITIES VERSUS READERS

While the creation of a database of consumers addresses the business interests of both publishers and their advertising base, it is apparent that publishers are also playing an important role as the organizers of online communities. In addition to delivering highly customized content around which these new communities form, publishers can organize online sites around existing "physical" communities, giving them a formal communications structure.

As more and more people get wired, digital communities will have increasing relevance. It's fast becoming a case of "so many people, so many interests, so little time." While virtual communities won't ever *supplant* the need for neighbors, parades, ski clubs, and bridge partners, they will *supplement* these kinds of social gatherings. In the physical world, you can't easily find a match in a group of people for your unique interests. And when you do, it tends to be limited to individuals or groups within your geographic sphere. However, on the Net, not only can you locate different people in each of your interest areas but you also can communicate directly with them on your own terms and at your leisure. Smart agent and collaborative filtering technologies of the future also may allow instantaneous matching of others with totally dissimilar interests, to potentially broaden experiences, as well as pinpointing information that others either like—or unlike—you have found interesting. The virtual community actually becomes the information provider!

The variety of communities that can be created on the Net is limited only by imagination and desire. High-rise apartment dwellers can create their own building community. Businesses can create communities of customers, as well as buyer-seller communities through an extranet.

In the New Jersey Online community, for example, "residents" can read local restaurant reviews from patrons, type their own reviews online, and participate in discussion groups ranging from sports to local politics. People raise their own issues, such as the widening of a local street that upset one nearby resident, and find all the information about local yard sales for the weekend. Since AT&T is one of the largest employers in the state, New Jersey Online even created a location called the Unofficial AT&T Insider, where people discuss the downsizing of American business, layoffs, unions, job opportunities, and news from or affecting AT&T. New Jersey Online, owned by Newhouse Newspapers, has created the organizational structure for the service, the platform on which New Jersey residents can organize.

Another example, Miami City Web, offers visitors language options, restaurant and entertainment information, classifieds, neighborhood maps, public transportation information, merchants listings and coupons, and a hotel/motel directory. The site also offers local residents and businesses a home page hosting service.

As readers spend more time on the Net, and away from traditional media, publishers will have to move into this new role of community organizer to protect their "timeshare." Some publishers are even going one step further by creating the actual tools for their readers to communicate with each other.

Consider Thompson Corporation, a $7+ billion publisher of daily newspapers, health, education, and legal information, and reference publications. The company expects that by the year 2000, 80 percent of its revenue could come from specialized or custom publishing. In its quest to assure that its content was properly aligned for the digital future, it developed its own digital asset management software to allow various subsidiaries access to company archives in order to facilitate group data sharing. Realizing that other owners of intellectual property on the Net could use the platform toolkit,

Thompson formed a group called Thompson Editorial Asset Management Solutions which created a commercial version of the software. In addition to other publishing companies, Thompson targeted aerospace, government, and medical organizations, as well as film and television companies. Going beyond both content provider and community organizer, Thompson saw an opportunity to become the creator of the tools that would allow companies to match information with users.

In somewhat similar fashion, the Sydney-based Australian Provincial Newspapers Holdings Ltd., views its move to the Net as a great opportunity to become a gateway for its consumers and take them online with them. "This is not defensive, this is a great way to grow our business," says Chief Executive Cameron O'Reilly. "60 to 70 percent of adults read us every day. We could be the gateway for all e-commerce in our community. Who else is going to tell you all about the Net? There are no limits to where we could go."

GLOBAL VERSUS LOCAL REACH

The Net has the unique—and somewhat paradoxical—ability to break market segments down to the individual while simultaneously reaching and uniting a global audience. In effect, what it does is make geography both relevant and irrelevant as an organizing principal. Audiences are disaggregated into small groups or singular units, and reaggregated according to common elements that transcend geography—or become directly linked to it. Consequently, local newspapers can become global, while publications with a more universal appeal can become localized.

The most obvious trend is the globalization of local publications. For example, in 1995, the Japanese newspaper *Asahi Shimbun* formed an Electronic Media and Broadcasting Division to take advantage of Internet technologies. Now, in addition to the more than 12 million copies—8 million in the morning and another 4 million in the afternoon—that come off the presses each day, an English and Japanese version of the paper is also posted to the Web for immediate global access.

The Abril Group, which bills itself as Brazil's leading Communications Enterprise, is a $1.5 billion media company comprising 200 magazines, with 30 million readers; a TV/video group with 1.25 million pay-TV subscribers and video sales of

$5.7 million; and a new business group with 9 million phone books covering 40 percent of all telephones in Brazil, 10 million people in Datalistas' database, and 12,000 subscribers to Brazil Online. Publishing accounts for 70 percent of the media conglomerate's revenue. In its quest to expand into the digital, interactive environment, the company created a large Web site, and quickly gained 22,000 subscribers. The communications company now can reach local-language audiences anywhere in the world. Dorival Dourado Jr., Information Technology Director of Abril, noted that executives say their biggest issues are how IT can support the organization, and "the need to have a more global vision."

Going in the other direction—from global to local—because audiences can be so effectively targeted, it will make sense for locally distributed publications to develop content online that can appeal to audiences globally. *The Macon Telegraph* (Georgia), for example, created an in-depth special report on a bicycle race in France featuring content that would be of special interest to French consumers.

Furthermore, it will be just as easy for a publishing company in one country to aggregate local-language content and customers in another, as it is for the local publishing company itself. On the Net, it doesn't matter where you are—the information and distribution infrastructure is the same, regardless of where you set up shop. This lack of geographic boundaries presents opportunities for new customer and revenue growth, as well as new opportunities for multinational alliances within the industry itself.

Take the multibillion dollar media empire News Corporation, for example. When it decided to enter the market in China, it did so by forming a joint venture with *The People's Daily*. Rather than offering information free to anyone, they decided to register users. Within a short period of time 7000 people were registered. Then, rather than repurposing material from the parent publications, leaders of the venture decided to create all new content, focusing exclusively on business.

Malcolm Colless, Director and General Manager of Corporate Development, News Corp., sees the venture as a major opportunity. "There is no limit to the amount and reach of information, because there is no newsprint cost. We have no print business in China, just the online product." In this way, not only can News Corp. afford to establish a local paper on the other side of the world, but it can also aggregate Chinese audiences in China and the United States. If it offered an English-language version of the paper, it could further aggregate audiences around the world based on its business-oriented content.

AGGREGATING VERSUS BRANDING

In just about every industry, companies setting out to do business on the Web have quickly come to realize that the Internet is a great equalizer. Small can be large, and vice versa, and competition can come from anywhere. But with everyone on the Net effectively a publisher, traditional publishing companies are perhaps feeling the most threatened by the Net's ability to level the playing field. However, what is not so easily acquired on the Web, especially when it comes to providing information, is authority. Over and above technical issues related to fraud and forgery, the challenge for all publishers—old and new—will be to earn *trust,* either by capitalizing on established brands, or by creating new brands. In both cases, the goal is the same: to be perceived as the best knowledge provider in the new medium.

With an almost limitless supply of information available on the Net, neither challenge is straightforward. While established brands carry more weight, the Internet constitutes an entirely new information infrastructure in which traditional measures of authority and credibility may not necessarily translate. Furthermore, any advantage may be short-lived, as newcomers eventually build trust and provide value in the new cyber environment.

For new publishers, such as CNET, the opportunity exists to create awareness, following, and trust as experts in the new medium. The company is well capitalized and seeks to do business only in the low-cost world of "bits." They are one of the new aggregators, whose mission is to capture the largest amount of information on a given topic or interest and neatly put it under one umbrella. Even with no brand legacy—which may actually work to their advantage—they could become the new information providers to beat.

But the opportunity to create new brands also exists for established companies, possibly more so than in the traditional business environment. Nonetheless, introducing a new brand on the Net risks damaging the core brand. Traditional publishers have huge amounts invested in their print production, and relatively little in Web publishing. Compared to newcomers such as CNET, which has millions dedicated exclusively to online publishing, products from traditional publications may appear less sophisticated. On the other hand, unhampered by tradition and customer expectations, publishers are freer to develop and define the new brand in this entirely new context. There is no way of predicting, just yet, how brands—old and new—will function in the new medium, but publishers are learning quickly.

For example, when Condé Nast Publications, publishers of *Vogue, Glamour, Details, GQ,* and *Mademoiselle,* put its brands on the Net, it started with both the Condé Nast Traveler Web site, named directly after its print publication, and Epicurious, a new brand. After newcomer Epicurious received four times as many visits as Condé Nast Traveler, the company moved Traveler under the Epicurious umbrella.

Time Inc. housed its well-known publications, including *Time, People,* and *Sports Illustrated,* on its umbrella site called Pathfinder. It became one of the most visited content sites on the Web.

When CMP, a Long Island technology publisher, entered the digital domain, it did so with a Web site called TechWeb. Later, as the Web matured, it created an umbrella site called CMPNet, under which it housed its publications, as well as TechWeb. The company branded its then two-year-old, knowledge-providing arm of TechWeb.

An even more interesting scenario involved the *New York Times* and its subsidiary, *The Boston Globe.* The *New York Times* launched itself on the Web under its own brand, at NYTimes.com. However, when *The Boston Globe* launched its publication on the Web it created a new brand, Boston.com. Under that brand, the company aggregated its competitors, *Boston Magazine,* WBZ Radio, WBZ TV, WGBH TV, as well as *The Boston Globe* itself. As the general source of news for the Boston area, Boston.com has covered the bases of aggregating TV, print, radio—all online. In this case, two completely different strategies were successfully used by brands operating within the same company. The *New York Times,* meanwhile, expanded on its tremendous publishing franchise by aggregating its own content, such as its book reviews and photographs. It partnered with bookseller Barnes and Noble so that it could provide total book service—from information through to purchase and delivery—as a new service to visitors to *The New York Times* site.

As publishers, new and old, battle for status as "trusted source," perhaps an even greater challenge involves vying for position as the final link to the customer, who remains a coveted target of Madison Avenue.

In addition to being aggregated by one another, publishers risk having their brands aggregated by new players. Total News, for example, aggregated the top brands in publishing and broadcasting, including *Time,* CNN, CBS, ABC, and Fox, putting the logo of each at its Web site. The major publishers sued, and ultimately settled with Total News so that the site could only *route traffic* to those sites, as opposed to "framing" the news of those publishers under the Total News logo, along with the rights to sell advertising on the content of those companies. Total News did, however, continue to reaggregate, or repackage the contents of the brands according to subject categories, such as Business, Sports and Politics, and sold advertising on each category. By breaking down the publications into individual articles and then grouping them all by category, Total News became a directory of news topics, with the ability to sell advertising on the basis of a highly targeted audience.

KNOWLEDGE VERSUS INFORMATION

As consumers gather more of their own information from an ever-expanding supply, there will be a real need for someone to put information in context, to help gauge its significance, and to add historical perspective and analysis; in other words, to create meaning. There will be a need to find, cultivate, and bring detailed, specific expertise to the marketplace, turning information into knowledge.

Book publishers in particular have a competitive edge in filling this role as knowledge provider. They have well-developed relationships with authors, and can act as aggregators of experts in specific fields. This may have implications for authors of the future, placing them in the position of becoming "experts" and "talents" around which publishers can aggregate audiences. Publishers are also adept at tapping into market needs for specific subjects, and at predicting future needs as well as creating trends. As the amount of information increases, and timelines for the whole publishing process shrinks—editorial, production, marketing—publishers will be challenged to integrate their legacy businesses into the instant, online environment.

Overall, the nature of the audience for information is changing quite radically. Publishers are facing a new kind of reader, one who absorbs information from multiple sources simultaneously. As we move from the "don't bother me, I'm reading the newspaper" generation to the "yeah, got it" sound-bite generation, publishers will have to adapt to a multimedia culture bombarded with information but lacking in knowledge. The need to provide directories of information about information, and the context to decipher—make sense—of all that information can be fulfilled by publishers.

CONCLUSION

As they approach the twenty-first century, publishers must cope with disintermediation, aggregation, and globalization. Furthermore, as empowered members of an increasingly multitasking, interactive generation that lives in electronic communities, their audiences are expecting unprecedented form and delivery of content and services. Only time will tell if the traditional publishing companies are up to the challenge. It is now that they must decide who and what they are in the new economy.

The traditional publishing companies will not necessarily drive publishing in the next millennium, although the opportunity is theirs to lose. It is they who have the opportunity to replace themselves as the Fourth Estate, and truly become the leaders in the Digital Estate.

NOTES

1. Martin, Chuck, *The Digital Estate: Strategies for Competing, Surviving, and Thriving in an Internetworked World* (New York: McGraw-Hill), 1997. For a detailed look at the growth of the publishing industry in the wake of the French Revolution, see Roger Chartier, *The Cultural Origins of the French Revolution*, trans. by Lydia G. Cochrane (Lafayette: Duke University Press), 1991.

2. Growing from five to 80 employees within its first year, iVillage received offers of up to $20 million in financing within 6 months of being launched. It took $11 million from the likes of TCI, the largest cable company in the world, Kleiner-Perkins, the premier technology venture capital firm in Silicon Valley, the Tribune Company, owners of the *Chicago Tribune*, and America Online. Later, it raised an additional $20 million from investors to fuel growth.

PICTURES IN THE DIGITAL ECONOMY

by Carl E. Gustin
Eastman Kodak Company

Pictures are powerful. They bring people to life in a grandmother's photo album; they help seek justice in a courtroom; they expose the horrors of war on a newspaper's front page. When a picture is taken it captures a memory, and a moment in time lives on.

For more than 100 years film and camera manufacturers have strived to provide consumers with easier and more affordable ways to capture the pictures they want and achieve higher-quality results. Early cameras were relatively large, cumbersome, and costly, and photographs were considered luxury items. It wasn't until George Eastman's invention of roll film at the end of the nineteenth century and his introduction of the Brownie box camera that photography started being accessible to the masses. Since then, professional and amateur photographers have enjoyed dramatic advances in quality (color, enlargements, and motion) and convenience (1-hour processing, easy loading, point-and-shoot cameras, and wide-latitude film).

But the best is yet to come. As this book outlines in detail, digital technology is already upon us in almost every realm of human activity. All forms of expression and communication—images, audio, text, and data—can now be captured, manipulated, and transmitted digitally. The implications for photography are clearly profound, and soon we will all employ digital technology to take, store, manipulate, and communicate photographs in ways Eastman would have never thought possible.

This doesn't mean a century of work by Eastman and his peers has been rendered obsolete. Conventional film will still be with us for many years. While digital technology is good and getting better, a low-cost point-and-shoot camera with traditional film can still record a scene in much greater detail than all but the most expensive digital cameras, and this will remain the case in the foreseeable future. When quality of the image is paramount, conventional film is the technology of choice. It is *after* the original image is recorded that digital technology truly shines.

Because the two technologies can happily coexist and complement each other, I see the growth of the global photographic industry proceeding down two almost parallel tracks.

In developed markets, digital imaging products and services will drive renewed interest in photography and increased demand for pictures overall. Home PC users are early adopters, editing pictures and adding them to e-mail, documents, and creative projects. But digital photography is much bigger than simply "PC photography"; many people, whether they're "wired" or not, will get the benefits of digital imaging from non-PC-based technology, such as Kodak's Image Magic systems in retail locations.

In developing markets—especially in growing economies such as Brazil, Eastern Europe, India, Russia, and China—conventional photography will grow much faster than digital imaging, since the traditional system is easier to put into place. Regular film needs only a supporting infrastructure of photo retailers and photolabs compared to digital imaging's need for telephone lines, computers with the necessary software applications, and retail services. This is a short-term barrier to a totally "wired world," but it is a reality that prognosticators of the digital way of life must face: Markets will move at different rates.

HOW PICTURES ARE USED

At Kodak, our business depends on understanding why and how people use pictures. The use of photographs generally falls into one or more of three categories: (1) information, including photojournalism, prepress, and business applications; (2) memories and personal sharing; and (3) entertainment.

PICTURES AS INFORMATION

Information flow in large businesses provides an example of pictures as information. In the emerging digital economy, pictures will be even more critical in helping organizations to communicate.

Two industries that already rely heavily on pictures are leading the way—insurance and real estate. In their attempts to take advantage of digital capabilities, they have learned that the payoff must be more than rapid access. Users in those industries are finding that the digital-imaging solutions they adopt must offer cost effectiveness by eliminating steps from the process, ease of use, and high levels of quality.

Insurance companies—property and casualty companies in particular—are in the information business. The more complete the information is, the better they can use it, and the more success they will have in processing claims, satisfying customers, and minimizing fraud.

The newest digital imaging systems for insurers enable them to take digital photographs of properties, record and attach voice notes during their inspections, link photos with other digital files, and automatically encode them with a security feature that alerts users to any alterations to the pixels in the image. And, insurance inspectors can use software, such as Kodak Digital Science intelligent image analysis, to take property measurement information right from their digital photos. This is a prime example of digital technology enabling organizations to improve their processes.

In a fast-moving real estate market, agents can move more decisively with digital imaging technology. They can take color pictures digitally or digitize conventional photos, and incorporate them into open house leaflets—printed digitally—for use the same day. The next step, of course, is to target the same information to registered house hunters who have specified parameters for their purchase, and to send the leaflet electronically to them over the Internet.

For online house hunters, real estate Web sites are very useful tools. To that extent, any realtor that has a Web site—incorporating pictures of agents and current properties on the market—enjoys a competitive edge over realtors who don't represent themselves on the Web.

It's possible today to use still pictures to provide an online tour of homes on the Web—complete with running commentary. Using highly sophisticated Web applications, specialized companies will eventually offer the option to agents and their potential buyers of taking virtual motion tours of homes. House hunters will be able to point to any direction in the house—even look out any window—and catch the view. Any "virtual" package on a property would, of course, include information on, or links to, maps, community information, pictures of the neighborhood, and whatever else the imaginative real estate agent can generate.

When it comes time for a real estate appraiser to submit a report to the mortgage lender, digital technology will be a natural time-saver. Pictures of the property—along with information on comparable properties from the neighborhood—are attached to the mortgage application, and printed as one document when needed. Today, storage of old mortgage applications—a requirement that varies from 3 to 5 years—is a space-consuming prospect, and retrieval is a task no one relishes. One file can be inches thick. When the whole application—including pictures—is digitized and stored on disk, the physical storage problem is resolved. Some appraisers are already doing this.

The ultimate application for digital imaging in real estate is the Multiple Listing Service, which can only be accessed by realtors and brokers. Currently, basic details of a house—floor space, bedrooms, etc.—are printed out in black and white text. A long-term goal is to put all this information plus color photographs online. By viewing properties online, purchasers and realtors will save time and money, can target their searches with purchasers' needs, and reduce the amount of properties a realtor has to show.

Home builders will be able to show people custom-built homes—even before the first shovel of dirt is moved—using a combination of photographs, drawings, colors, and textures. Home buyers will be able to view every element in their future home, from the siding and roofing to the color and texture of the carpeting.

Another useful model is catalog retailers, who have been heavy users of photography through the years. Naturally, many have embraced digital technology, not only for page layout but also for capturing the pictures they want, and, as a result, they have realized the process efficiencies of digital imaging.

Digital cameras today are in wide use by professional and news photographers. It was a novel occurrence when, at the 1991 Super Bowl in Miami, only one photographer—from *USA Today*—used a digital camera to take a picture of the game-deciding field-goal attempt. Using a telephone line in the press room, the photographer sent the picture to the newspaper's editorial offices in Virginia. In 1997, 48 photographers used digital cameras at the Super Bowl—the most popular single sports event in the United States. Virtually all of the thousands of pictures captured the same year by the Associated Press were taken with digital cameras. As early adopters of digital photography, news organizations now account for a large percentage of the pictures taken with digital cameras.

Digital imaging's original users—commercial printers and pre-press shops—will make even more progress in the digital age. Their processes will be faster and easier as more information comes from their customers in digital form. They are already starting to use direct-to-plate processes that cut out the middle film steps in print-ing, and they will pursue a distribute-and-print model that enables customers—even at the consumer level—to gather information cen-trally, then print it on demand at remote locations.

One popular vision is to have completely automated prepress software that contains process intelligence for layout and color—giving amateur layout artists professional capabilities. These wizard-based systems will emerge over the next few years, and will feature the ability to lead users through the layout process step by step, ulti-mately producing very good quality, template-based results.

Over the next 10 to 15 years, people will be able to purchase electronic magazines and output them on their own printing devices. Paper will support electronic media distribution, instead of electronic media supporting paper distribution.

PICTURES AS MEMORIES

Traditional photography has followed a simple process for decades. Shoot a roll of film. Deliver it to a photofinisher. Wait for the results.

In order to overtake film photography, digital imaging must bring even greater simplicity to the process, but a number of barri-ers have prevented digital imaging from gaining widespread popular-ity. High-resolution images contain lots of data, which generate large digital files that are cumbersome to process and transmit. Low-resolution images generate smaller files that are easy to use on the computer but cannot produce high-quality output. These quality issues, combined with the lack of standard formats for storing images and reproducing color, have forced users of most desktop imaging applications to make a lot of complex choices that often yield unpredictable results. The sheer complexity of the technology and the lack of compelling products have prevented more users from even trying to use pictures on computers.

Nonetheless, making digital cameras that equal or surpass the resolution of film is no longer the issue. The current challenge for Kodak and other manufacturers is how to make digital photography affordable and easy for people to use. The main limiting factor of image quality is the device that converts light into electrons. Kodak uses the charge-coupled device (CCD), a solid-state chip containing a series of tiny light-sensitive photosites, or pixels. After the subject is focused onto the CCD, the electrons then pass through an analog-to-digital converter which produces a file of digital information where bits represent the color and tonal values of an image. The greater the number of pixels, the higher the quality of the image. Currently, the CCD in a typical consumer digital camera handles around 350,000 pixels, compared to the 20 million pixels that would be required to match the quality of 35-mm film. A high-end digital camera today costs in the area of $20,000–30,000, and, some would argue, still does not fully match the quality of film.

The gap between quality and affordability continues to close, but in the meantime, tools that will help developers popularize digital imaging are hitting the market. One of these is FlashPix technology, developed collaboratively by Kodak, Hewlett-Packard, Live Picture Inc., and Microsoft. The FlashPix file format and imaging architecture is designed to serve as a universal standard, driving the development of applications that make digital imaging easy and fun for every-day computer users and more productive for experienced computer users.

High-quality color images still require large data files, but applications enabled by FlashPix technology allow users to access only the portions of the image they need at that moment. Images in applications optimized in the FlashPix format burst on-screen, transform instantly when edited, move rapidly over phone lines, and look great coming off the printer. FlashPix architecture has opened up new possibilities for online sharing, network image services, desktop applications, and "while-you-wait" retail kiosks where consumers can get a wide variety of digital photographic services.

Retailers provide three ways for people to access picture files enabled in the FlashPix format:

1. The Kodak Image Magic system FlashPix CD is an easy way to bring FlashPix images to the desktop. This represents one of many scanning services that make it easy for people to get their pictures digitized, simply by checking a box on their photofinishing envelope.

2. Other scanning services enable people to get their pictures loaded directly into password-protected Internet accounts in the FlashPix format.

3. Consumers can get lower-resolution scans on a 3.5-inch diskette that holds up to 28 images, or a single image on diskette at a higher resolution.

The lower-resolution scans (400 × 600 pixels) are suitable for use in documents, viewing images on-screen, printing small images, or transmitting pictures online. The FlashPix CD can contain hundreds of images scanned at 1024 × 1536 pixels, also available from photofinishers.

While these digitization options indicate that film will remain the capture medium of choice for many consumers, digital cameras also are making giant steps forward. Professional photographers can select from an extensive range of digital cameras or camera backs that fit on existing film cameras. In the newest models, resolution levels are climbing, ISO ranges are expanding so digital cameras can be used in lower and higher levels of light, and prices are moving inexorably downward.

Right now, most digital cameras are well-suited to applications where users are willing to trade off some image quality (compared to film) in order to get the images fast and in a form they can use right away on their computers. These include photojournalism, medicine, law enforcement, and a range of business applications such as catalog preparation.

The FlashPix architecture is one way of bringing digital photography to consumers, but there are many other facets to digital imaging that must come together to form usable systems for photographers at all levels.

For example, as people begin to use more and more digital pictures on their home computers, they will need convenient ways to access and store those pictures. The storage media for digital images have become smaller in size and larger in capacity. At about the size of a matchbook, Kodak Digital Science picture cards fit inside the Kodak Digital Science DC210 zoom digital camera and the Kodak DC25 digital camera. People can simply use the Kodak Digital Science picture card like a virtual roll of film: take it out of the camera and fit it into a reader/writer or the built-in PC card drive in a computer.

Industry standards play an important role in storage media as well as image files themselves. By employing standards, manufacturers can extend the use of image-storage products so that people can use the cards and card reader/writers with all kinds of desktop and laptop computer peripherals, without special drivers or software. In addition, users can take the cards to the thousands of retailers that offer Kodak Image Magic systems, where they can insert the cards into workstations to create instant digital prints—a real advantage for photographers on the go.

Of course, imaging software enables people to have more power over their pictures than ever before. Here are some examples of software utilities that make digital imaging more accessible:

Kodak Picture Easy software is designed to give those who use Kodak digital cameras the quickest and easiest way available to get pictures from their cameras into their computers, and save or print them.

Kodak Digital Science picture postcard software—which ships with many Kodak products and can be downloaded directly from the Kodak home page—makes sharing pictures via e-mail as easy as sending text.

Microsoft Picture It! was the first software application enabled with FlashPix technology to let consumers enhance, create, and share photographic print-quality memories in a fun, easy, and affordable way that requires nothing more than a typical home PC.

Kai's Power Goo from MetaTools is a creative entertainment software package that lets users distort pictures in a number of fun ways. For example, users can take a picture of a family member and transform that person into a caricature by stretching out their eyes and enlarging their ears.

For people who don't own a home computer, who don't want to take the time, or who want special output or other services, Kodak ImageMagic workstations make digital reprints and enlargements from existing photographic prints in minutes. More extensive projects might include repairing old or imperfect photos, or adding digitally designed borders. In addition, retailers can make posters with large-format color printers, scan images to Kodak Photo CD discs or FlashPix CDs, and output high-volume orders on minilab photographic printers.

As the number of home and retail options grow, Kodak sees a real need for retail locations that help people understand their personal imaging options. For that reason, Kodak is establishing cobranded stores that will bring the many imaging elements together under one roof. These include digital and film cameras; demonstration areas; photoprocessing and film-based photography products; and services for digitally transforming existing prints to produce custom digital creations such as wine bottle labels, personalized covers for the videotapes of family occasions (weddings, birthdays, etc.), photo collages, or simply applying a special border around an image.

The Internet is starting to play an extremely important part in helping people to share pictures in new ways—providing a digital alternative to the traditional sharing model based on the double set of prints and postal service.

The Kodak Picture Network enables people to share pictures at any time with friends or family around the world. Consumers simply get their pictures scanned and uploaded to the picture network at any one of thousands of retail locations, then use a claim number to access their pictures through a private network account at the Kodak Web site.

Initially, the Picture Network allows people to order reprints and enlargements electronically and to e-mail pictures to friends and family. When it's fully functional, the network will let people access and share images in new ways, such as creating online photo albums accessible to selected friends and family who can all order prints of any pictures in the album. People without computers at home will access Picture Network accounts through retail locations that sell and service Kodak Image Magic products.

As these digital products and services become available to consumers, Kodak and other providers are doing their best to anticipate market needs for consumer photography. Based on historic reaction to consumer-photography products, we can make some educated guesses as to what people will want to do with pictures using newer technology.

For example, people are accustomed to getting photographic products and services when and where they want them. The digital age of photography and the power of the Internet will not do away with the demand for opportunistic photographic services but will change the offerings.

Instead of buying a one-time-use camera at a theme park, perhaps consumers will rent digital cameras, then have the prints delivered to their hotel room or waiting for them as they leave the park. Maybe they'll pay a nominal fee to have those images uploaded to the Kodak Picture Network, or have them e-mailed to the destination of their choice. The film kiosk may also serve as a digital imaging enablement station, with all of the computer and communication power to deliver the right results.

PICTURES AS ENTERTAINMENT

Even as digital imaging technology pervades the entertainment industry, there is still no digital method on the horizon that will replace film in movie theaters for a long time to come. The coexistence model of film and digital imaging will apply here, as it does in consumer photography applications.

However, digital techniques today set the standard for special effects in motion pictures. In fact, the newest digital imaging systems for the motion picture industry offer astounding capabilities for creating special effects. The Cineon digital film system—made by Kodak—enables film producers to create special effects and seamlessly weave them into feature films. The Cineon system was first used on a feature-length film to restore the original footage of *Snow White and the Seven Dwarfs* and, more recently, freed Willy, enabled cartoon characters to slam-dunk in *Space Jam,* and put the underwater scenes in *Waterworld.*

Feature film studios, television networks, publishers, and advertising agencies can work with millions of images in databases by using emerging software and hardware that take advantage of FlashPix technology. Because text information can be embedded in an image enabled with FlashPix technology, users can manage and search image databases for specific dates, times, photographers, or other descriptive data. Eventually, similar applications may enable users to search huge image databases for nontext data, such as patterns, textures, or audio information—identifying, for example, only those pictures with a specific shade of sky, model of automobile, facial feature, or series of sounds attached.

Of course, all of this takes far more computer power than the typical desktop PC offers. But it illustrates how digital imaging works to improve what we're doing today with film—and as high-end digital capabilities "trickle down" to consumers, they show how compelling digital imaging can be for virtually everyone.

STRATEGIES FOR DIGITAL SUCCESS

Kodak is intensely interested in the future of digital photography—including digital images created from both film and digital cameras—and we think we have identified building blocks for its success. These include:

- Supporting established and emerging industry standards, such as the FlashPix technology discussed earlier.
- Sharing our expertise in color management by licensing technology to makers of operating systems, applications software, and computer peripherals—including scanners, monitors, and printers.
- Providing solutions that allow people to take advantage of digital photography through the existing photographic infrastructure—allowing people to receive the benefits of digital imaging from the photofinishers and retailers they already use today.

We also are providing the hardware peripherals—such as cameras and photo scanners—and software that enable people to produce digital pictures and share them in convenient ways. In short, we're planning to provide the means for people to take photography where they want it to go, and let them do exactly what they would like to do with their pictures.

Consumer research tells us, however, that, unlike the excitement that early adopters of technology show, most people are not going to embrace digital products just because they are new or offer improved capabilities. More than a century of experience has taught us to be acutely aware of the emotional attachment people have to their pictures, and of the psychology of introducing new technologies to the consumer-photography market.

We also know that no matter how much technology changes, the nature of relationships among people don't change—or at least don't change as quickly. The photographic business is also very much the relationship business. To that end, we must be careful how we ask consumers to change the behaviors that define relationships. Picture-taking and -sharing is one of those behaviors. Success will depend on whether we can enable people to do those things more easily and effectively.

Pictures make powerful impressions. For many years at Kodak, we have placed employee pictures on business cards, and we know that people are much less likely to throw them out. The perception is that if a document contains a photograph, it is of greater value than a document without one. We've been telling customers for years that products and services that use meaningful pictures carry a higher perceived value than other items.

As the digital age enables people to do more with pictures, we must work hard to give consumers the ability to use images in everyday life. And where Kodak doesn't supply all the pieces, we'll work with other companies that can help round out the offering. For example, we bundle software from makers such as Adobe, MetaTools, Microsoft, PictureWorks Technology Inc., and Storm Software with our hardware peripherals to make sure consumers get complete imaging solutions right out of the box.

As PC-based imaging solutions become more common, the trade-offs are beginning to become apparent to consumers. Getting started in digital photography requires a much greater investment (in time *and* materials) than traditional photography but digital technology enables people to do more with their pictures, faster. The digital economy truly will develop as the technology gains more power and appeal, and the trade-offs subside.

TO ADOPT—OR NOT TO ADOPT?

While it's important for companies such as Kodak to look to the future our more immediate challenge is to bring consumers and business customers up-to-date on the advances that already have been made. We try to keep in mind the time when personal computers were first introduced, and the distinction "user friendly," became necessary. Early adopters didn't mind struggling with the arcane commands required at the DOS prompt, but the mass market waited for Macintosh and Windows interfaces before they took the plunge.

For business users to adopt new digital imaging tools, those tools must improve a process or product significantly. Manufacturers and service providers must show businesses how to reengineer their processes using images, not just to add a layer of effort and additional expense.

For consumers, digital imaging must significantly enhance the enjoyment and usefulness of pictures. In both cases, imaging must be easy to use, or people won't be motivated to change.

Applications for Digital Pictures

Application	Immediate capture of...	Correcting/enhancing images to...	Digital accessibility means...	Digital sharing between...	Other benefits include...
Manufacturing (assembly line monitoring)	Critical points of assembly-line activity	N/A (images serve as record)	Continuous monitoring of process information; faster detection/recording of problems	Production workers and off-site management/experts	Quicker response to production problems; less down time
Real estate	Properties for sale	Improve aesthetic appeal	Pictures printed within documents—no more paper clips and file folders	Real estate offices, agents and customers; Web site access for property listings; remote home tours	More effective, memorable sales sheets with more pictures; lower design and production costs to use pictures
Security/ forensics	Personnel faces for badges; people/property under surveillance; crime-scene evidence	Create close-ups of surveillance scenes; reconstruct images, fingerprint ID from partial or damaged images	Immediate availability of personnel pictures, mug shots, missing-person images; controlling access to secure areas with picture IDs	Law enforcement agencies; regional corporate offices	More effient evidence collection; faster suspect ID; improved corporate-security
Property and business insurance	Cars, homes, etc.; before and after damage or loss	N/A (software prevents tampering)	Faster claims processing; company-wide use of images	Body-repair shops and claims adjusters; field agents/investigators and office	Automated measurement of damage to assess loss; reduced fraud; save on costs of film

Category				
Construction renovations	Prospect/customer properties	Show impact of design modifications, finished projects before work begins	Digital storage of blueprints and designs; ability to show customers previous projects easily	Suppliers, designers/architects, contractors, decision makers, customers	Faster, easier decisions on preliminary design parameters before detailed renderings; better customer understanding
Medical	Patient injuries; diagnostic images at accident scenes; remote-location telemedicine	Preview results of corrective surgery; improve diagnostic value of images	Improved patient record-keeping and accuracy with visual images supplementing notes and charts	General practitioners and specialists; collaborative diagnosis in different locations	Improved education; lower costs
Education	Student faces; class projects; field-trip images	Use images in newsletters, reports, etc.	Tracking student progress through student multimedia portfolios	Remote classrooms, teachers, schools and parents/communities (distance learning); Web sites for schools, classes	Learners have greater access to more information, including images and rare or remote objects and events
Consumer memories	Unique personal moments	Personal images in picture creations (posters, labels) and backgrounds (tourist attractions, with celebrities); correct common photo errors (red-eye, crop and zoom)	Ordering custom output and reprints online; online access to pictures after photofinishing; creating personal image databases	Selected groups of friends and family worldwide through online albums, e-mail	Retail workstations enable nonwired to benefit; cost savings over postal distribution of images; immediate viewing of digital pictures

Applications for Digital Pictures (*Continued*)

APPLICATION	IMMEDIATE capture of…	CORRECTING/ENHANCING images to…	DIGITAL ACCESSIBILITY MEANS…	DIGITAL SHARING BETWEEN…	OTHER benefits include…
Publishing	News events; catalog photos; feature photos	Correct color; create desired effects; edit images; design creative layouts	Online access to published works; anyone can be a publisher; fast, round-the-clock access to stock photos; creating personal image databases	Field photographers and office editors/printers for immediate publication; on-line collaboration among printers, prepress services and content creators, retailers and customers	Cost and time savings over traditional print production methods
Office workers	People and product images	Improve impact of business letters, reports, presentations	Fast access to central data-banks of images (employees, products, company logos, past designs, etc.)	Regional offices, customer locations, public Web sites, intranet sites; live desktop videoconferencing, online distribution of images	Improved telecommuting options; save money on face-to-face meetings and manual image distribution
Entertainment	Personal pictures for inclusion in games, movies and virtual-reality applications	Restore movies/shows; create movies/shows	Interactive, online movies and games	Content providers and consumers	Testing entertainment concepts with audiences

The adoption rate is a function of several key factors: the magnitude of the benefit versus cost, the quality of the result, and the ease of use. Ease of use is largely a function of how comfortably a new technology fits into a familiar process.

The television industry provides an example of how a significant benefit, quality, and ease of use came together to bring about the change from motion-picture film to videotape. While most TV drama programming still uses film, the switch among news organizations happened virtually overnight, because the immediacy of videotape and its ease of editing completely overshadowed the higher quality of film.

Just 10 years later, home video cameras also replaced motion-picture film cameras for home users. Again, the convenience of tape and viewing on the TV set was more attractive to consumers than the higher-quality images of film.

However, there is a threshold above which the highest quality is still important. There was very little drop-off in still picture-taking among consumers with camcorders. Film is easy, it is supported by a convenient infrastructure, and it affords the quality people want to capture their Kodak moments.

In the case of motion-picture film, that quality threshold is reached in the entertainment industry, where large-screen movies require the resolution that only film can provide. To date, no other technology can match it, and it will be a long time before motion-picture film is replaced for use in front of mass theater audiences.

Advances in imaging technology will continue to benefit other commercial and government applications—including the growing use of satellite and surveillance imaging. Once employed to unravel the secrecies of the Cold War, reconnaissance and surveillance imaging technologies now are serving a wide range of needs. From land, sea, air, and space, organizations take pictures for mapping, agriculture, forestry, atmospheric studies, and many other uses.

Digital technologies provide users with the ability to take these types of images to new levels of performance. For example, digital pictures taken in low-light situations are more likely to yield greater detail when users employ special software algorithms to enhance features that are, at first, unseen.

Just as digital advantages are combining with traditional ways of doing things for businesses and governments, in the mass-market consumer arena, people are adopting new technologies and products in a similar way. Even groups of competing companies are finding ways to work together to forge new directions.

But the largest potential market—populated by consumers at widely varying skill levels—is gaining momentum. In fact, the number of digital cameras available for under $1000 already substantially exceeds the number of the more expensive digital cameras used by photojournalists.

Today, they're for advanced users who create Web pages, e-mail their pictures, use pictures in documents, or like the speed of digital capture (plus the lack of film processing costs). For most of these users, the digital camera is an extra camera used specifically for PC applications. Over time, digital cameras will replace many film cameras.

What will consumer photography look like in 20 years? No one knows for sure, but we think we know many of the capabilities the photo industry will be offering, and how those capabilities will be received by consumers. Perhaps an equally important question is: What will the mass-market retail location of tomorrow look like? Because consumers and retailers are inextricably linked, it's important to consider retail concepts of the future.

For the past 100 years, the "killer application" that has driven the growth of photography has been picture-sharing versus -archiving. Whether people frame and place their pictures on their mantlepieces, or send them through the mail, sharing is a prime use for photos. While the Kodak Picture Network described earlier goes a long way toward helping people to do those things, the future likely will bring devices that will help people access the Picture Network and similar services more easily. Some experts predict that picture-viewing devices will be ubiquitous—cropping up everywhere from refrigerator doors and living room walls to office desks and suit pockets. It's no coincidence that these are the places people today like to place their most treasured pictures.

Today it takes a concentrated effort to share pictures with people who are far away. Imagine being able to access photos on the picture network, and to simply click a box (or give voice instructions to the computer/device) to send the picture to everyone in a selected circle of family and friends.

Another capability that should be available within 5 years is sending video clips over services such as the Kodak picture network. With new compression technologies that make it easier and faster to move very large files over the Internet, and with Internet pipeline sizes expanding, short video clips will be usable and movable by more and more people. Of course, using video clips on computers presents an ease-of-use challenge more daunting than still imaging. People are accustomed to the slick video edits of programs and advertisements on network television, so consumer expectations may be high for video performance.

Over the next 10 to 20 years, people will be able to sort video images using accompanying audio tracks. For example, during little Susan's birthday party, her parents capture a video of her waving her arms and saying hello to Grandma. A couple of days later Susan's mom wants to show this scene. She simply says, "Show me Susan saying 'Hello' to Grandma," and the imaging device displays it automatically.

While many companies are jumping on the digital-capture bandwagon with products of varying price points and quality, there exists a disparity in the price, quality, and convenience between the old and the new image-capture technologies. There is no way to predict the course of events with perfect accuracy, but given the historic pattern of similar product migrations, this "in-between" condition is likely to last for many more years. The coexistence of film and digital photography products makes sense for both platforms, since they are interchangeable at so many stages. For example, people can scan prints or negatives to convert them into digital files, just as they can make hard-copy prints of a digital image created on-screen.

This dawning age of digital photography has allowed the industry to make improvements on old concepts. Photo reprints are a perfect example. Kodak Image Magic systems, based at retail locations, enable people to make reprints and other photo products from existing prints. For example, one version enables retailers to provide "prints from prints" while customers wait; another gives retailers the ability to enhance and restore consumers' pictures; and a third gives consumers the controls, allowing them to copy, enhance, and customize their own pictures.

Event photography is another example—where photographers offer their services at special events or places such as theme parks or cruises. Digital cameras enable event photographers to take pictures, integrate them with a specific theme background or digitally created frame, and present them to the customer in just minutes.

THE FUTURE OF FILM

For many reasons, it seems clear that film will serve most applications well into the future as the capture medium of choice. Its benefits are numerous.

First, it's a low-cost proposition to use film for a wide variety of purposes, not least of which is the family snapshot album. Used with reasonable care, film cameras work for a long time, so there isn't a natural degradation point that would cause attrition to digital. More film is being manufactured today than ever before, so if nothing else, the perceived demand among manufacturers is there.

Film technology is something with which people are comfortable. Users don't have to understand photographic chemistry or science to operate a camera and get good pictures.

Film also provides high-quality images. Think of it this way: In contrast to today's digital technology, it takes about 4 MB of memory to provide an acceptable print for the average consumer, but it takes 100 MB of memory to store all the visual information available from one 35-mm frame of film. That's a lot of information packed into a small space.

For that reason, film is a dependable storage medium. With a historically long shelf life—and newer films provide even greater longevity—film serves well for storing family and professional photos, or document images and mainframe data on microfilm and microfiche. Many people are familiar with the use of microfilms in public libraries, but these specialty films are also routinely used to capture millions of check images each day in the banking industry, as well as documents used by insurance companies, government agencies, and other organizations.

Microfilms have been part of the digital transition for many years. Document-imaging systems allow electronic processing and distribution. But film is still used for archiving and during the transition. Users must be able to scan older film images into the new system. Because film images are easily converted to digital formats, whole industries have sprung up around the creation, storage, distribution, and digitization of microfilmed data.

A parallel development in the consumer photographic industry is the Advanced Photo System, developed by a consortium of companies consisting of Kodak, Canon, Fuji, Minolta, and Nikon.

Introduced in 1996, the Advanced Photo System was designed to address a number of outstanding consumer concerns through hybrid solutions. The new system features enhancements in film loading, picture formatting, and negative storage. Each of these and dozens of other improvements are specified as standards in the system. Now, licensed companies produce competing products—such as the Kodak Advantix system—based on those standards.

One Advanced Photo System innovation—a magnetic coating on the film—can be used to store vital information about each picture for use by photofinishers. The thin layer of magnetic particles can record information—such as the selected print format and lighting conditions—on each frame of the film. During photofinishing, processing algorithms adjust the printing equipment to optimize each exposure based on this information.

With the system's magnetics advancements, a 40-exposure roll of Kodak Advantix film has the ability to record more than 80 kb of this type of information. While initial Advanced Photo System products now employ less than 20 percent of that magnetics capacity, the technology makes Advantix films truly hybrid products.

In the migration to the digital economy, the digitization of film images is a critical capability for three basic reasons: (1) it takes advantage of a huge treasure trove of existing pictures; (2) people can still use film as a low-cost, high-resolution capture and storage medium; and (3) users don't have to invest in new cameras. Once in digital form, the productive and delightful things that can happen with digital pictures are beginning to take shape now, but they are just a hint of what will be available in a few years.

DIGITAL PICTURE STORAGE

What would happen if people digitized all of the more than 1 billion photographs taken each year? Digital storage would become an immediate problem, especially for home computer users.

One storage challenge relates to how it's done—identifying a workable storage method and providing enough media space to give users reliable, long-term access to large numbers of image files. At the desktop, CD (compact disk) and DVD (digital video disk) media will play a role. Services like the Kodak picture network can also meet consumer storage needs, using a client-server model.

Another difficult question is how to organize and classify digital pictures so that they can be easily retrieved. Experience with traditional photography shows that most people won't want to spend much time organizing and classifying their pictures. They will expect digital imaging systems to do it for them.

The answer to storage and retrieval lies in what the ultimate uses for specific pictures will be. People's organization of pictures will depend heavily on how they want to extract information from them. They will need, for example, automatic recognition of useful content. To the extent that we can encode what is physically represented in an image, we can meaningfully store and retrieve it. And in that challenge, there is more than meets the eye.

Effective storage and retrieval of images will involve organizing abstract concepts and definitions for the purpose of meaningful classification. When retrieving an image, a person might not exactly remember the scene, but may remember something about it in the picture. One way that computers will help retrieve the pictures people want is by association. In other words, finding one picture will lead to others in a group.

For example, a photographer takes a picture of Andrea in Tuscany on May 3, 1999. A year later, someone wants to find pictures of Andrea. The searcher could retrieve those pictures simply by entering "Andrea" as the search parameter, then the database might automatically bring up all pictures taken on May 3, 1999, because it would guess that Andrea is in a selection of those pictures. Essentially, the database will take logical steps to identify a set of pictures based on what it knows about individual photos.

What's more, computers will be able to interpret three-dimensional, real-world content to enable people to search still-picture or motion-video databases. Eventually, they will be able to search in three "dimensions"—digital video, still pictures, and audio—to locate a specific image. A person might not remember word-for-word a sentence used at a certain time, or the person the comment was made to, but searching all three dimensions together could locate the image.

This concept could extend to products such as custom television programming, wherein a person can select his or her own level of humor, eroticism, and violence, for example, then view only shows that contain those elements.

The concept of interactive television will enable people to become specific characters and to act out scenes or play interactive games on their computers. Other imaging technology will give people the capability to convert live-action movies to ones with animated characters for children.

Another way of classifying pictures is by the location where they were taken. In several years, cameras may be able to receive a global positioning signal from a satellite, and record the position of each shot. After the pictures are filed, users would be able to look them up by specifying a location, such as "Mt. Everest" or "San Francisco waterfront."

So, even if people don't remember the content of their pictures, they may remember locations, and with that information, they'll be able to retrieve their images.

As computers evolve to become user-friendly appliances—similar to cellular telephones—manufacturers will combine in them video, digital audio, global positioning, and perhaps even a small camera. These devices also will be able to communicate with each other, sending data and images from point to point for business, entertainment, and personal sharing.

FROM PRINTS TO SOFT DISPLAY

In the future, will people still want or need prints of digital images?

Some people are convinced that the photographic print will always be part of the cultural landscape. That's probably true for the foreseeable future, although digital technology will help consumers order only the prints they need and want, rather than every frame they shoot.

Conceivably, soft displays will reach a point where they offer the kind of resolution people are used to seeing in a print. In the meantime, their value is not as a replacement for prints but for other uses.

The psychological attachment to the print goes beyond the quality of the image it contains. People also value prints because of their tactile quality, portability, and low-tech simplicity, existing on their own, independent of a power supply to bring them to life. Today, even though many newspapers are available online, most people still prefer to digest written news in hard copy.

But there are reasons other than replacing paper to move ahead with soft-display research. While today's television screens and computer monitors use red, green, and blue dots next to each other to form colors, researchers are working on ways to superimpose colors on screens—the same way superimposed colors give film such great depth and richness. But most importantly, people will have additional uses for these new, high-quality reflective displays. This is where the potential for entirely new ways to *use* images becomes bounded only by our own imaginations. With the rise of the information appliance, any digital display device becomes a picture frame with interactive multimedia capabilities. For example, people may be interested in "picture frames" that show multiple pictures in sequence. Prints held up by magnets on a fridge could one day be replaced by programmable frames in the refrigerator door. The same technology also could be used for signage or other information. Entire building walls, for example, could display images, as seen in the classic futurist film, *Bladerunner*.

One thing seems certain as we move solidly into the digital age: no one provider can do it all. For that reason, Kodak will work through business alliances to enable digital imaging solutions in various products and services. The Kodak Color Management System and FlashPix technology, both mentioned earlier, are prime examples of Kodak-led innovations that are driving other manufacturers' digital products.

Inevitably, consumers will turn to providers who understand them as individuals—whether the extent of that understanding comes down to actually knowing consumer names, or simply recognizing the importance of specific behaviors such as hobbies and travel patterns—in order to communicate effectively with them.

Whatever technology we are pursuing, we must ask each day: How can pictures and images help people with the relationships they value, and empower businesses to serve their customers better? While the answers are not definitive, we surely have a wider-than-ever range of possibilities to leverage the ways people communicate in the digital economy, through the power of pictures.

THE GLOBAL LEARNING INFRASTRUCTURE

THE FUTURE OF HIGHER EDUCATION

by Carol Twigg
Educom

and Michael Miloff
Alliance for Converging Technologies

Today's production and distribution of information are undermining the traditional flow of information and with it the university structure, making it ready to collapse in slow motion once alternatives to its functions become possible.[1]

ELI M. NOAM

Society's higher education requirements are undergoing a fundamental transformation. A rapidly growing student population is becoming older and increasingly diverse. In addition, the new economy requires a workforce capable of handling an exploding knowledge base, and industries are looking to educational institutions to provide the necessary education and training. There is financial pressure, too: colleges and universities must control and even reduce costs, as well as manage new competitive dynamics, while responding to growing demands.

Emerging digital technology, especially the Internet, is ideally suited to meet the new learning needs by enabling a digital learning infrastructure. But such an infrastructure offers more than just education-as-usual on the Internet. It offers a set of extraordinary new tools: self-paced multimedia modules that deliver leading pedagogy, in-depth outcome assessments, and online interaction with fellow students and teachers that facilitates continuous feedback and improvement.

Currently, individual universities are bundling a number of functions, including standards setting, accreditation, content creation, and delivery and administration of instructional materials. With a digital learning infrastructure, these functions can be disaggregated, disintermediated, globalized, and carried out more efficiently by separate, specialized entities.

As a result, a student-centric global learning infrastructure extends far beyond the individual virtual university to include the new digital marketplace. With its emphasis on creativity and competition, it enables a wide range of players—universities, media, publishers, content specialists, technology companies—to market, sell, and deliver educational services online.

The potential for meeting the next century's educational needs is striking. But in transforming current teaching methods, the global learning infrastructure also challenges the educational system as a whole. Change will be rewarding but difficult.

Managing this transition will require bold leadership and public policies that find new ways to harness market forces and come to terms with emerging social, technological, and financial issues. Institutions of higher education and other players must rigorously assess their roles and niche competencies, and form new partnerships in order to contribute and compete.

CHANGES IN LEARNING REQUIREMENTS: TRENDS AND CHALLENGES

ACCESS

Increasing Numbers.   Today U.S. college students number more than 13 million—approximately 5 percent of the population.[2] Between 1996 and 2005, the number of high school graduates is projected to grow by more than 20 percent, to a total of 3 million by the end of that period.[3]

Currently, almost two-thirds of high school graduates go on to college, up from just 56 percent in 1980. The next decade will see college enrollments in this age group jump from 15 to 20 million students.[4]

Diverse Demographics.   Historically, undergraduate colleges catered to an exclusive group: white men under the age of 22. U.S. Department of Education projections suggest that in 1998, five out of every 11 students attending U.S. colleges and universities will be 25 and older; even more surprisingly, students who are 35 and older will outnumber those aged 18 and 19. This doesn't take into account an even greater number of adults who would like to pursue a college education but cannot, due to inconvenient class hours, campus inaccessibility, family responsibilities, business travel, or physical disabilities.[5] In the past 20 years, the number of women and members of racial minority groups has also increased: today 55 percent of undergraduates are women and over 15 percent are of nonwhite descent. As traditional barriers fall, the student population will become even more heterogeneous.

More Part-Timers.   What we think of as traditional undergraduates—those who are 18–22, attend full time, and live on campus—constitute less than one-fourth of all students in higher education. The "new majority" is over 25, attends part-time, and lives off-campus. Many of these students work or have child-rearing responsibilities; they place a premium on time management and on balancing education with other demands.

CONVENIENCE

Desire for Flexible Schedules.   In the past, education primarily took place during the 9-month academic calendar; now it's a year-round activity. Ever-more flexible calendars—evening, weekend, and summer sessions—are commonplace, and even more flexibility (24 hours a day, 7 days a week) is being demanded.

Growth in Off-Campus Learning.   Credit courses have moved out of campus classrooms and into workplaces, from offices and factory floors to submarines and malls, as well as the home. Because many adult students are enrolled only part-time, the need to live on or near a campus is reduced.

QUALITY

Explosion in Knowledge Sources and Communications Vehicles. In the past, universities were the primary source of up-to-date, specialized knowledge. Nowadays, vital knowledge is produced, stored, and disseminated by multiple sources around the world, including private companies, laboratories, and governments. There has been an exponential explosion in the amount of data being generated (for example, 10,000 scientific articles are published every day.)[6] Print, which has been the predominant mode for managing knowledge, is being supplemented and replaced by computer-mediated vehicles— presentation software, electronic mail, Internet sites, and CD-ROMs.

Continuous Learning.   Previously, students went directly from high school to college or university to prepare for a lifelong career; today, becoming educated is a continuous, long-term task. According to forecasters, the average worker of the future will have six or seven different careers, each requiring new skills, attitudes, and values. Although the core skills in science, engineering, finance, and law stay the same, rapid advancements in those fields make constant updating essential.[7]

Learning How to Learn.   As work becomes more knowledge-intensive, multidisciplinary, and collaborative, education must foster a new range of skills: how to find information, think critically, communicate effectively, work in teams, and manage projects. Change is constant, and makes educational upgrading essential. For example, the major accounting firms have declared that no one can master their discipline in an undergraduate education, because rules change so fast that there are always new ones to learn. Like many other professions, what these firms want is not graduates who know everything, but ones who have the capacity to learn.

Individualized Learning Styles.   Over the past several years, we have learned much about differences in learning styles and the virtues of customized approaches that accommodate the new diversity. There is also a significant difference between the abstract, reflective style of most college professors and the more concrete, active style typical of their students.[8] Howard Gardener argues that there are at least seven types of intelligence, but traditional Western pedagogy, based on lectures and textbooks, makes use of only two (verbal and logical).[9] Engaging the other five types of intelligence— spatial, musical, kinesthetic, interpersonal, and intrapersonal—will increase student success.

COST EFFECTIVENESS

Need for Cost Containment.   The current system is caught in a squeeze. In the past decade, government deficit reduction has led to sharp cutbacks in educational funding. At the same time, growing demand is putting ever-greater pressure on facilities. It will cost an estimated $235 billion to build campuses to serve just the new adult students, with a further $217 billion needed to operate them.[10] Classrooms are filled to capacity, and library collections haven't been able to keep pace with the growth in new resources. It is difficult to increase faculty course loads, but there are no funds for additional staff. Less financial aid is available, and students generally have less money.

MARKET RESPONSIVENESS

Student as Consumer.   Increasingly, students are taking a consumer approach to selecting schools. Adult students base their evaluations on a wide range of factors and are more likely to define quality on the basis of customer satisfaction than on traditional assessment criteria, for example, library size and staff-to-student ratios.[11] As the population ages, as the needs of the learner become more complex, and as the Internet reinforces a "consumer is king" attitude, students will become even more discerning in assessing educational alternatives.

New Competitive Dynamics.   In the past decade, hundreds of schools have closed their doors, unable to maintain depth and breadth of course offerings. Colleges compete fiercely for private funds, and try to attract benefactors and students by establishing distinctive identities. Faculty, especially younger ones, responding to academic uncertainties and business opportunities, take a more entrepreneurial approach to their careers and are less attached to the university. At the same time, institutions are facing competition from new educational providers—from corporations like Motorola to private institutions such as DeVry. Workplaces and professional training institutes are now perhaps the single greatest providers of management education. Many higher educational bodies are fighting back by expanding their continuing- and corporate-education programs.

MEETING TODAY'S LEARNING REQUIREMENTS WITH TECHNOLOGY

Despite its reputation as the best in the world, higher education suffers from serious deficiencies, as indicated by a failure rate of 60 to 70 percent among freshmen; a 28 percent drop-out rate between freshman and sophomore years; satisfactory completion rates for basic courses of only 64 percent; community college systems where only 9 percent of the students who want a degree secure one; graduation rates of 43 to 53 percent for all but the most selective schools; less than 40 percent of students obtaining a degree within 7 years at some baccalaureate schools; and freshmen and sophomores taught mostly by graduate students or temporary instructors. Funding can't meet current needs, never mind respond to future growth.

ACCESS

Through the Internet, it is now possible to offer instructional materials to anyone, anytime, anywhere. Students can access courseware or information 7 days a week, 24 hours a day. Many universities are now wiring their entire campus for broadband comprehensive access, and almost all institutions provide some access from major buildings or dormitories. Increasingly, schools like the University of Minnesota-Crookston, California State University at Sonoma, and Wake Forest University are ensuring that each student has 24-hour access to a laptop computer and the Internet.

Students are the demographic group most likely to use the Internet. According to Strategic Marketing Communications, the number of students logging onto the Internet at least once a day continues to grow, and may exceed 50 percent of all college students by the end of the Spring 1998 term. Of the more than 5 million full-time undergraduates in a 4-year program, 60 percent own a computer, with the majority of others intending to purchase one in the near future.[12] The plummeting costs of networked devices will make access even more affordable and widespread.

QUALITY

Massive amounts of information are now available on the Web, and more intellectual resources are uploaded every day. Soon, entire digital libraries of both general and specialized knowledge will be available. Instructional materials will never be in short supply. Digital learning applications are steadily improving:

- Search tools that enable complex and stored queries, as well as automated updates, are developing rapidly.
- Web-enabled presentation software is becoming easier to use, while facilitating the communication of ideas and information in ever more powerful ways.
- Hybrid CD-ROMs provide the multimedia richness of CD-ROMs and the up-to-date capabilities of Web sites; soon DVDs will carry up to 2 hours of video.
- Real-time audio can now be delivered through standard 28.8k and even 14.4k at radio quality; video, at 28.8k, now provides six to seven frames per second of about 2 inches square, combined with synchronized HTML (hypertext markup language) or PowerPoint presentations; at 56k, it's a quarter screen. Stanford and other universities already are deploying these technologies for selected courses. Virtual reality applications will offer additional enriching tools.
- Interactive databases, spreadsheets, and Java applications engage users with customized exercises, demonstrations, simulations, and tests.
- Collaborative applications enable students to interact with each other and with teachers. Features include topic threading and real-time chat tools. Web-based audio and video conferencing are now stable applications.
- Push technologies deliver software and local information (news, announcements, and other time-sensitive data), as PointCast does with its PointCast College Network. This and other push technologies can also be used to deliver instructional content.

The key challenge is to integrate these technologies into a coherent electronic learning environment. Such tools enable instructors to engage in a full range of teaching activities. They can make presentations using audio or video with synchronized HTML/presentation software; demonstrate concepts using shared electronic whiteboards; test students, including surprise pop-up quizzes; ask individual students questions; and provide individual feedback. Students can move through live or archived materials according to their own schedule and convenience, and communicate with teachers, other instructional resources, or fellow students.

COST

In most of North America, virtually unlimited access to public Web resources costs under $300 annually, about the equivalent of five textbooks. The browser interface has proven easy to use, and training is borne by individuals, typically on their own time.

High-performance servers will enable large volumes of students to reliably access course material while also participating in live events. Multicasting promises the efficient delivery of scheduled (broadcast or push) multimedia content to large volumes of users at reasonable telecommunications rates (and without congesting the Internet). Media-asset databases can help cost effectively manage materials for multiple courses.

MARKET RESPONSIVENESS

Due to its sheer size, the educational sector will drive some Internet innovation, but it will also be able to capitalize on innovation driven by even larger publishing, workplace training, and other knowledge-management applications. In addition, the Internet offers educational institutions unprecedented opportunities to efficiently collect, organize, and analyze real-time, large sample consumer research. Sources include:

- Responses to online surveys regarding student satisfaction and perceptions.
- Tracking of users' browser behavior on site: for example, on what learning points do students spend the most time; what is the sequence and pattern of interest; what questions do students ask?
- Transactional data on student registrations, drop-outs, completions.
- Interaction and outcome data generated from base-line assessments, exercises, and exams.

The potential breadth and depth of data will enable benchmarking and competency assessment, as well as tracking of topic, instructor, and resource selection. Because of the feedback available, digital products/services (for example, courseware and exercises) can be fine-tuned, and product development can be accelerated.

THE GLOBAL LEARNING INFRASTRUCTURE: A NEW VISION

We envisage the "global learning infrastructure"—a student-centric virtual global web of educational services—as the foundation for achieving society's learning goals. This contrasts with the bricks-and-mortar campus-centric university of today; it even goes beyond the paradigm of the virtual university, which remains modeled on individual institutions. The digital global learning infrastructure will encompass a flourishing marketplace of educational services where millions of students interact with a vast array of individual and institutional educational suppliers. It will be delivered through the Internet, by way of broadband cable, ADSL, and satellite; it is being developed in phases, but will ultimately cross all institutional, state, and national borders.

The global learning infrastructure draws its capabilities from digital technology and the Internet. It could not have existed 5 years ago—but it will be pervasive 5 years from now. Undoubtedly, individual institutions will exploit these technologies to advance their programs. But without conscious, concerted effort, the results will be a continuation of today's inadequate, piecemeal solutions. *The challenge—and extraordinary opportunity—is to develop the integrated digital learning infrastructure to meet the educational needs of the twenty-first century.*

At the technology core of the global learning infrastructure are fully interoperable modules and an enabling infrastructure.

MODULARITY AND STANDARDS

By a modular approach, we mean the unbundling of content and educational processes into their most basic components. Modules operate under interoperable standards so that they can be easily modified, replaced, and combined.

Modularity strengthens the educational marketplace's ability to stimulate and match distinctive supplier capabilities with customer interests. Suppliers can focus on their core competencies while customers need only purchase those services in which they are interested.[13]

In terms of course content, a modular approach involves its disaggregation into topics that can then be reaggregated into course modules. The same module can be used in different courses and certification programs. In the CUPLE physics educational project, for example, participant physicists create instructional modules according to an agreed-upon standard. These modules are reviewed by national peers before they become part of the body of material. Both creators and users are assured of consistency and quality. The result is a growing body of instructional materials that can be used in diverse settings.

Instructional modes can also be modularized, in effect, creating a separate marketplace for their creation and use, for instance:

- Delivery of primary instructional material
- Presentation of information on learning objectives, target groups, credit value, related courses, and programs
- Provision of secondary teaching resources including documents, library materials, Web sites, electronic newsletters, frequently asked questions, glossaries, and links to related professional/ career resources
- Provision of demonstrations, tutorials and exercises, and data sets for analytical research and exploration. For instance, the Calculus Consortium at Harvard University operates a Web site that provides nonroutine problems independent of the project's textbooks
- Evaluation through base-line and progress assessments, student benchmarking, learning diagnostics, quizzes, tests, and exams
- Presentation of instructional materials for different levels (for example, advanced, average, and remedial) and languages
- Description of course content and features to enable efficient searching of what ultimately will be tens of thousands of offerings

Open standards supporting interoperability also facilitate a "plug-and-play" approach to communication among instructors, teaching assistants, resource persons, students, and sysops. Features such as question and answer, information and idea exchange, coaching, tutoring, and collaborative class projects should be easy for suppliers to incorporate into courses and for students to use. Such standards should cover asynchronous and real-time, point and multipoint, text, audio, video, VRML, and pull and push communication methods while enabling integration with other knowledge resources.

Also critical to a positive online educational experience are software and navigation solutions that enable self-pacing, bookmarking, the creation of one's own links, and dynamic adaptation to different student technology configurations.

Standards for authoring, editing, and version control would enable geographically distributed suppliers to readily create, update, delete, and modify educational materials.

A modular or open standards approach would also facilitate the delivery of marketing, administrative, and educational support processes and services, including:

- Preview capabilities for interested users prior to purchase
- Registration and payment
- User tracking and feedback
- Reporting for instructors, students, and educational administrators to monitor individual (own) and group progress and compare to historical or normative standards
- Credit granting
- Application for financial aid
- Student counselling on courses and career

ENABLING INFRASTRUCTURE

Internet technology—with its low cost, anytime/anyplace/anyhow access, and the convergence of computing and television capabilities—is the foundation of the digital learning infrastructure. It offers a common base for developing and integrating software tools; however, what is still urgently needed is a set of higher-order specifications that will permit learners, teachers, software developers, and publishers to share and integrate learning materials from various sources and to manage the process from enrollment to certification.

Increasing broadband access is also important. Broadband is critical to rich multimedia and interactive experiences. A number of approaches will enable a significant proportion of students to gain access to these resources at relatively low cost. These include file transfer/push technology, hybrid CD-ROM/Web applications, penetration of 56k modems and ISDN, ever-improving compression technologies, spread of cable, ADSL and satellite technologies, and broadband wiring of campuses and workplaces. Many universities and large companies have, or will soon have, high-bandwidth connections to the Internet. Further development is needed to extend minimum standards to home use.

The value of stable, user-friendly systems is not to be underestimated. They are essential in ensuring that the "my dog ate my homework" syndrome is not replaced with its electronic equivalent ("my computer crashed"). Maturing technology promises to provide such a robust platform.

THE DIGITAL GLOBAL LEARNING INFRASTRUCTURE SCENARIO

Education no longer takes place within the silos of individual institutions (or even their virtual equivalents), but instead in a dynamic global marketplace of customers and suppliers. This shift is driven by:

- High front-end production costs, which force suppliers to seek larger markets

- Significant economies of scale and low marginal costs for incremental use, so that suppliers are motivated to achieve high market penetration and revenues

- Interoperable standards and modules that streamline production processes and expand the range of available products and services

- The global, real-time nature of the Internet which enables a critical mass of customers and suppliers from around the world to efficiently interact

ACCESS

The digital global learning infrastructure allows anyone to be a student. Millions of new users, especially those from disadvantaged groups and in remote locations, enjoy access that they could only dream of previously. Students use high precision search engines to find courses of interest or surf to see what is available. Consumer directories, credit ratings, and course previews and demos make it easy to make informed choices; recognized interfaces provide easy-to-use purchase and auditing options. Students register, apply for financial aid, and receive counseling online. The virtual school is open around the clock and throughout the year, allowing students to work at their own pace and convenience. Many adult students log on in the very late hours, after discharging family or work responsibilities.

QUALITY

No matter where they live, students can access the best resources from around the world. "IT will bring the best lecturers to students via multimedia anytime and anywhere so that, like the recordings of the country's most celebrated artists, those of the best will drive out those of the merely good."[14]

Students in small towns gain access to the world's leading content and pedagogy. Teachers, credit granters, and students disaggregate and combine modules to personalize learning packages. Gone are the days of "one size fits all" in course delivery. And modules are continually being updated and improved, since educational providers don't have to accumulate revisions and issue an expensive new book—with limited sales and revenues—every 2 years.

Measures of quality have also changed. Traditional measures such as the number of full-time faculty, number of books in the library, the size of classes, amount of student-instructor contact, and budget are no longer relevant. Fortunately, the new digital infrastructure enables the collection of a wealth of data on student progress (base-line assessments, exercises, and tests), user on-site behavior, and feedback. Students, instructors, accreditors, and consumer agencies all have access to this data. Courses and programs evolve organically, building on mountains of knowledge about users, and produced using sophisticated templates.

Concerns such as, "This is good for quantitative subjects like math, but can it really work for qualitative subjects?" or "How do you provide students with social contact?" are fully answered. In subjects such as the humanities, politics, and psychology, online interactive multimedia proves exceptionally effective—whether in the form of video clips from the Stratford theatre, up-to-date news clips, or minidocumentaries of family life. Online text, audio, and video interactions provide a rich, diverse social context and give students individualized support from instructors and teaching assistants. Parents' concerns as to how teenage freshmen can possibly be given full control of their educational experience are addressed by many institutions/degrees which require students to take highly structured, mandatory curricula, and provide stringent proof of competency to move ahead. New consumer reviews and advisory services help students (and their parents) effectively participate within the expanded marketplace of opportunity.

The digital learning infrastructure is not intended to replace all traditional pedagogy, but rather to expand and transform it, creating a new blend of face-to-face and electronic interaction. Instead of being eliminated, traditional forms of teaching are revitalized. Just as television brought new focus to radio, so digital education brings wiser use of personal interaction among instructors and students. Seasoned workplace trainers contribute their expertise to designing higher-education programs that integrate electronic and face-to-face contact for adult learners.

COST

Virtual publishing drives the costs of reproduction and distribution to almost zero, while, for cost reasons, admissions limitations nearly vanish. Authoring templates reduce the front-end costs for preparing instructional materials, and the ability to make small, continuous incremental changes encourages experimentation and innovation.

Initially, major investments are made where payoff is high, for example, for courses with high enrollment, standardized curriculum, a wide range of user types, demands for continuously updated material, effective measures of progress, and regionally distributed experts. For instance, approximately 50 percent of all community college and 35 percent of all baccalaureate enrollments are in one of 25 basic courses, for example, introductory studies in English, mathematics, psychology, sociology, accounting, biology, and chemistry. These courses are typically delivered through lecture presentations and weekly groups supported by a graduate student. Enrollment in these courses number in the millions. Revenues/cost savings of even $200 per student per year provide a cost-effective basis for investments in the millions of dollars for each of these courses.

MARKET RESPONSIVENESS

In the global learning infrastructure, the customer is king. Courses are self-paced and adaptable to a wide range of learning styles. Providers easily modify their material in light of data on student progress and feedback, as well as competitors' offerings. Within hours, resources are updated; within weeks, a team of experts, artists, programmers, and instructional designers develop and deliver substantial course material worldwide. Driven by knowledge-hungry workplaces, and the potential for national and international markets, new standards are defined. Some of these standards are elitist, aimed at competing with or exceeding those of institutions like Harvard and MIT in specialized areas, while others are aimed at mass markets. Although government approval is desirable, it is not necessary. Imagine the attraction of an Advanced Computing Specialization offered and cobranded by IBM, Microsoft, Harvard, and MIT.

A variety of academic and private agencies provide accreditation; similarly, instructional materials are diverse and are produced by a range of content creators. Some are modeled on standard pedagogical components (for example, demonstrations, tutorials, exercises, and tests), while others are more specialized (graphics, text, links, and individual demos). Compared to traditional print-based textbooks, the new pedagogy is highly multidisciplinary, requiring attention to design, interactive instructional design, multimedia graphics, and programming.

Distributors bring together consumers and suppliers, integrating all aspects of the educational process: accreditation, standards, content, and delivery. They include universities, specialized content providers, and publishing and technology companies. In response to low marginal costs of production and distribution and high economies of scale, providers madly rush to achieve a critical mass of users. A wide variety of pricing, branding, and partnering strategies are deployed, to the benefit of the consumer.

New services that benefit users and providers are available. Consumer services help students evaluate educational offerings according to cost, quality, outcome, and satisfaction. Academic credit banks function as trusted intermediaries, enabling students to deposit credits from any source and—when certain requirements have been

Comparison of Business Processes for Print Textbook and Digital
Interactive Learning Resources

BUSINESS PROCESS	TEXTBOOK	INTERACTIVE LEARNING RESOURCES
Content assembly skills	Subject matter expertise, print graphics, publishing, pedagogy	Subject matter expertise, graphics, audio and video, interactive instructional design
Pedagogical design	Linear. Can include an instruction manual.	Interactive. Can include online demos, exercises, tests. Includes links to secondary resources and online sharing of information with other students and resources
Field testing	Simple/limited	Complex/extensive/online
Product announcements	Direct selling, direct mail	Net-based
Preview	Exam copies	Browsing "live" demo
Decision maker	Faculty	Faculty/learners
Purchaser	Student	Student/institution
Timing of buying	2 × per year	Continuous
Distribution	Via intermediaries like bookstores	Net-based: directly to users
User support	Limited for faculty/none for users	Extensive, automated support
Product development/ market research	Expensive focus groups/ purchase behavior	Online focus groups: online questionnaires, user behavior (on site), outcome data
Updating	Periodic: only when it is economically viable to produce a new edition	Can be done on a continuous, incremental basis

met—earn an accredited degree. Broker services help the myriad of suppliers exchange information and products and work together.

NAVIGATING THE TRANSITION

The digital global learning infrastructure will transform both educational methods and institutional roles. Public leadership is required to identify and foster the conditions that will bring about such a system. Universities and colleges, educational publishers, and other potential players face unprecedented opportunities, as well as threats.

THE PUBLIC POLICY CHALLENGE

National and regional public policy makers face five key challenges:

1. *Create a climate for change.* Government must help educational institutions, the private sector, and the public understand the need for a new learning vision and the critical role that a digital learning infrastructure will play.

2. *Facilitate the creation and management of new market forces.* Government needs to deregulate education so that a wide range of providers can set standards, and accredit, develop, and deliver content. At the same time, accountability to the public and to student consumers needs to be established. Local and state regulation should be replaced by national and global frameworks.

3. *Facilitate the establishment of technical standards.* Critical to a successful digital infrastructure—and to truly unleashing market capabilities—is establishing agreed-to standards for telecommunications, file formats, and security, that enable high interoperability among instructional materials. Government can facilitate dialogue among colleges, educational publishers, and software and telecommunications companies. An important focus should be on developing multimedia capabilities for home-based students.

4. *Target financing to students and outcomes.* Current educational financing is provided to institutions on a per capita basis. Alternatively, funding can be linked to enrollment numbers by course or program—or even to the outcomes that students achieve. This approach harnesses market forces by rewarding success, that is, allocating more funds to those institutions or subject areas that attract the most students. Naturally, some funding can still be directed to support particular courses or programs that aren't in high demand but are perceived to be in the public interest.

5. *Develop appropriate social and economic policies.*   The digital education revolution is likely to have significant social and even economic impacts, many of them difficult to predict. Government needs to explore such impacts, facilitate public debate, and develop appropriate policy. Such issues include:

- The effect on communities where local brick-and-mortar institutions, unable to compete, are forced to close down
- Cross-border jurisdictional matters such as the development of export markets: regulation (if any) of courses taken by citizens of "unfriendly" nations; definition and protection of intellectual copyright of educational products
- Privacy and proprietorship concerns with regard to the volumes of student data that will be generated
- Copyright, royalty, and financing arrangements for contributors of products and services

THE EDUCATIONAL MARKETPLACE

The digital global learning infrastructure also poses tough challenges for individual educational institutions and private players and aspirants to the educational marketplace. Five key challenges are:

1. *Determine content and process roles.*   Higher education institutions need to decide what content areas to provide and what educational processes to offer. What role do they want to play in accreditation and standard setting? Do they want to concentrate on developing content or on organizing the delivery of content (produced by others)?

How will local institutions compete with multimillion-dollar interactive courses that feature the world's leading content experts, instructors, designers, and programmers? They need to recognize that, although their opportunities are global, they will also face new competitors unrestricted by traditional geographical boundaries.

Institutions need to determine their competitively sustainable core competencies.

Other current and potential players in the educational market face similar questions. For instance, where should private educational institutions and traditional textbook publishers focus their expertise? Companies already in the business of disseminating information—magazines, television, publishers, museums, knowledge-intensive private companies, such as consulting firms and non-profit agencies, and even government—need to consider the opportunities for repurposing and packaging their resources as instructional materials. Such materials may prove excellent tools for building customer brand and loyalty.

2. *Work with new partners.* The need for partnering is a hallmark of the digital economy. No single organization has all the capabilities for competing by itself. Take, for example, the production and distribution of Internet-enabled instructional resources. Universities may believe they have the internal experts (professors) and captive market (students) to engage in this undertaking. But they lack the full set of required skills. Textbook publishers, on the other hand, generally have a broader grasp of market opportunities across multiple institutions and jurisdictions, in addition to superior business planning and management skills. They are adept at outsourcing—typically including content experts from universities—and are capable of assembling the team to produce educational modules.

Global competition offers opportunities for both niche players and those who can effectively deliver on a large scale. The most successful products are likely to be produced through the joint efforts of multiple educational institutions and publishers. Other potentially valuable partners include technology companies able to develop and maintain appropriate applications and infrastructure, companies with strong electronic distribution and brands (for example, online media) who can provide content credibility and perceived market value, and private educational institutions experienced at niche marketing and delivery.

Institutions will need to grapple with the branding dimension of these partnerships. Traditional education constituencies will undoubtedly be nervous about excessive commercialism or being lost in the consortia with higher profile partners. Paradoxically, the need to partner will force higher education institutions and other players to crystallize their own distinctive role in this marketplace.

3. *Manage changing roles of faculty, physical plant, and technology.* The digital learning infrastructure will result in less need for lectures and presentation of material and even marking. Codifying knowledge into instructional resources will be critical, but it may require relatively few content and pedagogical specialists. More time will be available for coaching and mentoring whether face-to-face or electronically. However, many of these skills have little to do with research or even traditional lecture capabilities. These functions can be contracted out, or may even form integral parts of courses offered by others.

Providers must determine what types of skills and human resources are needed to excel at online education. Are the same number of faculty still needed? What is the ideal mix of full, part-time, tenured, and contract staff? How do you manage and evaluate staff in their new roles? How do you train staff, especially older ones, to effectively contribute to electronic strategies? What are the new student-teacher ratios?

Another challenge for higher-education institutions is deciding how much to invest in the physical plant. This depends on how rapidly the movement towards digital delivery takes place, and what face-to-face or residential role will continue to be provided.

All educational players need to decide whether to use the public Internet or establish private networks that use Internet technology but provide additional control, reliability, security, and bandwidth. This issue is intricately intertwined with broader concerns of role, target markets, management, and partnering strategies.

4. *Research the new pedagogy.* Electronic education is still in its infancy—there is much to learn about how to motivate, support, guide, teach, and test students. It is clear that research on the communications aspects of online learning is vital. Teachers and students must learn to identify and take advantage of online learning processes that enable and encourage interaction among students and between instructors and students. Building community among students, professors, and other partners will be crucial. Institutions need to review online pioneering initiatives such as the introduction of a dean's (electronic) honor role, distance learner success stories, and alumni discussion clubs.

All educational players also need to pay attention to the economics of online education. How do users like to aggregate or disaggregate instructional materials? Will they purchase services on a continuous or episodic (two or three times a year) basis? How will users gain information about quality and content? What will be the key decision criteria—quality, price, brand name, quality of experience? Will mass customization enable profit? How big is the market for specialized electronic instructional materials (for example, assessments or exercises) and for new consumer and advisory intermediaries?

5. *Gain new business competencies.*   In addition to traditional and new pedagogical capabilities, institutions need to develop business competencies in order to effectively build and participate in the global learning infrastructure. They must be able to:

- Spot and assess opportunities, evaluate new and fluid sources of competition and collaboration, determine the relative merits of various partnering strategies, and make the appropriate investments under what are still highly uncertain conditions
- Operationalize business models that appropriately allocate costs and revenues among business processes and partners
- Integrate physical and virtual brand and promotional activities
- Manage issues of knowledge access, competition, and exclusivity among partners and users

CONCLUSION

As we approach the twenty-first century, it is clear that the present system of higher education is in crisis. It is not adequately meeting current needs, and will face even greater pressures in the coming years. The learning requirements of society as a whole are changing, as is the demographic composition of the student population. The key to addressing these critical challenges is the development of a digital global learning infrastructure—which is able to move beyond the limitations of campus-centric models, engage diverse learning styles, and meet the demands of both an increasingly heterogeneous student population and a new economy. Reaching far beyond the traditional university to include a networked community of media organizations, publishers, content specialists, and technology companies, it has the potential to transform education in the new millennium.

NOTES

1. Noam, Eli M., "Electronics and the Dim Future of the University," *Science*, vol. 270, October 13, 1995.

2. Twigg, Carol A., *The Need for a National Learning Infrastructure* (Washington, D.C.: Educom), 1995, p. 3.

3. Green, Kenneth, "Money, Technology, and Distance Education," *ED Journal*, May 1997.

4. Green, Kenneth, ibid.

5. Vigilante, Richard, *The Virtual College* (New York: New York University), 1994.

6. Forman, David C., "The Use of Multimedia Technology for Training in Business and Industry," *Multimedia Monitor*, vol. 13, no. 7, pp. 22–27.

7. Verville, Anne-Lee, "What Business Needs from Higher Education," *Educational Record*, vol. 76, no. 4, pp. 46–50.

8. Schroeder, Charles, "New Students—New Learning Styles," *Change*, September/October 1993, pp. 23–26.

9. Gardener, Howard, *Frames of Mind: The Theory of Multiple Intelligence* (New York: Basic Books), 1993.

10. Dolence, Michael G., and Donald M. Norris, p. 7.

11. Jarboe, Patricia Kovel, "Distance Education Futures," unpublished paper, 1994.

12. From a December 1997 telephone survey conducted among 600 4-year, full-time undergraduates attending 100 representative schools nationally. The survey was undertaken by Strategic Marketing Communications as part of its *Student Monitor* publication. These results were reported on their Web site at www.smcinc.com/monitor/about.htm.

13. Working under the auspices of Educom's National Learning Infrastructure Initiative, the Instructional Management Systems (IMS) project will create specifications to support information exchange among learners, teachers, and educational resources. The IMS project brings together institutions (the California State University system, the University of Michigan, the University of North Carolina–Chapel Hill, Miami-Dade Community College, Buena Vista University, and the "Big Ten" Committee on Institutional Cooperation), companies (Apple, Farance Inc., IBM, International Thomson Publishing, KPMG Peat Marwick, Microsoft, and Sun Microsystems) and government (U.S. Department of Defense and NIST/U.S. Department of Commerce). The IMS

specifications will define the interface between systems and components, and describe the information that may be exchanged. The IMS is pedagogy neutral. It will enable communication among a wide range of content offerings, learning environments, and vendor products.

14. Massy, William and Robert Zemsky, *Using Information Technology to Enhance Academic Productivity* (Washington, D.C.: Educom), 1995.

CUSTOMER EMPOWERMENT IN THE DIGITAL ECONOMY

by John MacDonald
Bell Canada

and Jim Tobin
Bell Emergis, Bell Canada

> *In place of the expanding markets of the 1950s, 60s, and 70s, companies today have customers—customers who know what they want, what they want to pay for it, and how to get it in the terms they demand. Customers such as these don't need to deal with companies that don't understand and appreciate this startling change in the customer-buyer relationship.*
>
> HAMMER AND CHAMPY
> *Reengineering the Corporation[1]*

We're all probably a little tired of the word "empowerment," but we shouldn't write off the idea behind it just yet, especially as it takes on new meaning and relevance in the digital economy. Empowerment is no longer simply a term to describe the kind of power that management bestows upon the worker, or the power seized by workers from managers. In the digital economy, it is the consumer, both individual and business, who is gaining a new sense of power. Access to new and powerful technological tools is giving customers the ability to conduct transactions on their own terms. In short, technology is dramatically shifting the balance of power from the seller to the buyer.

Internet commerce already amounts to several hundred million dollars. In a few short years, it will be in the hundreds of billions.

As more consumers go online, increasing numbers of merchants will be drawn to this rich—and mostly untapped—new marketplace. But what they will discover when they get there is a new breed of consumer far different from any that has preceded it—more selective, better informed, and with a range of powerful tools at his or her disposal.

In the evolution from passive to assertive consumer, intelligent agents will play an important role. Already, software agents on the Internet can be programmed by the consumer to scan the network for the best price on many kinds of goods. Firefly, created by Patti Maes of MIT MediaLab, is the best known product, and now is believed to have 3 million users. Personal shopping agents will be very discriminating buyers, not only as far as price is concerned but also on the basis of their master's preferences. They will exclude any offers that don't precisely match their master's likes and dislikes and they will entertain only those offers that do.

All this is leading to a phenomenon we call *persona management*, where individual consumers create for themselves a personal electronic space (or several spaces) that dictates terms and conditions for interaction to the rest of the cybercommunity. This personal space can be thought of as an electronic profile that each consumer creates for him or herself—in essence, this is the consumer's face to the cyberworld. A few software partners and our development arm, Bell Emergis, began prototyping this capability in 1997.

Persona management promises to turn the traditional world of buying and selling upside down. Facing a consumer equipped with all this power, the seller's challenge of capturing attention becomes greater than ever. But opportunities do exist. Just as technology empowers the consumer, it can also empower the seller. Tools that track customers' and their agents' behavior on the Internet will give sellers the ability to tailor their own offerings to agent preferences.

In this rapidly changing environment, software and hardware developers have new types of opportunities—from the development of agents and security measures to new types of information appliances. As business models take shape and sort themselves out in this new frontier, we believe both consumers and producers will benefit. Since the continuing fragmentation of markets, industries, and corporations into units of one is inevitable—take micromarketing and teleworking, for example—this new producer/consumer balance becomes a principle tenet of online commerce.

CASTING THE NET: ONLINE SHOPPING

Nobody knows how big Internet commerce will eventually become, but in October 1997, Forrester Research predicted consumers will spend more than $17 billion online by 2001.

Many customers have become accustomed to complementing their physical shopping experiences with mail order and, more recently, telephone order. People routinely dial 1-800 and 1-888 numbers to purchase products and services.

But Internet shopping has the advantage of being seamless and occurring in real time. The customer orders and pays for the product on the same medium that he or she uses to view the actual product offering. Wal-Mart anticipates retailing 10 million SKUs over the coming 5 years. Internet shopping most closely resembles actual store shopping, where viewing and buying are combined, as opposed to catalog or TV shopping where the process is spread out over several media.

For sellers, large and small, the Internet is a unique distribution medium. It lets them "hang out their shingle" around the globe without investing in a physical presence. This is especially true for intellectual property such as music, software, and information. Following the McLuhanism "the medium is the message," here, the product *is* the channel, and vice versa. Traditional advertising metrics are also changing. Companies that run the most popular home pages charge a premium for an advertising banner or hot link because of the number of eyeballs or visits they can deliver.

Beyond obvious marketing opportunities, many businesses are trying to determine how new technologies can provide a competitive edge for existing markets and customers. Many companies are setting up Web sites, but few are sure of why they have one, or the impact it has on their operation. Everyone is searching for the key to successful business in this new medium.

Business leaders need to step back and take stock of what the rise in Internet commerce and the evolution of the digital economy, in general, means to their business. Simply transposing the traditional buying/selling/servicing models formulated around brick-and-mortar and broadcast communications will not be the winning approach. Businesses must pay attention to the changing buyer-seller relationship, as customers become increasingly empowered through enablers like software agents and persona management.

EMPOWERMENT—THE HUNTER VERSUS THE HUNTED

Technologies like data mining and data warehousing provide new opportunities to target customers more precisely. According to an *Information Week* article in November 1997, of the five top opportunities to be gained from implementing corporate Web sites, number one was better customer service using data mining and number three was intranet access to data warehouses. The ability to zero in on individual customers lets marketers perform "surgical strikes" instead of "carpet bombing"—and gives marketers a lot more bang for the buck.

For the customer, it seems there is no place to hide. Nearly every transaction we make leaves an electronic record, creating vast storehouses of information about our spending patterns, our product preferences, our purchasing power, and even personal data like marital status or religious affiliation. A new database marketing industry is growing out of this vast accumulation of consumer information— and this data is scrutinized, refined, and analyzed with powerful technology tools and increasingly sophisticated analysis techniques to yield astonishingly detailed portraits of individual consumers. And this is worth doing. Capital One, a U.S. financial services company built completely upon data mining capabilities, is one of the fastest growing companies in its sector; going from nowhere to a top-10 ranking among all U.S. credit card issuers in less than 3 years.

Such detailed information about customers provides an opportunity to create custom value propositions aimed at increasingly smaller segments of the target market. The idea, of course, is to "hook" the buyer by tailoring a product offering. Such mass customization could even target a market segment of one—a single individual.

Put simply, new technologies place more accurate guns in the hands of the hunters. While this means better service to the customer, the specter of Big Brother looms large.

However, there is another vision which we and many other service providers aim to realize, where the balance of power shifts to the customer. The same technologies that enable better target marketing can also place more power into the hands of customers to give them a more selective and active role in determining which marketing messages they receive, and when.

In this view, customers accept proposals on their own terms. They can filter out marketing messages that are of no interest to them. They gain control over their profiles and individual information and prevent others from using this information for other purposes without their explicit permission.

This scenario may not need to wait for legislative action to prevent misuse of information, as some people are advocating. Market forces will rule: businesses that don't play by the rules will be ostracized by customers. New technologies equip the hunted with better camouflage—perhaps turning the tables completely: the hunted becomes the hunter.

Which scenario will prevail? We believe the balance will tip in favor of the second view, that of customer empowerment. We also contend that, although perhaps not initially obvious, this will benefit suppliers over the long term. Why will customers win? Because they will have the earliest possible access to better shopping and purchasing tools.

Furthermore, consumers are becoming more aware of and concerned about the misuse of what they consider personal and private information. Many surveys have shown that consumers increasingly believe their personal privacy is being eroded by technology. Those same surveys suggest that incumbent communications companies are preferred keepers of private information, the holders of "digital safety deposit boxes."

THE NEW MEDIUM IS A MESSAGE, "SATISFY ME!"

The Internet, along with venues like America Online, has become a vast collection of gathering places where people with common interests can exchange views and actively participate in discussions, instead of just absorbing what is pushed at them by traditional media. The experience is both liberating and empowering. Not only do you, as a participant, make your voice heard, but you see how others react to you and to what you say. The "virtuality" of these communities minimizes recrimination and face-to-face confrontation, so free speech grows.

But how do these electronic communities relate to the business of buying and selling? Consider for a moment an interest that one of the authors of this chapter, John, shares with thousands of others: motorcycles. On the Internet, he can go to any number of locations to learn about motorcycles. He can read reviews of new models, browse the Web sites of bike manufacturers, and chat with other motorcycle afficionados. Such communities of interest can easily become buying groups, for example, flexing their combined purchasing muscle for better prices or customized products.

John is now a more informed, powerful buyer. If he wants to buy a particular model, but finds out from other owners on the Internet that they have had nothing but trouble with that bike, he will probably think twice about making that purchase. The Internet signals the end of an era when manufacturers could hope to get away with producing poor products. If you, as a producer or seller, alienate even one customer, you risk alienating your entire buying community.

Sellers can also use the new online medium to participate in customer communities. The simplest example is providing an e-mail conduit through the corporate Web site, where customers can voice their displeasure or register their approval. This kind of direct feedback loop provides great insight into what your customers want and can help you create more compelling products and services. It can also quickly alert you to problems with your product or service and suggest ways to improve it.

The Internet also enhances the power of choice. Today, a consumer in the market for a travel product, for example, has the choice of going online, or going to a travel agent. Many such online travel services—such as American Airlines' Travelocity—are enticing consumers with things like air miles points, in lieu of actual cash discounts. In the grocery business, urban professionals are taking advantage of online shopping services like Peapod—and saving valuable time and energy. In other retail areas, online shoppers find lower prices and better selection as online merchants in an increasingly competitive market pass on their cost-savings directly to consumers.

Transactional sites are proliferating. Meanwhile, special interest communities will continue to flourish in the online medium and will play an increasingly powerful role in the buying/selling process. Both of these trends will combine to propel consumer empowerment forward.

THE PUSH AND PULL OF INTERNET COMMERCE

Traditional advertising uses an information push model, where a message is created and broadcast over mass media channels such as television, newspapers, and radio. Success is achieved if that message interests a significant number of consumers. If the supplier is able to predict who might be interested in the product, more targeted means—such as direct mail—may be employed, although this is still a push model.

The Internet can also be a push environment, using technology that automatically delivers content to users who choose to accept this kind of delivery. In simple terms, the push model can be described as the "couch potato" scenario, while the Net's more common pull model can be thought of as the "couch commando" scenario, where the consumer takes control of the information environment.

Both of these delivery models will have a place in an ever-expanding universe of online information, entertainment, and commerce. In entertainment or news, for example, push frees the user from the bother of going out and gathering the content for him- or herself. But if the individual user wants to find a very specific piece of information, or buy a product or service, he or she will probably choose to browse the Internet and pull in only the information that is of interest. Some pundits believe that a broadcast or push model is inevitable for any mass market; we think that ignores the generational shift under way. Kids as young as 2 years of age already find normal TV frustrating due to the lack of control. They have already learned to prefer their CD games and videotapes. When they get older, will this "pull" approach be more pervasive in society?

In the combination of push and pull models, information is pushed at the consumer, but the consumer decides what gets through. The most notable example of this is the PointCast service which allows the user to apply a filter, or personal profile, to the content that is automatically downloaded and displayed on the PC. Another, less well-known example is Televitesse, a software product from a small Canadian company that monitors television broadcasts for users. The system lets the user build a keyword profile which is then used to monitor encoded information related to the video broadcast. When there is a "hit"—when one of the key words comes up in a broadcast—the software automatically records the video and audio clip. The result is that the consumer is no longer the prisoner of real-time TV.

In the course of establishing personal profiles for filtering information, users may post detailed information about their own preferences on the Internet. Companies that store this information have at their disposal a very valuable marketing database that could be sold to others—perhaps without the user's knowledge. The irony is that, even as they are taking control of their incoming information, users may unwittingly be giving suppliers the power to target their markets more precisely. We suggest that there is nothing wrong with this outcome, as long as users are aware, and agree the information may be used for these purposes. Several companies, notably Netcentives and Emaginet, have gone as far as offering rebates, coupons, or other forms of reimbursement for customer information they request. The notion of valuing personal information is making its way into consumers' daily lives. More significantly, it underlines the increasingly interdependent nature of the relationship between consumers and sellers in the electronic marketplace.

SILICON SALLY, MEET ALEXIS AGENT

There's no question that the Internet has become an overwhelming environment of possibilities—which means consumers will increasingly look to sophisticated technology tools to sort through information, as well as products and services offered for sale. That's the idea behind software agents, which can be viewed as the next evolutionary stage in information filtering.

The idea of autonomous software agents has been around for several years, beginning with General Magic's Telescript technology in the early 1990s, which envisaged software objects, or agents, that would reside on a communications network and perform tasks for their users. Although General Magic's plan for a proprietary information network was quickly superseded by the explosion of the public Internet, the idea of network agents has taken hold. A growing number of agent technologies are available on the Internet today.

Andersen Consulting, for example, has developed an agent prototype it calls BargainFinder, designed to help consumers shop for music CDs. BargainFinder comparison shops various Internet stores to find the best price for any given title. Users can first shop in an electronic store that offers reviews, ratings, background information—and at some time in the future, probably samples and clips. Then BargainFinder goes out on the Internet and locates the store with the cheapest price.

What is interesting about this experiment is that some stores have tried to block BargainFinder agents. However, the agent would notify the user that it was blocked from obtaining access to a particular store. Given a critical mass of customers, it would be difficult for stores to resist such agents without alienating a large part of their customer base.

What's much more difficult is getting an agent to make a "judgment call" on your behalf, such as recommending a film that you might like. How does the agent know what kind of film you will like? If you program it with very specific instructions—such as: "I like James Bond movies when Sean Connery is in the lead"—the agent can go out and find something that will meet that criteria, but you have limited its functionality to a very narrow range. What about all the films that you might enjoy, but don't know about? If the agent isn't informed about them, it won't consider them and you won't be any further ahead in your quest to find an enjoyable film without spending a lot of time searching.

In this kind of situation, what is needed is an agent that will infer what you might like or dislike. A good way to find out is to compare your likes and dislikes to people with similar preferences. That's the idea behind Firefly, an agent-like tool that performs "collaborative filtering." Once you create your initial profile—by filling out an electronic questionnaire—Firefly makes recommendations on the basis of the stated preferences of participants with similar profiles. For example, Firefly will recommend to you a film you have not seen, based on reviews submitted by a set of people who have seen the movie and historically share your tastes in movies. The software is also designed to continually learn from the choices the user makes and the feedback he or she provides, constantly refining the user's profile and becoming ever more accurate in its recommendations. Meanwhile, improvements in the overall technology will be rapid as the software developers and market builders benefit from the accumulated learnings in various agent offerings. Idealab's RecoMentor and Amazon.com's use of profiling and collaborative filtering show this trend of progress.

But sellers can also benefit from the same technology by zeroing in on the particular segments of customers they are seeking. An example of this is SelectCast for Ad Servers, from Aptex Software.

This product, developed in partnership with Infoseek, continuously evaluates user profiles as users click ads. Following an analysis of the characteristics of users, it delivers the same ads to similar users. It targets audiences by developing profiles for all site visitors, analyzing and grouping profiles to identify users with similar interests, and then delivers designated ads to users in selected groups. The use of "cookies"—small text files a Web site can use to recognize a repeat visitor while that visitor's personal profile is masked—has proliferated and changed confidence levels for the better.

Future versions of agents with greater intelligence and more power could even band together to form electronic buying groups that could demand quantity discounts. If you're in the market for a certain kind of PC, for example, there's a good chance there are dozens, maybe hundreds of other consumers looking for exactly the same kind of PC. What if your agent could quickly find them and negotiate a discount with the supplier? Such buying groups could even use their leverage to influence suppliers to create products that previously did not exist, such as a group air fare for 30 people traveling from Toronto to New York, for example. Your agent and those of the other passengers could get together to solicit bids from various carriers on such a transaction. When, in the next few years, encryption technologies and digital cash are more widespread, we expect these activities to experience explosive growth.

YOUR OWN CYBERSPACE COCKPIT: PERSONAL ELECTRONIC SPACE

Where is all of this technology taking us? Imagine a future where people deal not with computer operating systems but rather personal operating systems. In this future, people will be able to establish a personal electronic space that works at making their lives simpler, not more complex. They will be able to create what we call a number of different "persona," each with a specific profile with defined interfaces to communities of interest. Electronic agents will become a key part of this scenario, roaming the network searching for information, completing transactions, and negotiating with other agents.

These persona management systems have a standard protocol that contracts between buyers and sellers. Unsolicited offers from businesses would be rejected unless permitted by the consumer, under terms dictated by the consumer.

For example, a consumer would be willing to entertain a sales offer only if there is something in it for her. It could go as far as being paid to view an advertisement. This is not too far-fetched really—after all, consider broadcast TV, where businesses indirectly offer free programming to consumers in order to get them to watch their ads.

The notion of persona management recognizes that an individual may adopt different persona at different times. For example, you may be at home acting as both a member of the household as well as a teleworker representing your company.

The most important attribute of all is that the consumer is in complete control of their communications and network space. This means that others will be unable to communicate with them or use any information about them without their explicit consent. The full realization of this concept also recognizes and allows for such variables as geographic independence, appliance independence, network independence, personal and geographic communities of interest, and context sensitivity. Let's examine these in more detail.

Geographic Independence. Whether at home, at work, or on the road between the two locations, as long as we have access to an information appliance, our persona manager is at work. If we travel to a distant city and happen to walk up to a next generation pay phone/kiosk, we can log on to the persona manager by inserting either a smart card or perhaps alerting it through a voice recognition agent. What appears on the screen are things that are not determined by the local geography—they are things that are of particular interest to the user. The same holds true when we check into a hotel room. As long as there is access to a networked appliance, we can communicate with the same ease as from home or the workplace.

Appliance Independence. When it receives messages, the persona manager can adapt communications automatically based on the capabilities of whatever appliance is being used at the time. If the user happens to be using a simple telephone, the communication of a particular transaction will use voice and possibly a text display. The same transaction, when delivered to a multimedia PC, will use voice, text, and video. When sending messages, appliance independence means we don't have to create a new "log-on script" tailored to the appliance used. We can gain access to voice mail, e-mail, and video mail from different types of appliances without having to create a unique profile by appliance type.

Network Independence. A user's persona manager doesn't care what type of network he or she may be using at the time—such as wireless or wireline, for example. It doesn't care who is transporting the underlying bits, just that they are being reliably transported. The key is that the underlying networks have standards-based interfaces to persona tools accessible on servers or other network-resident repositories. This "middleware" build out is a much more profound development in the communications sector than the rollout of broadband infrastructure. Since the middleware's existence will commoditize underlying networks, service providers will be faced with the challenge of creating enough demand for personalized services and content in order to justify commitments to broadband deployment. The industry will be revolutionized more by technology than by regulatory reform.

Always-On, or Always "There." Our persona manager does not sleep. You don't have to boot it up to get it going. You simply use it when you want to. It makes resources available to you as you need them. You don't have to order a capability that you only use once in a blue moon. It's there when you want it—you may just have to pay a transactional rate for using the resource. If you use the resource frequently enough, you may choose a monthly rate rather than a transactional rate.

Personal and Geographic Communities of Interest. Geographic communities of interest will always represent an important dimension to individuals. Our homes, schools, hospitals, and workplaces—and the people who inhabit them—have historically defined our physical sense of community and they will continue to do so. But in the age of the Internet, people are increasingly creating bonds with individuals and groups who are outside their physical community.

But just because these communities exist only in cyberspace doesn't mean they can't have a sense of place. A Web site can easily be dedicated to a particular physical community such as a city, a town, or even a country. For example, Zip 2 hosts local Web directories of community events and information. Canada's Sympatico Web site, which pulls together Canadian-related content from a variety of sources, is an example of applying the idea of community on a national level. Their award-winning Healthy Way area for personal health information represents a strong and growing community of interest. Persona managers will be aware of the different kinds of communities we belong to and will be able to provide appropriate bridges and linkages between them.

Context Sensitivity.   In its simplest sense, context sensitivity involves technology adapting itself to the needs of the individual rather than the other way around. The best current examples involve telephony, and they are harbingers of what is coming in terms of data networks. Everyone is familiar with the notion of caller identification (name or number). One of the limitations of current technologies is that the technology does not really authenticate the individual calling—it identifies the electronic name or address associated with the physical port on the network. It also sends the same name and address information regardless of who the individual is calling.

A persona management system could, first of all, break the linkage between the geographic port and the individual. It would also be able to change the information sent depending upon who was being called.

For example, when assuming one's business persona, and calling a supplier, the supplier's phone display would show "Jane Doe of Consolidated Enterprises." But when Jane Doe assumes her family persona and calls her daughter, from the same telephone, her phone would display "Mom Calling." This dimension of persona management is very powerful. The key will be to make it as simple as possible for an individual to communicate with their persona management system and indicate preferences relevant to individual transactions.

Remember, the most important attribute of this new system is that the consumer is in complete control of his or her communications and network space. This means that others will be unable to communicate with them or use any information about them without their explicit consent. This can transform society as well as commerce.

Until now, we've been giving examples of consumer/business relationships, although persona management can be applied just as effectively to relationships among businesses, or relationships between consumers and government bodies. In the latter case, governments could conceivably feel uneasy about the power of persona management to restrict the use of an individual's information.

Witness the debate in the United States about public/private key encryption, which has resulted in court challenges, considerable press attention, and ample bandwidth consumption on the Internet through the mobilizing efforts of the Electronic Frontier Foundation and others.

Another important dimension of persona management could be in personal relationships. People would be able to control how others access their personal electronic space. Depending on the person calling or attempting to make contact, the receiver will be able to choose from various transaction modes. For example, a person could program the system so that only particular numbers may ring the appliance directly. Others would be intercepted by some mode of nonreal-time communications, such as voice mail. Another option would be to receive *all* electronic mail, but in the future, unwanted mail may be deleted automatically.

THE SELLER IN THE NEW ONLINE WORLD—CHALLENGES ABOUND

Persona management could be a frightening proposition for many businesses—this technology will create virtual gated communities for consumers. In the traditional media the consumer has few defenses against bombardment by commercial messages. Sellers will have to adapt to the empowered consumer to succeed in the digital economy.

Other threats to sellers include the emergence of network-based intermediaries who may replace, or disintermediate, traditional business facilitators, like retailers and wholesalers. Network service providers, for example, by virtue of their management of the "electronic landscape" could begin to play an important role in buying/selling transactions between their customer base and outside sellers. Network service providers are becoming increasingly important, not only because they facilitate commerce and host persona management systems but also because the accumulated know-how from hosting persona management activity (that is, learning networks) can enable an ever-increasing consumer empowerment. In other words, networks are now learning from usage. They put every new set of lessons learned into the hands of the end customer. These come in the form of successively more empowering releases of various software applications, which could pose a new challenge to both established distribution channels and the ultimate product or service manufacturer. Here the power in the buying/selling relationship rests with the service provider on behalf of the end consumer. And if service providers command a significant enough customer base, they can become very powerful when negotiating prices on behalf of their customers.

One question is, how much of the existing marketplace will move to the electronic domain? Will it be just a niche, or will e-commerce become the dominant model? Will online travel systems seriously affect existing travel agents, particularly those who are slow to adapt? Probably. Will online grocery shopping put established grocery chains out of business? Perhaps not. The real barriers to electronic commerce growth are the current lack of user-friendly interfaces and engaging, "dramatic" processes. Retailers and wholesalers who can migrate these "look-and-feel" characteristics to online business will flourish.

For product and service manufacturers, disintermediation creates significant challenges. If a company is on the receiving end of a customer-launched agent query searching for the cheapest car, airline ticket, hotel room, PC, or communications service, or just about any other product or service, then that company has just been relegated to the role of a commodity provider. Perhaps the most serious implication of this is the possible devaluation of brand identity—as consumers turn to their technological tools, instead of to a trusted brand name, to find assurance of quality and satisfaction.

If the customer is launching agent queries from a network service provider (NSP), this could cause the customer loyalty to shift to the NSP and away from more traditional channels. The probability of such a shift and the resulting impact on the supplier depends upon two things: the ability of a particular product to become a commodity and the place that a supplier occupies in the perceived distribution chain.

Of course, the value of a commodity product is in the eye of the beholder. To some, an airline ticket is just an airline ticket. To others, an airline with an exemplary safety or on-time record matters a great deal.

The biggest impact of a shift to commoditized products will be in distribution. In one scenario, the customer has already decided to buy a specific branded product but is looking for the cheapest source of supply. In another scenario, if the customer sees no value in the brand, suppliers at the manufacturing end will be hurt. In either case, the greatest risk is to the distribution channels, who will be challenged to present the customer with an enhanced value proposition.

This suggests a bifurcation in the nature of suppliers serving empowered customers. Some suppliers will focus on serving markets based on commodity pricing approaches. They will be the low-cost providers, substituting electronic overhead for bricks and mortar, and developing massive scale economies by serving a large market base. They will likely be new entrants aiming to displace existing channels and will concentrate on niche markets. These will be the new "rogue" retailers.

Other established suppliers, no matter what position they occupy in the distribution chain, will aim to move away from the commodity game by differentiating their value proposition from other suppliers. They will try to create brand loyalty and avoid, if possible, being at the receiving end of an agent query. They will do their best to keep their branded icons on their customers' appliance. They will want a customer to click on their WonderBank logo rather than on an unbranded icon for Financial Transactions, or even worse, an electronic bazaar for financial services. New value-added intermediaries are arising, too. Key influencers, such as product reviewers, online value-added resellers, solutions or content aggregators, and community-of-interest organizers are becoming powerful players.

How can the supplier achieve an effective presence in the electronic marketplace? New forms of brand awareness will be a key factor. If the consumer is using persona management and agents, the seller wants the buyer's agent to pick up their brand. In this environment, the brand will have to be much more than the result of creative advertising and promotion. It must become a true value proposition, a well-articulated representation of a provider's entire business system from product development through to customer after-sales service and support. Since agents can be very particular in their online hunts, sellers will need to specify what differentiates their offerings. The "me-too" offering that today's consumer often accepts will rank second in the future agent's search.

In essence, companies that want to create binding relationships with their empowered customers must master the protocols of emerging electronic distribution channels. The key will be to get your icon on the appliance and keep it there through meaningful association between that icon and the experiencing of real value by the consumer. Companies also need to recognize that, rather than wait for their customer to initiate a query in cyberspace, they can take advantage of electronic channels to narrowcast messages and propositions to their customers—with the customer's permission of course. A continuous loop of information from company to customer and back again will create the greatest opportunity for creating customer loyalty.

All this is driving the development of technology tools that enable the supplier to understand the needs and desires of customers in the electronic marketplace. These tools will help the seller to identify and target consumers by tracking the behavior of their agents or persona management systems. Data mining and similar technologies will play a big role.

But all sellers will have to join the Internet chaos if they hope to understand the new marketplaces and address their customers with some semblance of order and presence. Seller business systems must be modified continuously and rapidly to suit this highly dynamic environment, because there is too much momentum in this adaptive direction to expect that the Internet can ever be "controlled." Smart sellers will find ways to play into individuals' persona management systems through their own such personalization. For example, banks could easily replace their call center approach to customer service with "patch-in" communications taking their customer directly to the most logical bank source for tailored problem resolution.

OPPORTUNITIES UNLIMITED...

There is a growing specialized area of online commerce related to intellectual property. In its first incarnation, it involves electronic software distribution, an extension of downloading and shareware, e-zines, and subscription-based services such as AOL and Canada's Sympatico. At least one company, Idea Market, is extending the concept to allow payments to flow for "premium chat," serialized interactive releases by prominent authors, and other forms of intellectual property. In this environment, the product is the channel and vice versa.

Opportunities abound for software developers to facilitate customer empowerment. There is great promise for everything from the development of agent systems, systems for payment and e-commerce, privacy protection, and negotiation systems, right up to full-blown persona management environments.

We believe the same to be true for hardware providers. The big opportunity will be to develop appliances that are much simpler to use and have a significantly lower "personal energy factor"—the amount of energy a consumer must spend to get results. Remember, that for true customer empowerment to flourish, a critical mass of customers is needed. This will not happen until more comsumer-friendly appliances appear.

To examine other potential opportunities, one must first envision the business models that are likely to emerge. One model allows the consumer to acquire software and appliances that will enable them to create profiles and agents on their own. In this model, there is no middleman. Consumers would initiate transactions directly against suppliers and filter incoming messages on their own. However, this model has some shortcomings. What happens when the consumer is mobile? How are multiple appliances handled? How are communities of interest nurtured? It seems this mode would best be supplemented by a secondary service provider.

One can imagine two different types of service providers that would act as focal points for both consumers and businesses. One type would be a utility for maintaining consumer profiles and all of the capabilities to ensure independence of appliance, geography, and time. It would have simple consumer interfaces and be the repository of the consumer's persona, under the strict control and management of the consumer.

Another type would be more application-specific and deal either on a general or specific basis in serving the needs of the consumer. This kind of service provider might be more closely focused on a particular area of expertise—such as travel or entertainment—and would provide agents for the consumer to use. There could be significant overlap between these two types of service providers, but the consumer is still in control.

For example, a customer may want to be served by multiple NSPs and have access to a number of transactional services for traveling, entertainment, etc., and may not wish to duplicate his or her persona across each service provider. A central repository, with interfaces to other service providers, may be the best solution in this case. The additional advantage of the centralized repository is that developers can tap the aggregated set of online experiences as content or even "lines of code" for new applications. It would allow a persona manager to deal not just with the online world but also be active in managing real-time voice and broadcast communications spaces on behalf of the customer.

A third business model involves the consumer having a direct relationship with an end supplier. Here the supplier maintains its icons on the customer's appliance by virtue of a superior value proposition. It could be a bank, an airline, or a telecommunications company. A company that can achieve this would reintermediate itself with the empowered customer.

In tomorrow's environment, there will likely be more than one winning model or solution. In any case, the balance of power between producers, consumers, and intermediaries has changed irreversibly. Ultimately, the consumer will benefit, as will businesses that embrace the brave new world of consumer empowerment.

NOTE

1. Hammer, Michael and Jean Champy, *Reengineering the Corporation: A Manifesto for Business Revolution* (New York: HarperBusiness), 1994.

THE NEW LOGISTICS

SHAPING THE NEW ECONOMY

by Dennis H. Jones
Federal Express

Mastery of logistics is as vital to success in the digital economy as it was to the extraordinary success of the Roman Empire.

FREDERICK W. SMITH
Chairman, President and CEO, FDX Corporation

THE CLASSIC CASE FOR LOGISTICS

The Roman Empire was more than a triumph of warfare and military might. It was a triumph of logistics—breathtaking in its scope and scale.

Through the course of five centuries, the Romans maintained order and nurtured a growing commercial economy over a massive region spanning three continents, millions of people, dozens of cultures and languages, and hundreds of political entities.

All this was achieved in an era of primitive transportation and limited literacy—an era when Rome had no particular advantages in weaponry or numbers of troops and horses. In fact, Roman armies were vastly outnumbered by existing and potential forces in virtually every corner of the empire.

Logistics was the key—mobilizing and moving information, resources, troops, administrators, and money when and where needed to quell insurrection, maintain orderly rule, and develop successful trade. Rather than maintaining a full standing army in every province, the Romans assembled forces as needed from legions and materiel stationed in various locations. They achieved this through efficient organization and communications, essentially replacing inventory with information—inventories of troops and materiel with information as to where they were located and how they could be mobilized.

The linchpin for this triumph of logistics was a sophisticated network of roads, planned and built across Europe, Britain, the Middle East, and North Africa. As the earliest "World Wide Web," it enabled highly efficient routing and shipment of information, troops, goods, and money. The Romans also developed ways to move information and money more efficiently around their Empire—by establishing Latin as the first universal language, developing a literate class of military and civic administrators, creating a common currency, and maintaining a well-organized courier service.

The Roman Empire eventually imploded as its colonies evolved and learned that the economic benefits of the imperial system were not shared equally. However, it lived on as the basis for the Western economy and successful global commercial empires through to the twentieth century, as the colonies of Spain, Portugal, France, Britain, and Germany in turn colonized the world.

Superior logistics was the basis of power and commercial success for each of these empires.

THE NEW LOGISTICS

The achievements of the Roman Empire were remarkable, and the lessons to be drawn are profound. In our postcolonial digital economy, the legacy of the Roman Empire lives on in the mastery of logistics. Integrated with information and communications, logistics has become the foundation of the successful commercial enterprise today.

Technology has made it possible to "shrink" the world, and information and money have been digitized. Many of today's products and services exist in digital form and are consumed in the digital domain, for example, music, software, and financial services. But our physical goods must still be manufactured, assembled, mobilized, and moved. Beaming up physical matter remains a *Star Trek* fantasy, but the new logistics moves closer to that vision by making it possible to have products materialize intact in shorter and shorter time frames, anywhere and everywhere in the world.

More importantly, advances in telecommunications and computer technology have enabled the integration of various logistical functions from managing the entire supply chain through to distribution and beyond. This can include customer services, transportation, warehousing, inventory management, order processing, information systems, production planning, and purchasing.[1]

While integrated logistics effectively improves transport and storage, it reduces the buildup of inventory: mass is replaced with information. In other words, if you know where your goods are at any given time and how long it will take for them to reach their destination, it minimizes the need for a warehouse of safety stock. "If you think about it," says Frederick W. Smith, Chairman, President, and CEO, FDX Corporation, "a warehouse is nothing more than a place to put something so you know you've got it. Well, I figured if we could provide the same degree of assurance to people, electronically, that their goods are 'in the FedEx warehouse'—be it on one of our 500-mile per hour planes or a 50-mile per hour truck—then they would no longer need to have it in a warehouse."

Over the last two decades, this simple premise has had a profound effect on the U.S. economy. In 1980, the United States spent 10.8 percent of gross domestic product (GDP) on inventory—a big chunk of money for goods that just sat in warehouses. By 1995, that figure had dropped by more than half to just 4.3 percent. At the same time, spending on logistics in the United States—as a percentage of the GDP—dropped from 17.2 percent to just 9 percent.

Clearly, gains made in logistical efficiency have largely reduced inventory costs, and businesses are no doubt more productive and much more competitive in the global marketplace. But even so, U.S. companies still spend $700 billion a year (1996) on inventory and moving it around. There are still lots of gains to be made in the business of logistics.

But improvements in the efficiency of logistics—mostly due to improved information technology—are only half the story. Replacing inventory with information not only saves money and lowers the cost of finished products but also opens up a whole new world of possibilities, where logistics becomes an integral part of business strategy, and ideas and knowledge become the real capital base.

For logistics companies, this means facilitating an entire retooling of the conventional business order with services that make the Internet a key component of commerce in the future. Nonvalue-add intermediaries and expensive warehousing will be a thing of the past. Organizations will increasingly be in the business of design, packaging, and promotion, with customers able to order goods online and receive delivery straight from the manufacturer's assembly plant, or eventually, from assembly points managed by logistics companies like FedEx. In the future, the traditional roles of manufacturer, distributor, direct marketer, or retailer will blur significantly.

For FedEx, taking on the role of a logistics provider has been a logical extension of our services, and indeed, a vibrant part of our electronic commerce. Nonetheless, it is not as simple as that. The Internet has certainly made the job easier by providing a standard platform for communication, but trust remains a key issue. How far will a customer want to let you in to their back operations? And what about FedEx? There was concern that if we link the Internet to our internal systems we could be exposed to the risks of fraud by hackers. But because of our heritage of sharing information through our proprietary networks, further integration via the Net was truly a natural move for both FedEx and our customers.

LOGISTICS IN THE INFORMATION AGE: THE FEDEX CASE

The success of FedEx is, in part, a product of the growth of information technology and the burgeoning computer industry. In 1973, Fred Smith started the company based on an idea that anticipated the high-speed, high-tech world of today. The company was built on his astute observation: as computers became an integral part of everyday business operations, it would become crucial to have quick and reliable parts delivery so that a company's operations didn't collapse during a computer breakdown. No company, however, could afford to keep the inventory of parts that such on-call maintenance required. Express delivery of replacement parts from manufacturers was the solution. And given the growing importance of computers for business operations, high-speed, higher-value forms of shipping and distribution were justified.

In this environment, Fred Smith founded Federal Express as a shipping company based on airplanes rather than traditional ships and trains. Speed and reliable delivery were the expected competitive advantages. Higher-value transportation would provide the speed, but information management and telecommunications were essential for the reliability.

As we built a physical network of planes and distribution centers, we developed an electronic network to efficiently manage the physical one—and, at the same time, allow customers to better manage their inventory and supply chains.

The FedEx information network began in the 1970s with an internal system, COSMOS, which integrated the two essential information streams that are central to the new logistics. The first stream is information about goods being shipped (contents, special handling requirements, origin, and destination); the second is information about the transport system (carriers, shipping routes, schedules, pick up and transfer points, storage centers, customs clearance, and so on).

By bringing these two streams together with COSMOS, we managed our own business far more effectively while providing package tracking information to customers—information that is key to inventory and supply chain management.

In the early 1980s, FedEx took a major step forward with bar code scanning, improving our efficiency by further automating our processes and enabling us to provide more detailed information to customers. But the greatest leap was linking customers into an interactive information network in the mid-1980s with a program of automated shipping programs called FedEx PowerShip. This program enabled customers to prepare their own shipments, print their own bar-coded labels, track the status of their own packages, and produce their own invoices.

That was before the networked world of today: bringing customers online meant providing them with hardware, software, printers, and network connections. PowerShip required an investment of millions of dollars, and initially, we could only afford to extend the program to major customers who shipped more than 100 packages per day. But the benefits for FedEx and customers were immediate. Our own efficiencies improved as customers performed many functions that we had previously processed internally, while customers were able to make major improvements in shipment processing productivity, allowing them to gain greater control of their inventories and supply chains. Providing millions of dollars of computers to customers was considered a bold idea, even inside FedEx, but the cost savings to both our customers and FedEx, and the incremental shipping this convenience supported made the program a major success.

But it also had a revolutionary effect that in many ways foreshadowed the networked world of today. By linking customers through FedEx PowerShip, we immediately transformed our customer base into a network. Customers were able to interact with our system and turn their mailroom into a veritable FedEx outpost, and we were able to download software and shipping information into their systems. The benefits of sharing information were clear. For customers, the system was sophisticated enough to tell them when they typed in a wrong zip code, for example. A reduction in errors on the front end quickly translated into increased on-time deliveries.

The next step was to extend these benefits to all our customers. By 1994, PCs had become so prevalent and networking had become so advanced that FedEx was able to bring even the smallest customer online. We developed FedEx Ship, providing software and toll-free dial-up access to our network.

By late 1994, with the spreading use of the Internet, we began to provide interactive services through our Web site, boosting customer access and reducing costs even further. Though the Internet poses some challenges, it holds extraordinary potential for the logistics industry. Since the Internet is ubiquitous, the cost of bringing customers online is significantly less because software doesn't have to be created to support separate networks for each new customer.

Furthermore, the Internet makes it easy to consolidate the information gathered from our automated users. This information has been almost as valuable to us as the packages we send. Through automation we're able to track who is shipping where, how often, and in what quantities. This helps us to spot trends and identify our customers' needs early.

We've also been able to manage our day-to-day operations more efficiently. Data from international shipments is updated to FedEx and electronically sent to the destination country's customs organization prior to the actual shipment, expediting clearance. And, there are fewer surprises. Instead of a dock manager in, say, Austin, calling late in the day to tell our ground operations that they're going to exceed the plane's capacity, we'll get an indication through our computer system much earlier in the day that Austin is going to go into overflow and can plan to provide the needed service.

With the continued development of both our physical and information networks, FedEx has become a major force. By 1997, we were picking up and delivering nearly 3 million parcels a day in 212 countries around the world; we were operating a fleet of close to 600 planes and 40,000 trucks and vans; we were managing 140,000 employees and had distribution facilities located in all major global markets; and our annual revenues had reached the level of $11.5 billion.

But even more important than our current status is our positioning for the future. We have become a key participant in the new economy. Through online commerce we can become full-service logistics providers to our customers, specializing in orchestrating the flow of goods and information between customers, retailers, and suppliers. *Wired* magazine has described us as a "network amphibian—equally at home with the task of switching packets of cardboard or packets of electronic data." We're comfortable in each arena because we have had years to develop our operations in the two fields and refine how each relates to the other.

VERTICAL INTEGRATION REVISITED— SUPPLY CHAIN MANAGEMENT

Through the industrial era, the ultimate corporate model was vertical integration—companies that owned their entire supply chains from manufacturing through assembly to marketing. Vertical integration was the best way to control the production process. It provided a formidable competitive advantage to big companies through critical mass and economies of scale.

Because of shipping costs and constraints, manufacturing operations were typically located as close to raw materials and/or markets as possible. Entering new geographic markets generally meant duplicating vertically integrated manufacturing facilities within those markets.

As technology advanced and we entered the information era, new approaches became possible. Ongoing development of logistics information systems, linked to physical distribution, allowed for the move to just-in-time inventory management, providing more control and efficiency, and reducing reliance on in-house production and warehousing facilities.

Manufacturers could reach further and further afield for parts and components, from internal or external suppliers—purchasing what was required, when required from producers offering optimal price and performance.

Increasingly, the manufacturing supply chain was outsourced: car manufacturers became assembly plants, using parts provided by a host of suppliers; consumer products companies became brand managers, using custom manufacturers for everything from soap powder to paint, breakfast cereal, and running shoes. The trend is pervasive—successful companies like Nike and Sun MicroSystems outsource all their manufacturing, focusing their attention and energies on design, marketing, and distribution.

Vertical integration is being replaced, inexorably, by *virtual* integration, where value-leading businesses focus on a limited set of core competencies and outsource virtually every other function. Thanks to the new logistics, they are able to source components and services from wherever in the world they can be most efficiently produced and they can market their products and services wherever demand exists. Logistics is the key to the virtual corporation.

Examples of adding value through integrated logistics abound. In a 1995 article in *Logistics Information Management*, Robert Halhead of GE Information Services cited dramatic improvements at three multinational companies:

- Benetton, the Italian fashion retailer that operates in 100 different countries utilized electronic services to revamp its order through delivery process—reducing ordering time from an average of a week to a matter of hours, increasing manufacturing efficiency and reducing inventory levels.

- Peugeot Citroen, which assembles 2 million cars a year with 60 percent of components from outside suppliers, cut its inventory cycle from 8 days to 5, reduced the number of unassembled vehicles (waiting for delayed delivery of components) on its assembly line by 70 percent, and boosted the number of different car versions it offered to customers by 30 percent.

- GE Aircraft Engines' integrated logistics solution reduced its purchase order cycle time by 15 to 30 days and reduced the costs of issuing a purchase order from $100 to $5.[2]

OUTSOURCING THE LOGISTICS FUNCTION ITSELF

While the logistics function is the underpinning of outsourcing, it is increasingly outsourced itself. Physical distribution has long been outsourced—no company that is not in the transportation business could possibly afford to maintain the in-house fleets of trucks, planes, and ships that are essential to participating in the global economy. Now, as well as outsourcing physical distribution, more and more companies are outsourcing the entire logistics function as part of their logistics strategy, since, as a business process, it has no value add.

Those with the most to gain are small- to medium-sized firms that must compete with industry giants but who do not have the scale of activity to support internal logistics functions. Precise logistics are particularly important with the rise of globalization. As the ability to reach international customers grows, the need to understand customs and duties, find overseas storage facilities, and reduce shipping times increases exponentially.

A prime example is National Semiconductor (NSC), a global producer of computer chips used by customers around the world—for everything from computer components to consumer electronic equipment. As Kelvin Phillips, director of worldwide logistics put it, "We recognized our competency was building semiconductors, not doing logistics."

In 1992, NSC was managing a complex supply chain through chip production and delivery to manufacturers around Southeast Asia—a never ending obstacle course of airplane, train, and truck schedules, and customs and clearance hurdles through multiple markets, each with unique languages, cultures, rules, and infrastructure.

The NSC supply chain cycle averaged 60 days—a major constraint in an industry where product lifecycles are collapsing. Recognizing that its core competency was developing and marketing semiconductors, NSC decided to outsource its logistics management and execution to FedEx.

By using our global information systems, a dedicated warehouse in Singapore and a well-established transportation network throughout Southeast Asia, we were able to collapse the supply chain.

The cycle time is down to 2 *days,* from 60, and the ramifications have been felt through the entire supply chain. NSC's warehousing, inventory, and transportation costs have dropped while responsiveness to their customers has increased. NSC customers and suppliers can now schedule production around their own customers' orders, rather than by guessing what requirements may be 2 months down the road, when chips on order may already be outmoded, or when their customers' requirements may change.

Outsourced logistics management is still in its infancy: third-party providers represented just 6 percent of the $500 billion logistics industry in 1996. But that was up from 2 percent just 5 years earlier. And the growth potential is enormous—as is the potential for customer savings and efficiencies and marketing improvements.

Outsourcing distribution alone can greatly increase the manufacturer/marketer's customer fulfillment. We have seen this throughout our network of 25 FedEx Express Distribution Centers around the world, where our customers can store fast-moving merchandise right at our transportation hubs in order to get their products to their end-use customers more quickly and easily—and at less cost.

These centers greatly enhance a company's ability to operate in different global markets without infrastructure costs—and allow for order fulfillment in different time zones. For example, Cisco Systems, a California-based maker of networking equipment, uses the FedEx Express Distribution Center in Memphis to fulfill orders until 1 a.m. Central time. And staff at our centers also perform final configuration work on products ordered—allowing for immediate customization and further shortening Cisco's response times.

ELECTRONIC COMMERCE: THE IMPACT ON RETAILERS

Collapsing the supply chain has been a function not only of speeding up the cycle between the different links but also, in some cases, of eliminating links—the nonvalue-added distribution links between the manufacturer and the marketing company, and between the marketing company and the retailer.

Now, with electronic commerce—particularly direct marketing via the Internet integrated with logistics—along with more mature forms of direct marketing (cataloguers operating by mail and telephone)—the store-based retailer (the intermediary between manufacturer/marketer and customer) can be bypassed for a growing range of products. With integrated logistics, direct marketers can source products directly from manufacturers and route them directly to customers—perhaps via a distribution point that allows for custom assembly of products for individual customers. This is the basis of mass customization.

The benefits to the end consumer are clear: lower costs through elimination of nonvalue-added steps, greater convenience through direct delivery, and more choice through the customization.

Online commerce is growing explosively, and is accelerating the growth of all nonstore retailing which had already captured a 15 percent share of the $3 trillion worldwide retail market in 1996. Some forecasters estimate the number could reach 50 percent by 2010.

This is already the reality for banks, which are providing more and more transactions electronically, rather than through the expensive brick-and-mortar of their retail branches. Of course, banking *is* electronic commerce, as money and financial instruments have long been digitized. They are not physical objects which must be physically delivered to the customer. But with the advances in integrated logistics, electronic commerce is also supplanting in-store retail for physical products.

With the trend toward direct marketing and electronic commerce, there will be many winners and losers in the traditional supply chain. Others are responding to the challenge by becoming more efficient and adding value to their physical locations.

The value of retail stores, for many customers, is the credibility of an actual location where physical objects can be touched, and where there is accountability and guarantee of service, and perhaps, advice. Cyberspace does not yet deliver that sort of comfort level. Store locations may also add value by responding to broader cultural needs for socialization. Consumers can now buy books on the Internet, but at a bookstore complete with cappuccino bars and music, they may enjoy a social atmosphere.

NEW RETAILING APPROACHES: THE MONORAIL STORY

New companies are emerging to create hybrid approaches that recognize and maximize the value of bricks and mortar retail while enjoying the benefits of integrated logistics and electronic commerce.

One such example is Monorail, a PC supplier founded by Doug Johns, a former Compaq executive, in 1996. The premise was to mass customize low-cost PCs—delivered to retailers within 24 hours. Demand for mass customization in PCs had already been established by Dell, but Monorail focused on an important niche that wasn't being served: the customer who wasn't comfortable buying a big-ticket item over the phone or the Internet. Such customers want the security, real or perceived, of entering a store, dealing with the vendor face to face, and physically handling the products.

Monorail, which has no manufacturing facilities, is a prime example of integrated logistics and virtual integration. All computers and components are outsourced. Direct sales are handled by the retail chains like CompUSA. Electronic commerce and logistical requirements are handled by FedEx, which delivers the computers directly to the individual stores as needed, rather than to a retail chain's central warehouse.

With this level of outsourcing, Monorail can focus on its core competencies, which are design, marketing, and managing the relationship with retailers. With a staff of just 40 people, Monorail gives customers the option of walking into a store and purchasing a Windows-compatible Pentium PC for under $1000—a significant price breakthrough in 1997. Customers may either buy off the shelf or order specific custom configurations—delivered within 48 hours.

In its first 40 days of operation, Monorail achieved sales of $10 million. Again, the benefits were clear through the supply chain: manufacturers build computers to order rather than maintaining inventory that quickly becomes outdated, and retailers such as CompUSA are selling more computers with lower inventory and distribution costs.

FEDEX VIRTUALORDER FOR THE VIRTUAL COMPANY

FedEx has responded to the trend towards virtual companies—and accelerated the trend—by developing offerings for the Internet that enable the smallest companies to participate in electronic commerce. In 1997, we developed FedEx VirtualOrder, a back-end electronic commerce software system that automates the interaction between our customers and their customers and suppliers.

With FedEx VirtualOrder, we provide the tools for a commerce-enabled Web site, hosted by FedEx and linked to our network. When a consumer places an order on this system, FedEx automatically processes the shipment, conveys the order to our customer/merchant, and issues a tracking number to the consumer who can access the status of their order at any time.

With such systems, direct marketers with no Internet or electronic commerce experience can immediately set up shop in cyberspace—using a series of computerized forms which enable them to transfer their paper catalogs to the Web.

FedEx VirtualOrder provides some of the missing links that had constrained Internet commerce: customer service and fulfillment, quick and reliable delivery of custom products, and the comfort level of a respected brand name. For small merchants, being supported by the FedEx brand name is a major advantage. In fact, even some firmly established cataloguers report higher order sizes and response rates when they use FedEx to fulfill online shopping orders.

CHALLENGES OF ELECTRONIC COMMERCE—SHARING THE BENEFITS

With FedEx VirtualOrder, FedEx is playing a new role in the value chain—we have assumed a retailer role on behalf of merchants, with direct contact to customers. While this increases the viability and scope of electronic commerce, it also raises serious issues and challenges.

We see two key issues. The first goes back to the level of trust required between FedEx and its customers. FedEx, by being the final link to the customer, has access to valuable information including postal codes, frequency of purchases, dollar value of purchases, etc.

Second, there is a competitive threat to all participants—including logistics suppliers—as barriers to entry in all parts of the value chain are reduced by technology and electronic commerce.

This is uncharted territory, and the issues are just beginning to emerge. The approach at FedEx is to remind ourselves constantly that we are in the integrated logistics business. We are not in competition with our customers. We believe success for each member of the value chain depends on sharing the benefits. As observed at the outset, the Roman Empire ultimately imploded because the economic benefits were not shared with the colonies.

The change in barriers to entry is the other major challenge of electronic commerce. The ability to create a virtual company and use the Internet to assemble a supply chain and sell products is the great equalizer. The playing field is readily accessible by all. Traditional competitive advantages—from manufacturing capabilities to retail brick-and-mortar—have been largely eliminated.

For the logistics industry in particular, we no longer enjoy the competitive advantage of our vast investments in proprietary computer systems linked directly to customers. However, the basic advantages of those systems can potentially be replicated on the Internet. Just as the banking and financial services industry has seen new competition spring up from unexpected quarters, contenders in this space will find that long-held notions about doing business will be turned upside down by the Internet. An example of this is Microsoft's sudden interest in the logistics business, in the form of their ValueChain initiative. Other examples include Pandesic, and Actra, the Netscape/GEIS combination which Netscape later acquired. Their goal of creating a software product that seamlessly and effectively integrates multiple carriers is an aggressive vision, but it remains to be seen whether it becomes a reality.

Certainly, the recent closing of Encompass, a joint venture between American Airlines parent AMR Corporation and shipping giant CSX Corporation, which focused on providing computers and software that allowed companies to manage their use of transportation providers, and GE Info Systems' retrenchment of its logistics tracking system, both imply that meeting this objective is easier said than done.

Nonetheless, while electronic commerce eliminates barriers to entry and poses difficult challenges, it also opens up new opportunities.

Although a shared network takes competitive advantages away from the owner of proprietary networks, it has the long-term effect of reducing costs, improving efficiencies, increasing competition, and spurring greater overall growth of a market or industry. Railway companies saw this in the nineteenth century when they linked and shared their proprietary rail networks, greatly enhancing the long-term development of rail travel. Banks saw this when they shared and linked their ATM and debit card networks, leading to a quantum leap in usefulness and usage. And electronic commerce, using shared networks, will spur long-term economic growth—not for every participant, but for those who focus on their core competencies and respond to change.

The digital economy and the new virtual corporate structures that are arising within it have already moved us into a postindustrial era. Electronic commerce will drive economic growth from now on—and the rate of technological change makes it impossible to predict how far and how fast the world of commerce will change.

THE PHYSICAL NETWORK

What often gets lost in discussions about Internet commerce and the digital economy are the physical aspects of doing business. The Internet has engendered a feeling that anyone can start up a Web site to sell widgets, and instantly they're worldwide marketers. Much attention is being paid to how potential customers will even become aware of these Web marketers. Assuming an answer is found to that challenge, their issues are not totally resolved. What happens when they get an order from Singapore or Germany? They don't have an international shipping department. They haven't thought through the logistics.

To succeed in Internet commerce, we believe a company has to be as effective in the physical world as they are in the electronic arena. The ability to move information around the world at the speed of light is a great enabler to commerce, but it breeds a corresponding need for the physical goods. The information network needs a physical network: FedEx's 596 planes, 38,000 trucks, and 17 distribution centers provide a way to act on that information. The Internet will change the way the world buys and sells its collective production of goods, but its benefits will only come to full fruition if the physical network can keep pace. The key is the ability to move fast, and, luckily, moving fast is what we're known for.

It's likely that airplanes and trucks may soon be replaced with more efficient air-, land-, or water-based vehicles. We can no better visualize transportation two or three decades hence than the Romans could visualize the cars that now travel on the roadways they engineered 2000 years ago. But whatever our tools may be—and whoever the competition may be—integrated logistics will remain central in the new economy.

NOTES

1. Gustin, Craig M., Patricia J. Daugherty, and Theodore P. Stank, "The Effects of Information Availability on Logistics Integration," *Journal of Business Logistics,* vol. 16, no. 1, 1995, pp. 1–21.
2. Halhead, Robert, "Breaking Down the Barriers to Free Information Exchange," *Logistics Information Management,* vol. 8, no. 1, 1995, pp. 34–37.

PART THREE

ENABLING THE INTERNETWORKED ENTERPRISE

The chapters in this section address the intersection of information technology and business strategy, that is, the role of infrastructure, enabling technologies, and applications that together, deliver a company's business solutions. Perspectives vary from the subtleties of user interface and information design to the overall approach to business.

THE COMPUTING MODEL FOR THE INFORMATION AGE

by Raymond J. Lane
Oracle Corporation

50 YEARS AGO

In 1948, invention was on the move. The Polaroid camera and the long-playing vinyl record both made their debut, and Bell Labs announced the invention of the most important technology of the twentieth century: the transistor. With it, the information age was born.

Or was it?

Thirty-five years ago those transistors found their way into computers. This helped IBM make corporate computing routine, by providing a more economical platform for processing business transactions. Maybe this was the start of the Information Age?

Or maybe it started 15 years ago, as the PC proliferated throughout corporations, growing computer usage tenfold.

I'd like to suggest a different view. We are not in an information age at all, as conventional wisdom would have us believe. Rather, I think we may just be entering this era as we begin the new millennium. An information age can only be defined as the time when access to information is low in cost and simple.

Today's world doesn't meet those criteria. For one thing access to digital information is through personal computers, and PCs are not ubiquitous. Telephones, radios, and televisions are found throughout the developed world, even in less developed countries.

But less than 3 percent of the world's population uses computers. In the richest country in the world, the United States, two-thirds of the population don't use computers. In California, home of the computer industry, even if we put a computer in every classroom, students would still have only occasional access to the Internet. This doesn't sound like an information age to me.

The PC is creating a planet of *haves* and *have-nots*. In today's complex world, those who are cut off from information may be cut off from participating fully in the business and civic life of our society. We won't have an information age until everyone can participate. And that can't happen until we can substantially reduce the cost and complexity of computing so we can extend access to more people.

NETWORK COMPUTING CHANGES EVERYTHING

The solution to this challenge is already reshaping the world in which we live and work. The World Wide Web, constituted from the standard and open disciplines of the Internet, is a marriage of the computer and the communications network. For the first time in computing history, it creates an environment with the economies of scale and ease of use that can alter the fundamental economics of how information is gathered, shared, stored, and transported. Almost overnight, it has changed the rules in nearly every industry, from publishing and entertainment to retail and high tech.

The Web's power is rooted in a simple model for sharing digital data: *network computing*. Network computing is a way of managing information that is easier, less expensive, and more reliable than personal computing and private networks. Network computing is truly the first opportunity since the telephone and television to revolutionize the way we conduct business and the way we communicate. It is based on the concept of using Internet standards and powerful, professionally managed networks to provide information. People who need access to the information on the network will use a variety of devices from personal computers to network computers to a new generation of Internet-enabled phones and television sets. Getting information will be as simple as turning on the television. Transacting business will be as easy, at significantly lower cost.

The Web started with the idea that a common language could enable users to view documents stored on remote computers anywhere in the world. The widespread deployment of the Mosaic browser, public-domain software developed at the University of Illinois in 1992, made this vision a reality. With Mosaic, a scientist in England could share documents with a colleague in Hong Kong and not have to worry about whether they both had the right computer, the right configuration, and the right version of the software. Documents could be marked up in a simple language called HTML (hypertext markup language), that gave users an easy-to-learn tool for formatting documents. Those documents could then be placed on a server, a computer attached to the Internet network, and made available to anyone with access to the Internet. Any computer user with an HTML-compliant browser like Mosaic could view and read the documents. This concept allows viewing of information by "tuning in" rather than needing the information and the software to view it on every individual computer.

YOU SAY YOU WANT A REVOLUTION

The network computing model works on the same powerful but simple idea as the Internet and the Web. Anyone with access to the network can create and store work files, exchange information, and communicate with anyone else on the network. They are all using the same standard software—a Web browser—and connecting to a network based on Internet standards. The data and applications they need reside on servers—powerful computers that can securely store and "serve" the data and applications as users request it—connected to networks. The user's computer can be a full-blown workstation, a desktop PC, a diskless network computer, or even an Internet-enabled TV. It doesn't matter. All that is required is a standard browser, sufficient computing power to download and display Web pages, and a network connection.

Using open Internet standards and open tools like Java, the programming language developed by scientists at Sun Microsystems in 1995, the software developer creates programs that can be accessed by any Web-enabled device. The user's computer runs simple-to-operate programs such as Internet browsers and Java viewers (programs that can download and run Java applications) to access corporate applications, corporate databases, personal files, or the Internet itself. The user gets all the power of a typical desktop PC, but is freed from dealing with application upgrades and other complex maintenance chores. Network computing users can create documents; communicate with coworkers, friends, and family members; browse for information in corporate systems or online applications; order merchandise; and find out the latest sports scores from anywhere in the world. And they can do all this with very low-cost devices that will expand access to more people. In today's economics, this translates to a few hundred dollars versus a few thousand dollars, with the costs falling fast.

At Work and At Home

Imagine a world where employees can access applications and data on remote networks and can work from any machine in any office anywhere in the world. All they need is an Internet connection and a password for the company network to access their files and the company's information systems. Imagine a world where parents can turn on the television set and review their child's homework assignments, plan a vacation, or find out how to treat chicken pox. Imagine a world where a child from a low-income neighborhood has access to the same information resources as the child from an affluent neighborhood. These things are all possible with network computing and low-cost Internet appliances.

Network computing is based on an established distribution model. The network itself is complicated, but the point of access is a simple, easy-to-operate device. This is exactly the way today's networks operate. Take television as an example. Think of broadcasters such as CBS and CNN as the servers, the airwaves as the network, and the television set as the access device. All the complexity of creating and storing the shows, broadcasting, and managing the transmission networks is left to professionals. The television set runs the interface. It is a simple on-off device that works without fail nearly every time you use it. It's easy, intuitive, and, thanks to economies of scale, relatively cheap. You don't need to configure it, upgrade it, reboot it, or inoculate it with antiviral software to get it to run. You don't need to carry your own TV with you to have access to its data when you are traveling. The data comes to you via a network. This network model is repeated in most of our major public systems: the radio network, the telephone network, the public water supply, and the electrical grid. It will work for information as well.

The Best of Two Worlds Forms a New World

From an architectural standpoint, network computing offers a fundamental break with the past. It represents a third stage in the evo-

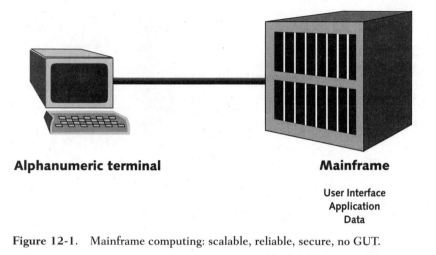

Alphanumeric terminal   **Mainframe**

User Interface
Application
Data

Figure 12-1. Mainframe computing: scalable, reliable, secure, no GUT.

lution of our interaction with the three key elements of computing: data, which is the information we collect and use; applications, which are the tools for analyzing and manipulating data; and interfaces, which present the data to us.

The first era of computing was the mainframe era, which stretched from the dawn of computing to the late 1970s, when the corporate database, the applications, and the presentation all resided on the same machine. Mainframes looked like big refrigerators, and were housed in special, climate-controlled rooms where they were cared for by teams of programmers. Mainframe computing was a one-tier architecture (see Fig. 12-1). All of the processing power and storage was in the mainframe. Users accessed the mainframe via terminals—dumb machines that could only present a picture of text data that resided on the mainframe server. It was like viewing a window into the mainframe. Users could interact with data in very limited, predetermined ways, such as entering orders or creating invoices. There was nothing personal at all about the experience. There was no graphical user interface. Programmers had to learn cumbersome computer languages to develop applications, and most companies could never keep up with the demand for business applications. There were some advantages, however. Mainframe computing consolidated a company's data and applications, so that they could be professionally managed, and users' terminals were inexpensive, low-maintenance devices, even though access was limited and the user experience was poor.

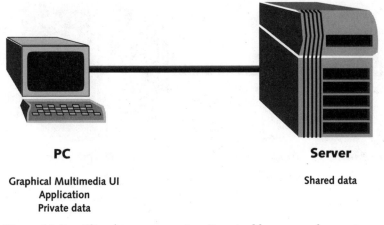

PC   Server

Graphical Multimedia UI   Shared data
       Application
       Private data

Figure 12-2. Client/server computing. Promised lower cost than main-frame, unmanageable without MIS.

In the 1970s this paradigm began to be replaced, first with the introduction of the microcomputer, the first single operator machine, and then the personal computer, which gave birth to the client/server computing architecture. In the client/server model of computing, which is found in most businesses today, corporate databases still reside on servers, which can be mainframes, minicomputers, or even in some cases PCs. However, the applications and the interface now reside on the client machine, typically a desktop PC (see Fig. 12-2).

Client/server computing brought graphical user interfaces—the familiar Macintosh and Windows look and feel—to computers. These user-friendly environments vastly improved the user's experience. The downside of client/server computing is that it has added tremendous complexity to the tasks of managing data and applications, and its ultimate scalability is questionable. Even today, client/server applications do not scale to mainframe levels. Typically, companies have thousands of desktop PCs, each with a different configuration, each with its own unique data and applications. And PCs have an unfortunate tendency to crash, freezing data and applications and rendering the computer useless, at least temporarily. Managing hundreds or thousands of PCs and upgrading applications on every one of them can be a logistical headache, and it adds tremendous labor overhead at a time when qualified labor is scarce and expensive. And outside the corporate environment, PCs are too

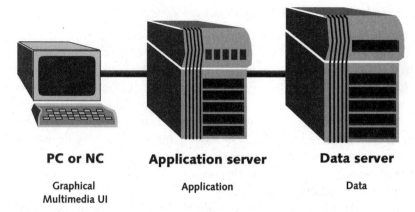

PC or NC   **Application server**   **Data server**

Graphical   Application   Data
Multimedia UI

Figure 12-3.   Network computing: simple appliance—professionally managed network.

expensive and complex for the vast majority of the world's population to buy and use.

Network computing borrows the best of both the mainframe and client/server paradigms. It makes computing more manageable while preserving the attractive user experience with graphical user interfaces. And because it lowers costs, access can be extended to many more people. Network computing explodes the client/server paradigm by separating the client into two parts. The interface still resides on the desktop computer, which can be a traditional desktop PC or any new network computing device, but the applications now reside on their own server on the network. It is a three-tier computing architecture (see Fig. 12-3): data servers hold all of the information, such as parts and pricing for an auto supply store; application servers hold all of the software applications, such as an order entry form; and clients simply run a browser-based user interface.

This model takes advantage of the biggest computer trend of the decade—the migration of value from the computer to the network. Ten years ago the greatest value came from computation: having the fastest computer, the best operating system, the latest software tools. That was a technical advantage. Today, a computer's greatest value derives from the networks to which it is connected. The key value for consumers and businesses lies in having access to the information that resides on networks, whether it is the corporate network or the public Internet.

Information Is Where the Value Is

Applications and servers must conform to the needs of the data, because that is what users care about most. Data is what companies gather, store, manage, and manipulate in order to create better products and deliver better services. Data is what consumers access and browse to help them buy a car, book a trip, find more information about a medical condition, or get in touch with others who share a common interest. Data is what enables us to decide where we want to go and what we want to do. The value to companies and to consumers lies in the information—and knowledge—they can glean from the data they can access.

Imagine a 360 degree view of your business and your customer, from information that could be mined easily by anyone in the organization who needed it—when they needed it—to make the best decision. Imagine hundreds of field offices with immediate access to promotion results as they develop on a daily basis. Imagine halving support costs as your customers opt for "self-service" over the Web by mining the right information when they need it. Imagine Chinese children having access to American university content, or a repository of the world's most current medical practices—as available in the third world as it is in the most developed countries.

Think about it this way. Which is more valuable, the piece of technology you bought from a third-party hardware or software vendor, or the information you gather and store about your customers, your products, your services? Because it is the data that carries the greatest value, the point of integration in network computing is the information itself, not the operating system.

One hundred percent of Fortune 500 companies use multiple operating systems today. It just doesn't make sense to integrate systems around the low-level code that runs a computer, especially given the variety of computers and operating systems in use, with different operating systems prevailing for different tasks. Every organization needs to build systems around the information they need to operate and thrive rather than around a piece of equipment or software. And in today's world of multinational business, mergers, acquisitions, and consolidations, the integration of diverse business operations is enough of a challenge without the added worry of what operating system, what computer hardware, and what applications each division is using.

With intelligent systems built around the information people value, and Internet-based networks as a readily available distribution channel, all people need is access. With network computing, all they need is any browser-based device, or network computer, and a connection.

What Is a Network Computer?

A *network computer* or network appliance, sometimes called an NC, is a low-cost device based on Internet standards. Though almost any computing device can conceivably function as a network computer, there are specifications designed for various NC devices. The NC reference platform, controlled by an industry standards organization called the Open Group, laid out a basic design for a diskless computer with random access memory, Ethernet connectivity, and an operating system that is compatible with Java and standard Web browsers. Manufacturers may customize these designs for specific applications. For example, some network computers are designed to act as Windows terminals and run Windows applications stored on a LAN server. But as long as such devices maintain Java and Internet compatibility, most of the benefits of network computing are available to them.

Critics of network computing say it looks a lot like a return to the mainframe era. But users of traditional dumb terminals were severely constrained in how and even when they could interact with data. Network computer users, on the other hand, have all the benefits of a friendly, graphical environment and the power to run applications and work with their own files.

The network computer runs on the same powerful microprocessors as the traditional PC, so it's fast and can run familiar applications like spreadsheets, word processors, and e-mail. But users access data and applications and store their files on a professionally managed network of many computers that have specific content, rather than one general-purpose mainframe as in the past. As with any professionally managed network, this leads to much greater security and reliability in the long run.

Most of us feel more secure with our money in a bank account rather than stuffed under our mattresses. We use an ATM card and our personal identification number to access our account through a network of bank machines around the world. Network computing is like a bank for users' data and applications. It keeps information secure and private and ensures that only those with the appropriate authority can access it.

Network computing is more reliable, too, because professionally managed networks are less risky than stand-alone systems. The power goes off a lot less often than a PC crashes. And when the power goes off, you don't have to go out, find the source of the problem, and fix it. That's done by professionals. So it is with network computing. With fewer systems to manage (servers on the network, as opposed to thousands of individually configured PCs), network computing is more efficient and cost-effective.

SAVING MONEY WITH NETWORK COMPUTERS

Though the first network computers only recently made their debut in 1997, the savings and advantages of NCs will become an irresistible lure for corporate IS shops. While the cost of PCs is dropping rapidly, it's not the initial purchase price that causes corporate nightmares. According to the market research firm IDC (Framingham, Massachusetts), the total cost of ownership of a PC is as much as $14,000 or more *per year*. And lower PC prices don't help much, because most of that cost is in the labor needed to upgrade PC software, back up desktop data, and do everything else necessary to keep PCs running. Analysts agree that moving from client/server to network computing can save up to 40 percent in the total cost of ownership. Many companies are swayed by this arithmetic. At Federal Express, the company is reportedly replacing thousands of 3270 terminals and PCs with network computers. The devices run Java applications, Internet browsers, and legacy applications. Federal Express reportedly hopes to save $250 million per year.

At another company, a large flower telemarketer, the company is replacing 2500 dumb terminals with NCs. Unlike the terminals, the NCs can run multimedia browsers and modern applications with a friendly, easy to learn graphical user interface. The NCs save in several ways. Because users access a new customer service application via a familiar Web browser, they can learn to use the new application rapidly. That keeps training and maintenance costs low. And, because the NCs themselves are inexpensive, the company can cheaply scale up its telemarketing operation during busy times of year, like Valentine's Day or Mother's Day.

A common thread among network computers and network computing is Java, the first programming language specifically designed to enable people to create applications once and deploy them on any computer, regardless of its operating system.

THE ROLE OF JAVA

If the Internet is the earthquake of the information age, then Java is its major aftershock. The Web browser is the universal platform for network-centric computing and Java is becoming a key language for developing Web-based applications. Understanding how it works is important to an understanding of how computing is evolving.

Java was originally designed as a way of delivering applications to small devices, such as handheld computers or interactive set-top boxes for television. It is an interpretative language—it translates its code into the native code of the computer on which it is running. It is designed to run equally well on any microprocessor in any operating system. In other words, it is operating system independent. Operating systems, such as Unix, Windows, and MacOS, ship with a Java Virtual Machine: a program for interpreting Java code. Because of these capabilities, programmers can write Java applications, or "applets," that download in real time and run on the user's machine. Using Java, programmers are creating applets that allow users to access remote databases via a Web browser, regardless of the hardware or software configuration of the machine they are using.

One of Java's great benefits for software developers is that it really levels the playing field. Until now, a large part of any programmer's job was porting: writing computer code that allowed applications to run on various computing platforms. At Oracle, we have often had programmers working to port applications to more than 20 platforms. With Java's "write once, run anywhere"[1] capability, programmers can develop applications more quickly and skip the porting process. In addition, Java is object-oriented, which means that programmers can write pieces of code that perform specific functions and reuse them in many applications. For example, a programmer can create an object called *Customer* that includes all of the information the company has about a customer (name, address, etc.). Then every programmer creating applications that involve customers can simply include the *Customer* object, considerably speeding up programming time and lowering the cost of new applications.

More than a million programmers have downloaded the Java development kit from Sun's Web site since February 1997. And, in a Forrester Research (Cambridge, Massachusetts) survey of *Fortune* 1000 companies, more than 60 percent already use Java for application development. Java is not the only open, object-oriented solution for creating write-once, run-anywhere programs. For a technology that is less than 3 years old, its adoption curve has been incredible.

MAKING PCS MORE EFFICIENT

The PC has brought enormous power to the typical business user. Unfortunately, it has also brought the complexity of a mainframe to every desktop in the corporation. According to a recent survey, on average, an employee using a PC loses 100 minutes a week during the first month a new system is introduced. The Gartner Group, a technology industry analysis and consulting firm based in Stamford, Connecticut, estimates the futz factor—the time users waste futzing with their computers instead of being productive—at $5600 per year.[2]

In the client/server model, every desktop computer in an organization is different from every other desktop in the organization. Each machine can be uniquely configured with hardware add-ins, such as CD-ROM drives and modems. Users can bring new software (and viruses) from home or download them from the Internet. If a user's PC malfunctions during a critical deadline, he or she can't get at their data or applications until they resolve the problem or an expert comes and fixes it. In the client/server world, managing upgrades and maintaining systems is extremely difficult, time-consuming, and expensive. And most companies' MIS departments just can't handle the load efficiently.

Most workers need to run spreadsheets, word processors, document layout programs, and e-mail. Many workers use only one or two applications heavily, especially in functional areas such as order entry or accounting. Likewise, personal computer users routinely use less than 5 percent of the data stored on their PCs. These characteristics make personal computing very expensive. The vast majority of workers at the vast majority of businesses can perform these tasks with low-cost network computers, or with PCs configured as network computers. Any PC can be used as a network computer—all it needs is a Java-enabled Web browser to gain many of the benefits of network computing and to maximize the return on existing hardware investments.

In the network-computing world, if a machine malfunctions, a user can walk over to another identically configured network computer and keep on working. If there's a new version of an application, MIS places it on the application servers on the network and every user automatically gets the new version. When the database is updated, every user has immediate access to the most current information.

With data and applications stored on the network and accessible to all users as needed, you can ensure that everyone has the right tools for the job when they need them. You can also ensure that everyone has access to the right version of a document or presentation, because it is stored on the network.

The network computing model is simple. All the desktop computers are the same from the point of view of the software developer and the network administrator. They are based on open Internet standards. The developer can write an application that he or she knows will need to run on multiple platforms and be certain that it will work. The network professional can focus on keeping the network running and improving performance rather than installing software on thousands of PCs. Network computing lowers the costs of creating, distributing, upgrading, and maintaining software and systems. Network computing lets your scarce MIS resources focus on creating business applications that add value to your organization rather than simply trying to keep everyone's computers up and running.

WORLDWIDE POTENTIAL

The increasing use of Internet and Web technology to create company intranets (connecting all workers to company data), and extranets (allowing companies to work more closely with supply chain partners), is leading to savings that go way beyond shaving computer costs. In the field of education, network computing offers to extend important information resources into all classrooms equally. The low cost and ease of use of this computing model at home means that the potential exists for network computers to become as ubiquitous as televisions. Often, these are thought of as U.S.-centric phenomena or trends. But examples of the emergence of network computing and its impact can be found throughout the world.

QUILMES BREWERY

In 1996, Quilmes Brewery in Argentina faced a challenge. The company needed to establish a better communications system with its network of 500 distributors stretched across a country that is 2000 miles long. Like all businesses, Quilmes needed to find ways to trim the costs of distribution and become more efficient at getting the right products on the shelves at the right time. And the old combination of phone calls, mail, and information conveyed from in-person sales representative visits to the distributors was no longer fast or efficient enough.

Quilmes chose to implement an extranet—an external private Web site accessed over the public Internet. Programmers connected the Quilmes order and inventory systems to the Web site. Distributors can log in to the site from any Web browser, using a private name and password. Once on the site, distributors can access records and statements, place orders, track inventory and pending orders, get information about ship dates, find out which promotions and advertising offers they are eligible for, and request help with special needs or orders. The system was an immediate success. Within 3 months of its launch, Quilmes had connected 150 distributors, representing 70 percent of the company's revenue.

Quilmes estimates the company saved $250,000 over non-Web solutions in the initial installation and that the company has saved $3 million in the first year of use via greater efficiencies in areas such as manufacturing and inventory. For Quilmes, an information system based on the network computing model has lowered costs and complexity and provided greater efficiencies and higher quality service. And it has begun to effect changes in the organization. Easy-to-use information systems mean that salespeople can spend more time on higher-value activities—selling more products to more customers—and less time attending to routine information chores.

Educating Children on 7000 Islands

Network computing promises to have an even greater impact on education. For educational institutions to integrate computing into the curriculum, technology has to be much lower in cost and easier to use. Many schools in many countries around the world simply cannot afford personal computers and don't have the skills or resources to manage them. Even schools that do have PCs and computer networks struggle to keep them up and running. Network computing can bring all of the resources of the Internet to any student, in any country, at any time.

One example of this can be found in the Philippines, where network computing is reaching university students all over the country through a project called Phil-Net. The Philippine Long Distance Telephone Company (PLDT) and Oracle are jointly developing a network computing infrastructure for the Philippines that will extend literacy, education, and commerce throughout this nation of more than 7000 islands. Phil-Net will provide broad access to the Internet via low-cost network computers and a modern networking infrastructure. The Phil-Net project has started with major universities and will expand into other educational institutions. For a country like the Philippines, which is on the brink of becoming a hub for commerce in the Asia-Pacific region, the low cost and ease of use provided by network computing is the only way to raise the level of computer literacy and access for Filipinos.

BECOMING A HOUSEHOLD NAME

If network computing did nothing more than lower the cost of desktop computers and enable more flexible information networks for corporations and educational institutions, it would be a remarkable success. But it still wouldn't be enough to enable an information age. That will come when we put the power and simplicity of network computers into consumer information appliances and make those appliances broadly available.

In the consumer electronics industry, mass market purchases increase once the price point drops. That was the case for VCRs, televisions, and other consumer electronics. The trend is holding for computers, too. As computer prices have dropped, more households have purchased them. But the majority of households still do not own a computer, and the average computer is still too complex. Network computers, which are less expensive and easier to set up and use than PCs, are already available for less than $300. And they are flying out of stores faster than manufacturers can make them. In the first 4 months since RCA's NC debut in October 1997, it quickly sold out in every store.

What can you do with an NC? You can browse the Internet, book a vacation, send e-mail to friends and family members, track your investment portfolio, check out your bank account, or follow your hometown sports team. And the RCA NC is only one type of network computer. There is a whole class of emerging network computing devices that are as low cost and easy to use as the average household appliance.

THE INFORMATION APPLIANCE

Imagine computers that are integrated with our telephones, faxes, and televisions, costing a few hundred dollars. Or less. Companies are working on these and other information appliances today. Networked information appliances are designed to bring the power of computing to everyday tasks on the job and at home.

At last count, there are already more than 100 different devices that don't meet the traditional definition of a computer, but have the capability to access the Net. Today, these include Internet-enabled cellular phones that handle voice, fax, and e-mail from a single device; Internet-enabled television set-top boxes that provide Web access via your television and a remote control; game machines with built-in modems; personal digital assistants like the Newton, Psion, and Palm Pilot; and even LCD projectors with built-in connectivity.

In the next 5 years, we can expect the number and variety of information appliances to expand exponentially. Key technology developments such as ubiquitous smart card readers; faster, energy-efficient microprocessors; lighter, thinner materials; and new display technologies for small devices will spawn a wide range of new appliances, including:

- Specialized single function Web devices such as electronic phone directories.

- Electronic checkbooks that communicate wirelessly with your bank's financial networks via ATMs or wireless Internet connections.

- Car computers that can access updated road and weather information as you drive. Cars may even have built-in networks with information appliances at every seat.

- Wearable computers that are no bigger than a typical Walkman.

- Electronic schoolbooks: portable readers that access CDs and the Web so that teaching materials are always up to date.

- Multifunction devices: handheld devices with built-in cameras, television receivers, or audio recording capability that will let people send multimedia messages from anywhere.

The impact of networked information appliances will be more dramatic than the impact of the PC itself. Certainly, they will sell in greater numbers because they will be consumer-oriented and lower priced than traditional computing devices. And they will be integrated into devices people already are familiar with, such as cars and televisions. People will want to own more than one, so they will never be out of touch with vital information, similar to how more affluent families today equip their teenagers with pagers and cellular phones. While the total number of mainframes sold to date numbers in the millions, and the total number of PCs sold totals a couple of hundred million, billions of information appliances will ultimately be sold. They will reach the economies of scale we associate with radios, phones, and calculators.

OBSTACLES TO THE INFORMATION AGE

The network-computing model is going to be the dominant technical paradigm, there is no question of that. But there are still many obstacles to the information age. Some of these are technical; others are political, economic, and cultural.

The core technologies for putting network computing to work in every sphere of life are sound, but all are enabled by bandwidth—the ability of our data networks to carry information. Bandwidth has to grow in three areas to keep up with the demand for information: inside the corporate network, in the home, and on the public backbones. It is estimated that traffic on data networks is now doubling every year. That means we must double capacity every year. And that's what is happening in our fiber optics networks. In fact, optical capacity is growing even faster than microprocessor capacity, which doubles every 18 months (Moore's Law), while the price is halved.

Inside the enterprise today, most medium to large businesses are already on high-speed phone lines. And the prices of those services are dropping quickly as competition becomes common in telecommunications markets. The same will happen to bandwidth for the home and on public networks.

REACHING THE HOME AND SMALL OFFICE

Developing a low-cost "last-mile" pipeline into the home and small office is a great challenge. This last mile is not only vital due to the growing SOHO (small office/home office) workforce, it's also where consumers are. Until homes have higher-speed access, business-to-consumer electronic commerce won't reach its full potential. However, as new players enter the field (cable, wireless), competition will drive down the price of home high-speed connections, just as it has driven down the costs of long-distance telephone calls.

Wireless and Satellite

If homes don't get wired quickly enough, consumers may just jump to wireless services. Today wireless is helping emerging countries and companies leap into the information age without the investment in physical plant. Soon, we will be able to use satellites to deliver information to customers. Firms such as Motorola are launching major low-orbit satellite services aimed at voice and data. It is likely that by the year 2000, high-speed satellite services will be putting lots of competitive pressure on land-based services. By early in the next century, satellites may offer more bandwidth than cable or phone lines do today.

Cultural Legacy Issues

Each revolution in computing faces cultural obstacles. When the PC was introduced, enthusiastic users literally had to sneak them into some businesses. Organizational attitudes have changed in the past two decades, though. Today, it's likely that managers—many who have grown up with technology—will push hard for IT investment in order to stay competitive.

Some workers may react negatively to network computing. There is a generation of computer-knowledgeable people who may find it difficult to change. A lot of people liked radio in the 1950s and did not want the change that television represented. However, most users care only if their computer helps them be more productive and makes their work easier. Soon, people won't want to store their data locally any more than they would want to keep their money in a piggy bank. Data is safer on a professionally managed network.

Secure Transactions

Consumer and business concerns about security are real. But overall, the protocols and infrastructure for secure transactions are in place. For most end users, the convenience and benefits of electronic commerce will soon outweigh the risks. According to Forrester Research, we are on the verge of an Internet commercial explosion. Revenue will rise from $10 billion in 1997 to $327 billion by 2002.[3]

TRUST, PRIVACY

Privacy of communications and personal information must be protected at all costs. Consumers are already distrustful of a credit system that piles up enormous amounts of data about each of us. Preventing abuses will require a combination of software safeguards and ethical business practices. Ultimately, consumers should control their own information online, giving out their personal profile only to whom they want and protecting it from prying eyes. There are no technical obstacles to this, only political and commercial ones. The Open Profiling Consortium, endorsed by more than 100 computer industry companies, has affirmed a consumer's right to not be spied on by Web site owners. This should be standard business practice.

CENSORSHIP

We all have a stake in securing a free flow of information around the globe. Many countries have already learned that it is impossible to fully police Internet content at national borders. However, bringing a communications network connected to the entire world into your home can be dangerous. Parents clearly want to be able to protect their children from pornography or inappropriate material without monitoring their every keystroke. Freely available smart filtering software should ultimately take care of many problems but corporate accountability and strict enforcement of laws will also be necessary.

COPYRIGHT

The laws we now have on the books are quite specific when it comes to protecting the rights of creators, but the Internet provides new opportunities for mischief. As we move toward digital distribution of recordings, movies, and other entertainment, rights holders will want unambiguous protection of their works. Laws designed for protecting print works in previous eras can't be guaranteed to provide adequate protection for digital works. Copying ideas and information can be done at little or no cost, so revenues will be vulnerable. Methods to protect this wealth should be instituted and executed worldwide. It is critical to all of us.

TAXATION WITHOUT REPRESENTATION

There is another obstacle in terms of how taxation is handled when everything is digital. Consider a piece of music created by a German artist, produced in French, that sits on a server in the United Kingdom and is downloaded by a U.S. consumer in California. It's a thorny problem that will require international agreements and laws to ensure that everyone involved in a transaction gets the value they are due.[4]

HAVES AND HAVE-NOTS

The PC revolution has bypassed the majority of the world's citizens due to cost and complexity. It's truly unacceptable that less than 3 percent of the world's population has access to computers. Standard computers connected everywhere by a standardized, reliable network must be available if we wish to grow and distribute wealth everywhere on the planet. In a networked world, everyone really is right next door to everyone else. We cannot afford to deny participation in the information age.

It makes economic sense to extend access and opportunities to more people. If every child has access to better educational resources through network computing, they will grow into better educated, more skilled, more employable adults. A well-educated and skilled workforce will increase economic output. We can use network computing to provide opportunities to people who are disenfranchised today. Poor children will have better tools in school. Workers will be able to learn the skills they need more rapidly and at much lower cost.

There's a school in south central Los Angeles, George Washington Carver Middle School, that shows the promise of network computing. Oracle installed network computers in several classrooms and wired the school for access to the Internet. Children at Carver are now exploring worlds of information they had never seen before. When I visited Carver in October 1997, I watched a young girl, Sandra Hernandez, as she followed the journey of Sojourner, the Mars explorer, online. Sandra lives in a community that doesn't even have a public library. Through network computing at her school, Sandra can learn about space in ways she only dreamed about before. And she can learn what it takes to be an astronomer, or an astronaut, and what colleges offer the best programs for students interested in space. Network computing didn't just open a window of opportunity for Sandra and the other students at Carver. It opened up a world of possibilities by enabling them to participate in the information age.

GIVE US A PLATFORM

More than 2000 years ago the Greek mathematician and philosopher Archimedes expressed the principle of a platform when he said that with a lever long enough and a point to stand on he could move the world.

A platform, then as now, implies strength. It is something you can stand on, build on, depend on. With a strong platform and enough leverage, you can move anything.

We now have the power to bring the information age to every person, every school, every village, every business. The low-cost network computer is its platform; the Internet provides the leverage.

Now, let's move the world.

NOTES

1. "Write once, run anywhere" is a Sun Microsystems trademark.
2. Rowan, Geoffrey, "PC Wastes Worker's Time," *Globe and Mail,* September 19, 1997.
3. For a detailed discussion on Internet security, privacy, copyright, etc., see Chap. 19, "Stranger than Truth or Fiction: Fraud, Deception, and the Internet."
4. For a detailed discussion on managing international electronic transactions, see Chap. 18, "You Can't Declare Cyberspace National Territory: Economic Policy Making in the Digital Age."

MAKING INTRANETS OBSOLETE

EXTENDING THE ENTERPRISE TO PARTNERS, SUPPLIERS, AND CUSTOMERS

by William J. Murphy
Hewlett-Packard

With the promise of universal connectivity made possible by the Internet, a new era of competition and commerce is upon us. As the traditional boundaries between businesses, suppliers, customers, and partners collapse, the same challenges that encouraged businesses to make intranets a strategic imperative are now making today's intranets obsolete.

The opportunity in the decade ahead will be to leverage the Internet and existing IT investments to extend the enterprise beyond the corporate firewall, improving global competitiveness as well as reaching new markets and customers. Moving beyond the intranet entails the birth of new internetworked virtual enterprises that encompass channel partners, remote workers, suppliers, distributors, and consumers through a secure Web-based global network capable of defining a new era of e-business and competition.

This new model is based on the idea of *inclusion* rather than *exclusion*. The networked economy of the future will depend not on our ability to lock people out but on our ability to integrate partners and customers securely and seamlessly into the enterprise through ubiquitous, personalized security. This paradigm will not only require new technologies, it will also require new attitudes toward information sharing and collaboration. The key to this new model is trust.

For decades, companies have been searching for ways to address the challenges of corporate growth by implementing new decentralized business models and coordinated communications frameworks. These efforts have been hampered, however, by the lack of a technological infrastructure capable of supporting and integrating such large-scale distributed organizations. The Internet and the World Wide Web provide this infrastructure, and they do so in a way that addresses the long-standing need for improved operational effectiveness and global competitiveness.

The key to competitiveness will lie specifically in internetworking capabilities and new organizational models. In the digital economy, organizations will compete together in groups, or e-business *communities*, rather than as individual companies.[1]

As the Director of Marketing for Hewlett-Packard's Internet Program, I have had a unique opportunity to observe how emerging Internet standards and technologies are changing the way businesses access information, collaborate on projects, and conduct core business transactions, not just within the corporate firewall, but beyond it, reaching out to partners and consumers through the internetworked enterprise.

My goal with this chapter is not only to define the internetworked enterprise but also to describe Hewlett-Packard's unique experience and competencies in helping to develop a range of technologies and solutions that will be the essential building blocks for the business models of the twenty-first century.

LAYING THE FOUNDATION FOR THE INTERNETWORKED ENTERPRISE

The ideas that I have been putting into practice are based, to a great extent, on the practical experience I gained as Founding President and Chair of the National Information Infrastructure Testbed (NIIT). The NIIT, now called InfoTEST International, is a private industry-led consortium that tests how large corporations and other institutions can gain a competitive advantage using Internet technologies. Our original goal was to evaluate how the Internet and other information technologies could improve internal operations and strengthen enterprise marketing, sales, customer service, and other essential business priorities. To achieve this we implemented a range of collaborative business trials involving large distributed applications.

In the early 1990s, the Internet was undergoing a major transformation—from a relatively obscure and technical communications medium used primarily by engineers and academics, to a mainstream business tool. Many people in business were still confused about what this new infrastructure was capable of achieving. One of the most popular visions at the time focused on the idea of using the Internet as an interactive entertainment medium, pumping out 500 channels and endless interactive video games. This vision, which is still with us today, is a fairly shallow one.

At the NIIT we believed that a more serious approach to the national information infrastructure was crucial to the country's future. Instead of barraging consumers with 500 channels of eye candy, the various projects of the NIIT set out to improve the quality of the environment, improve medical diagnoses, and improve the access of remote locations to the libraries of the world.

EARTH DATA SYSTEMS: CHANGING THE WAY SCIENTISTS CONDUCT RESEARCH

The NIIT's first project did not result in blazing headlines about megamergers or interactive entertainment. Instead the group quietly labored on something of far greater importance to the country—the environment.

The project, called *Earth Data Systems* (*EDS*), was the first in a series conducted by the consortium. EDS was conceived as a multimedia workgroup application that enabled geographically separated users to work collaboratively with large amounts of environmental data and computing resources. The project joined eight sites across the country using sophisticated software and computer communications equipment contributed by the member companies. Participants shared satellite images of ocean currents, coastline and river data, weather statistics, salt levels, fishing yields, and other crucial environmental data.

Research of this kind has been conducted for years without the use of sophisticated information systems. What has changed, however, is the pace at which information can be gathered and shared, and scientific discoveries made. NIIT identified three ways in which EDS had the potential to change the way scientists worked.

First, many important scientific investigations never take place because the data cannot be located, or finding the data for an investigation among a multitude of different databases is too time-consuming. To overcome this problem, the EDS network was designed with an intelligent query capability which takes a single request for information and then automatically queries multiple sources and databases to find it. The user only has to know what he or she is looking for, not where it might be located.

Second, many scientists are used to working on their own, yet there are vast resources to be tapped through real-time collaboration with scientists from related fields. Effectively, scientific research could now take place in "virtual labs" for the duration of the study.

Finally, scientists have reached a point where the ability to collect information exceeds their ability to make sense of the data. The sheer volume of data collected in the earth sciences field has grown dramatically, making it difficult to interpret all of the information. This is a common problem in many disciplines, including financial markets trading. EDS made use of an increasingly effective solution to this problem, called "data visualization technology," which converts tables into simple graphical symbols. Such symbols could be as simple as a bar graph or as sophisticated as an animated, three-dimensional representation.

We chose EDS as our first reference model for several reasons. First, issues of global environmental change have increased the urgency of extending and applying our knowledge of how our planet works. Secondly, as a useful and relevant large-scale application, EDS provided a real-world context to help us better understand and deploy fundamental information infrastructure services that meet the requirements of users who need to efficiently accomplish real work.

IMPROVING THE QUALITY AND ACCESSIBILITY OF HEALTH CARE

For me personally, the most important project of the NIIT involved the use of the Internet to achieve new breakthroughs in health care.

In September of 1994, in a dramatic demonstration to the Medical Technology Caucus of the U.S. House of Representatives in Washington, D.C., we showed the real-world potential of telemedicine. Using satellite and high-speed ATM terrestrial services, NIIT created a simulated "emergency room" in the foyer of the Rayburn Congressional Office Building, which was linked electronically to the Los Angeles County/University of Southern California Hospital; a medical clinic in rural California; NASA's Jet Propulsion Laboratory in Pasadena; and the Johns Hopkins University Hospital in Baltimore, Maryland.

More than 300 people, including various members of Congress and Clinton administration officials, watched as USC physicians performed an end-to-end telemedicine scenario in which a patient from Maryland, who was injured in an automobile accident in rural California, was treated by the physicians in Los Angeles. The Rayburn Building foyer became a simulated trauma center with the physicians demonstrating several telemedicine technologies.

First, the doctors used "smart" cards to access medical records and radiological images stored at various places and in different formats. They then engaged in three-way cross-country video consultations and rendered three-dimensional images of the victim's chest and abdominal cavity generated in real time by a Cray T3D supercomputer provided by NASA. This demonstration attracted national and international attention as the first ever end-to-end telemedicine network integrating terrestrial ATM with satellite services.

This project represented a pivotal change in my view of the Internet. I could see then that the Internet could enable fundamental changes in the way health care is delivered. This was not just a new marketing or entertainment paradigm. Here was technology that had the potential to save lives and forever change the way people work and communicate. And, even more significantly, the same ideas could be applied in other areas of endeavor. That, to me, was an epiphany. I brought these ideas back to HP where I have done my best to become an evangelist for the Internet.

Many of the lessons we learned at NIIT have now come into mainstream use in the form of corporate intranets, which have become an integral part of most enterprises. More and more companies, including HP, are running their businesses on their intranets instead of on mainframes. Here at HP, over 140,000 users are on our intranet, one of the world's largest, transmitting 10 terabytes of information every month and 1.5 million messages every day.

TOWARD PERVASIVE COMPUTING

One of the most important observations we can make about the Internet is that it is not just a technology phenomenon; it is changing the way we think about business in general. The Internet has had a profound effect on how we think about competition, for example, by lowering the barriers to entry in many types of businesses, such as retailing and banking, where new entrants can set up shop for a fraction of the cost of a traditional brick-and-mortar operation. While this creates opportunities for imaginative entrepreneurs with new ideas, it also means that the established leaders in almost every industry now have to think about where new competition might spring from.

The Internet has also ushered in a whole new way of thinking about how a business interacts with its partners, suppliers, and customers. In today's competitive business climate—created in part by the Internet—the need for effective business collaboration and communications has never been greater, both within the enterprise and among different companies that are linked together in a business chain—the internetworked enterprise. Furthermore, groups of internetworked enterprises will compete together as e-business communities.

If we look at the evolution of business computing over the last several decades, we can see several distinct eras, or waves of changes, from batch computing on mainframes, to distributed minicomputers, to PC-based client/servers—all of which have helped to pave the way for truly pervasive access to information and computing.

The impact of PCs in both the enterprise and the home has revolutionized how we create, access, and use information. PCs today have greater power, speed, and memory, and can handle many of the applications that used to be reserved for larger computers. As PCs become more powerful, two environments are merging together: the personal computer, based on Microsoft and Intel technology, and the systems model, based on RISC (reduced instruction set computing) and the Unix operating system.

The Internet is another major shift in our computing paradigm, perhaps the most far-reaching and significant yet. Like most major shifts, it is associated with chaos and upheaval, as existing technologies, systems, and processes are uprooted. But the chaos will eventually have a positive impact because it will recast old computing paradigms and cause the formation of new structures and alliances that will provide secure, personalized access to new services, information, and content.

The Internet also brings us one step closer to a vision of truly pervasive computing—universal and ubiquitous connectivity. By the next decade, computers will be as commonplace in your home as electric motors are today. We will all own hundreds of them. A few will be directly visible like the PCs and workstations of today, but most will be embedded in information appliances that will perform any number of specialized tasks, and they will be embedded in the networks to which these appliances connect.

In the era of pervasive information systems, these information appliances will be supported by a global, digital information utility, which will dispense multimedia information the way today's infrastructures provide electric power, water, and telephone service. Like them, the information infrastructure will be dependable, consistent, ubiquitous, and will feature standardized interfaces.

The digital information utility will blur the distinctions between home and office, laboratory, school and library—it will make physical location much less important.

Some of the most radical changes, though, are taking place within enterprises. Organizations are recognizing the tremendous potential of this increasingly pervasive infrastructure to cultivate a range of new business alliances, new supplier and partner relationships, and new ways of reaching out to global customers through online commerce. Some of these enterprises are interested in selling information or entertainment content, while others want to sell goods and services using this pervasive infrastructure. But they are all looking for complete, open, and secure technology solutions with advanced systems management that will enable them to do this.

PRESENTING THE INTERNETWORKED ENTERPRISE

It is not difficult to see why networked computing is enabling the internetworked enterprise. From a macroeconomic perspective, every individual enterprise is just one part of an interlinked business ecosystem, if you will, each one dependent, in one way or another, on the others.

In this sense, the internetworked enterprise has existed, to varying degrees, since the beginning of commerce. What networked computing and the Internet are bringing is a degree of interconnectivity that was not possible until now. This means that companies can explore entirely new ways of collaborating with each other and can design new kinds of supra-enterprise structures and entities in order to gain competitive advantage in the market.

This new paradigm enables a world where everyone is closely connected:

- Within organizations via intranets

- Across businesses, suppliers, and customers via business-to-business networks called extranets

- Across organizations, businesses, homes, and consumers via the public Internet

In its simplest sense, the internetworked enterprise is based on transacting business through Web-based networked computing. The starting point, for most companies, is the corporate intranet that allows employees secure access to corporate resources anywhere and at anytime.

The next logical step is to extend that capability—via secure Internet links—to business partners, suppliers, distributors, and retailers—as well as outsourcing partners, remote workers, and customers. It also means supporting electronic business solutions, in order to reach new markets and customers in the electronic market place.

Finally, the internetworked enterprise encompasses the service providers who deliver the supporting Internet infrastructure and value-added technology services. This includes access providers, interexchange carriers, payment facilitators, and others who will offer a plethora of enabling services for this electronic market place.

From a business perspective, the internetworked enterprise gives companies the ability to configure and manage themselves in whatever way best suits their business goals and the desires of their partners and customers.

INFORMATION: A CRITICAL STRATEGIC PRIORITY

Looking back on the information technology revolution, it was more than just technology that provided companies with a competitive edge; it was information itself. Walter Wriston, the former CEO of

Citicorp, has said, "Information about money has become almost as important as money itself." That remark is inscribed in the lobby of New York's Library of Science, Industry, and Business. Now, companies everywhere are focusing on information as a critical, strategic priority. How valuable is information about its customers to a bank, for example? Clearly, possessing such information and being able to study and analyze it in powerful new ways leads directly to valuable knowledge about what kind of products customers want and when they are likely to buy them.

But just having good information isn't enough—equally important are the technology tools needed to gather, store, analyze, and channel that information in a productive way. It's not surprising that industries that rely most on information are also the biggest buyers of information technology. The banking sector, for example, is among the biggest buyers of information technology in corporate America—spending $18 billion in 1996. Chase Manhattan and Citicorp each spend about $2 billion a year on IT. Today's banker probably spends more time thinking about how to harness technology than thinking about how to avoid bad loans or hedge against abrupt changes in interest rates.

And as computing becomes pervasive, these same managers must think not just about how to work with information effectively but also how to keep information intact and secure. In a networked world, the notion of "mission critical" must expand to encompass the entire network infrastructure—including the home as well as the enterprise. The same requirements for up-time, high availability, performance, and scalability—which previously mattered in only a few specialized applications—will become crucial across the Internet as it becomes the platform for pervasive computing, electronic commerce, new broadcast models, and emerging communications channels.

Within the enterprise itself, e-business will bridge all organizational functions: sales, customer service, operations, purchasing, supply, manufacturing, production, transportation, finance, accounting, and personnel.

As information systems become increasingly heterogeneous and decentralized, IT organizations need to shift to an architectural role, planning and designing the corporate network rather than implementing it. And as IT begins to take on the role of business enabler for the digital economy instead of being merely a productivity tool, the IS architecture must evolve from a technology-driven to a business-driven model. This means that the IS architecture needs to be developed in close cooperation with business decision makers.

NEW ORGANIZATIONAL STRUCTURES IN AN AGE OF COMPLEXITY

If the way we use both technology and information is changing, it must logically follow that the way we organize our business structures must also change.

In the past, organizational structures were typically described using a mechanical metaphor. Organizations were seen as something that could be taken apart and put back together according to a straightforward set of rules. But the study of organizational systems has led, in recent years, to a much more complex and organic view of organizations. This view holds that organizations are actually complex systems and, like all complex systems, are subject to unpredictable interactions between their various elements.

An emerging field of study, known as complexity theory—drawing inspiration from disciplines as diverse as biology, physics, philosophy, economics, and computer science—represents a shift from our traditional perception of a world of simple systems that are linear, closed, and predictable, to a view based on complex systems that are nonlinear, open, and interactive. Author and researcher William H. Roetzheim defines complexity theory as, "The study of emergent behavior exhibited by interacting systems operating at the threshold of stability and chaos."

Today's management principles are trying to reflect more realistically what happens in complex organizations. One of the guiding principles behind this view is the idea of self-regulating, self-organizing systems. The science of self-organization tries to explain how novel structures and forms emerge from existing forms.

Self-organization in business means that each department evolves by creating something new from within itself. Change is not brought about from outside but emerges from within. In order to maintain its position, any successful organization will need to constantly self-organize. This is particularly true in today's environment of increased deregulation and networked interdependence.

REINVENTING THE SUPPLY CHAIN

Another important outcome of the internetworked enterprise is the transformation of the supply chain as we know it. Because the Web provides consistent standards that can be used by everyone, regardless of their geographical location or industry, the traditional supply chain disappears in this new environment, and businesses can create their own linkages. Organizational boundaries are blurred. Any entity can communicate with another, creating virtual teams and supply chains.

Let me give you an example of how the internetworked enterprise is enabling a fundamental reinvention of the business supply chain. Around the globe, today's major retail chains import nearly 30 percent of their products for resale. With increasing price competition at the retail level, buyers are constantly looking for more cost-effective sourcing. Enter WOMEX, a business-to-business trading service that brings together buyers and manufacturers from more than 135 countries in an online community.

The WOMEX Online Global Merchandising Communications System was launched in mid-1996 to meet the growing need of international export manufacturers to reach a larger buying community, and for import buyers to locate more sources of potential products. WOMEX's services make it possible for exporters to market and importers to source on a global basis—enabling the parties to communicate directly with each other with no intermediary.

Retailers can compare products from over 135 countries and negotiate product requirements, pricing, and contracts directly with manufacturers. The system offers a product database, a commerce information database, a state-of-the-art communications network, and a news section. It features digital photos of products and factory facilities, product specifications, manufacturer contacts, and e-mail addresses to facilitate direct communication.

Initiatives like WOMEX point to a retailing future that revolves around improved business processes, better cooperation among trading partners, and, most importantly, improved customer service. It shows that successful retailers are taking a "process view" of their business across the internetworked enterprise.

E-business solutions such as WOMEX are leading to an unprecedented level of enterprise, as well as industry, integration. In the near future we may see the melding of today's vast network of small businesses, government agencies, large corporations, and independent contractors into communities of interest revolving around a common business thread. All participants will have the ability to communicate and perform transactions with one another seamlessly across any computer platform. And, clearly, there will be exciting new vistas of opportunity if companies can combine their talents and resources to go after opportunities normally beyond the realm of any one organization.

The time is right for businesses and industries to capitalize on the convergence of commercial interchange, consumer markets, distribution channels, and processing centers. It is time to recognize that the benefits of Internet technology are not limited to one isolated segment of the enterprise. The Internet provides a unifying communications and coordination infrastructure that allows organizations to bring the benefits of distributed decision making not just to remote workgroups but also to business partners and even customers. It empowers every level of the enterprise, providing greater flexibility and the ability to respond more effectively to rapid changes in the global market.

TRUST AND SECURITY

In the world of the internetworked enterprise and e-business communities, businesses are going to have to adjust to a more open way of doing business. Information will be shared, not just within the tightly secured boundaries of an organization but also with partners and customers.

This new openness is going to require a much higher degree of trust. But people are still very distrustful of the Internet and seem to be willing to tolerate far less risk than they would in person-to-person commercial exchanges.

Contrary to popular perception, the Internet itself is fairly safe compared to real-world commercial transactions. Most of us think nothing of handing our credit card to a waiter in a restaurant or giving the number out over the phone to a mail-order clerk, yet these provide far easier opportunities for fraud than sending our credit card number over the Internet.

Another misconception is that most attacks on computer systems come from outside—if we can just keep all the bad guys out, everything will be fine. In reality, the majority of attacks on corporate IT come from *inside*, not outside, the corporate network. Some of the biggest threats to computer security are from mistakes made by poorly trained or careless system administrators and, to some extent, end users. Examples of this are administrators who grant supervisory privileges to inappropriate personnel or allow the use of tools that circumvent LAN security.

Underlying all of this is the need for easy-to-use, scalable security solutions. Security is essential to any successful commercial use of the Internet. As electronic commerce and online transactions become more sophisticated and pervasive, security will need to evolve in lockstep.

But the challenge of security boils down to engendering trust in all the parties that use the system, both within the internetworked enterprise and among consumers. Although the technology measures employed to assure security may already be in place, it won't make much difference as long as users still feel vulnerable.

BUILDING THE INTERNETWORKED ENTERPRISE INFRASTRUCTURE

The construction of a robust public infrastructure that will fully support the concept of the internetworked enterprise can be described in terms of a three-level model. The first level consists of the network platforms and devices that allow end users and customers to easily tap into the power of the Internet. The second level encompasses a range of enabling technologies that must be leveraged in order to spur the growth of strategic new Internet applications. The third level is the convergence of platforms, technologies, partners, applications, and services to provide customers with total solutions in such areas as collaboration, electronic commerce, and electronic publishing. I will discuss all three levels here, with particular emphasis on the second level, the enabling technologies.

LEVEL 1: NETWORK PLATFORMS AND DEVICES

This is the foundation level for any internetworked enterprise and consists of Internet and Web-enabled platforms and devices, ranging from portable hand-held devices to high-end enterprise servers running both Windows NT and Unix. Scanners and digital cameras act as digital on-ramps, channeling multimedia information into the electronic infrastructure. Networked printers act as digital off-ramps, allowing you to print information where and when you need it. To provide a solid foundation for an internetworked enterprise infrastructure, every part of the enterprise needs to be focused on Web- and Internet-enabling products and platforms—even testing and measurement instruments need to have Web front ends to ensure they fit in smoothly with the rest of the parts.

The simple reason is that the Web and Internet standards are the universal bridge that allow interconnection among all kinds of different enterprises and computer systems. Imagine if every house or office used its own unique electrical outlets. It would be impossible to use any of your neighbor's power tools or appliances. That's precisely the situation that exists today with computers—with a multitude of incompatible platforms and applications.

LEVEL 2: ENABLING TECHNOLOGIES

The next step is to take these platforms and create an enterprise-wide, mission-critical infrastructure (see Fig. 13-1). This is the second layer—the enabling technologies and middleware solutions that are needed to create the internetworked enterprise. There are three key technologies here: management/measurement, digital imaging, and security.

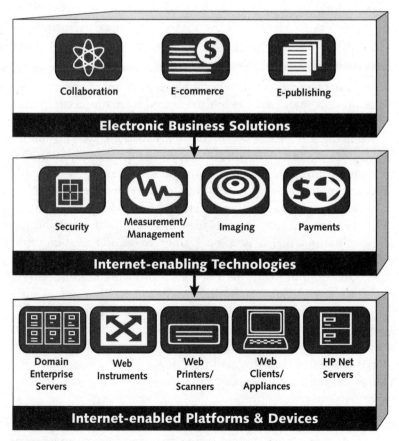

FIGURE 13-1.   The internetworked enterprise infrastructure.

Measurement/Management.   Management and measurement technologies apply to two distinct but related environments: network management and process management.

Network Management.   As corporate networks increase in size and complexity, businesses must be able to manage and integrate complex environments that may be a mix of Windows NT, Unix, and mainframe architectures.

Network management also entails performance issues, which is where test and measurement comes into play. If you can't measure it, you can't improve it. The idea of distributed measurement and control is now becoming a reality, using new types of smart sensors that can be linked throughout the enterprise. Working alongside real-time applications that collect data, such a system would couple the information from the physical world to the business information systems of the enterprise.

The combination of measurement and management also allows network managers to visualize how their intranet is performing— including response times of critical servers, what applications are being used most, and when peak usage occurs.

Process Management.   The second element of management consists of the process management tools required by manufacturers and service providers to build collaborative solutions across their supply chain. By placing key processes at the heart of their system, manufacturers, resellers, and distributors can integrate the key planning activities for production. Such a consolidated view of the supply chain creates many benefits, including shorter production cycles, reduced inventory, faster time to market, and increased market share.

At HP, we are now applying this idea by enlisting the distribution channel as a manufacturing partner. Using cross-enterprise communications, we have developed a Virtual Supply Chain Management capability. This communications backbone provides manufacturers with real-time knowledge of supplier inventories, changes in customer demands, and knowledge of distributor capabilities.

The result is more efficient process management and it allows HP's vendors to take a more active role in the assembly of PCs and servers. HP estimates that this will produce a 10 to 20 percent cost saving based on reduced inventory, price protection, returns, freight, and warranty reimbursements.

Digital Imaging.   Digital imaging is also becoming a key technology for the Internet. Most people agree that the key to successful commerce on the Web is compelling content. The majority of companies today either have, or are developing, strategies to put their content on the Web as catalogs, applications, or marketing materials.

But currently, most of the images on the Web are not of photographic quality, mainly because it would be impractical to download or print them at modem speeds. To complicate matters, there are a wide variety of image file formats but few mainstream applications that support them.

But new technologies are being developed by a range of industry players, including HP, to make visually rich media more practical and ubiquitous for business on the Web. Looking forward, we can expect to see a new class of commercial image applications for the Internet, including image publishing and distribution, catalogs, gallery and museum applications, stock imagery, personal photography, real estate, and many others.

Security. As I have already stated, security is perhaps the most critical enabling technology for the internetworked enterprise. Security solutions fall into three categories: gateway services, platform security, and security management:

1. *Gateway services* include products that secure an enterprise's perimeter and provide secure transactions.
2. *Platform security* secures the application server, client, network appliance, and network communications.
3. *Security management* provides the central repository from which authentication, authorization, general security policy administration, and monitoring take place.

A good example of a company employing the latest security technology to define new markets and achieve new efficiencies is Security First Network Bank (SFNB), the first online banking site to be certified by the Office of Thrift Supervision (OTS). The certification assures customers that the bank is backed by the government and that its security infrastructure is solid.

Customers of this new online bank write checks and pay bills electronically, have access to all current rates and promotions, and because it is all done online and in real time, they enjoy perpetually balanced bank accounts. Best of all, this is one bank that never closes.

None of this would be possible without efficient, effective security. SFNB has provided a total security solution for their banking customers, and addressed the security challenge at all levels, sys-temwide. In fact, the same technology that keeps classified govern-ment information away from unauthorized personnel now keeps bank information protected and available only to valid users of bank applications.

The bank server runs on a trusted operating system, called *CMW+*. Security First is the first commercial application of trusted operating system technology. Developed as a multilevel security platform for government installations by Security First, CMW+ provides a hierarchy of authorizations and privileges that protect the system's functions from outside interference. Further protection from intruders exists in Security First's system of firewalls and filter-ing routers. Each presents an additional barrier between the Internet and the internal bank network. Finally, Security First uses secure sockets layer (SSL) technology to implement the rapidly emerging technology of public key cryptography, used for client and server authentication.

LEVEL 3: SOLUTION FRAMEWORKS

Now that I have laid out the enabling technologies, the next step is to take that infrastructure and its constituent pieces and mold them into electronic business solutions that provide a real business advantage to customers. The three key application areas in the internetworked enterprise will be collaboration, electronic com-merce, and electronic publishing.

In terms of collaboration, technology solutions need to give businesses the capability to break through both organizational barri-ers and geographic obstacles. Clearly, there is a real business advan-tage in being able to tap into expertise, regardless of where it's locat-ed—both within and outside the enterprise. The ability to quickly join forces on a design project with an outside partner, for example, could be done by linking engineers and designers over a networked application that allows each participant to share images, data, and video in real time. The key to this kind of solution is overcoming the incompatibilities of existing platforms and data formats and making meaningful collaboration as easy as plug-and-play, regardless of what technologies the various participants are using.

Solutions for electronic commerce also must act as a universal bridge between incompatible technological standards, if they are to tap into the full resources of the internetworked enterprise. These solutions will also need to address the myriad of different ways that individuals and corporations will want to interact with each other. A consumer may be content to browse a vendor's Web page and order products online, but a business customer will probably have a need for access to much deeper information. This could include accessing detailed product specifications from the vendor's product database or real-time information about the vendor's movement of goods, in order to synchronize the customer's own production facilities.

In the realm of electronic publishing, business solutions will need to support the needs of both the providers of information and content and the consumers of that content, whether they be individuals or businesses. The paradox of our information-rich society is that the more information we produce, the more difficult it becomes to connect the right information with the right seeker. Since the ultimate goal of the internetworked enterprise is to leverage the power of information in a useful way, the ability to organize and channel information effectively through electronic publishing will become imperative.

LOOKING FORWARD: THE FUTURE OF THE INTERNETWORKED ENTERPRISE

Perhaps the best way of predicting the future of the Internet is to understand what is on users' minds today and then projecting technological advances forward a generation or two to see if normal incremental progress is likely to satisfy those needs. When it does not, we must try new things to create the future that users want.

What follows is a glimpse of just a few of the technologies HP is currently working on to address the issues that are at the top of our customers' lists.

MORE NETWORK BANDWIDTH AT FAR LOWER COST WITH UNIVERSAL AVAILABILITY

The rapid increase of multimedia information, richer user interfaces, and the advent of network-based distributed applications all require increases in bandwidth at much lower cost. Because of this, the futures of the computing and communications industries are now tightly linked. Important developments are now taking place in optics technology that could have a huge effect on the telecommunications system.

The theoretical capacity of fiber-optic cable is vast—something on the order of 25,000 gigabits per second, only a fraction of which is actually used today. Thus, if we can find a way to send and switch more signals through a fiber-optic cable, we could increase the system's capacity by at least two to three orders of magnitude.

This suggests that an all-optical system is needed, and the most promising approach is called "wavelength division multiplexing." This is not a new idea, but it is now becoming realistic to think of such systems being deployed in the next decade or so.

Fiber technology has advanced over the last 20 years to the point that the distance across which a usable light pulse can be sent has grown from a fraction of a kilometer to hundreds of kilometers, and the cost has plummeted concurrently. If we could transmit and then select all the theoretically possible frequencies, then the system could work the way that a radio does. At one end, a particular station chooses its frequency; at the other end, the user has what amounts to a big dial. Depending on whom you want to be connected to, you turn the dial and change the frequency of the receiver. Sometimes a movie comes over the pipe, sometimes a newspaper, sometimes the results of an economic model from a distant supercomputer.

There are still technology problems that must be overcome, but once they are, the results will be dramatic. Just one strand of fiber, in principle, could carry 2.5 million separate audio telephone calls—all the phone calls for a large city. Many users of the digital information utility will want enough bandwidth for high-resolution real-time multimedia—say a 100-megabit-per-second-wide channel. That's 10 times an entire Ethernet for each user. With wavelength division multiplexing, a single optic fiber could carry a quarter of a million of these superbandwidth channels.

Other bandwidth-related technologies that are currently under development include infrared diodes for point-to-point communication among devices which are more than 10 times faster than current versions, and 28-gigabit-per-second wireless links for faster, cheaper, hub-to-home service.

MORE ROBUST AND SECURE NETWORKS THAT ARE EASIER TO INSTALL AND MANAGE

Open networks, including the Internet, have other serious problems besides being too slow and expensive. To be more usable for electronic commerce and mission-critical applications, they must be more secure, better at recovering from errors, and easier to install and manage. Users will expect the quality of service they now get from their telephone system. The Internet is nowhere near this today.

Network measurement and management are an important area of research. It's clear that using Internet-based technology can reduce the complexity and lower the cost of system management. In fact, HP has built a very successful prototype of such a system that is operational today in a London cellular trial. This operational trial uses a novel sampling technology, capable of viewing the behavior of the entire network, but with the ability to zoom in to the level of a single call if desired. The reduction in cost and improvement in resolution compared to traditional methods is startling. We have developed technology to rapidly search and sort huge databases of call data records to feed relevant information to associated applications.

As you can imagine, visualizing this mass of information is a difficult challenge, but this novel radar-like display lets operators discover problems at a glance and then click on the relevant part of the display for more detailed information. The entire system can be monitored from a single operator station, which can be located anywhere and replicated as desired.

GREATLY DECREASED TOTAL COST OF OWNERSHIP

Open, distributed client/server networks offer users the benefits of better price/performance than centralized mainframe solutions, but often the resultant network complexity raises the total cost of ownership. In the internetworked enterprise, cost of ownership will be an important competitive differentiator. The Internet offers us an opportunity to achieve dramatic reductions in cost of ownership.

Today, the Internet and the World Wide Web deliver and distribute multimedia information and provide a crude means of asynchronous communication. The infrastructure will evolve to function as a true information utility—it will provide information on demand, just as today's utilities provide electricity, water, or telephone service. But this utility can provide more than just information; it can provide computation on demand as well.

In other words, users should be able to access the utility to solve their computing needs, as well as access information. This means that computing could become a competitive service, rather than the capital investment it is today. Users would pay for computing by usage, as they do for other utilities, and it would no longer matter where the servers were located.

Client utility is a major paradigm shift in computing. It will gradually restructure the industry into utility operators, content and computation providers, solution providers, and the technology suppliers to all of these.

MORE POWERFUL, FAR LESS EXPENSIVE SERVERS

While both the price and performance of computers continue to improve, a major step—similar to the introduction of RISC technology—is needed to address the huge increases in scale that lie ahead. Network servers, in particular, need dramatic gains in performance at both the processor and system architecture levels.

At the network systems level, we are experimenting with new architectural concepts that break the server into separately optimizable functional components. If we are successful, this will allow flexible, dynamic allocation of resources like computing cycles, memory, I/O (input/output), and storage bandwidth in response to individual user requirements and changing system loads.

LESS EXPENSIVE, EASIER TO USE CLIENTS AND MOBILE APPLIANCES

PCs and portable computers have become smaller and cheaper, but they are still far from ideal for mobile applications—in terms of cost, size, computing power, and wireless bandwidth. Their interfaces are often too difficult for the general population to understand.

It seems inevitable that most computers will evolve into information appliances—devices which are dedicated to a particular task, and whose usage seems quite natural to ordinary people. After all, users tend to think in terms of the task at hand and not in terms of how the appliance works. As a result, information appliances will impose much less learning overhead.

In all cases, we imagine very powerful optimized processors supporting rich sets of user interface technologies, such as speech recognition and synthesis, gestures, handwriting, and intelligent, cooperative agents.

Such processors, working as cooperative elements of conventional computers, will energize servers and network elements. As the heart of portable appliances, they will be power-rich intuitive interfaces that use recognition technologies.

We have grown used to the shape and appearance of portable computers, but consider for a moment the idea of a disaggregated computer. What if a computer could be constructed so that the components that are physically and logically integrated today (like the processor, display, keyboard, memory, and storage) could be physically distinct while retaining full interoperability.

A disaggregated approach to appliance architecture will enable truly wearable computers that are unconsciously portable, like watches, fountain pens, and wallets.

Network Boundaries Blur as Security Becomes More Personalized and Ubiquitous

Today it makes sense for us to segment the internetworked enterprise into a series of interlocking components including corporate intranets, business-to-business extranets, and the wide open world of the public Internet. It will not be long, however, before these distinctions start to dissolve. New personalized security technologies such as smart cards and public key cryptography will allow individuals to securely access any device on any network to which they have authorization.

The use of public key security technology provides strong authentication to help protect information and transactions, as well as digital signatures to improve data integrity, ensuring nonrepudiation of electronic transactions. However, this approach does not fully address application requirements demanding that security be more flexible, portable, and easy to use. The combination of proven public key security features with the ease-of-use and portability of smart-card technology is now expected to provide the best approach to meet the broad-based corporate security challenges of the future.[2]

Similar in appearance to a credit card, a smart card stores information on an integrated microprocessor chip located within it. Although still a fairly new technology in the United States, smart cards have been around since 1974 and are commonly used throughout Europe for banking and pay phones. Smart cards currently represent a $4 billion global market that is expected to grow 220 percent by the year 2001.

ARE INTRANETS OBSOLETE?

Intranets became popular quickly because they allowed people to do things that they had dreamed about doing for years, but lacked the standards-based network infrastructure to make them a reality. The reasons for implementing a corporate intranet are well documented: centralized control of information, faster time-to-market for e-business solutions, cost-effective implementation and maintenance, and exploitation of open client/server standards and technology.

While these gains have been significant, the challenge in the next decade will be to leverage the Internet and existing IT investments to move beyond the isolated intranet, surrounded by its moat-like firewall.

For some, the idea of intranets becoming obsolete may seem like a radical proposition, but I am not proposing that companies throw out their intranets. On the contrary, intranets provide the foundation for the internetworked enterprise. In this new era of e-business on the Internet, an isolated, centrally managed intranet is not sufficient. The same decentralized business models that have enabled the rapid adoption of intranet technology must be internetworked beyond the firewall through the use of secure authorized access by authenticated individuals.

The ability to create an internetworked enterprise helps businesses to change the rules of competition. You decide where you want to compete today and the internetworked enterprise makes it possible to shift your market direction online. These changes represent both an opportunity and a threat. Those who embrace the new technology will create vast new opportunities for growth and profitability. Companies that do not embrace change will face new forms of competition for which they are unprepared. There is a fork in the road and the only viable choice is to embrace the new technology. Yesterday's recipe for success will not yield good results in this time of dramatic change.

NOTES

1. For a detailed discussion of e-business communities, see Chap. 1, "Joined at the Bit: The Emergence of the E-business Community."
2. For a more detailed discussion on cryptography, see Chap. 19, "Stranger than Truth or Fiction: Fraud, Deception, and the Internet."

THE NETWORK IS THE BUSINESS

by John Roth
Nortel (Northern Telecom)

One evening not long ago, I decided to log on to the World Wide Web with my home computer and check a competitor's site. Unfortunately, the Internet was having one of those nights. After several tries I managed to connect with the Web site I was interested in. Each time I clicked on a new page and waited for it to download, it was like watching grass grow. I could have walked my dogs in the time it took to download just a few pages. Then, just when I found the information I wanted, a "transfer interrupted" message appeared on my screen and I lost my connection. It was a frustrating lesson in why people call it the World Wide Wait. It's all maddeningly slow and dull to time-conscious business people used to working in a nanosecond environment driven by the accelerating pace of change.

Don't misunderstand me. I think the Internet is one of the great inventions of the modern age, and the World Wide Web is one of the most innovative business opportunities we have witnessed in decades.

But for a business on the Web to realize its true potential, the Internet has to become as reliable and easy to use as the telephone. Pick up the phone and there's the familiar tone letting you know that your system is ready to make the connection you specify. It's always on. It's instant, reliable, secure, and simple to use as an interface. The telephone system has enough capacity for you to carry on an uninterrupted conversation for as long as you want and it's rare to be dropped off the network in the middle of a call. It offers easy access to a wide choice of connections to other phones and to a wide variety of network services and information directories.

Compare this with the present state of Internet access, today's rudimentary form of what I call webtone. If you use the Internet, you're probably like me—you have a love/hate relationship with it. It's an incredible source of information and connection. But the downside is the delays, broken connections, and overall slowness of the system. This includes the World Wide Web, which lacks many of the fundamentals essential for e-business.

Obviously, the Internet is a far richer experience than plain old telephone service (POTS), and the Web is rapidly developing multimedia capabilities. But the fact is that today it's barely adequate for displaying still images. It's totally inadequate for viewing full-motion video, despite recent advances in video-streaming technology.

Webtone today is comparable to the state of the telephone system in the 1930s and 1940s. In those days we placed our calls through operators, coped with line congestion and outages, and used primitive hand sets. We could not have predicted that 60 years later we'd be able to call anywhere in the world from a wireless phone that fits into a shirt pocket. Or that public carrier networks would be so reliable that system downtime would amount to no more than a few hours over a 40-year period. Webtone capabilities have to evolve to this level of instantaneous access, simplicity, and reliability.

You should be able to turn on your information appliance—your personal computer (PC), personal digital assistant, palmtop, or Internet phone—and there's the Web. You should be able to interact instantly with a multidimensional world that contains voice, text, graphics, sound, and moving images, including 3D. You should be able to rapidly browse a Web site or interact with a real-time presentation that includes full-motion video without being told that you have to download a new plug-in or that your transfer has been interrupted.

And you should be able to accomplish all this in a wireless environment. Although optical fibers will play an important role in telecom infostructure for some time to come, the individual should not have to be tethered to this infostructure by a wire. As quickly as possible, we need to make *air* the medium of choice for webtone capabilities.

A lot of digital infostructure has to be put in place around the world before we reach that stage. But we're headed in that direction. Around the end of 1996, we reached the historic milestone when, for the first time, data accounted for more than 50 percent of the traffic moving over the average cross section of the public network in North America. Data has been growing at about 30 percent a year since we've been able to measure it. Voice grows at almost 3 percent. So data's share of traffic on the public network will grow quickly—to 75 percent by 2000, rising to 90 percent soon thereafter. We've entered a new realm where there are more electronic interactions between computers than there are voice conversations between people. This is the foundation for webtone.

Now why am I putting so much emphasis on moving from dialtone to webtone networks? Because the faster we can move to true webtone, the more quickly we can realize the benefits of an interconnected network of global communications, a world of networks connected to other networks that have the bandwidth—communications capacity and power—to move almost any form of digital information in real time.

The Internet is the fastest growing and most talked about part of this world of networks. In business, the Internet has led to intranets and extranets that are having an impact on how we develop local area and wide area networks. Data is increasingly migrating to networks optimized for Internet protocol (IP) traffic that will carry voice as one among many applications. The Web has already begun to replace the PC as the engine that drives the IT industry, which lends even more credence to Scott McNealy, the CEO of Sun Microsystems, who claims that "the network is the computer."

However, at this point I think the network has evolved beyond that definition. Computers, faxes, telephones, personal digital assistants, white boards, video-conferencing equipment, even TV sets—all these devices have become nodes on this much larger entity that we call the network. The network is more than the computer. In today's world, the network is the business.

This was all really driven home to me one weekend when I was doing some woodworking and needed a piece of hardwood for a project. I live in the country, a fair distance from the main shopping centers. One option was to get in my car and drive from lumber yard to lumber yard until I found what I needed. Instead, I turned on my computer, checked out the Web sites of specialty wood suppliers without any thought as to their physical location, compared quality, prices, and delivery capabilities, and ordered what I needed with a credit card. The wood was shipped overnight by courier. The search and solution took about 20 minutes. The rest of the day was mine.

The whole experience was made possible by the network. It provided the essential link between me, the consumer, the wood supplier, Federal Express, and the financial institutions that handle the money end of the transaction.

But, is FedEx a courier system or a communications network? Can you separate the network from the business? The goods they deliver, and the planes and trucks they operate, are all part of a sophisticated network that links every part of FedEx's highly successful operations and allows customers to track their own deliveries online. Without the network, FedEx would not be in business.

I paid for my wood with a credit card issued by a company whose operations are indistinguishable from the network. This company is part of an international financial system where trillions of dollars a day flow across the network between banking and other institutions around the world. Their network is their business.

The retailers I visited online are at the forefront of a growing trend toward electronic commerce and the disintermediation of business—in other words, cutting out the intermediary and lowering costs by direct selling electronically.

Web shoppers are expected to be some 75 million strong by the turn of the century. By then, annual revenues for online commerce could reach $150 billion. But these consumer transactions are just the most visible evidence that the networked digital economy is becoming a reality. The strategic impact of networks is totally changing the way companies do business. This is especially true with transnational corporations, a fact that is reinforced every day at Nortel. As much as any company, our network is our business. We're totally dependent on it.

THE NORTEL EXAMPLE

We built our internal network based on the transmission control protocol/Internet protocol (TCP/IP) in the mid-1980s, so we could capitalize on Internet technologies and applications very quickly. But when it came to deploying them effectively, we ran into a common business problem. We had overlapping networks for voice, data, fax, and video traffic. In 1993, we did a study that found

Fortune 1000 companies maintained an average of 6.7 separate and distinct networks. We had 7.

We soon decided to build an ATM-based very-high-performance wide area network that handles voice, data, and video traffic between 60,000 personal computers and workstations at more than 250 locations around the world. On top of this network, we built our intranet. It was our move from dial tone to webtone. By the end of 1997, we were shipping 4 terabits of information on our backbones every month, supporting 22 million call-minutes, 6.7 billion data packets, and 18,000 audio conferencing hours.

This reconfigured network connects a global corporation of employees, management teams, R&D labs, and manufacturing operations. Everything is on the network, from production schedules and purchase orders to human resource profiles, design files, sales reports, and financial results. When we expand into a new country, we put the network in place before we start hiring sales people because we know that, without the network, the sales force will not be productive.

We're a more effective company because the network provides us with a custom-built approach to workflow and project management. It helps us get maximum efficiency from all functions and departments, no matter where they're located, and it drives decision making down several layers in the organization, closer to the marketplace. The network encourages more coordination, collaboration, and use of virtual teams.

Our information systems group, for example, created a computing platform that software developers can use to design the network-oriented applications we need to run the business better. Purchasing groups created a Web site that cuts the time from initiating a purchase requisition to delivery of the goods by 80 percent.

Expense reporting is now virtually paperless. Call the application by computer or phone, and it adds up expenses, converts currencies, and processes payment to whatever account the employee specifies. About 40,000 employees complete about 18,000 expense transactions every month.

Our real-estate managers track facilities and generate reports with a project-management application. Space planners navigate inside buildings, moving to any floor to view layouts and workspaces with a few clicks of a mouse. Reworked layouts are called up by future occupants at their desktop. We've found that lots of costly trips between sites are no longer being made.

At our major labs, the local library used to be charged with meeting the information needs of our knowledge workers. Material often had to be sent via mail or fax and, as we expanded globally, the time between the request and the receipt of the materials began to lengthen. With the new network in place, our information resource group was able to set up a Web site so employees could have desktop access to market research, competitive intelligence, technical journals, conference proceedings and reports, standards documents, and general business information.

Given the intense competition in our industry, we've had to tighten communications between our customers, sales force, and business units. A company such as ours has thousands of products that are continually changing. An application called sales.com gives 6000 sales and marketing staff around the world access to up-to-the-second Nortel product information and data on what the competition is offering. They can monitor the status of customer orders and create orders directly through the application.

Sales.com provides us with a lot of competitive benefits. Our order processes are continuously improving, our sales teams are more responsive to their customers, and we deliver information to partners, joint ventures, distributors, and major customers instantly. Through improved productivity, performance, and customer service, we estimate the value of this tool at around $50 million annually.

We're also utilizing an interactive broadcast-quality video network, called *Nortel Vision*, which delivers programs over a combination of digital fiber and direct-broadcast-satellite networks. We've delivered product training to more than a dozen customer locations simultaneously, run distance-learning courses internally, and held meetings between senior executives and employees at sites on different continents.

Now that the Internet is more secure, we're also creating additional linkages to customers and suppliers through extranets. Customers want open systems, uninterrupted service, and support wherever they do business, all customized to fit their individual requirements and priorities. That makes it critical for us to collaborate with them to know their needs and expectations. Both of us depend on the timely flow of information that extranets provide.

Working within agreed-upon security systems, we go deep into customers' databases to understand their needs and download the information—a far simpler and less costly process than having armies of our people descend on the customer. The network provides the real-time dialog we need to deliver the kind of solutions and services that lead to long-term relationships. On the other side of the equation, customers access our databases and become far more involved with customized product design. Our suppliers and distributors also use the network to determine what we need.

The competitive benefits of the network are obvious. But we're also seeing real productivity gains. The transformation of our network in early 1996 resulted in first-year operational savings of $5 million. Even a productivity increase of as little as 2 percent of revenue saves a company the size of Nortel nearly $300 million a year. But we're not alone. At Nortel and every other global corporation, the network has become the business.

Why has networking become so mission-critical for so many industries? There are a number of energizing forces causing us to reframe the familiar:

- Topping the list is worldwide deregulation and global competition

- Equally important is the decreasing cost and increasing power of technology, including wireless technology

- The networking phenomenon of this decade—the Internet and its corporate counterpart, the intranet

DEREGULATION

The telecommunications industry isn't just being deregulated—it's being revolutionized. With 70 countries signing on to the World Trade Organization's agreement to open up telecommunications markets, there'll be far more global competition and many more network service providers. Deregulation is happening all over the world as a vast tangle of technical, economic, and political problems get solved. Deregulation throughout the European Union, starting in 1998, is transforming the once bureaucratic, slow-moving postal, telegraph and telephone companies (PTTs) as it did in the United Kingdom in the 1980s. Telecommunications acts have been passed in Canada and the United States creating fiercely competitive markets. In the Far East, Australia, Hong Kong, and the Philippines have taken their place among the most deregulated markets in the world. In Japan the unthinkable is happening—NTT is being privatized. More than 16 Asian countries are planning some form of deregulation or privatization of their telecommunications services.

With deregulation, network operators such as Bell Atlantic, Ameritech, BellSouth, and British Telecom, know they're going to lose market share at home, so they're looking to build their business and generate revenues elsewhere. These companies, along with network suppliers, such as Nortel, are showing up in Eastern and Central Europe, the Middle East, Asia, and Latin America. As a result, we'll soon be seeing developing countries with networks as good as or better than many networks in the most advanced industrial countries.

For 20 years the International Telecommunication Union (ITU) has insisted that developing countries can compete in the global market only if they have strong information-based economies glued together by information networks. In other words, they must invest in infostructure. China, for one, has taken that message to heart and has targeted the creation of telecommunications networks as the top priority in its economic planning. China is not alone. Most nations of the world are acknowledging the essential role of network technology—more than $3 billion a week is being invested in information networks.

Nearly as many new public networks will be built between 1997 and the year 2000 as have been built in the last 100 years. With undersea optical fibers, satellite arrays, and new wireline and wireless networks, we're about to see a huge increase in the capacity of global communications. The amount of traffic on public and private networks is expected to increase tenfold by the turn of the century, with most of that traffic associated with high-speed data, video, and interactive applications.

TECHNOLOGY

The advancement and decreasing cost of technology is making this possible. Yesterday the high costs associated with technology meant that our basic product—bandwidth—was a scarce resource and had to be closely managed. In that environment, the best solution was the creation of monolithic communications companies that operated as monopolies.

Today, everything has changed. Networks are evolving toward multimedia applications—expanding the volume of networked voice, graphics, data, and video traffic at an accelerated pace and increasing the pressure for even greater bandwidth. As this happens, communications and computer technologies are becoming closely intertwined.

The cost of technology has plummeted while its capabilities have soared. Bandwidth and processing resources continue to become cheaper and more plentiful. Network service providers are focusing on delivering better and less costly services of greater value to the users. And users want everything in real time, characterized by microsecond delivery of digital information in the form they want it and when they want it.

Telecommunications technology in general is advancing along the same exponential curve being followed by computer technology. Computer technology has been driven by advances in microprocessor technology predicted by Moore's Law: that the density of transistors on chips—and therefore the performance relative to the price of computers—doubles every 18 months. Moore's Law may be superseded by Intel's new technology. The new development alters the basic physics of chip design and essentially doubles the storage capacity of each transistor on a chip. This means that instead of 18 months, microprocessor performance could double every 9 months or less.

In the telecommunications world, the cost—though not necessarily the price—of transmission is being cut in half about every 3 years. This has been going on since the first transmission across the Atlantic in 1901, sent from Cornwall, England, and received by Marconi in St. John's, Newfoundland. In 1997, Nortel began deploying OC-192 digital systems that delivered 10 gigabits per second. With wave-division-multiplexing technology, the OC-192 can be scaled up to deliver 80 to 160 gigabits.

Right up there on the leading edge is one of Nortel's customers—Qwest Communications, a carrier's carrier in the United States. Qwest is building a prototype network for the twenty-first century using fiber-optic technology. At its core are two dozen pairs of hair-thin strands of glass that can carry 25 million voice calls simultaneously. More than 80 billion bits of information can move down the pipe every second. This is just the starting point. Qwest will be able to boost the network's power to terabit speeds, moving 1 trillion bits per second.

In the mid-1990s, all the phone networks in the world combined only carried an average of 1 terabit per second. One terabit is equivalent to all the voice traffic in Europe. Two terabits is equivalent to all the voice traffic in North America, switched and routed every second. At that speed, the network could deliver the contents of the U.S. Library of Congress across the country in 20 seconds.

That kind of capacity is reshaping the economics of the traditional telecommunications industry. Let's put this in another perspective. Consider the cost of a long-distance call. In 1915, the average cost of a peak-hour, weekday, coast-to-coast 3-minute call was $20.70. It dropped to $9.00 in 1930, $2.50 in 1950, and $1.45 in 1974. By 1997, rates were being advertised at 10 cents a minute. Competition and deregulation are bringing wholesale costs down to 1 or 2 cents a minute. Internet telephony and Internet fax, just getting underway, will change the equation yet again and prices will plummet even more.

Distance will no longer be a factor—city to city, coast to coast, or continent to continent, it just won't matter. With the death of distance, organizations operating on a global scale will be able to reach customers, suppliers, and business partners they were never able to communicate effectively with before. And advances in data communications have already created a whole new breed of virtual office workers—from road warriors with laptops to home office entrepreneurs and telecommuters.

Wireless communications technology is also advancing rapidly, letting new networks roll out more quickly and inexpensively, while creating a new mobility. In Finland and Sweden, there are now about 30 cellular and PCS subscribers per hundred people. In Canada, we're at about four to five subscribers per hundred people. Worldwide, one new telephone subscriber in six purchases a mobile phone.

Wireless has grown from a blip on the radar screen in the early 1990s to a $2.5 billion business today. And the growth curve is accelerating. By the year 2000, the number of cellular subscribers may reach 400 million. Early in the next century, there will be as many wireless networks in the world as fixed wireline networks. As the digital revolution proceeds, virtually all personal voice phones will be wireless.

THE INTERNET

Of course, the key driver fueling the appetite for more bandwidth is the unexpected champion in the world of networks, the Internet.

Who would have thought 10 years ago that the Internet would undergo a metamorphosis from an arcane academic and military network for information exchange to the most exciting force in business today, with its incredible growth rate continuing.

Back in 1993, the year the Internet was poised for takeoff, there were about 1.3 million host computers. A 1997 survey conducted by Bellcore's Internet Architecture Research Laboratory indicates that the number of host computers grew to 26 million as of September 1997, up from 14.7 million a year earlier. In another report issued in 1997, the research company, IDC, states that the Internet is evolving into the largest construction ever conceived. The number of Internet users is expected to increase from 75 million in 1997 to 250 million in 2000.

The Internet, by doubling every 12 months, seems to be following the dictums of Metcalf's Law, named for Robert Metcalf, the father of Ethernet and a founder of 3Com Corporation. Metcalf's Law states that when you connect any number, n, of machines, you get n squared potential value. It does not matter what the machines are—cars, telephones, or computers. Cars without roads and telephones without networks are of little use. Provide the infrastructure, or in the case of telephones and computers, the infostructure, and their value grows at an exponential rate.

It's companies recognizing that kind of value that are now in the vanguard of Internet development. They're looking at the Internet as a new medium for reaching employees, customers, and suppliers, and they're demanding a higher class of network than the Internet can now provide. They're pushing for greater availability and integrity, and they want to make sure the security systems are in place before they put sensitive information on their intranets and extranets.

But the value of intranets has been demonstrated so well that a new intranet is created every 4 minutes. Every four-tenths of a second, another user comes online. This is a good sign that more companies realize the network is the business and that they ignore this new paradigm at their peril.

Companies are also leading the way to webtone capabilities with ever increasing speed. One example that I'm familiar with is the network Nortel created for the Dallas Cowboys football team (*www.dallascowboys.com*). Business-to-business transactions can take place, while fans visiting the Web site can take a virtual reality tour of the stadium, watch quick-time videos featuring the Cowboy's players and cheerleaders, check out player bios and statistics, and purchase tickets and Cowboy-related merchandise.

To provide that kind of instant, accessible, and feature-rich webtone in the public network, the network is going to have to be transformed. Right now, it simply can't supply the service levels required, but there's a kind of chicken-and-egg situation. If the network and content providers can respond faster and offer more services, usage will grow. And more usage can fund the network's increased capabilities. But, if the response time chokes and services suffer, people will lose interest and usage will fall off.

This is a catch-22 situation for the telephone companies. The business case for participating in the Internet is not always clear and it's not always good. They're finding that a lot of the capacity they have developed for voice traffic is being sucked up by the Internet, so they add switches to handle more voice and right away more Internet users come online. The problem is that the revenue streams from the Internet are pretty small—it is certainly not throwing off enough money to let the telephone companies make massive investments in infostructure. So the business problem that has to be solved is this: how do the organizations responsible for carrying Internet traffic realize a reasonable return on their infostructure investment?

Another tough problem relates to the growth of the Internet backbone infostructure. International service providers are faced with the fact that the Internet is far from a global enterprise. More than half of the intra-European and intra-Asian Internet traffic is routed through the United States. Outside of America, there is a lack of high-quality, affordable, and easily available infrastructure. All of this could slow down the globalization of the Internet as nations outside the United States attempt to link with a North American infostructure that's already beginning to show signs of strain.

As the network becomes the business, there is a downside. If your network crashes, you're out of business. That's one of the reasons why Chief Information Officers and Telecommunications Managers are on 24-hour call—if the network burps, the whole organization gets a stomachache. Business over the Internet is no exception. As it's presently configured, the Internet could soon suffer a severe case of the hiccups as consumer and business traffic swells.

We have to build networks that have the capacity, reliability, security, and quality of service to make business more competitive. Webtone networks should be as robust as the public carrier networks that are the foundation of modern telecommunications. They operate 24 hours a day, 7 days a week, with down-time measured in a few minutes per year. This is in contrast to some data networks in service today, which measure downtime in hours per month, sometimes per week. This will not be acceptable as companies, large and small, recognize that the network is the business. Like connectivity and open architectures that enable internetworking, reliability will be a key factor in determining which vendors and service providers find success.

Fortunately, technology is up to the challenge. New high-speed switches and routers are being developed. New routing schemes are being designed that will create paths for high-bandwidth multimedia traffic which are separate from the links handling low-bandwidth transmissions such as e-mail. At the core of these networks will be incredibly fast switches using ATM and IP technologies. High-speed Ethernet is making an impact on corporate intranets. Routers of gigabit and eventually terabit class will handle the traffic at the edges of the network. Computers, network computers, multimedia devices, white boards, even the most powerful parallel processors, will all become subsystems of the network. Higher-speed access technologies—from broadband wireless to cable modems to compression technologies that deliver broadband over copper wire—are beginning to be deployed.

A particularly promising development is progressing in the academic community, where more than 100 universities in the United States have joined forces with a range of corporations to form a consortium to deliver information 100 to 1000 times faster than today's Internet. Internet2, as it's being called, will initially connect participating campuses at 600 million bits per second—enough to transmit a 30-volume encyclopedia in less than 1 second. Internet2 is planned to reach speeds of 2.4 gigabits per second. That's 2.4 billion bits a second compared with the 56,000 bits per second being piped through the fastest modems now generally available.

At this speed, Internet2 can handle a range of broadband applications including online collaborative research, distance education, and video conferencing. Although Internet2 will be a vast improvement, it's still limited. It's when you venture into the terabit range that bandwidth constraints really begin to disappear and the use of the network becomes limited only by your imagination.

Internet2, like the original Internet, is designed to improve communications and network access for the academic community but its developments will quickly spread to the business community and everyone will benefit. It's not just multimedia and virtual reality applications that are motivating us to take a new approach to network technologies and architectures. Even relatively pedestrian applications—like order tracking or adding mobile workers to the Net—are pushing the envelope. We need to be able to create network solutions that can handle 100 percent growth in traffic every year for the foreseeable future.

Even if Moore's Law isn't repealed by the new Intel technology, we are still looking at the creation of ever more powerful PCs and servers. More MIPS (millions of instructions per second) means more powerful, varied, and demanding networked applications. The Intel breakthrough will make it happen all the more quickly. These advances in microprocessor technology will allow us to transmit and receive full-motion video with the quality of high-definition TV backed up by crystal-clear sound. We will be able to move our businesses closer to our customers and provide service no matter where we are and where they are—at work, at home, or on a ski slope in Colorado. We'll be able to design networks that are flexible and that can be tailored to meet the personal needs of individual users and help them be more productive.

We'll be able to do all this and more, but only if the network can support this explosion of data-communications traffic. That means developing intelligent networks that make network-based applications instantly available to users, whether in the home or on the job.

One ramification will be the demise of some network vendors. Developing integrated networks on a global scale is a complex undertaking requiring competence in dealing with a range of technologies such as photonics, software-system design, microwave, silicon, digital signaling, and wireless. Many companies won't have the depth of experience or the critical mass of R&D to develop such highly sophisticated, business-critical networks.

From the user's standpoint, there's nothing but good news. The constraints of physical distance will disappear. It won't matter whether you're in Toronto, Thailand, or Timbuktu. You will interact with your colleagues, customers, friends, and acquaintances using the appropriate network subsystem—whether it's your PC or a virtual reality machine—at the speed of light.

It's a fairly straightforward progression to arrive at this point. We must build the network infostructure and the networking capabilities—particularly the Internet capabilities—that will create fully functioning webtone, interconnect the business world with power networks, and, in the process, bring about the death of distance.

What is not straightforward are the social and economic changes that these technological advances will bring about. How will they alter the patterns of people's lives and work? What will happen to national borders and the way trade is conducted? With the advent of global communications, will cultures tend to become more diversified or more homogeneous?

I don't like to use the phrase "paradigm shift" indiscriminately. But in the case of webtone and IP networks—with the impact they'll have on the way the world communicates and exchanges information—I think we're looking at a shift of that magnitude. It's also a fundamental shift in the economics of telecommunications that will result in changes in the structures of industries and companies.

Here's another aspect of the shift that will have a significant impact for business and society: mass electronic communication is profoundly liberating, empowering, and democratizing. This has tremendous implications for how our companies are organized and structured, as well as for society.

Obviously, we're faced with great challenges as we move from dial tone to webtone. But we're being presented with even greater opportunities. And as we approach the turn of the century, what could be better than facing that world of opportunities and realizing the potential of the digital economy, which has reshaped business and is already touching every aspect of our personal lives.

CYBERCOMMUNITIES

BETTER THAN
BEING THERE?

by Robba Benjamin[1]
Sprint

Despite the hype surrounding today's digital "everything," the real secret to charting a successful course in cyberspace lies less in the paradigm of technology than in the construct of community. Think about it; we may communicate more easily and frequently with more people across geographic, cultural, economic, and political boundaries, but how often do we really *connect*?

The true "killer app" of tomorrow's cyberspace will be a blend of hardware and software that lets us communicate easily, immediately, universally, inexpensively, and—most importantly—on our own terms. It will effectively allow us to be in one, two, *many* places at once; open more doors to communication while giving us more control over our environment; enrich and multiply the contexts for meaningful personal and commercial transactions; and provide us with the opportunity to participate more fully and freely in society.

Consider the following: During a break in a typically hectic work day at my office in Kansas City, I want to visit my grandmother who lives half a continent away. She has always been a central part of my life as a friend and confidante. It's not the scheduled visits on holidays I miss, but the spontaneous expressions of love that breathe life into a relationship.

Currently, I have three options, none of which is satisfactory. I can shirk my business responsibilities, drive to the airport, and arrive at my grandmother's house several hours later for a rushed visit. Or, I can call her on the telephone and simply speak with her in the single dimension of voice. Or, given the effort, limitations, cost, and frustrations inherent in the first two options, I can let my impulse to visit my grandmother pass and turn back to my work, comforting myself with the hope that I will see her soon enough and call her on the weekend. Sadly, I usually default to the last choice. It shouldn't have to be that way.

My vision of cyberspace is one that will allow me to take advantage of that work break to visit my grandmother at her home in Portland without leaving my office in Kansas City. I want to be there in three dimensions, using five senses. I want visual and auditory clarity so that I can see and hear nuance. I want true-to-life color and texture and fluidity of motion. In every way I really want to feel as if we are in the same room. I want to be part of the same family—the same community—not just on special occasions, but every day, at the same time fulfilling my business obligations. I want to be in many places at once to accomplish all my goals.

This illustrates the true promise of cyberspace—infinite opportunities for human interests and activities to be shared. What we are doing today—building infrastructure, gaining access, and publishing information—is merely the first phase of this communications revolution. The ultimate goal is to create a cyberspace that enriches and transforms our various and overlapping relationships and associations—to create community.

CREATING COMMUNITY IN CYBERSPACE

Not everyone shares my enthusiasm for this exciting new realm. Some critics see cyberspace as somehow destroying the "real world," and replacing it with a faint, electronic simulation that is less "real," less personal, less human.

Typical is *War of the Worlds: Cyberspace and the High-Tech Assault on Reality*[2] by Mark Slouka. He writes, "It is possible to see, in a number of technologies spawned by recent developments in the computer world, an attack on reality as human beings have always known it."[3] He worries that reality "may one day come with an asterisk"[4] and that we will increasingly choose "simulations" over the real McCoy. "Instead of exploring a local farm pond, or catching praying mantises in the park, today's eight-year-old can explore the world on the computer."[5] By allowing us to evacuate the world of shared experience and ignore the fact that most of the "human race [is] more immediately interested in survival than transcendence," argues Slouka (and most cybercritics), cyberspace undermines responsible community and fosters fragmentation and alienation.

I don't share this view. In my mind, cyberspace cannot and will not replace the "real" world. Cybercommunities will *supplement,* not *supplant,* existing communities. By allowing more people to interact in more ways and in more settings, cyberspace facilitates greater communication, more participation, deeper human connections, and, by extension, community.

I think that the rise of virtual communities will actually result in an increase in "real" communications. Because of greater opportunities to connect in cyberspace, people may follow up with face-to-face meetings more often, whether for business or pleasure. Furthermore, so-called real communities will be better supported because of their virtual emanations, and vice versa.

Make no mistake: communications technologies may make us more "efficient," but they will not necessarily make us "better" human beings. Our vices—and our virtues—are likely to continue to achieve full expression through this new medium, and there will be new issues to resolve in cyberspace such as digital fraud and forgery, cyberstalking, flaming, etc., all of which have real-life consequences.

But it is also my belief that cyberspace enables and advances the positive elements of community while minimizing some of the traditional negative elements. For example, territory (as we know it) is not an issue in cyberspace. There is room for everyone and there are no "national" borders, at least not yet.

Furthermore, because cyberspace does not require its "citizens" to forgo ties to other places, real-life communities may be more easily preserved. For example, a person can still leave "home" for extended periods of time, yet continue to work and/or play—cheaply, easily, and, one day, literally—with family and friends left behind.

One important issue, however, is the preservation of uniqueness when the elements of community—existing as bits of data that share a common language (TCP/IP and HTML/HTTP, for example)—become even more easily exchanged in cyberspace. Homogenization is always a risk with increased interaction and exchange, therefore, the challenge will be in providing the tools that enable heterogeneity and unique expression within cyberspace.

For me, the question then, is not whether cyberspace is "good" or "bad," but how to best maximize its potential. People are already meeting each other, forming relationships, marrying, contributing to causes, making purchases, getting burned, being rejected, having a great time, starting businesses, and even making a living in cyberspace. Indeed, cyberspace—sometimes rightly castigated for being as cold and sterile as the dark side of the moon—must always be seen as the technical means to very human ends. The main advantage of cyberspace is that it allows us to belong to thousands of communities at once, greatly multiplying our connections and enriching our lives. It preserves local cultures while granting access as never before to—literally—a World Wide Web of new cultures, people, ideas, and experiences.

REQUIREMENTS OF COMMUNITY

Communication and community share far more than a common etymology. Communication is a prerequisite for community, just as community provides a context for meaningful communication. Community is a prerequisite for the trust and interdependence that sustains both personal relationships and a market. Though distinct from their traditional analogs, online communities share the same essential characteristics. Both have similar requirements for success. Communities, whether "real" or virtual, are defined by:

1. Shared space
2. Shared values
3. Shared language
4. Shared experiences
5. Shared purpose

At a national level, for instance, Americans inhabit defined boundaries (neighborhood, city, state); generally ascribe to a common set of values (life, liberty, and the pursuit of happiness); speak largely in various dialects of English; believe themselves to speak a common language of optimism and hope for a better future (The American Dream); and have bonded over tragedies (the Kennedy assassination), triumphs (the moon landing), and common activities (voting, the Super Bowl). Without always being able to define the nuances, we know what it is to "be an American."

It is important to see that membership in one community, especially in the case of cybercommunities, need not preclude inclusion in another. It is common for people to "belong to" many communities. On one level, we may define ourselves as American. On more local levels, we may define ourselves as midwesterners, say, or as Kansas Citians. All such designations carry their own values, languages, and experiences. Community need not be tied to geography: lawyers, Boy Scouts, and Roman Catholics all occupy similar spaces (courtrooms, camps, and churches), share certain values, speak a certain vernacular, and undergo common experiences all over the world.

While shared spaces, shared values, shared languages, shared experiences, and a shared purpose may be prerequisites, by themselves they do not guarantee "community." A commuter bus stop, for instance, fulfills all the criteria: The same people occupy the same place every weekday morning. They mostly talk the same language, share the same values (hard work, reliability, diligence), and they share the common experience of waiting for the bus, if nothing else. But no one would confuse such a setting with a community. One could say the same about most sites on the World Wide Web today. While they provide a common space for individuals who share many things, they are more like bus stops than communities.

That's because there are other crucial, defining elements of community. First, individual members must feel the group has a high degree of *relevance* to their identities or goals. Put another way, we could ask why individuals choose to join particular communities. What does someone get out of being an American, living in Kansas City, going to Mass, shopping at Nordstroms, drinking Coke, buying only Apple computers? After all, these are, for the most part, voluntary associations.

People join communities because they must. As sociologists and philosophers have remarked throughout time, human beings are social animals with needs that cannot be met adequately in isolation from one another (except possibly for the rare ascetic or saint). An individual joins *particular* communities because she expects to find them self-affirming and satisfying. They are avenues through which she can actualize her potential. She acquires a certain identity, gets a certain pleasure, a certain status from seeing herself as an American, a Macintosh fanatic, a Buddhist. In the end, communities are tools through which members can experience themselves—who they are and who they might become.

That leads to the second condition for sustainability of community—active engagement. One can find relevance in a library or newspaper or online publication if the content resonates with the reader's interests, goals, needs, and aspirations. However, it is when the *community member* actively engages with others, helping to establish direction, goals, policies, content (whether directly through production or indirectly through selection), context, and, especially when the individual gives and receives recognition for the effort as well as takes pleasure in the results, that a sense of community is established.

Thus, relevance, social engagement, and participation in direction are necessary to sustain community. They are determined not by the community developer but by the community members. What transforms a supermarket into "my grocer," for example, is not necessarily the merchandise or the display or the prices or the location (although these are all important). What transforms a place into a community is its gestalt: one's perception of, and resonance with, the people, the merchandise, the methods, the texture, the very rhythm of the place, the degree of one's participation in and perceived impact on the environment.

CYBERCOMMUNITIES TODAY

Until recently, scenarios of multidimensional, full-sensory presence of the sort required to support my vision could rightly be dismissed as fantasy, the province of comic books, science fiction novels, Hollywood movies, and wild-eyed visionaries. However, there are an increasing number of interesting explorations and first attempts to create community online that illustrate not only the potential for cybercommunities to evolve, but also the ability to overcome some of the barriers that would prevent these communities from emerging in the physical world.

Consider Starbright World, a multimedia network that creates a virtual playground for seriously ill children hospitalized for extended periods. The result of a collaborative partnership between The Starbright Foundation, Sprint, and Intel, the network will link over 100 children's hospitals across the United States by the end of 1998. With the guidance of filmmaker Steven Spielberg and others, the Foundation is responsible for designing the world and the children's experiences.

The Starbright Network features a three-dimensional play space where children in different hospitals can actually play with one another in real time. Through a unique application of game technology, participants communicate with one another through a personal computer controlled with a mouse or joystick.

The children represent themselves through "avatars"—special screen icons representing a chosen character. They can select familiar figures such as E.T. from a menu or scan images into the system and create their own avatars. Since many of the children have undergone chemotherapy or other physically debilitating treatment programs, the avatars allow them to interact less self-consciously. Ironically, they can be more themselves when freed of their physical bodies. Through the avatars, they can explore several environments: Tropical World, Cave World, Sky World, Game Arcade, and Building Zone. The view of the shared online environment is from the perspective of each of the participants. Therefore, the children can see one another approaching and choose whether or not to interact. They also have the option to appear in their physical forms through a simultaneous video/audio conferencing tool.

Starbright Network links children to a peer group that shares similar challenges and experiences. Early indications are that this contact could have beneficial medical effects, helping in areas such as addressing isolation, pain distraction, and socialization skills. Starbright World demonstrates how even a rudimentary cyberspace can facilitate a virtual world that improves upon the "real" world. The children share the common language not only of their exploration of the online experience but also of their aliases.

The lesson for community builders of the future is to keep the community member's needs and values paramount. To succeed in any sustainable way they must supply all the tools required for people to form *their own* successful sustainable communities. Starbright is successful because it brings together members of the same peer group who would otherwise remain physically separated.

Another unique and promising multimedia platform is Pebbles (Providing Education by Bringing Learning Environments to Students), a research project coordinated by Ryerson Polytechnic University in Toronto. The Pebbles project seeks to use multimedia technology and robotics to provide a means for students to be virtually present in the classroom through a semi-intelligent mobile video conferencing system that permits a student to attend class, even be positioned in the normal seating area and to "walk" about the classroom interacting with others as required. The student, absent from the physical classroom, maintains contact, presence, and social participation with his community in a form more closely reflecting the ambulatory first-person perspective. The Pebbles project suggests a way of maintaining a community that has already been established in the "real" world.

Sprint developed one of the first fully integrated platforms for networked virtual work groups. Sprint's Drums network allows real-time collaboration between geographically dispersed participants. Drums is particularly useful to the highly competitive entertainment and advertising industries, since creative and production houses are often located on opposite sides of the country—or even different continents—and time frames and budgets are always tight while the demand for creative excellence and control is always high.

In the Drums environment, each user sits in front of a computer monitor that displays a common set of icons. Participants can see and speak to each other. They can search for, select, display, and edit digital images, text, or film on a shared workspace, which all participants can manipulate in real time. Drums allows collaborators to meet face to face, voice to voice, or product to product without traveling; to draw on a common pool of resources; to remove the time lag built into overnight shipping of copy or tapes; and to boost productivity and efficiency by speeding up planning and production times. For instance, a traditional creative cycle in television advertising consists of making a "cut," shipping it out overnight, and waiting for comments sometime the following day or two. With Drums, users can go through three to five such cycles in a single 8-hour period. It effectively squeezes a work week into a single day.

While the time savings are important, it is really the sense of creative control as well as the benefits of creative collaboration that makes Drums so valuable. The network is a system specifically designed to help people with similar skills, needs, interests, aims, and language build a community of the best, most creative forces in the world. The community members design the interface; they decide who to invite into the community; they share their triumphs and tribulations with each other. The members maintain their own black book, circulate a newsletter that contains information, news, and articles about new and different applications of the program. Like Starbright and Pebbles, the Drums network has created a virtual environment in which otherwise geographically dispersed people can come together to pursue common goals, purposes, and activities.

MULTIMEDIA DIALTONE

Despite all the progress that has been made, we must recognize that we are only at the very early stages of development. As Clifford Stoll, a University of California astronomer, long-time Internet user, and author of *Silicon Snake Oil: Second Thoughts on the Information Superhighway*,[6] has written, "A computer network is, indeed, a community. But what an impoverished community! One without a church, café, art gallery, theater, or tavern. Plenty of human contact, but no humanity. Cybersex, cybersluts, and cybersleaze, but no genuine, lusty, roll-in-the-hay sex. And no birds sing."[7]

Stoll is correct that the information highway is an "impoverished" community, but only because it exists today as a community of computers. My goal is to take this complex network of connections to a whole new level—from infrastructure to superstructure.

Over the past few years, cyberspace *has* developed from a text-based medium without much sound or texture (the Internet) to a much richer multidimensional forum (the World Wide Web). This converging connectivity foreshadows the emergence of a unified platform to support rich, relevant, and productive individual and group action online and provide infrastructure conducive to sustainable cybercommunities—what I call Multimedia Dialtone.

Multimedia Dialtone will allow instantaneous, zero-loss, simultaneous translation of protocols, computer languages, human languages, emotions, gestures, mood, interfaces, middleware, operating systems, and networks according to users' individual preferences. Just as all networks, computers, and operating systems will be able to connect, so too will everyone on the planet who is connected—through voice, vocabulary, color, tone, texture, gesture, and posture.

Multimedia Dialtone will be as simple or robust as the user desires. There will be immediate access to full-sensory environments for those who want them; anonymity and a safe haven for those who prefer it; safety and protection from duplicity for those who require it; the immediacy, energy, and spontaneity of a chance meeting or the controlled, deliberate environment of a letter; and a defined set of regulating devices and governing norms to provide a comforting sense of order.

As Fig. 15-1 illustrates, the Multimedia Dialtone system consists of a Core Fabric (that is, the basic transportation medium) surrounded by several layers, starting with the IP Layer. The IP Layer

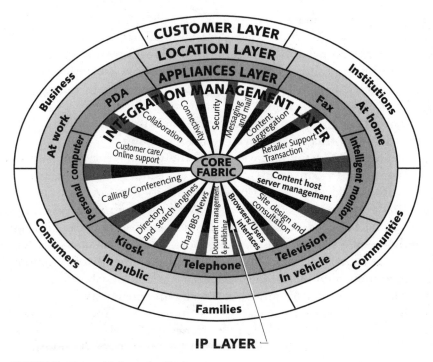

FIGURE 15-1. Multimedia Dialtone.

can be described as the internetworking protocols conversion layer. It assures that all parts of the global network interconnect seamlessly, irrespective of the carrier (for example, Sprint, AT&T, WorldCom, or any Internet Service Provider). The IP Layer enables and assures open communication among the various network and system protocols so that bits of data are carried from sender to receiver—even if they hop from one provider's transport fabric to another's. Next, the Integration Management Layer will provide the various communication services ranging from simple connectivity to content host server management and collaborative applications of the sort described earlier in the chapter.

The Appliances Layer consists of the myriad information appliances from which to access services. User interfaces will be standard but uniquely applicable to the user's style and tasks. Push systems like PointCast and Backweb, advanced programming languages like Java, and profiling and updating systems like Firefly, Castanet, and Tribal Voice provide a glimpse of the future world of simplicity and elegance which will make networked personal computing systems as ubiquitous as telephones and televisions. Speech-driven systems will render keyboards optional accessories, not necessary evils, and personal computers will appear much more holistic and intuitive to the user. I believe that the screen itself will eventually disappear as visual computing becomes embedded into a new breed of digital media we have yet to discover.

The Location Layer represents the various access points, be it your car, your office, a café, even your very person.

Finally, the Customer Layer shows the various user groups, who will continue to consist of traditional consumers and businesses, but, with the development of cybercommunity networks, will form a multitude of distinct yet interchangeable groups. Enabled by multimedia dial tone, participants will at once engage as colleagues, as family members, as friends, as neighbors, as club members, as fellow students, as cyberpals. There will be infinite points of commonality around which individuals will come together in cyberspace.

The system will be intuitive, intelligent, imaginative, and will enable full sensory interaction. The more we can stimulate our senses for total communication, the richer our experience, the more enjoyable our cybercommunities will become. Indeed, solutions aimed at improving the "richness" of cyberspace are in various stages of development. Deutsche Telekom, the German communications giant, even has a patent on a sensor that essentially allows a computer to pick up smells in a remote location.

Most important, if Multimedia Dialtone is going to enjoy widespread use, particularly by ordinary consumers, it must be as easy to install and operate as today's telephone. We cannot expect today's users, consumers, and businesspeople alike to sit down and read a manual to learn to use a new communications device.

Nor can we expect them to worry about managing their communications systems. Devices connected to Multimedia Dialtone networks will be on and available 24 hours a day, just like telephone and cable systems. They will be capable of providing the precise amount of bandwidth required for any given application. The network will host and distribute software as needed. Upgrades will be continuous and determined by the usage patterns of the individual. It will actually be possible to determine the need for and value of future features sets and release schedules based upon information gleaned from the network.

Although it will be decades before we can install a "true to life" system like the one I envision, the rapid global adoption of an open architecture combined with technological advances in data compression, optical fiber, high-speed multimedia switches, digital television, and satellite broadcasting suggests that Multimedia Dialtone could become commercially viable within a decade.

THE NEW COMMUNICATIONS PARADIGM

A number of factors delay widespread deployment of full, multi-sensory communications. Barriers include the massive initial and ongoing capital investment required to provide multimedia network and access infrastructure; the lack of simple holistic intuitive multimedia operating and navigation systems and interfaces; the difficulty of converting existing content from analog to digital form; the challenge of integrating so many disparate complex elements; the need to generate profits quickly—to name a few.

But, the biggest challenge is not directly related to technological development or business models; rather, it concerns our ability to embrace a new communications—and community—paradigm. As technology continues to advance, we must keep our minds open to new possibilities and not be bound by the frameworks and achievements of the past. Today, people *do* want to time-shift, to get more done, to be three places at once. Businesses *do* need to create 24-hour-a-day work groups to gain and keep a competitive edge. Customers are demonstrating their desire for solutions by signing onto the Internet in record numbers, irrespective of the installation problems they encounter, and by using the Internet with increasing frequency, despite its quality problems.

Perhaps most telling, people are substituting time spent in front of the television, talking on the phone, and going to the post office with time on the Web. That trend is the first evolutionary step toward Multimedia Dialtone and a virtual world every bit as stimulating as the "real" one. But just as early incarnations of telephone service, personal computing, and television programming pointed to, yet did not define today's huge markets in each, it would be a mistake to confuse today's Internet experience with the ubiquitous multimedia platform of the future.

In fact, it does not even come close. The technology that enables communication in the future will have to be true to life and entirely transparent to the end users. Busy signals, slow transmission speeds, lack of touch, taste, smell, or anything that takes us out of the experience, gets in the way of why we are online in the first place—to communicate and interact.

There must be a similar transparent quality when it comes to information. In a large sense what we must do is create workable templates for cybercommunities that render the technological infrastructure transparent and are seamlessly integrated with the real world.

Additionally, we will have to seriously consider what it means to be not just an *inhabitant* but a *citizen* of cyberspace, with full-fledged rights and responsibilities. As Miller also notes, "If people are to homestead the cyber frontier and build communities, we need to figure out how to extend the citizenship of the physical world into its virtual counterpart," and I would add, *transform* it.[8]

IF YOU BUILD IT, THEY WILL COME

Like their real-world counterparts, cybercommunities—public and private, personal and commercial—will be built from the ground up, on ascending levels of infrastructure, platform, and content. Think of a house. The infrastructure consists of the prerequisites for building a *home:* a strong foundation, adequate plumbing, proper electrical wiring, and a blueprint that integrates all the elements. The platform consists of the building itself, its form and structure. The content is what you bring to and create inside the house.

Figure 15-2 illustrates the three phases of construction of a cybercommunity. Phase 1 comprises the building blocks of basic universal connectivity and access—the foundation of bandwidth on demand upon which communications, collaboration, and content provider value can be built. This foundation consists not only of interconnected, interoperable technologies, hardware, and software but also of services that enable and assure stability, that is, network and protocol integration (gateway services), network management services, and application integration services.

Phase 2 of the diagram shows the components of real-time communications, primarily software-based client and server tools to broadly facilitate two-way and broadcast communications, collaboration, entertainment, information search, delivery and analysis, and commerce.

Although Phases 1 and 2 together constitute Multimedia Dialtone—the delivery of just-in-time sufficiency for connecting,

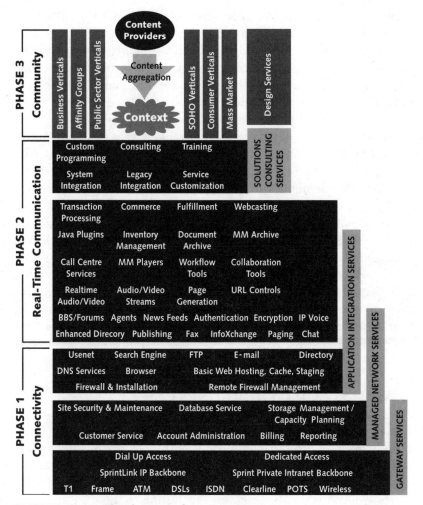

FIGURE 15-2. The elements of community.

communicating, and collaborating—Phase 3 shows the necessary additional components required for valuable cybercommunities. In Phase 3, process tools, systems, client/server software, network connections, and hardware introduced in Phase 2 are customized to suit the needs of groups and individuals. It is in this last phase that the emphasis shifts from technology to community requirements. To complete the house-building analogy, Phase 3 is the stage during which the roof tiles, the trim paint, the furniture, and the flowers in the garden ultimately, along with other personal details, distinguish my 3000-square-foot house from my neighbor's 3000-square-foot house. In this phase, excellence in programming, content aggregation, integrated gestalt marketing, and form factors and appliances will determine success more than ever. Custom profiling, tracking, and programming, and solutions consulting and marketing services will also take on new significance.

Finally, Fig. 15-2 is shown as a linear model with each phase neatly built upon the previous. It is more likely that development of the phases will be iterative and occur simultaneously. As new construction technologies and techniques are invented and business models mature, elements will be upgraded to keep pace with market demand.

As long as the builders of Phases 1 and 2 keep the end game—community—as well as their immediate customers' needs in focus, the Multimedia Dialtone will get built. The question, then, is not whether markets for cybercommunities will emerge, but at what pace the superstructure will evolve, and what shape it will take. This will be determined, just as it is in the home-building industry: by both the buyers' and builders' access to capital, their determination—and their creative vision.

DRUMMING UP CYBERBUSINESS

The final question I would like to explore is how we might incorporate such insights around community building into business practice. Businesses hoping to incorporate cyberspace into their activity must recognize that they, too, are in the business of building communities. At the industry level, as the Drums network illustrates, professional communities are emerging as partners, and suppliers and customers become increasingly linked through network technologies. In this final section I will focus specifically on the role community plays in the customer relationship.

Although business communities track along slightly different lines than personal communities, the concept of *relevance* remains absolutely crucial. Regardless of the product or service, ultimately, what customers are purchasing is self-actualization. Indeed, businesses must recognize that community is a precondition of a market and must strive relentlessly to create a sense of community both within the firm (often called a "team" or "family") and in their customers. In other words, they do not merely hawk goods and services; rather, they sell an overall experience, a sense of belonging, a set of feelings and attitudes that transcend a one-dimensional seller-buyer model.

In fact, cyberspace turns this model on its head, providing the first example of a buyer-controlled commercial environment. This is a radical shift not to be taken lightly. Consider a contemporary car dealership, which is perhaps the epitome of a seller-controlled environment. Amplifying the dealer's information advantage is the physical site of the dealership: Walls decked out with posters and exhortations to Buy! Buy! Buy! Now! Now! Now!; flags and eye-popping stickers galore; salesmen roaming the grounds like predatory animals; an in-house credit shop schooled in hard and soft sales—and everything in between.

Sales resistance is the automatic response of a customer accosted in such a manner. Such a reaction imposes extra costs all around. Sellers must work harder for a sale; buyers are less likely to browse around.

Now imagine the same situation brokered through a community-oriented online environment. Faced with the growth in information—and, by extension, educated customers—we can expect that car dealers will begin to offer services that will put prospective buyers in direct contact with satisfied customers, and also to come clean with all sorts of inside information. Web sites offering similar services, like Edmund's New Cars, for example, already exist today (although not provided by dealers themselves). The Edmund's site lists not only what the dealer pays for a particular model, but what he pays for option packages and up-to-the-minute announcements of manufacturer rebates to dealers. The site also includes independent reviews of new and old cars and detailed specs and comparisons. There is a "town hall" that allows visitors to the site to exchange views. The result is a car buyer who, through increased access to information combined with the exchange of information among fellow buyers, has seriously equalized the information equation and is arriving at the point of sale knowledgeable and motivated.

In the future, these types of services will involve not only virtual interaction with a community of customers, but also the choice to virtually test-drive a car from wherever they are—in whatever setting they choose. Prospective buyers will be able to get a feel for how the car handles with different engines and options. They will see instantly what it looks like with a range of equipment packages. Financing will be automatic, and car manufacturers will develop just-in-time delivery systems to bring their product directly to the customer's driveway.

The key—and the challenge—for businesses is to cater to the changing demands and needs of customers, providing quick, impersonal service at one moment and longer, more personal attention at another. This is no simple task and is best accomplished by allowing customers to choose among a number of contact points, ranging from face-to-face interaction to telephone services to Web-based menu plans. Hence, cyberbusinesses must take advantage of cyberspace to fully personalize their contacts, realizing the ultimate marketing dream: affordable narrowcasting to a market segment of one. At the same time, they must exploit its rich interactive potential, effectively creating a commercial community—a place to go and have a fully engaging and efficient shopping experience.

Safeway grocery stores, for example, are piloting a program that allows shoppers to place a detailed order online and receive it, at home, the next day. Amazon.com boasts a virtual inventory of over 1 million book titles which far outstrips those of traditional brick-and-mortar superstores. Its delivery policy allows it to reach bibliophiles who live outside high-density areas that support conventional stores. Amazon.com is also pioneering various narrowcast innovations that have transformed it from a commercial site to a commercial community. In addition to sophisticated search tools, Amazon.com also features (and solicits) reviews by professional journalists and readers alike, and invites authors to comment on their own work. The result is an interactive site that engages the customer, puts her in touch with other like-minded people, and continually updates its content—and a significant competitive threat to two massive, entrenched incumbents.

At Sprint, our Web site creates a sense of community by allowing cybercustomers to instantaneously interact with their supplier and with each other to secure vital services. Twenty-four hours a day, 7 days a week, customers—again at their own initiative and convenience—can do the following: change their service arrangements; check the status of their accounts; sign up for new services; send messages and account inquiries; participate in forums on matters of interest to them; and share their experiences, opinions, and suggestions with each other.

It has become clear that businesses that simply transfer their catalogs from paper to the Internet, for example, will add little value. Interactivity means engaging the business prospect in the process of building, changing, and customizing the product—all right before the prospect's eyes. In the future, this could mean anything from virtually test-driving a car on the Autobahn, listening to different sound systems in their living rooms, seeing how an antique table fits in their dining room, or even visiting a resort when planning their vacation. In the future, it will also mean offering related products on a just-in-time basis.

The same customers who cybershop at Sprint, Safeway, or Amazon.com today will demand similar services of other retailers tomorrow. They will demand brands they know and trust as well as responsive and individualized service and attention. They will demand shared spaces, shared values, shared languages, and shared experiences. In short, they will demand not just a particular cut of meat, or a particular book, or a particular phone service—they will demand a community that gives them something they can get nowhere else. The companies that deliver that community will prosper; those that fail to will languish.

BETTER THAN BEING THERE?

Cyberspace is far more than a set of related technologies. It is a set of potential communities and a set of emerging markets populated by individuals and institutions behaving, interacting, and transacting independently with one another. The challenge will always be trying to understand how, when, why, and where people communicate, collaborate, and conduct business. Those of us in the communications technology business see ourselves in some ways as the Interstate highway builders of the 1950s. We, too, are working to construct the infrastructure that will move goods, services, and people from one place to another, but we must also look beyond the individual connections to the new worlds that will emerge from this infrastructure.

Cyberspace is sure to grow and evolve over time and space. Future Netizens will demand services and responsiveness we can scarcely imagine today—the store with only the products they love, the doctor's office with the world's best physicians, a family reunion on top of Mt. Everest. This much is certain: cyberspace will function as a supplement to the "real" world in which we live, work, love, and die. It will allow us to add infinitely to our lives and to enrich our contacts, connections, and communities.

We will be able to be here *and* there—and wherever else we choose. We will be able to upload ourselves onto a broadband network so ubiquitous and efficient as to be invisible. It will make it easier for me to visit with my grandmother in Portland while at the same time it makes it easier to establish and maintain all sorts of personal and commercial ties. It will enable individuals to launch the social applications they need to create the communities that will let them save time, save money, control their environment, and realize their full potential while not limiting their ability to carry on with "real" life. The challenge is not simply to devise more sophisticated ways of delivering on the slogan that electronic communication is "the next best thing to being there." It is to envision and to deliver on how technology can enable interactions and help build virtual communities that may actually prove to be *"better* than being there."

NOTES

1. This article was written by Ms. Benjamin when she was Senior Vice President of Sprint and President of its Multimedia Group. She has since resumed an active role as Partner with the firm Benjamin/Nair, Inc.

2. Slouka, Mark, *War of the Worlds: Cyberspace and the High-Tech Assault on Reality* (New York: Basic Books), 1995.

3. Ibid., p. 4.

4. Ibid., p. 7.

5. Ibid., p. 115.

6. Stoll, Clifford, *Silicon Snake Oil: Second Thoughts on the Information Superhighway* (New York: Doubleday), 1995.

7. Ibid., p. 47.

8. Miller, Riel, "Rules for Radicals—Cyber-Citizenship," http://www.intellectualcapital.com/issues/97/0911/icbusiness.asp.

CENTER AND PERIPHERY

BALANCING THE BIAS OF DIGITAL TECHNOLOGY

by Mark Weiser
Xerox PARC

and John Seely Brown
Xerox PARC, Xerox Corporation

Imagine the following experiment; or if you are brave, try it. Find two empty cardboard toilet paper tubes and tape them over your eyes, like a pair of binoculars. You will see only a small, circular view of what is directly in front of you. You can't see what is above or below, to the left or right.

Now try walking. What happens? Everything that you see pops into your field of vision unexpectedly. Your head must constantly swivel to see where things are coming from, and what lies ahead of and around you. Otherwise you will trip, run into things, miss people passing you, and generally bumble. You have lost your peripheral vision. After a few hours you will feel exhausted and highly anxious from simply trying to keep up with your world.

Wearing cardboard tubes is much like living in the digital age. More information hits us each second during a walk in the woods than in an hour of Web browsing, yet, after surfing the Net, we're exhausted from "information overload" and having to constantly pay attention. This is because today's digital technology and delivery

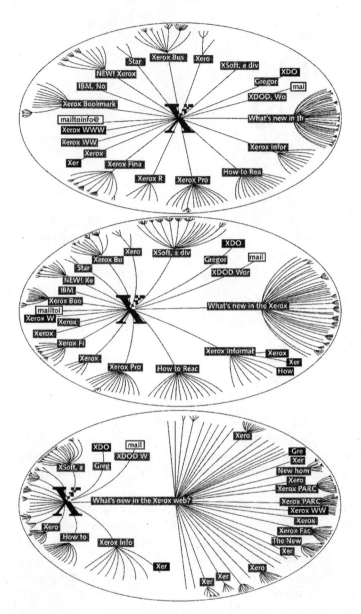

FIGURE 16.1.   Hyperbolic browser.

mechanisms tend to flatten and push all information to the center of our awareness. This bias effectively cuts out the periphery, which provides the context required to make sense of and anticipate the world around us. Without it, we are lost and confused.

While we tend to take our existing computer devices and interfaces for granted, digital technology is not a neutral medium for delivering information. As already described, pouring data through today's clumsy screens and computer interfaces distorts that information subtly, yet profoundly. Today's interfaces are not the ultimate in digital media design; nor is the desktop computer many of us use in our daily lives the only possible apparatus for delivering information. Although newer technologies, such as ubiquitous computing and "things that think," will not be widely available soon, at Xerox PARC, we believe that balancing deep technology with deep design and an understanding of work processes can greatly reduce digital distortions.

For example, Xerox's hyperbolic browser (Fig. 16.1) avoids the cardboard tube effect caused by most browsers or user interfaces. Functioning on the perceptual level, the hyperbolic browser presents a kind of fish-eye view that shows thousands of related Web nodes at the same time. The nodes that most closely match a particular search are found at the center of the browser screen and are larger. Unlike a fish-eye, the hyperbolic browser maps an infinite space to a single view integrating a rich periphery that supports the focus and adapts as focus shifts. However, balancing center and periphery on the perceptual level alone is not enough. As we will see, digital technology affects our ability to communicate on the conceptual level as well.

In this chapter, we will identify and discuss the 10 biases in today's digital technology that contribute to unbalancing center and periphery. We describe the domain of conscious, symbolic thought and action as the center; the domain of flow, context, and intuition as the periphery. In other words, the center tells us primarily "what" and "who," the periphery tells us "how" and "where." The 10 biases we have identified are:

1. Saying
2. Homogenizing
3. Stripping
4. Reframing
5. Monosensing
6. Deflowing
7. Defamiliarizing

8. Uglying

9. Reifying

10. Destabilizing

The first six of these—saying, homogenizing, stripping, reframing, monosensing, and deflowing—are less likely to disappear in the immediate future. They very much represent the limiting factors of current digital technology. The last four—defamiliarizing, uglying, reifying, destabilizing—will improve as digital design evolves as an area of practice.

Each of these biases, on its own, can be employed to produce an appropriate or desired effect. But in excess, and in combination with the others, they distort how we perceive and interact with digital information.

SAYING

Digital technology tends to explicitly "say," rather than imply, hint, suggest, or offer. It has difficulty leaving anything unsaid, except by mistake. Yet, in human communication, what is not spoken or heard—the pregnant pause, the dramatic glare, the rests in music—makes up the periphery that sometimes "says" more than we can explain.

It is especially when authenticity or integrity need to be communicated that nonexplicit expression is crucial. What is your reaction to someone you don't know very well who says, "trust me"? Your trust in them probably goes down. Earning trust requires more than someone just saying so: trust is inspired when the information captured by all our senses, together with our intuition, past experience, and stock of knowledge, tells us whether someone is trustworthy.

Consider video conferencing. It was once thought that it would lead to less air travel. Instead, because opportunities to connect with people have increased, the number of situations where people need to follow up in person to establish trust and personal connection have likewise increased. It is impossible to fully reproduce periphery-rich physical meetings through digital technology.

Authority is another quality that is largely communicated through peripheral cues. For example, imagine an online dictionary that, as you start it up, says, "contains 257,452 words." What does this mean in terms of authority? Is this a comprehensive dictionary? Are the definitions of all those words exhaustive or cursory? Without any reference points, it's hard to tell.

Now imagine that you see a huge bound dictionary on a stand in a library. Its privileged position on a podium, your knowledge of the possible cost and effort that went into producing such a physical object and compiling its contents, along with its sheer size relative to all the other dictionaries you have ever used, create an immediate impression of the dictionary's authority. This happens within milliseconds without once thinking consciously and explicitly about these elements—and without having to count the words.

One way of substituting for this kind of nonexplicit authority in the digital economy is through branding. The brand embodies a history of experiences, knowledge, and identity. Nike, for example, stands for quality and excellence—both in its products and their users—and a particular lifestyle. *Time* magazine represents a source of credible and authoritative information. Branding will be especially important for conducting business on the Web, where other signs of trust and authority are lacking.

As Web design (and interactive multimedia design in general) evolves, Web pages are starting to contain nonexplicit, formal elements to give a site authority. When frames and Java, for example, first appeared, they conveyed a certain sense of sophistication. However, since their code is easily copied, they have become more common and their authority has diminished. Much more effective is good, original design. Pages with a combination of elements that are tasteful, simple, attractive, and interesting are the most effective, although still rare on the Web. These design elements are not easily duplicated because they exist as a combination of content and carrier that cannot be copied like a piece of HTML. Eventually certain "looks" will function as brands on the Web, like the *Wall Street Journal*'s distinctive font and layout does now in the world of newspapers, or *Wired* in the magazine world.

Two technologies currently under development in research labs around the world may eventually resolve the problem of communicating authority in the digital age. One is telepresence, the other, ubiquitous computing. Telepresence is advancing digital, audio, and robotic technology to connect participants to remote locations in sensory-rich environments. Although similar to videoconferencing, telepresence differs in its aim to create true "being there," not just a representation of being there. Current telepresence still has a long way to go, but, eventually, if we came to trust telepresence technology as we now trust "real" presence, it could replace many live encounters.

Much more advanced is the more modest technology of ubiquitous computing, which imbeds computational abilities in everyday devices designed to perform specific tasks. The combination of the digital and the physical provides a much richer media space to work with. For example, even the best designed Web page is still limited by the confines of the screen and pixels. On the other hand, physical design can use size, weight, form, and all the other elements of industrial design and art to deliver its message. Delivering a digital dictionary in a handheld "package," for example, conveys more authority through its physical formal elements than it does online through a computer screen. We expect the development of ubiquitous computing to accelerate as it becomes recognized as an opportunity to even out the distortions in digital communication.

HOMOGENIZING

Digitization also leads to a homogenization of the world. Homogenization flattens, or reduces all information to a monotone—bit by bit, word by word, all center, without context or periphery. In today's world of e-mail, homogenization is clearly illustrated: all information arrives within the mail reader in the same font and format. Furthermore, it comes as part of a stream of messages, with "To" and "From," a "Subject" line, a few short paragraphs, and a signature. The subject line offers the only opportunity for differentiation, through the "headline" style in which it is usually written. Contrast this to the world of paper mail, where information comes in a myriad of envelopes and paper stocks, with distinctive textures and weights that tell us something about the sender. The fonts or handwriting, colors, postmarks, and envelope sizes combine with the enclosed explicit messages to influence our response.

Homogenized information is prone to misunderstanding because there are few and limited ways to imply meaning through things like intonation, volume, etc. For example, discussion groups on the Internet go through disasters called "flame wars" in which e-mail of progressively angry and inflammatory content is exchanged. This happens, in part, because all information is delivered in neutral, plain text ASCII code, which allows the reader to project any emotion onto a message, frequently one unintended by the writer. Explicit "saying" may tend to increase the amount of homogenization in communication, but the two differ in that "saying" limits *what* is said, while homogenization limits *how* it is said.

Of course the homogenizing effect of the bit is, at the same time, its incredible power. The Web is a perfect example. The most effective and accurate way to understand the Web is to think of it as an agreement on how computers will talk to each other. Agreements have enormous power; think of the Magna Carta, the U.S. Constitution, the European Union, and NAFTA. The Web is a worldwide agreement that every computer will speak the lingua franca of IP, TCP, HTTP, and HTML. The specific technologies are much less important than the existence of this agreement. In other words, it is the agreement that created the explosive commercial and technological opportunities, not the other way around.

It is this aspect of homogenization—agreement—that has led us to think that the digital challenge lies simply in "capturing" information and, in effect, reducing everything to bits. This can be efficient for some aspects of life and work, but not everything can be homogenized into the same form. The fact is that digitization is not enough: for this agreement to be useful, we must balance center and periphery so that information can be differentiated.

For companies doing business in the digital economy, heterogeneity will become a crucial way to position and differentiate their products and services. Those that take advantage of the tools of heterogeneity, such as Java or advanced HTML, will have a competitive advantage.

The next few years will see the emergence of a variety of solutions to homogenization, including advances in Web design, new software tools, ubiquitous computing, and eventually telepresence. Nonetheless, we expect to see an increasing premium on interesting, creative writing on the Web as a factor of heterogeneity and quality. At least for the time being, there is little else by which to truly differentiate digital information.

STRIPPING

Any preexisting periphery tends to be stripped away when it enters the digital realm. The video conference, for example, limits our view to the "head shot," or what is directly in front of the camera. We can't always see everybody in the room, we may not get a full sense of the participants' corporate culture, or we may miss subtle yet significant details about participating individuals, such as their full body language or even their footwear. Furthermore, the video conference does not allow for the physical possibilities of reaching out a hand, of catching a glance from someone who could otherwise be sitting next to us, or of meeting a colleague in the hallway or on our way to the conference. The exclusion of these peripheral cues and physical possibilities drastically affects the tone and potential outcome of the meeting.

The presence of these kinds of possibilities can be very powerful. We like to use the word attunement to describe subconscious attention to the less apparent and unofficial possibilities inherent in any situation—those not on the explicit agenda, so to speak. Being attuned to certain possibilities is distinct from attending to what is visibly and consciously the focus of our attention at any given moment.

Driving down the expressway, for example, you are likely to be attending to the road, to the cars around, to the next exit. What happens if the engine suddenly makes an unfamiliar noise? Effortlessly, you shift your attention, listen for what hazard it might signal, and take appropriate action. But how is it that you heard the noise at all? You were not listening for it, yet it got your attention nonetheless. The answer is that it was part of your periphery, and you were attuned to it.

Attunement is the unconscious connection we have to those parts of our periphery that we can quickly attend to with a simple shift of attention. We can attune to much more than we can attend to. Think back to the car on the expressway: What are the variables that might cause you to shift your attention? Weather conditions, noise, other cars, changes in road surface, unusual billboards, interesting words or music on the radio, a funny taste in your mouth, a sudden unbidden memory. For highly attuned individuals, there are infinite opportunities for a deep and wide connection with a greater part of our environment.

Too often designers of digital media only consider how to transmit the center. This reduces attunement by representing only the more obvious elements of a situation. This is why flying blind is very difficult, in spite of all the required information displayed on the cockpit instruments. Furthermore, digital technology can strip meaning from the absence of information, or change its meaning altogether. For example, even when driving a car by telepresence, silence may just mean the microphone is broken, whereas when actually in a car, the absence of loud engine noises means the car is running smoothly.

If you believe that optimal functioning always involves ignoring everything that's not part of your focus, then you are missing the opportunity to greatly expand your attention and enrich your experience.

REFRAMING

Digital technology, once it has stripped away the periphery, compounds the problem by supplying a new periphery, or "frame," which often changes our conceptualization of information. A computer screen frames an article from an online publication, for example, in a way that conveys a completely different meaning than the one we get when the same text is printed on an $8\frac{1}{2}$- $\times$ 11-inch piece of paper. Similarly, the frame of e-mail and ASCII paragraphs, compared to envelopes and hand-signed letters, conveys a different message.

Consider the musical background to a movie. We are not always 100 percent conscious of the music, but it is part of the periphery that surrounds and frames our experience. Dark, moody music in a film noir connects us with the dark minds of the characters. Suspenseful music can make us cringe in anticipation of a violent act. Imagine the famous ending to *Casablanca*, when Humphrey Bogart says good-bye to Ingrid Bergman at the airport. The music is sadly sincere, then patriotic. But imagine if it turned ironic, or comedic. The change in frame might lead us to perceive Bogart's character as self-serving instead of self-sacrificing. Frame as much as center contributes to our interpretation of the message.

Another interesting aspect of the frame of digital technology is that it can sometimes be falsely authoritative. Once upon a time computers were considered nearly infallible; whatever the computer said was considered to be the "truth." Today, in a somewhat wiser era, some of us are likely to view what comes out of a computer with a bit more skepticism. Yet the frame of the computer, and the power of the pixel, still carry inappropriate weight. Rumors on the Web, such as a missile bringing down the TWA flight, get picked up and repeated as truth by the media, without much question.

At the other extreme, the frame of digital technology can sometimes be falsely discrediting. Is everything on the Web bunk? Is all computerized information subject to falsification, viruses, and tampering? Although these kinds of incidents are uncommon, or at least not more common than in the analog world, encryption technology is providing both the technical and conceptual frames for interpreting information as authentic. For example, IBM's Cryptolope provides a frame for transmitting digital information over the Internet within which content, sender, and recipient are guaranteed. This way, information arriving in a cryptolope will immediately be considered legitimate. A key technology associated with cryptolopes is Xerox's Digital Property Rights Language, which allows the creator of digital information to specify the rights for using that information. A frame that indicates the material is under copyright travels with, and surrounds, the information. Functioning on both a cognitive and technical level, it helps deter and prevent copyright violation.

MONOSENSING

Digital technology, for the most part, delivers information to the fovea, the center of the eye. While sound is becoming part of more and more digital media content, our peripheral vision and sense of touch, taste, and smell are rarely, if ever, stimulated. The computer speaks to us as though we were barely alive—just an eye in a box. The predominance of one sense over others distorts our perception and therefore our ability to make intelligent decisions.

Monosensing overloads one part of the brain while leaving others underutilized. Since the brain is never still, unstimulated senses will compensate by activating their own frames. Music or peripheral sounds, smells, the feel of our chair, will be integrated into our experience and influence our perception of the visual stimulation. Although we might sometimes attribute these displaced responses to "mood," it is often a natural result of mixing sensory input from within and outside the frame of digital technology.

Monosensing also leaves vital sources of intelligence untapped. It is well known that styles of learning and comprehension differ among people, with some more verbally inclined, some visually, some kinesthetically, and so on. By delivering information to only one sense we make many of our employees or colleagues appear less intelligent than they are, and less intelligent than we can afford them to be.

The overall value of a company's workforce would multiply if a diversity of sensory modes was used in digital work tools. Future documents may generate multiple renderings of themselves, so that they can be understood through multiple senses. For example, audio tracks or interactive elements could become part of the user interface. By using several different forms of a document, we get a more complete message than either could convey alone. As a multibillion dollar expense, training could also be greatly enhanced and costs reduced, using multiple-sense training tools and materials.

DEFLOWING

Digital technology tends to be delivered as a series of snapshots. Not only do these snapshots contain explicit information that has been stripped of context and, furthermore, reframed into the screen, but they also lack flow. Lack of flow is worthy of mention because flow is so essential to effective human communication and action.

The psychologist Mihaly Csikszentmihalyi describes a human condition called the "flow state." In the flow state our conscious attention partially vanishes, yet we fully martial a great deal of knowledge and skill into effective action that is deeply attuned to the current set of circumstances. For instance, the experienced downhill skier is not consciously thinking about the position of his or her skis or what muscle to move next, but is more likely to be looking further ahead at the slope and the mountain overall. Yet the whole body is expertly controlled, oriented, and balanced from one millisecond to the next. Similarly, the computer programmer or business strategist may need to take enough time to get immersed in the details of a problem and achieve the flow state before making significant creative progress.

One can reconstruct flow from a series of snapshots, of course, but it requires mental effort. The exhaustion we feel after spending time at a computer comes partly from the energy spent creating flow out of snapshots. The pleasure of skiing and most forms of entertainment is partly in their flow, which seamlessly integrates with the natural flow of our minds and bodies. An unexpected event, phrase, sound, or person, disrupts our flow state.

Context switching also disrupts our flow, something digital technology often demands of its users. Think of the "pop-up" messages on computer systems to which one must respond "OK." These are rarely part of the flow of our current task, and include messages of varying levels of importance and urgency.

An example of digital technology that alleviates the burden of context switching is the electronic "room." A set of digital tools and related works in progress on a screen can be thought of as a room. One can switch from room to room, with each room retaining the configurations of its last use each time it is entered. Unlike "windows," a room contains multiple active applications and documents, much like a real room.

One of the key values of faster computers and bandwidth is reduced context switching. A rule of thumb in the design of interactive computer applications is that a delay of $\frac{1}{10}$ second is imperceptible and does not reduce flow, a 1-second delay is noticed but without distraction, and a 10-second delay will cause the mind to wander and totally disrupt concentration. Faster computers and faster bandwidth will shorten most of our disruptions to 1 second or less.

Compared to the biases discussed up to now, the next four biases—defamiliarizing, uglying, reifying, and destabilizing—will describe more transient aspects of digital technology. They are less inherent in technology itself, and more related to how it is used. As applications become increasingly sophisticated, some of these characteristics will vanish with time.

DEFAMILIARIZING

The majority of protocols and conventions associated with digital technology are new to us. Ordinarily comfortable and familiar behavior, such as negotiating a contract or engaging in conversation, become strangely fraught with confusion when carried out over e-mail, for example. Simply put, work practices are different in the digitally mediated world. As the next generation—who will have been computing most of their lives—enters the workforce, this problem will lessen, but in the meantime the effects of defamiliarizing must be taken into account.

Digital technology leaves us uncertain of our information types and formats—genres—and their identifying characteristics. A genre can be thought of as comprising the elements and characteristics that define a "text," or document type (whether a letter, a short story, a financial report, a spreadsheet, etc.) within a particular context in which it is meaningful. For example, a corporate strategy document opens with an executive summary, whereas a detective novel would not begin with a plot summary. We understand the significance of the presence of a summary in one genre and its absence in another.

Identifying genres in our digital world is difficult because their attributes are largely triggered by peripheral cues. These cues, through homogenizing, stripping, and reframing are, for the most part, lost.

One of the difficulties of searching the Web is that documents are word matched and delivered without regard to genre. Memos, high school theses, learned journals, maniacal rantings, and personal home pages are all dutifully indexed by Web search engines, and likewise served up to the eager person looking for Web information. Search engines cannot tell the difference between a learned article on "technology and education" for example, and a brochure offering courseware on a company's Web site. Yet a quick look distinguishes these genres.

The problem is that existing technologies are not very good at searching through significant peripheral cues. Work underway at Xerox PARC and elsewhere is aimed at actually searching on aspects of document genres, not simply the content of words and phrases. Genres are complex linguistic phenomena that are not easy to identify or code digitally. To search on genres requires linguistic and metalinguistic knowledge in the search engine (for example, style of sentences), not just word or part-of-speech matching.

Genre is only one way of categorizing a series of documents. Other peripheral criteria, both conceptual and physical, can group documents as a collection. For example, all works by an author, whether essays or novels, comprise a collection. All documents residing on your hard disk or your bookshelf—regardless of their genre or author—are also a collection. Collections themselves can be parts of collections—the works of all Irish authors, for instance. And so on, to collections of collections of collections—for example, all female authors writing about technology. Whether we realize it or not, we are attuned to the collection from which our current documents were selected, and it influences our interpretation of its contents—for better or for worse. More powerful search engines will eventually be able to search for aspects of document collections, giving us more control on how we gather and create meaning out of information.

UGLYING

A lot of digitally delivered documents are not pleasing to the eye. As both designers and readers become more sophisticated in their understanding of digital technology, this will improve. But meanwhile, "uglying"—largely a result of ignoring the periphery in design—is an unfortunate side effect of the digital age. Uglying goes beyond the inadvertent clumsiness inherent in "saying" and "homogenizing" by actively (if unintentionally) creating poor design.

Good design is largely about engaging the periphery and creating a context that supports a message and enhances its meaning. The design of *Wired* magazine, for example, nowhere explicitly says "future," or "confusion," or "fast-paced," nor would it be as effective if it did. But by using a loud, chaotic feel with shocking colors, font, and layout, a certain context is created within which these elements are understood by the reader. Most of the articles in *Wired* would have trouble being reprinted in *Reader's Digest*—its peripheral elements would not support *Wired*'s message.

We've had thousands of years of experience in designing physical documents, from clay tablets to newspapers and magazines. Part of the designer's skill involves placing elements in the periphery so they insinuate instead of shout. There is now a rich array of design nuances in fonts, layout, materials, color, etc., that, in the hands of the skilled designer, work together to meet us at the boundary of document and mind.

Part of the art of newspaper design is to use the physical, non-symbolic elements of the paper layout to strategically place articles and photographs to guide the eye's flow over the page and to take advantage of such physical attributes as above-the-fold and below-the-fold. A large amount of the ease and pleasure of reading a physical newspaper compared to its online equivalent results from the attention given to selection and layout of articles, which provides an overall designed experience of reading.

On the other hand, digital technology has far less history. We know little yet of the interactive experience and using digital media to create peripheral cues that hint, imply, invite, or calm. The lack of control over the actual consumption of information, that is, whether it will be viewed on a monochrome laptop computer or a color HDTV screen, further complicates digital design challenges. Information appliances, as mentioned earlier, will give the designer more control over how information will be received, however, this particular area of industrial design is also in its infancy.

REIFYING

Digital technology emphasizes the explicit. It recognizes only what is officially authorized through digitization. For instance, business processes can now be cast in self-enforcing computer programs. Reifying is the process by which digital technology reduces and restricts our range of activities to those existing in the digital domain. In other words, it offers no possibilities outside the boundaries of what has been digitized. This system closely resembles "work to rule."

In real life, however, business processes are always in a symbiotic relationship with emergent, self-organizing communities that are practically engaged in specific work processes. Overly reifying the processes may kill the symbiote, and so the whole organization. The more complete the process being reified, the higher the risk. When everyday business processes are "digitized," because of the ease with which this system expresses rules and eliminates imagination, there is a tendency to encourage rules-based activity and incite a "work to rule" organization.

In this way, reifying can discourage trust and creativity. If someone is told exactly what to do, and does it perfectly, without creativity or passion, there is no way of knowing at what point they stop simply following instructions and start employing initiative. In practice, we can never tell anyone exactly what to do. In every human activity there is much left unsaid—even the most detailed instructions to an employee involve huge amounts of common sense understanding that we cannot put into words. The more trust we have in an individual, the less needs to be said. Hundreds of millions of dollars have been spent attempting to teach computers common sense, so far without success. It is by trusting colleagues and employees to respond and carry out what we cannot explicitly command—what we cannot formulate as a rule—that work gets done.

As another example, consider the organizational diagram, or the "org chart." The org chart shows the official relationships comprising the explicit, or "authorized" organization—that part of the organization that functions according to the rules. But the org chart is only part of a system that is assumed also to have many unrecorded relationships. If individuals could only talk to those directly connected to them, above or below on the chart, most organizations would grind to a halt. For the org chart to function, the presence of another part of the organization is required: the part that self-organizes; that is focused on the goal, not on the rules; the peripheral organization that gets things done and supports the explicit, authorized organization.

As the lifeblood of any successful organization, the peripheral, or emergent, organization grows through relationships that are either "accidental" or defined. Location, or who one meets in the cafeteria, by the coffee machine, or at a conference often forms the basis of an emergent organization. The flow of information, materials, or revenue can generate an emergent organization through, for example, a salesperson or engineer making direct contact with the manufacturer of the product they are selling or using. Shared activities—across geographical, departmental, organizational, and industrial boundaries—are another emergent organizing principle resulting in what has been termed "communities of practice." Within Xerox, for example, those engineers that deeply understand the chemistry and physics of xerography form a geographically disperse but emotionally and intellectually bonded community. An organization's core competencies may be built and sustained upon such emergent communities of practice.

The emergent organization is one area in which digital technology can help. E-mail is perhaps the easiest and most common way for information to cross geographic and organizational boundaries, however, intranet/extranet applications, corporate "push" technologies like Backweb and Marimba and other more specific applications are also being developed. For example, at Xerox we created a system through which field service people could share repair "tips." This system, called "Eureka," depends upon its users contributing and using information horizontally—among themselves. Realizing that field service people get lots of valuable information from informal conversations with their colleagues, the most difficult part of creating Eureka was recreating an equally informal social context while permitting tips to spread throughout and be used by the sales force. For example, Eureka provides no cash payments for submitting tips—the service reps themselves rejected these—but it does give credit in the form of bylines to those who contribute a tip. Piloted in France using the Minitel system, Eureka is now being deployed in the United States on the Web.

DESTABILIZING

The biases discussed so far—saying, homogenizing, stripping, reframing, monosensing, deflowing, defamiliarizing, uglying, and reifying—together create a destabilizing effect.

Lack of flow, lack of familiarity, and lack of good design contribute to our unease with information. A homogeneous, explicit, symbolic, monosensory channel unbalances our ability to respond, while constant psychodynamic disturbance[1] leads us to the ultimate destabilizing condition: information overload. We are left upset, frustrated, and exhausted. There is no calm place to turn within the technology that connects us with our core.

A CALL FOR BALANCE

The 10 biases of digital technology described here all contribute to the imbalance between center and periphery. The former is emphasized at the expense of the latter. Saying omits the powerful context provided by what is not said. Homogenizing reduces all information to the same level of importance. Stripping removes context, while reframing imposes a new confusing or inappropriate context. Monosensing underutilizes the majority of our senses, leaving important sources of intelligence untapped. Deflowing constantly interrupts our focus and mental processes. Defamiliarizing leaves us lost, while uglying leaves us uncomfortable. Reifying leaves us untrusted or untrusting, and finally, destabilizing leaves us overwhelmed and stressed out.

There are many levels at which center and periphery can be out of balance. At the perceptual level we can lose peripheral vision, as in the cardboard tube experiment described at the beginning of this chapter. At the conceptual level we can lose the context that gives meaning to information, as the stripping and reframing examples illustrates. At the social level we can exclude significant dynamics of human interaction through reification, or become uncertain of the etiquette or protocols associated with new communication tools

The 10 Biases of Digital Technology

Bias	Effect
Saying	Only explicit information is delivered. Implied messages—sometimes more powerful and important—are communicated less effectively, or not at all.
Homogenizing	All information is flattened or reduced to a monotone. Differentiation between levels of importance of messages or tone (e.g., complimentary versus insulting) is lost, often resulting in miscommunication.
Stripping	When the periphery is cut out, or "stripped," the context needed to create and support meaning is lost. In interactive communication, stripping also eliminates serendipitous opportunities for making connections.
Reframing	Replacing the context, or frame, in which a message was originally created with another (e.g., printing a Web page on 8-1/2″ 11″ paper) can alter our conceptualization of information. On another level, the frame of technological media can be either falsely authoritative or discrediting.
Monosensing	Monosensing overloads one part of the brain, distorting our perception and leaving important sources of intelligence untapped.
Deflowing	Creating flow out of "snapshots" of information requires mental energy. Pauses as well as context switching constantly interrupt our focus and mental processes.
Defamiliarizing	Digital technology leaves us uncertain of our information types and formats. Genre-specific peripheral cues are lost through homogenizing, stripping, and reframing. Search engines, for example, can't tell the difference between business documents and journal articles.
Uglying	Interactive, multimedia design is still in its infancy, leaving most digital design awkward and clumsy. The result—uglying—is most often caused by ignoring the periphery.
Reifying	Reifying reduces and restricts our range of activities to only those that have been digitized or are digitizable. This system closely resembles "work to rule," thereby discouraging trust and creativity, and suppressing the opportunities for emerging processes, activities, relationships, etc.
Destabilizing	All biases together create a destabilizing effect leaving users upset, frustrated, and exhausted.

through defamiliarization. Digital technology unbalances us at all these levels. The long-term result is that we really don't know—deep in our souls—where we are, where we have been, or where we are going. We become frantic, instead of calm.

At Xerox PARC, we try to keep periphery and center in balance by mixing technology research with other activities less prone to imbalance. We increasingly view our activities at PARC as stirring a creative cyclone of deep technology, deep design, and a deep understanding of work.[2]

CONCLUSION

Understanding the power of balance between center and periphery can be a tremendous source of advantage in the digital age. Digital technology, through its ubiquitous and voluminous provision of information, must engage a richer periphery. Trying to focus on the increasing volume of bits can overwhelm us, and we can badly misuse our intelligence by ignoring attunement, community, and peripheral awareness. The opportunity for focus is greater than ever before, but only if we recognize that focus only exists in relation to a periphery. As management catches up to the digital age, and as tools are developed that engage the periphery as well as the center, we can expect a world of greater satisfaction and effectiveness—if we can stay in balance.

NOTES

1. See Hirschhorn, Larry, and Carole Barnett, *The Psychodynamics of Organizations* (Philadelphia: Temple University Press), 1993, for a description of the role of emotions, interpretations, projection, and the whole space of psychological effects. Exacerbation of these effects through digital technology will have a profound effect on the people in our organizations, and so the effectiveness of the organizations themselves.
2. The cyclone concept was originally formulated by researcher Eric Saund at Xerox PARC.

PART FOUR

GOVERNANCE IN THE TWENTY-FIRST CENTURY

As the world becomes wired, many important thinkers are forecasting a fundamental transformation in the structure and function of government. Debates rage on how much to regulate the Internet, if at all. This section addresses two principal themes—the future of government and the overall development and governance of the Internet itself. A variety of issues from civil disobedience on the Net to questions of "cyber citizenship" and national jurisdiction provide a "big picture" view of the future sociopolitical context.

GOVERNMENT AND GOVERNANCE IN THE NETWORKED WORLD

by Michael R. Nelson[1]

Governments are in the information business. The U.S. Federal government spends a major portion of its budget collecting, processing, and disseminating information—whether tax records, weather data, research results, or economic statistics. Likewise, state and local governments generate terabytes of data each year in order to collect taxes, register real estate transactions, deliver welfare benefits, and carry out dozens of other functions.

Just as information technology is profoundly changing the structure of American business, we can expect new computing and communication technologies to dramatically change the structure and function of government at all levels. Yet, most government officials have been slow to recognize the changes that are afoot. Rather than consider how digital technologies will change the role of government, the United States and most other national governments have focused on two related near-term questions. First, how can government facilitate the development of the digital economy by spurring the deployment of the information infrastructure required for electronic commerce, online education, telemedicine, and other applications.[2] Second, how can government use information technology to fulfill its current missions more quickly and cost effectively?[3]

While these questions are critical, this chapter will explore an issue which, in the long term, could be even more significant: how will information technology and the development of the digital economy lead to fundamental changes in the expectations of their citizens and the way governments work?

A LITTLE HISTORY

Throughout history, governments have evolved as new inventions and technologies have provided new tools and increased their power. In particular, advances in information technologies have changed the structure and scope of government. The Roman road network speeded communication and transportation, enabling Rome to extend its influence over an empire stretching from the British Isles to Persia. The printing press fostered the nation-state by enabling a central government to easily and quickly disseminate its edicts. Newspapers advanced democracy in Britain, its North American colonies, and elsewhere, by giving ordinary people the facts they needed to cast informed votes. The worldwide telegraph network of the 1800s helped Britain and other European nations control their colonies around the world.

In general, faster, cheaper forms of communication have enabled bigger, more centralized government. The ability to collect information more easily has given central governments more control over their citizens.

Today's typical government has access to a mind-boggling assortment of information. Some it collects itself, some it obtains from commercial data-collection companies, the media, and other organizations. This information gives governments ever more power to tax, regulate, and control its citizens.

But interestingly, new information technologies are now shifting the balance of power from the central government toward individual citizens. The reason is simple—these technologies give individual citizens more access to information. Individual citizens now have much better information on what their government is doing. They can more easily mobilize to oppose government actions they disagree with. They also have the tools and the information they need to perform some of the services that they previously relied upon government to provide. The result could be a massive change in the way government does business. Functions previously performed by national governments will devolve to local or state government. Others will shift to private companies and organizations.

INFORMATION IS POWER

Power for the Boss. Traditionally, government bureaucrats have treated information as a source of power. If you knew something someone else did not, you had power. The further up on the organization chart you were, the more information (and thus power) you had. The job of a manager was to integrate the information flowing upward from subordinates and pass it on up the pyramid. Very little information flowed back down, and even less flowed across the organization to other divisions.

Power for the Government Worker. Office local area networks and the Internet are changing all this. Now it is so easy to share information widely that enlightened office managers and government executives realize that information power can and should be shared with everyone in the organization. The result: more and more problems are resolved at lower levels in government agencies, the ranks of middle management can be thinned, and internal squabbles between different parts of an organization, fed by misinformation or a lack of information, have become less common.

Power for the Citizen. New information technologies, especially the Internet and World Wide Web, have enabled U.S. government agencies to much more quickly and inexpensively distribute information to the public. The White House home page (*www.whitehouse.gov*) provides Presidential speeches, press releases, administration reports, a virtual tour of the White House, and even a picture and recording of Socks, the First Family's cat. Created in late 1994, the site hosts tens of thousands of visitors every day. The White House home page links to every agency and department of the U.S. government. In all, several hundred thousand government documents are available online.

This online information is enabling U.S. citizens to better understand and influence the policies of the Federal government. It is enabling citizens to locate resources they need, such as tax forms, information on where to get a small business loan, or educational materials.

By serving as a clearinghouse, Federal agencies enable citizens to solve their own problems at the local level, rather than trying to solve them from Washington, D.C. By fostering this kind of grassroots approach, agencies can stretch their tight budgets and help more people more effectively.

THE CHANGING ROLE OF GOVERNMENT

The digital economy has engendered a growing debate about the changing role of government in the networked world. This debate, which rages on various mailing lists and chat groups on the Internet, in the pages of *Wired* magazine, and at increasing numbers of conferences, pits two groups with quite different philosophies against each other. Ronald Brownstein calls them cyberlibertarians and technocommunitarians.[4]

Cyberlibertarians claim that the Internet, encryption, and related technologies will so empower the individual that government will become powerless or at least irrelevant. Some argue that digital cash and electronic commerce will make it increasingly difficult for governments to tax their citizens or regulate commerce. As a result, governments will slowly wither away. A variant of cyberlibertarians might be called "cryptoanarchists." They predict that unbreakable encryption on the Internet will make it impossible for government to detect or prevent a range of presently illegal activities, including tax evasion, child pornography, theft of trade secrets, and theft of private, personal information (for example, medical records).

Technocommunitarians, on the other hand, see information technology as a powerful new tool for enabling society to better govern itself. Not only will information technology make government more efficient and effective, it will enable citizens to get more involved in decision-making processes. The technocommunitarians argue that individuals have always looked to government for certain services that cannot be or have not been provided by the private sector. They argue that there is no reason to assume that those needs will disappear or that companies will suddenly begin providing services that are not sufficiently profitable. Although economists agree on few things, almost every economist agrees that there are common goods that the market will not adequately provide.

Let us consider the functions that governments have traditionally fulfilled and how information technologies could affect each of them. Throughout the developed and developing world, governments play a prominent role in:

1. National security
2. Personal security (for example, law and order)
3. Physical infrastructure (transportation, sewers, water)

4. Commercial law

5. Public health and safety

6. Education

7. Research and development

8. Economic development

9. Disaster assistance

10. Environmental protection

For each of these functions, we can speculate on how information technology could change government's role.

NATIONAL SECURITY

Even the most ardent cyberlibertarian will usually admit that governments will have a continuing role in national security. The debate instead focuses on what is worth protecting. Is it necessary to merely protect your own country's borders or does a wealthy, powerful country like the United States have responsibilities overseas as well? Globalization, driven in part by the digital economy, means that the economic vitality of the United States or any developed country is increasingly dependent on its trading partners. That argues for a more coordinated, global approach to security and that has been exactly what the Clinton Administration and previous administrations have been pursuing, through NATO, the United Nations, and other bilateral and multilateral alliances. Clearly, information technology, by facilitating coordination and intelligence sharing, is making this easier.

The growth of the digital economy also means that there are new national security threats. In particular, information warfare—attacks on a country's information infrastructure—are a growing concern. Malicious hackers, often just bored teenagers armed only with $2000 personal computers and modems, have demonstrated the vulnerabilities of both commercial and government computer and communications systems. It is clear that a foreign government could, with a focused effort, disrupt and damage parts of the U.S. telecommunications system and possibly affect the air-traffic control system, the electric power grid, and the oil and gas pipeline networks. For this reason, in July 1996, the White House created the President's Commission on Critical Infrastructure Protection, which, in October

1997, submitted a classified report with recommendations on how best to protect the U.S. information infrastructure.[5]

There are different approaches being considered. One is a top-down approach in which a new government agency monitors the security of the nation's networks and critical infrastructures and responds to any attacks or disruptions. A second grass-roots approach provides industry with incentives to monitor their own systems and improve the security and redundancy of the infrastructure. An example of this latter approach is the Computer Emergency Response Team (CERT) at Carnegie Mellon University, which monitors security breaches on the Internet. CERT provides information to managers so they can take steps to better protect their networks and computer systems from hackers, computer viruses, and other threats.

Not surprisingly, the private sector favors an industry-led approach. But such an effort will only work if the people who run the networks understand the threats and are motivated to address them. Governments can help by sharing information on the threats to and vulnerabilities of the global information infrastructure, by taking steps to secure its own information and telecommunications systems, and by promoting the development and dissemination of new technologies for protecting information systems and networks. As the number of individuals and organizations participating in the digital economy grows, it becomes increasingly difficult for all of them to cooperate to ensure network security and reliability. Yet, such cooperation—between government, industry, and users—is critical if the infrastructure upon which the digital economy depends is to be robust and secure enough to sustain it.

PERSONAL SECURITY

Since the first tribe formed, people have relied on governments to protect them, their families, and their possessions from harm. One of the oldest written documents is the first legal code promulgated by Hammurabi almost 4000 years ago to ensure law and order in ancient Babylon.

Law enforcement agencies invest heavily in information technology—computer systems, networks, wireless communications systems—so police can track and apprehend suspected criminals. In recent years, police departments have also started to use the Internet and computer networks to better inform citizens so they can help the police and so citizens can take steps to prevent crime. The National

Center for Missing and Exploited Children's Web site (www.missingkids.org), for example, is a vital resource to help law enforcement agencies locate missing children, and, more importantly, it informs parents about steps they can take to prevent kidnapping.

Local police stations are now making crime statistics available online. Citizens can be alerted if there has been a rash of burglaries or auto thefts in a certain neighborhood, and can take additional precautions. In this way, the Internet can help connect the police department to the community. By mobilizing the eyes and ears of hundreds of citizens, the Internet is strengthening community policing efforts around the country.

Law enforcement agencies also need to learn to deal with new, digital manifestations of crime. Information technology makes the theft of private information, personal information, or intellectual property easier and harder to detect. Child pornographers and extremist militias have demonstrated that the Internet can be a powerful medium for online conspiracy and the distribution of hateful, dangerous, or illegal content. Yet law enforcement agencies and the judiciary are only now learning how to address these critical issues.

Surveys have found that privacy, piracy, and pornography are the most serious concerns of Internet users. The increasing number of newspaper and magazine articles about online privacy and the need to protect children from adult material on the Internet reflect and accentuate the public's anxiety. Citizens expect their government to "do something." In response, the U.S. government and others are working with the private sector to find and promote new technological and legal solutions. But such solutions will have to be international, since neither the Internet nor cybercriminals respect national borders. And such solutions will have to be consistent with the widely varying national and local laws protecting freedom of speech and freedom of the press.

INFRASTRUCTURE

Governments have traditionally built the roads and bridges, water and sewer systems, and harbors and airports needed for a modern economy. These are shared facilities, which need to be available to all citizens for maximum societal benefit. It is hard to see how the private sector could assume more than a fraction of this role.

However, in most countries, the information infrastructure needed for the digital economy—the "information highway"—will not be built by government. Government needs to support the development of the information infrastructure and, in particular, take steps to ensure that all citizens have the opportunity to get connected. In the past, to achieve this goal, government would either (1) build and run communications networks itself, or (2) grant telecommunications companies monopolies and then regulate them to ensure they served all citizens for a reasonable price. Neither approach makes sense today, when many companies are using various technologies (telephone, cable TV, wireless, satellite) to compete for customers.

Some governments are starting to take a bottom-up approach that empowers individuals, not monopoly phone companies. One example is the decision in May 1997 by the Federal Communications Commission (FCC) to help schools and libraries get connections to the Internet. In the United States, most schools have lacked the resources to pay for Internet service and to install the inside wiring needed to connect to the Internet. Yet, without access to the Internet, students will not be well equipped to work in the digital economy.

To fill this need, the U.S. government could have set up a nationwide program which would have sent its employees or contractors into the schools to wire the classrooms and connect them to the Internet. Instead, the FCC took a grass-roots approach. It set aside $2.25 billion a year from the Universal Service Fund, which each telephone company contributes to in order to ensure telephone service to customers living in poor or high-cost areas. This money is to be used to pay up to 90 percent of the cost of inside wiring and Internet service for schools that apply for the program, with the poorest schools getting the largest subsidy. Schools are free to contract with whatever provider gives them the best price for the service they need.

Such a market-based approach encourages competition and ensures schools get the service they want at a reasonable price. For this approach to work, the government also needs to ensure that schools have the information they need to be informed buyers. Here, again, the Internet helps, by enabling schools to get answers to their questions, both by contacting the government and by communicating with other schools who have successfully wired their classrooms. Without such information, a decentralized, market-based approach does not work.

Many developing countries recognize that development of their national information infrastructure is essential if they are to join the developed countries in the digital economy. In many of these countries, the government is debating whether to follow the old top-down approach of empowering monopoly telecommunications companies to build the information infrastructure, or the new bottom-up approach of empowering consumers by giving them the choice of a number of competing telecommunications service providers. Those countries, such as Chile, that have chosen the latter approach have seen a stunning increase in the amount of investment, the quality of service, and the number of customers served. Countries that are willing to abandon the models of the past will reap most of the benefits of the digital economy.

COMMERCIAL LAW

A modern economy depends on government providing a framework for legally binding contracts. It is hard to see how businesses could function without such contracts.

However, in the digital economy, electronic commerce will be global. It will not be clear whose laws apply to a particular transaction. If a person in Germany buys software from a company in the United States using a server run by an Internet service provider in Canada, whose laws govern the purchase? Where does the customer go if he or she encounters a problem?

The global nature of online commerce could mean that commercial codes of conduct will begin to augment national contract law. Companies will agree to abide by a code of conduct specifying how it will treat customers and suppliers and a third party will validate that it is abiding by the code and investigate complaints if it fails to do so. For instance, such a code would ensure that an aggrieved party had recourse in case of breach of contract.

Consumers who wish to protect themselves would seek to do business with companies who have agreed to abide by such a code of conduct. While such codes would not be legally binding, companies will abide by them in order to attract customers and maintain their reputation in cyberspace. In this way, global competition in cyberspace, coupled with the ability of potential consumers to easily determine who is and who is not practicing fair business practices, will provide a replacement for contracts enforced by governments. It will work in much the same way as the Better Business Bureau does today. Individual consumers shopping online will have the information they need to find reliable, ethical vendors.

Consumer advocates have started to use the Internet to publish ratings of different products and services, everything from Internet service and modems to laundry detergent and automobiles. The next generation of Ralph Naders is busy using the Internet to publicize poor quality, overpriced products, and unethical business practices. By providing consumers with more information about the products and services they buy and the companies that make them, the Internet will make it much more difficult and less profitable for companies to defraud the public.

That said, government will still need to find and punish companies that deceive consumers. In particular, they will need to monitor online commerce in order to find, publicize, and arrest those who would use the Internet for digital scams.

PUBLIC HEALTH AND SAFETY

The digital revolution does not present any new threats to public health or safety. Nor will it dramatically change the function of public health and safety agencies or the expectations that citizens have of them.

However, new information technologies provide new tools that public health and safety agencies can use to disseminate health advisories and consumer information. The Center for Disease Control and Prevention, the National Library of Medicine, and other agencies have created effective Web sites to keep health care providers and the general public informed about a wide variety of topics.

In addition, thousands of private-sector Web sites providing health information have sprung up. Both traditional and alternative medicine are well represented on the Web. Some governments are worried about the quality of medical information available to Web surfers and fear that the advent of telemedicine could enable "cyber-doctors" to practice medicine without a proper license or training. Protecting consumers from quack remedies and unproven treatments will be increasingly difficult in a global electronic marketplace.

EDUCATION

In the United States and most countries, government-run school systems educate the majority of the country's children. The digital revolution promises to both improve the quality of education and to provide competition to the public school system.

Computer technology and the Internet enable teachers and students to enjoy access to a wide range of educational materials. Web pages, online courses, and video conferencing enhance what the classroom teacher can provide.

Such resources are available not only in public schools but also in private schools and to home-learners. Whittle Communications attempted to revolutionize the school system by using computer-based instruction to dramatically cut the annual cost of private schools by thousands of dollars per pupil. Like many revolutionaries, Whittle may have tried to do too much too soon. While he was not able to realize his dream in the early 1990s, since then the cost of computing has dropped and the quality and variety of educational material on CD-ROMs and the Internet has improved. Future entrepreneurs are expected to use information technology to improve the quality and substantially reduce the cost of private schooling.

We are already seeing an up swing in the number of children being taught at home. This reflects both growing dissatisfaction with the quality of public school education, and the fact that new tools make it easier for parents to give their children a top-notch education. However, the development of standards that validate the quality and content of educational software packages will be critical to educators and parents.

It will be interesting to see if, in the future, governments not only fund the public school system, but encourage alternative schooling by helping ensure that high-quality computer-based educational materials are affordable to all students.

RESEARCH AND DEVELOPMENT

The Internet is one of the best examples of the value of long-term government investments in research and development. Started in 1971 as a U.S. Defense Department research project, the first national computer network, ARPANET, evolved into NSFNet (funded by the National Science Foundation) and was gradually privatized in the early 1990s. Today, tens of millions of people around the world use commercial Internet service providers.

Long-term research projects such as ARPANET are unlikely to be funded by the private sector, especially in those industry sectors where increased competition is shortening the time horizon. Yet at the same time, more and more of the gross domestic product in industrialized countries is generated by high-tech companies that rely on innovation. For these reasons, all indications are that the importance of government research funding will increase as the digital economy develops.

Information technology will provide new opportunities to disseminate research results and better link government research programs to commercial and societal needs. There is every reason to believe that information technology should significantly shorten the "time to market" or commercialization of research and development efforts that will benefit both industry and consumers.

ECONOMIC DEVELOPMENT

Conservatives and liberals alike agree that the free market is a powerful mechanism for generating wealth and jobs. But the market only works for those who can fully participate. The Housing and Urban Development Web site is designed to help individuals in poor communities get the tools they need for job training and job finding. Similar state and local government efforts have used schools and libraries to give unemployed people access to the Internet and a wealth of information on job opportunities.

The digital economy offers new opportunities for economic development for communities that are otherwise outside the mainstream. The Center for Civic Networking helps small businesses in remote areas sell crafts or specialty food products online. Businesses that could never afford national advertising now have global reach. Other similar grass-roots efforts have started, often with seed funding from local, state, or national governments.

Again, government's goal should be to give individuals the information and the tools they need to help themselves.

Success will ultimately depend on the digital economy's ability to satisfy not just economic aspirations but also social, linguistic, and cultural needs. Some nations and cultures might resist the individualistic view of the Internet, looking instead for ways to more closely bind their social fabric.

DISASTER ASSISTANCE

Government has always provided emergency assistance in natural disasters, such as floods, earthquakes, and hurricanes. Although insurance increasingly covers the costs of repairs, government will continue to help citizens deal with unforeseen or unforeseeable disasters.

The digital economy does not present new challenges for government agencies responsible for disaster assistance. However, information technology does provide new opportunities. In the United States, the Federal Emergency Management Agency (FEMA) has been quite effective in using information technology to accomplish its mission.

FEMA was created during the Cold War to coordinate civil defense efforts and to prepare for and respond to natural and man-made disasters. Until the 1990s, it was notorious for being secretive, politicized, and poorly managed. Since the end of the Cold War, FEMA has shifted its focus from thermonuclear war to natural and man-made disasters. In addition, it has given much higher priority to disaster preparedness and prevention, rather than just disaster response.

Information technology has played a key role. The FEMA Web site is a source of information on what home owners can do to prepare for earthquakes, floods, and hurricanes. It provides online assistance for people whose homes or businesses have been damaged by natural or man-made disasters. The site links FEMA employees to one another, to state and local emergency preparedness officials, and to the public. FEMA has ended its top-down culture of secrecy and become a customer-focused organization.

ENVIRONMENTAL PROTECTION

Information technology is enabling the U.S. Environmental Protection Agency (EPA) and state environmental protection agencies to adopt new approaches. Traditionally, EPA has sent inspectors into the field to monitor emissions and fine factories violating pollution standards. As long as citizens want clean air and water, and as long as some factory owners disregard emission limits, the EPA will need inspectors in the field.

Increasingly, environmental agencies rely on self-reporting by businesses. One of the most cost-effective EPA programs in recent years has been the Toxic Waste Emission Database. Each year, businesses submit information on toxic waste emissions from factories. The EPA verifies the data and posts the results on the Internet. As a result, citizens can find out which businesses in their communities are polluting the environment. They can compare them to facilities in other communities. And they can use the information to pressure businesses to do a better job of reducing emissions, even when emission levels meet EPA standards. By providing local communities with information, government enables local action and reduces the need for top-down solutions.

TOWARD MORE WIRED, MORE EFFECTIVE GOVERNMENT

It is hard to see how information technology will end the need for government. Citizens will continue to look to government for a wide variety of services. And as long as that is the case, the cyberlibertarian's dream of government withering away will remain a science fiction fantasy.

However, it is clear that information technology provides a chance for government to work much more effectively and to find new ways to fulfill traditional roles. In the examples previously given, there are recurring themes:

1. Government will devote more resources to collecting, verifying, and disseminating information which citizens and communities can use to address problems at the local level.

2. Grass-roots programs tailored to unique local needs will replace top-down national programs. Information technology will enable local organizations (both governmental and nongovernmental) to obtain the expertise and information previously restricted to national and state agencies. They will combine this with knowledge of community needs to find effective solutions to problems.

3. Information technology will allow more effective sharing of information among local groups striving to tackle similar problems. This will eliminate the need for some national and state programs. This has been happening in K-12 education as teachers and school administrators go online and share experiences.

4. For such solutions to work, there must be equal access to information resources. Thus, there will be a continuing and increasing role for government to make sure the poor and disadvantaged can be full participants in the digital economy. Market mechanisms can work magic, but only if everyone can participate.

CONCLUSION

It is clear that over the next 10 to 20 years, the role and function of government will change more than it has over the previous 200 years. New digital technologies will change the ways in which government collects, processes, and disseminates information, and will empower individuals to find new ways to solve problems. That said, citizens will still look to government for a core set of functions—national security, personal security, commercial law, education, R&D, help for the disadvantaged, and environmental protection.

But in many of these areas, rather than expecting top-down solutions emanating from their national capitals, citizens will look to their national government to give them the information they need to leverage the resources, organize themselves, and solve their own problems. National government will distribute fewer dollars but much more information. If this is done properly, the result could be far more cost efficient and more responsive.

In 1793, Alexander Hamilton, then the U.S. Treasury Secretary, wrote "A Report on Manufactures,"[6] his attempt to chart a course for the United States at the start of the industrial revolution. Hamilton understood the profound changes that the industrial revolution would bring to both the economy and the government of the newly independent nation. His report was intended as a blueprint for government actions needed to fully realize the potential of that revolution.

It is clear that a similar report is needed today, one that reexamines the role of government in the digital economy. Such a report would attempt to design a new form of representative democracy from the ground up. No doubt such a report would be controversial since it would challenge the assumptions and power of many existing government agencies and other institutions. And, like Hamilton's report, parts of it would be wrong. In an interconnected, globalized world, this report would also need to recognize the collective aspirations of individuals and nations representing a wide variety of ideologies.

It is not easy to predict how technologies will develop. It is even harder to predict how they will be used. Yet we need to start now to assess how the new digital technologies can and will change the way we govern ourselves.

NOTES

1. The opinions and conclusions of this paper are those of the author and do not necessarily reflect the views of other FCC staff, the Commission, or any of its Commissioners.
2. See "The National Information Infrastructure—Agenda for Action," "The Global Information Infrastructure—Agenda for Cooperation," "A Framework for Global Electronic Commerce," July 1, 1997, Organisation for Economic Co-operation and Development, summary of National Information Infrastructure plans, Paris, France.
3. See the National Performance Review.
4. Brownstein, Ronald, "Rage Against the Machine," *Fast Company*, August/September, 1996, p. 94.
5. For a summary of the "President's Commission on Critical Infrastructure Protection," see http://www.pccip.gov/summary.html.
6. Hamilton, Alexander, "Report on Manufactures," 1793.

YOU CAN'T DECLARE CYBERSPACE NATIONAL TERRITORY

Economic Policy Making in the Digital Age

by Stephen J. Kobrin
Wharton School

A Wall Street financial analyst notices problems with an important program. Before leaving for the day, she e-mails a support firm in India, requesting that the bug be fixed. The programmer in Bangalore turns on his computer, connects to the workstation in New York via satellite, and by the next morning the program has been repaired. Payment is then transferred electronically from New York to an account in Bangalore.

A teenager in Germany buys an album from a French virtual music store by downloading it from a Web site maintained in India. Using her smart card, she pays with electronic cash—perhaps in marks, perhaps in dollars—which she deposits in a bank in the Cayman Islands. Sometimes she downloads and records an entire album, and other times she simply listens to a selection of popular songs.

Both of these transactions took place in cyberspace—a marketplace unlike any other in history. No physical product crossed a geopolitical boundary; no paper currency changed hands. In fact, no slip of paper may even exist on this planet as a tangible record of either transaction. Now, consider the staggering and perplexing economic implications of billions of similar transactions which will take place every day in the new digital economy.

My main concern here is not what is going to happen but what might be possible. The general outlines of our digital future are becoming clearer, even if precise shapes are not yet evident. The emerging electronically networked global economy will affect how we are governed and how we live. Policy makers, technologists, managers—each of us, for that matter—must confront the political and economic implications of digitization if we are to shape the twenty-first century societies in which we will work and live.

I will begin by looking more deeply into our first two scenarios.

THE INDIAN SOFTWARE INDUSTRY

Although India is among the world's poorer countries, it has several excellent technical institutes and universities which produce a large number of well-trained and productive programmers who are significantly less expensive to employ than their European or North American counterparts.

The sector has grown dramatically, from a total turnover of $10 million in 1986 to $1.2 billion in 1996; the estimate for the compound growth rate for the first half of the 1990s was 46 percent per year. The industry is export-driven: exports, primarily of software services, have grown at over 60 percent per annum in recent years, rising to $734 million in 1996 and accounting for about 61 percent of total turnover.[1]

A number of factors are responsible for the dramatic growth of Indian software service exports. Most relevant here, however, is that India's communications infrastructure has developed to the point where reliable high-speed international data links are readily available, at least to the extent necessary to support growth of this industry.

How are these software services exported? The Indian industry has relied on the two obvious methods. "Body shopping"—sending Indian programmers to on-site locations—accounts for about 60 percent of exports. On the other hand, offshore services delivered via direct satellite links have been growing rapidly. As late as 1990, offshore services accounted for only 9 percent of exports; by 1996 they accounted for 40 percent.

One potentially huge source of revenue for the Indian software industry is the "millennium bug," the problems older computers will face when dealing with dates after December 31, 1999. It is not unlikely that Indian firms will develop a "product" that solves the problem and subsequently be swamped with requests for their "product." A host of programmers in Bangalore could be logged onto computers all over North America and Europe 24 hours a day to fill the demand, being paid by electronic transfer of funds from their clients' accounts to theirs.

MUSIC OVER THE WEB

Music is hot on the Internet. A simple Alta Vista search for the word "music" resulted in over 6.5 million hits. There are any number of Web pages that are devoted to artists, innumerable categories and subcategories of music, and countless opportunities for fans to chat about music and their favorite stars.

There are also an increasing number of sites, such as CDnow and Tower Music, that sell CDs. These online music stores offer a great deal of information and some clever ways to find music you would not normally come across on your own. Although they are innovative in many ways, the process still boils down to a virtual mail-order business. Consumers select CDs and pay for them with their credit cards using a secure browser. The CDs are then shipped to the buyer. While 1997 online sales of recorded music are estimated at only about $47 million, the market could grow to about $1.6 billion by 2002, or about 7.5 percent of total volume.[2]

It is of interest here that some of the largest music companies such as Warner and Sony have established virtual retail stores on the Web. Anticipating the next step in the digital music market place—delivery of music over the Net to the listener's computer or audio system—they are selling many of their titles directly to the consumer. Sony's TheStore, for example, offers prices competitive with major retail outlets and other online sellers.

Since almost all music is now digital, existing as 0s and 1s on a CD, it is easy to bypass or "disintermediate" all of the traditional intermediaries. The music could be listened to immediately, saved on a hard drive for later enjoyment, or recorded on a CD.

Although a number of "cyberjukeboxes" currently offer music over the Internet, they have been hindered by the amount of time it takes to download even a relatively short song, the poor quality of the sound, and all of the obvious problems of illegal copying and distribution. (It is far from clear that all of the current sites are concerned about this last issue.)

Most of these problems are in the process of being solved. Cable networks and other sources of wider bandwidth have reduced the time required to download high-quality audio to well within acceptable limits. Sound quality is improving rapidly due to advances with computer-based sound systems and the means by which computers are linked to audio systems. While copyright protection is a more difficult problem, solutions include embedding a digital signature or watermark within the music to identify the copyright owner, and technologies that prevent unauthorized reproduction.

An interesting test of direct digital delivery of music was conducted in France in the summer of 1997. Eurodat's Paris Music project reached about 400 homes connected to the Cybercable network in Le Mans, Strasbourg, and Paris. After sampling a selection, consumers could download songs to their hard disk for prices ranging from 6 to 15 francs, depending on the popularity of the title. The music could then be played either through the computer's sound system or by connecting the hard drive to an audio system. A 3-minute song would take about 90 seconds to download; 300 songs consumed about 1 gigabyte of memory. Encryption software prevented the music from being copied from the receiving hard drive.[3] Like software services, payment occurs through the transfer of electronic cash.

ELECTRONIC CASH[4]

As the digital economy grows, and purchases of products and services over the Internet becomes an everyday reality, the typical means of payment will be some form of electronic cash. Electronic cash is not new. Most money in the world economy has been digital for some time, transferred electronically from bank to bank, computer to computer. Only a small proportion of the trillions of pounds, dollars, yen, and marks circulating around the globe each day actually takes tangible form in checks, cash, and coin.

Of interest here are the new forms of electronic money, such as smart cards and digital cash, which really do represent new modes of payment. Smart cards, or "electronic wallets" (Mondex, for example), are plastic cards with an embedded microchip that can electronically store all sorts of data—medical information and security devices—as well as acting as electronic wallets.

Money can be downloaded to a smart card directly from an ATM, or, using available card readers and a personal computer, over the telephone or the Internet. Funds can then be spent at merchants or vending machines with appropriate scanning devices. Used this way, smart cards are not very interesting; they are merely debit cards which do not require approval for each transaction. They have the potential, however, to do a lot more than transfer funds from one bank account to another.

Electronic wallets such as Mondex allow direct and anonymous user-to-user transfers. Banks, or any other firm, for that matter, could download funds to your smart card as a loan or payment for products or services. You could then transfer funds to any other cardholder via a small two-card reader or your personal computer. As long as confidence is maintained that funds can be redeemed or spent at will, dollars or marks or yen could circulate from card to card almost indefinitely. (The Mondex card can hold up to six currencies in its "wallet.")

Must wallets continue to bulge with plastic in the digital age? Why not just eliminate the card? Electronic cash could take true digital form as units of value stored on the hard drive of your personal computer, either downloaded from your account, obtained as a loan from a bank or a nonfinancial institution, or transferred over the Internet as payment for consulting services or supplies. Whether or not it must be backed up by reserve accounts of "real" money is still an open question. What is critical is that there is confidence that it is authentic—that the payee can be sure it is real—and that it will continue to be accepted in the future.

What might a world where electronic cash is an everyday reality look like a few years into the future? Again, my concern here is not what is likely, or perhaps even immediately feasible, but scenarios that are within the realm of the possible:

- Multiple "brands" of e-cash exist. Most of the major banks have created e-currencies, but they face stiff competition from Microsoft, General Motors, and a variety of other institutions.

Some electronic currencies exist on their own; they are no longer backed by "real money" and are not denominated in units issued by a central bank. The better known brands of e-cash are very liquid and universally accepted.

- Peer-to-peer payments are easily made. Digital value units, or DVUs, can be transferred to any computer anywhere in the world with the stroke of a key; anyone with access to the Internet can now transfer funds across borders electronically. DVUs are easily divisible, making it simple to purchase a snippet of information over the Net, even if it costs only a few cents.

- E-cash is secure and easily authenticated. It is also anonymous. Public key encryption technology and digital signatures allow the receiving computer to know the e-cash is authentic without revealing the identity of the payer. E-cash can be exchanged any number of times without leaving an audit trail behind.

THE ECONOMIC IMPLICATIONS OF THE DIGITAL ECONOMY

Cyberspace is intangible; you cannot ask where a transaction took place. Yet, effective economic policy making depends on the fundamental assumption that, even in the global world economy of the late twentieth century, all transactions take place *somewhere*. That all production, sales, loans, and currency exchanges can be precisely located in two-dimensional space. That at the end of the day, one can determine jurisdiction: whose law and regulations apply.

The World Bank's 1997 World Development Report[5] argues that the unique strength of national governments—the power to tax, prohibit, punish, and require participation—results directly from its monopoly over law enforcement and rule making within their boundaries. Thus, the emergence of an electronically integrated digital economy renders geographically rooted jurisdiction and, by extension, territorial sovereignty problematic, to say the least. This basic disconnect between geographic space and cyberspace raises fundamental questions about national economic control, and indeed, the very meaning of a national economy.

Obviously, the location of a business is the critical factor in determining who gets to regulate and tax it. The U.S. tax code, for example, uses such terms as "permanent establishment" and "fixed place of business." Where did the transaction occur? Where was the income generated? Where is the business located? Where is the firm incorporated? The "where" is always in terms of borders and national territory.

But we must remember that the "blurring" of national borders is not new. As business has become more international, and capital, technology, managers, and even labor more mobile, jurisdiction has become increasingly ambiguous. Is the Canadian subsidiary of an American multinational an American firm subject to tight U.S. regulation prohibiting trade with Cuba, or is it a Canadian firm subject to Canadian law? Do multinationals slip between tax jurisdictions or do they get caught in a tangled web of multiple taxing authorities? Whose environmental law applies? Whose standards of worker rights?

In the new digital economy borders and jurisdiction are *irrelevant*, rather than ambiguous. Transactions cannot be located in geographic space because they do not take place *there*; "electronic commerce doesn't seem to occur in any physical location but instead takes place in the nebulous world of 'cyberspace'."[6] The problem economic policy makers now face is the absence of jurisdiction rather than interjurisdictional conflict.

In this next section, I would like to explore the problems electronic commerce poses for policy making in a world where law and regulation is firmly rooted in territorial sovereignty.

MANAGING THE NATIONAL ECONOMY

Although the end of the Cold War ushered in the era of the global market, all governments continue to take responsibility for some degree of management of the domestic economy, at a minimum, trying to assure macroeconomic stability. Most governments go further, accepting varying degrees of responsibility for societal health, welfare, and well-being. In every country, however, the spread of e-cash and e-commerce will raise some serious questions about the role of government in a market economy.

If digital cash becomes widespread, central banks may find themselves competing with a number of private electronic currencies issued by a variety of institutions. Some or even many of these may be beyond the reach of the state. How will central bankers exert control over the size and rate of growth of the money supply if the "national" currency loses its monopoly position?

The problem may be compounded by a loss of control over financial institutions; indeed, by a significant dilution of the meaning of that term. Take one example: Could U.S. reserve and reporting requirements be applied to Microsoft's and General Motors' e-currencies? While current U.S. regulations apply to anyone who "acts like a bank"—that is, takes deposits—it is far from clear what "acts like a bank" means in a digital economy. All that can be said at this point is that it is unclear whether the current system of regulation of "financial" institutions will apply to everyone who issues e-cash.[7] Indeed, we are still far from sure what "issue e-cash" really means as well.

E-cash and e-commerce will make it increasingly difficult to define and measure both monetary aggregates and national income and wealth. Defining and measuring the domestic money supply certainly will be problematic. However, one can go further and ask if any of the traditional measures of the size and rate of growth of a domestic economy (gross domestic product, for example) will retain meaning if electronic commerce and electronic cash become widespread.

How will governments track electronic transactions paid for with electronic cash? Many of the commercial and financial institutions which record and report transactions will be bypassed in the emerging digital economy as direct e-cash sales to consumers become the norm.

TAX COLLECTION

The new digital economy puts some serious obstacles in the path of the tax collector, be it a locality, state or region, or national government. Electronic commerce gives new meaning to the term "mobile capital." Moving the "location" of a business may mean no more than electronically transferring key files to a new computer. It will be easier than ever to "flee" jurisdictions with high tax rates and relocate in those with low ones.

Tax evasion will be a very serious problem in an economy where e-commerce and e-cash are the norm. If encrypted, anonymous transactions are the rule, audits will become increasingly problematic. In many countries, tax reporting and collection is dependent on all sorts of intermediaries: merchants who collect a sales tax or firms that report payments to individuals, for example. As already noted, many of these reporting institutions may be bypassed by direct sales over the Net. Electronic commerce transactions which involve the exchange of information for information—digital data for electronic cash—may be especially problematic in this regard.

Who is going to report and collect the sales or value-added tax our teenage consumer owes when she downloads an album from the French company? A mail-order supplier, whether conventional or Web-based, always knows where the product is being shipped. However, if information is being downloaded over the Web, the seller may have no idea where the buyer is actually located and vice versa.

How will the French tax authorities be able to track revenue generated when a customer "buys" an album from a computer located in India and pays by transferring e-cash to a Cayman Islands bank? If the album originally resides on a music company's computer in Ireland and is then sent via the Indian server through the French company's Web site to the German consumer, do each of the four governments get to tax the transaction?

"THE SCENE OF THE CRIME"

"Returning to the scene of the crime" is a well-worn plot device in murder mysteries. The assumption that crimes take place "somewhere" is so basic it does not need to be stated, but it is critical: it determines which authority has jurisdiction, and, indeed, whether or not the act is a crime under the law. Again, while there may have always been some ambiguity here (whether state/provincial or federal authorities have jurisdiction, for example), that ambiguity generally does not involve "the scene of the crime."

Let's assume that our German teenager is defrauded. What happens if she transfers payment to the Cayman Island bank and then finds that the album is not delivered as promised? To whom does she turn? German authorities? French? Indian?

From the viewpoint of law enforcement authorities, a world of e-commerce and e-cash combines all of the problems of cyberspace with those of a cash economy. While the issue of privacy versus the needs of law enforcement authorities is far from resolved, money laundering would become child's play if digital cash remains anonymous and untraceable. The electronic transfer of funds, which at this point is the privilege of banks and other large institutions, will be available to anyone with access to a computer and the Internet. Large sums could be transferred at the touch of a key anywhere in the world without an audit trail. Digital counterfeiters, for example, could work from anyplace in the world and spend any number of currencies anyplace. New forms of fraud and financial crime will certainly appear which will be hard to detect.

Germany now appears to be the epicenter of attempts to control Internet content through criminal prosecution. German prosecutors have tried to block access to material that is considered obscene, violent, or a danger to society; for example, anything that glorifies the Nazis or neo-Nazis.

If our German teenager downloaded or even just listened to music with a Nazi theme, that clearly would violate German law and she could be arrested. But the Web site, in France or India, is outside of the reach of German jurisdiction.

At first glance there does not appear to be much difference between accessing a Web site and listening to proscribed music on short wave radio. However, there is a fundamental difference between music broadcast over the airwaves and music that is downloaded from the Internet. A host server can be accessed from everywhere and anywhere. And almost anything is likely to be illegal someplace in the world.

In one case, a young German woman was arrested for maintaining a link on her Web page to a Dutch site which provided access to *Radikal*, a left-wing newspaper that contained information about making bombs and derailing trains—illegal in Germany. Her defense was that the Dutch site exists, whether or not her home page is linked to it. Going one step further, German authorities threatened action against the Internet provider for not blocking access to the site.[8]

Any Web site, regardless of where it is "located," can be accessed from any computer anyplace in the world. Does that make every Web site subject to the laws of every country in the world? Does everyone have jurisdiction? Does *anyone* have jurisdiction? Does jurisdiction, a geographic concept which entails control over discrete territory, even apply to the digital world of cyberspace?

SEPARATING THE DOMESTIC FROM THE INTERNATIONAL

Our earlier example of an Indian programmer in Bangalore working to solve the millennium bug on a bank's mainframe computer in New York raises some fundamental questions about the very meaning of the term "international trade."

An export or import is an international or cross-border economic transaction—which assumes geographic jurisdictions and discrete borders. The idea of finite goods crossing a discrete and effective national (jurisdictional) border is critical; an export is produced in one market and consumed in another. For example, an automobile produced in Germany physically crosses the U.S. border when it enters the American market. And even though my copy of the *Financial Times* does not cross the U.S. border in a physical sense when it is transmitted via satellite to an American printing plant, given that a tangible product is sold by a subsidiary of the British company, it fits the definition of export closely enough.

But, according to the U.S. Treasury, "the Internet has no physical location. Users of the Internet have no control and in general no knowledge of the path traveled by the information they seek or publish."[9] Do India's offshore software services then, represent exports and imports? If the packets of bytes comprising the instructions or new code from the computer in India travel through five different countries, do they really cross five borders? Is it reasonable to even describe this phenomenon in terms of international trade in services?

If governments cannot control, or even track and measure, critical cross-border flows, the idea of a domestic economy or national market loses all meaning and it becomes difficult, if not impossible, to talk about international or cross-border trade and investment.

"Foreign" Exchange

What about electronic transfers of digital cash? As already discussed, digital cash will "democratize" cross-border electronic funds transfers; anyone with a PC and access to the Internet will be able to send funds anywhere in the world to another compatible computer. Peer-to-peer transfers of digital value units (DVUs), however, are not necessarily official foreign exchange transactions in any real sense. If I have $200 of DVUs on my hard drive and buy a computer program from a German programmer, we will agree on a mark/dollar exchange rate. However, when I transfer my DVUs to Germany, I send them over the Internet to my German supplier's hard drive. No foreign exchange transaction need take place; the DVUs are simply revalued as marks rather than dollars. If the German programmer then pays a bill in Paris and transfers those DVUs to a French firm's computer, they would be revalued again as francs.

The critical point here is that no official foreign exchange transaction has taken place. DVUs—bytes on a hard drive—have simply been renamed dollars, marks, and then francs, and valued accordingly. It is certainly reasonable to wonder how long it will take for universally denominated DVUs to emerge. If electronic currencies develop that are independent of central bank currencies, why should they be called something different in each national market? While it is far from clear that governments have any real control over the tremendous volume of cross-border flows of funds at this point, it will be virtually impossible in a world of digital cash.

Perhaps even more important, governments may not be able to track flows of "money" across their borders. If e-cash is anonymous, states will not be able to account for much of these cross-border flows. "Official" reporting will be bypassed when direct peer-to-peer transfers take place. If a cross-border flow of information—software for example—is paid for with e-cash, the entire transaction may be beyond the reach of the state.

CYBERSPACE AND SOVEREIGNTY

"Disintermediation" is a word that comes up frequently in discussions of electronic commerce.[10] Downloading albums from Sony's Web site, for example, disintermediates, or bypasses, retail music outlets. Similarly, downloading software directly from Microsoft's or Netscape's site disintermediates computer stores and mail-order houses.

But on a much larger scale, the emergence of a digitally networked world economy may eventually disintermediate geography or territorial sovereignty. Once again, it is important to understand that the issue here is not simply the increased *permeability* of borders or the increased *mobility* of capital, technology, and information in an electronic age; it is that e-cash, e-commerce, and electronic markets may render territory—and with it, *sovereignty* itself—irrelevant.

It is hard for us to imagine a world where politics and economics are not organized geographically, in terms of territories bounded by discrete borders. However, both nation states and national markets are relatively recent creations.

While countries such as France and England have existed in some form for much of the current millennium, the modern concept of sovereign states is only about 400 years old, conventionally dated from the Treaty of Westphalia which ended the Thirty Years' War in 1648. Territorial sovereignty is certainly not privileged historically; other political systems have existed in the past and others may well come into being in the future.

Over 65 years ago, *The Economist* observed that the tension between a political system partitioned into "sixty or seventy" sovereign national states and a single all-embracing world economy has been producing "a series of jolts, jars and smashes in the social life of humanity." Much more recently, the U.S. Comptroller of the Currency echoed this argument in contemporary terms: "E-money and E-banking are fast making geography irrelevant…Unfortunately, while geography may be becoming irrelevant from the standpoint of business operations and communications, it is still very much a part of the laws and regulations that govern the provision of financial products and services in this country." He goes on to note that "the legal structure that governs our activities as regulators and the activities of the institutions we regulate still has geography at its core."[11]

Both *The Economist* and the Comptroller of the Currency point to an emerging asymmetry between economics and politics. The former is increasingly global rather than transborder, and organized in terms of electronic networks. The international financial system, for example, is comprised of hundreds of thousands of screens located all over the world. It is the first major electronic market and certainly will not be the last. It cannot be described in geographic terms: the international financial market does not exist in geographic space.

Politics, however, is still overwhelmingly local and geographic. The problem we face is that territorial sovereignty is no longer a viable basis for exerting control over an economy or economic activity in a world of electronic cash, electronic commerce, and electronic markets.

In one sense the U.S. Congress is 100 percent correct on this issue. American sovereignty is being compromised daily by the emerging electronically integrated global economy. So is that of every other nation state in the system. The tide, however, cannot be stemmed by yelling at the surf. *We cannot declare cyberspace national territory.*

Nation states will be with us for the foreseeable future; they are not going to fade away. However, that does not mean that what states look like and how they function today will remain the same.

CONCLUSION

My focus in this chapter has been the problem rather than the solution. However, it is reasonable to ask: What will replace territorial sovereignty as the basis for economic governance? I think that the answer has to be coordinated transnational solutions to problems that can no longer be resolved uninationally.

Three types of international action would seem warranted. At the most basic level, there is a need to harmonize national legislation. The U.S. Government's "Framework for Global Electronic Commerce," for example, calls for governing commercial transactions on the Internet by "consistent principles across state, national, and international borders that lead to predictable results regardless of the jurisdiction in which a particular buyer or seller resides."[12]

This will help prevent the use of electronic networks to "slip between the cracks" of national jurisdiction on the one hand, or the hindrance of the development of electronic commerce because of a fear of getting caught between jurisdictions, on the other. Harmonization, however, assumes cross-national agreement on basic principles such as content or taxation. European-American disagreements on encryption and privacy—which are being aired as this chapter is written—are examples of the difficulties we will face in this area.

Second, more substantial steps towards governance will require markedly strengthened international institutions such as the World Trade Organization. Effective governance of a digital world economy will require institutions with the authority to collect data, to regulate, and, perhaps, to tax. International institutions provide the possibility of a nongeographic mode of governance layered on top of territorial sovereignty where it remains effective. Again, the issue is not whether states cede sovereignty but whether they are willing to act in concert to buffer it with an effective nonterritorial mode of governance.

Last, the erosion of territorial sovereignty raises the possibility of an increased role for "nonsovereign" actors in the international system to oversee "international agreements" between all sorts of nongovernmental and private institutions. An example is provided by international finance where the Group of 20, a consortium of leading banks from Europe, North America, and Japan, have agreed to set up a mechanism to develop real-time settlement of foreign exchange transactions to minimize the problems of settlement or "Herstatt" risk in foreign exchange markets. The action came in response to demands by central banks that the private sector find a solution to the problem posed by settlements in yen, marks, and dollars taking place in different time zones.[13] (There could be a serious shock to the system if a bank collapsed in one time zone, leaving its trades unsettled in another.)

An interagency working group of the U.S. government preparing the framework for global electronic commerce concluded that "the Internet has become the vehicle of a new, global digital economy which has enveloped the physical world, altering traditional concepts of economic, political and social relations." It has transformed our concepts of space and time. In doing so, it renders territorial sovereignty, the basic underlying mode of modern economic governance, problematic.

The question we ultimately face is how economic and political governance will be organized in our digital future when geography is no longer a valid or viable mode of exercising economic and political authority. How will the disconnect between geographic space and cyberspace be resolved? How will we govern ourselves and how will we organize the type of societies we will want to live in?

NOTES

1. The data on the Indian software industry is drawn from: Nicholson, Mark, "India Emerges as a World Centre for Software," *Financial Times,* July 7, 1996, p. 4, and Taylor, Paul, "Exports are Surging Ahead," *Financial Times,* Survey: India's Software Industry, November 6, 1996, p. 1.

2. Rawsthorn, Alice, "Online Music Sales to Reach $1.6bn in US," *Financial Times,* June 20, 1997, p. 4.

3. See Henshaw, Lee, "Farewell CDs, Hello Hard Disk," *The Independent,* June 17, 1997, p. N6 and Covington, Richard, "French Company Launches On-Line Jukebox," *International Herald Tribune,* April 7, 1997, p. 11.

4. The discussion of electronic cash in this chapter is drawn from Kobrin, Stephen J., "Electronic Cash and the End of National Markets," *Foreign Policy,* Summer 1997, pp. 65–77.

5. The World Bank, *The State in a Changing World* (New York: Oxford University Press), 1997.

6. Department of the Treasury, "Selected Tax Policy Implications of Global Electronic Commerce," Washington, D.C., November 1996 (*http://jya.com/taxpolicy.htm*).

7. See Hayes, David G., et al., "Introduction to Electronic Money Issues," a paper prepared for the U.S. Department of the Treasury Conference "Towards Electronic Money and Banking," Washington, D.C., September 19–20, 1996.

8. Andrews, Edmund L., "Germany's Efforts to Police the Web are Upsetting Business," *The New York Times,* June 6, 1997, p. A1.

9. "Selected Tax Policy Implications of Global Electronic Commerce," op. cit., p. 14.

10. The term "disintermediation" originally referred to the shift of funds from savings accounts in S&Ls and banks to direct purchases of treasury bills or money market accounts when interest rates rose beyond the regulatory ceilings imposed on some financial institutions.

11. *The Economist,* October 11, 1930, p. 652. Also see remarks by Eugene A. Ludwik, Comptroller of the Currency, before the ABA Conference on Financing Commerce in Cyberspace, Washington, D.C., May 8, 1996, *Office of the Comptroller of the Currency Quarterly Journal,* OCC OJ LEXIS 313.

12. Clinton, William J., and Albert Gore, Jr. "A Framework for Global Electronic Commerce," Washington, D.C., July 1997 (*http:///www.iif.nist.gov/eleccomm/ecomm.htm*), p. 4.

13. Graham, George, "Top Banks Approve Global Settlement Service," *The Financial Times,* June 27, 1997, p. 6. Herstatt risk refers to the collapse of a Cologne bank in 1974 with dollar liabilities left unsettled due to the time difference between Europe and the United States.

STRANGER THAN TRUTH OR FICTION

FRAUD, DECEPTION, AND THE INTERNET

by Vinton G. Cerf
MCI Communications

Where is the wisdom we lost in knowledge? Where is the knowledge we lost in information?

T. S. ELIOT

Though the lament of America's most famous expatriate may be decades old, his words have a newfound resonance when we consider how today's digital technologies are affecting the way we perceive and shape reality.

Among many of my colleagues, there is a feeling that the widespread use of the Internet will usher in a new technological utopia. Part of this attitude stems from a belief that somehow the Internet is not rooted in reality.

While I share much of this enthusiasm for the future of the Internet, I find I have to temper this view with the understanding that this so-called virtual world is firmly grounded in the mores, customs, and frailties of the real world. It is not, as some metaphors tend to suggest, a separately existing platonic world of perfection, but rather, exists in continuum with our everyday, sometimes messy reality. As a consequence, we are subject to many of the same hazards we experience in the real world.

However, when we travel in cyberspace—whether for personal or business purposes—we must come to grips with the fact that, as communications and information technologies merge, blur, and meld into ever more powerful forms, we are going to be subject to increasingly clever and insidious types of digital harassment, fraud, and deception. And with the Internet open to all, the opportunities for information abuse increase a million-fold; human interaction and commercial activity will discover their online vulnerabilities and aggressions, while the line between truth and fiction will become finer.

In this chapter, I will explore some of the abusive behavior we have seen to date, and the potential for fraud on the Internet. What I hope to offer is a glimpse into the technical, legal, and social solutions to governing this new space without destroying its democratic nature.

INTERNET ABUSES

Consider the travails suffered by an author from Maryland.

In early 1996, the author received an e-mail from a literary agency in New York. After contacting them to inquire if they would be interested in representing her, the agency asked the author for a $225 reading fee before reviewing some of her work.

Requiring fees before agreeing to represent a writer is a common scam in the literary industry, and the offer made the author wary. So, using postings to USENET groups, she began to spread the word to warn others of possible wrongdoing. Although she was by no means the only author to warn others about the agency, she was targeted for anonymous harassment for her efforts.

Over the next few weeks, e-mail addresses used by the author, her literary agent, and a university where she was a teaching assistant were inundated with messages—a particularly odious practice known in the field as "mail bombing." In addition, racist messages were posted to newsgroups using the author's name. Finally, a sexually suggestive posting in the author's name included her address and telephone number, and led to harassing phone calls and unwanted magazine subscriptions.

Making the situation even more frustrating was the fact that the harassers had altered their e-mail addresses to conceal their identities. Eventually, with the help of some Internet-savvy friends, the author was able to track down her harassers.

In January 1997, she filed a $10 million lawsuit in the U.S. District Court of New York, naming the literary agency and its associates as defendants.[1]

There are other examples. One Georgia woman got into an argument on a USENET newsgroup on advertising, and soon found herself on the receiving end of a barrage of hostile messages from the person she had been arguing with. Later, more messages were sent through an anonymous remailer—a service that can conceal the original source of an e-mail message. Further, the woman eventually discovered her name and e-mail address had been posted on the Web along with the photo of a nude woman and text offering to have sex with visitors to the Atlanta area during the Olympic Games—a posting that generated thousands of unwanted e-mail messages.

While cases like these are by no means the norm, they point out that the sort of localized boorish behavior we see in society at large can take on overwhelming forms when carried out in the realm of the Internet and digital technology. In addition, it is not only individuals who are subject to these sorts of attacks. Businesses, as well, can be victims of mail bombing and libelous attacks on newsgroups, Web pages, or distribution lists.

Many of these abuses have counterparts in older media (e.g., crank calls and poison-pen letters) but we have more well-established means of combating abuses and/or prosecuting abusers in these other media. Part of the frustration with more serious forms of Internet abuse comes from the inability of law enforcement to help. In both the examples cited here, no real physical threat had been made. Furthermore, laws concerning Internet-based harassment are neither uniformly on record nor well understood or applied.

The lack of a developed legal (and moral code), combined with the ability to quite easily conceal one's identity, can encourage gross and even illegal conduct on the Internet. In addition to simple, aggressive behavior as illustrated here, one of the most prolific misuses of anonymity is the distribution of junk e-mail, or "spam." Although not illegal (yet), spam is usually even less useful than the regular junk mail we receive in our snail mail boxes at home. Furthermore, spam can actually cost the recipient more to read and process than the sender. In addition, by falsifying return addresses, senders of spam either render the messages "unreplyable" or victimize the alleged senders who receive irate responses from the targets of the original spam.

Despite such drawbacks, anonymity does have its benefits. Many thousands of users enjoy anonymous subscription to newsgroups. Anonymity can allow for free and frank discussion of contentious issues. It can also aid law enforcement by encouraging whistleblowing and anonymous tips.

While the sort of abusive activities I described here could not be described as rampant, it is clear that the threat is real and growing. As the Internet continues to expand at its current exponential pace, we can expect the opportunities for this kind of behavior to increase exponentially as well.

DIGITAL FRAUD AND FORGERY

Combating the kind of malicious or annoying harassment previously described is only one challenge on the Internet. There are also those of fraud and forgery, not to mention the more naive propagation of misinformation. With ever increasing processing power, the desktop PC now has the power to alter or fabricate all types of information. Future advances in PC technology will only make uncovering digital forgery more difficult. Connecting the PC to the Internet further allows easy and rapid distribution of information on a global scale, from an increasing number and variety of sources. Plainly, we will be confronted with the need to authenticate the purported sources of online information. The ability to forge source indications is one obvious area needing attention. Once again, digital signatures may prove very useful in effecting the validation of origin and integrity of online material.

We do know for sure that we will be dealing with a blizzard of information as individuals and Internet-enabled devices interact in ways we have only begun to imagine. Already, industry observers have begun discussing just how we can expect to cull useful information from mounds of data. Many of us eagerly await the arrival of the digital snowplow, but in the meantime, we will apply the same techniques we use today to cope with the information reaching us by radio, television, newspapers, magazines, books, and telephone.

GAINING CREDIBILITY

As in our noncyberspace meanderings, we will no doubt come to rely on trademarked publications and their editors to guide our selection of content. We will rely on friends and recognized authorities to help find reliable information sources worthy of our trust and attention. There will always be a role for individuals who serve as "filters" of information—whether they perform that role for a traditional publication or an online information service. In fact, we've already seen many mainstream media outlets migrate to the Web and take the credibility they have earned with them.

Today, for example, when we pick up *The New York Times*, the brand conveys a reputation for credibility that is decades old. When we access *The New York Times* over the Internet, that hard-earned credibility is readily transferred to the new medium.

However, with the advent of digital technology, we should pause for a moment to consider two things. First of all, it is relatively easy to forge *The New York Times'* Web site—much easier than it would be to print and distribute a fraudulent version of the actual newspaper.

Second of all, it is not yet clear how the credibility of traditional media—like *The New York Times*—will translate or may be affected by the new information infrastructure in the long term. One of the great advantages of the Internet is that it offers every user the potential to become a publisher. We've already seen more than a few enterprising individuals begin to publish materials exclusively on the Internet and distribute them via electronic mail or over the Web. Consequently, new communities or constituencies of "readers" are emerging that could, in effect, undermine the previously exclusive authority of traditional providers of information.

On the other hand, as new online "publications" emerge that have no analog reference or established reputation to build on, cultivating from scratch the same kind of authority and credibility enjoyed by traditional media may pose a challenge. The transformation of information into "legitimate" knowledge on the Internet is a complex process whose dynamics operate as much outside the realm of technology as within. Overall, with so many sources of information receiving equal distribution on the Internet, there may be a certain leveling of the playing field when it comes to authority of information. Nonetheless, it is more than likely that some form of hierarchy of credibility and authority will evolve on the Internet, but its establishment remains to be seen.

In the meantime, we must address the risk of tampering with the digital raw material itself—the data from which information is gathered and knowledge created—as it becomes subject to increasingly sophisticated methods of digital forgery and instant global distribution.

THE NEW AGE OF CRYPTOGRAPHY

Clearly, as Internet technology becomes more ubiquitous, we will need to build an infrastructure that secures information, assures its integrity, and verifies and authenticates the identity of both the sender and recipient—the latter will be required to determine that the recipient is a legitimate subscriber. With this, we must turn our attention to an area formerly the exclusive province of mathematicians and intelligence services: cryptography.

The most popular type of encryption in use today in the financial industry is called symmetric key cryptography. In this system, the same "key" or "code," is used to both encrypt and decrypt data. The most popular form of this sort of cryptography is called DES, or data encryption standard.

DES, which became the worldwide standard for encryption 20 years ago, may nonetheless not be a perfect solution for securing Internet commerce for several reasons. First, many feel DES is just too simple to break. And, those critics do have a point. As of 1997, the limit on symmetric key export permits only 40-bit algorithms, which, in a number of incidents, have been deciphered using brute-force decryption techniques. Most recently, a brute force attack using computers working together over the Internet was able to crack 56-bit DES. Today's cryptographic cognoscenti recommend no less than 90-bit keys for symmetric algorithm strength, and there is no way of knowing how long this limit will remain adequate.

A second problem with symmetric algorithms involves the need for all parties engaged in secure communication to have access to the symmetric keys. For private, pairwise communication security, each participant needs a key for each possible pair of communicating parties. That requires the distribution in the order of N-squared keys. For even a small company of 50 individuals, that amounts to over 1000 keys. Moreover, these keys need to be securely distributed, which usually rules out the use of the Internet itself for distribution because of the potential exposure of the keys while in transit. Key distribution is the bane of all cryptography-based security methods.

Another solution, a form of asymmetric cryptography called public key, may fit the bill for widespread consumer use. This is how it works: Suppose we wanted to construct a secure method of distributing bank account information over the Internet. First, a bank customer would generate two keys—one "private" and the other "public." The "public key," associated with the recipient, and generally available in an online repository, would be used by the sender to encrypt the sensitive information. Next, upon reception, the bank customer would use his or her "private" key to decrypt the message.

When it comes to authenticating documents, a new digital watermark process designed to help enhance copyright protection might provide some answers. Again, with the relative ease in which digital images can be copied, verifying the source of information and enforcing copyright protection is often a difficult task.

A digital watermark can be embedded in a still image, video or audio, and must be detected with specialized software. It has to be able to resist alteration, yet still be invisible, inaudible, and present throughout the data. When images from the Vatican Library were put online, digital watermarks were used to authenticate their origins, while discouraging unauthorized duplication and display. Unlike its analog counterpart, the watermark can be specific to a particular recipient and, through suitable cryptography, can be made unforgeable. Removal or forgery of watermarks might be a problem unless the image bits chosen to implement the watermark can be unpredictably varied along with the values of the bits making up the digital watermark themselves.

Unfortunately, many of these technological solutions are still in their infancy. In addition, many of the cryptographic programs available are not exactly known for their ease of use, and may be of limited utility to a wide swath of Internet users for some time. Finally, ensuring the reliability of all these new technologies will require the development of an extensive administrative infrastructure. Growing pains like this will become more common as the Internet continues to expand, and we can probably expect many of the debates about cryptography to mirror much of the contentious debate over reform of the Internet domain name system.

ELECTRONIC COMMERCE

Nonetheless, the urgency for reliable cryptographic methods is there. Although many businesses have set up shop on the Web with transactional sites, the majority remain hovering in cyberspace, waiting for the green flag. As bandwidth increases, and online business models develop, security of information is still one of the primary factors preventing full-scale online commerce.

It is no surprise that, in today's wired world, cryptography is most often being applied to the fledgling field of electronic commerce. Despite the remote chances of interception of confidential financial information, such as a credit card number, many individuals still do not trust the security of Web transactions. At this early stage of the medium's development, it is crucial to adopt structures that verify that all transactions are between legitimate and authentic parties.

Some in the industry have already anticipated the need to provide secure cash transactions for mainstream consumer purchases. Companies like Cybercash, DigiCash, and E-Cash are all looking forward to the day when online shopping is commonplace.[2] In fact, it seems that the development of systems that can handle "micropayments" may even engender the rise of new products unique to the online world. Such systems may give new life to the digital version of the "penny novel" so popular around the turn of the twentieth century.

Despite the opportunities for growth in consumer applications for the Web, the leader will be business-to-business commerce. The area where this could reach its greatest potential is in vertical industries like aerospace and automotive manufacturing. To give one example, the Automotive Industry Action Group[3] is currently working on a set of standards and processes that enables suppliers to accept orders electronically. The Internet-based standards they are working on, including provisions for security, will have a huge impact on the industry. Considering that the industry consists of thousands of suppliers, and accounts for about $300 billion in goods and services annually, even if 10 to 15 percent of their ordering were done over the Internet, the effect would be quite significant. Current estimates indicate that about $500 million of business in the automotive industry was done over the Internet in 1996. If Internet commerce takes off in the automotive industry the way I think it can, $20 billion a year by the end of the decade is not out of the question and some estimates (for example, Forrester) exceed $320 billion per year.

Despite this tremendous upside, we need to remember the critical need for securing these transactions. We need to realize that while the amount of hacking needed to steal one credit card number may not be justified to the digital thief, the potential for mischief if many falsified online purchases were to result would almost certainly destroy the utility of electronic commerce. Opportunities for industrial espionage (details of future car models, production costs, and other specifics) raises equally chilling concerns.

THE CRYPTOGRAPHY DEBATE

While the particulars of cryptographic methods may be bewildering, the implications are not. In a nutshell, the conundrum is this: encryption protects the law breaker as well as the law-abiding citizen. It protects both the online shopper and the child pornographer; it ensures the safety of the legitimate international businessman and the international drug dealer. In fact, it seems that we are in a way reenacting the debates many Western democracies had over issues of privacy and civil liberties—except now these debates are occurring in a whole new domain.

Certainly, in the United States, these issues have drawn the attention of both Congress and the executive branch. To address both business' need for security, and the government's need to conduct surveillance for law enforcement, first the Bush, and now the Clinton, administration proposed a series of solutions.

The proposals, once dubbed "Clipper," have undergone a gradual evolution since their introduction in 1992. In the latest iteration, cryptography will no longer be considered a munition—and thus subject to export controls—unless created specifically for military purposes. Second, responsibility for commercial encryption policy will now reside with the U.S. Departments of Justice and Commerce. Finally, and most critically, export of 56-bit encryption will be allowed for the next 2 years, contingent on a company's promise to provide "key recovery" products after that 2-year period expires. In early 1997, in an amendment of the policy, key sizes greater than 56 bits were permitted only if, during a 2-year period, exporting U.S. companies committed to develop some sort of "key recovery" capability.

"Key recovery" refers to establishing a system whereby the "keys" to a cipher will be accessible to the government under suitable conditions (for example, court order). Previous incarnations of the policy had the responsibility for this "key escrow" function residing with the government or government-approved escrow agents.

For several reasons, the administration's original proposal met with heavy resistance from both the information industry and civil liberties advocates. Those concerned with privacy issues questioned whether or not the government could be trusted to act responsibly if they had access to virtually any electronic communication. Considering both past domestic surveillance activities during the civil rights era, and the new potential for abuse by government agencies, it seems that some of these concerns may be warranted.

A second argument against the administration current restrictions concerns U.S. industrial competitiveness. The U.S. computer industry obtained its dizzying lead in computer science in the absence of government regulation. If the government continues to insist that encryption techniques for export be strictly limited, with keys accessible to the U.S. government, potential customers inside and outside the United States may resist the use of such products out of a concern for abusive access to the encrypted information. The U.S. computer industry runs the real risk of falling behind in what is sure to be a key component of future information technology. The extent of the software industry's concern was underscored when Microsoft CEO Bill Gates and Intel CEO Andrew Grove both trekked to Washington in the spring of 1997 to push for liberalization of the government cryptography export controls.

It is important to note that U.S. law does not limit domestic use of cryptography. And already a company has taken advantage of the loophole. C2Net Software, in conjunction with UK Web, has introduced a suite of encryption products they call Safe Passage. Developed entirely overseas in undisclosed locations, Safe Passage utilizes a variety of ciphers, including 128-bit RC4—a cipher that appears to be much stronger than 56-bit DES.

It seems clear to me that C2Net may only be the first of many companies developing encryption software that will relocate overseas in order to export their products worldwide. They may not succeed entirely in this. France, China, Russia, Singapore, and other countries have very strict domestic limitations. Moreover, as the United States discovers that export controls in other countries fail to limit what Americans can access, there might be legislation in the name of law enforcement and antiterrorism which tries to restrict import. I think such a move would be very strongly opposed by civil liberties groups among others.

In addition, reports are coming out of Germany which indicate that companies there are freely exporting 128-bit encryption software, while U.S. companies—under no such domestic restrictions—are barred from foreign sales.

Clearly, there are serious obstacles that the U.S. government must overcome to convince our allies overseas to adopt a "key recovery" infrastructure worldwide. While the United Kingdom and the European Union share many of the same concerns about the unfettered distribution of strong encryption around the world, it seems unlikely that other governments will sanction the use of cryptography that the U.S. government could access but others could not.

On the domestic front, the war over the fate of U.S. encryption policy will be fought in Congress. Ironically, the battle lines in this fight seem to be crossing traditional party loyalties. Proponents of freedom of encryption and the tight regulation of its use and export can be found on both sides of the aisle. In addition, the Clinton administration has found allies for its position among some congressional Republicans.

In testimony before the Senate Commerce Committee, FBI Director Louis Freeh proclaimed the FBI's opposition to unfettered distribution of encryption. "If technology prevents law enforcement from gathering evidence of crimes, it may be impossible to save potential victims—whether the victim is a kidnapped child or the target of a terrorist act."

Indeed, the same technology that protects the international bank from electronic theft protects the international drug lord when he wants to launder his money. DigiCash, in particular, has constructed a cipher so complicated that it can't track how customers spend their money. DigiCash calls its system "one-way privacy," in that funds are only tracked when deposited, not removed.

Interestingly, the international banking system typically cooperates with governments to report transactions above a certain size, so governments don't really need the ability to decrypt such transactions to track them. And as a result, relaxation on the import, export, and use of cryptography to protect banking and other financial transactions is common. It is this sort of spirit of cooperation that needs to be injected into the often absolutist debate over cryptography.

SUGGESTIONS

While some of the problems outlined here are merely pranks (satiric spoof Web sites like Stale, or irritating spam), we need to recognize that the unchecked growth of fraud can seriously undermine the credibility of Net-based services, and ultimately retard the growth and utility of the network. With that in mind, I'd like to offer some commonsense suggestions to combat these problems.

Certainly, the passage of new laws regarding Internet fraud and their vigorous enforcement could be part of the equation. However, simply because your neighborhood has a police patrol does not mean you can leave your door unlocked at all times. Clearly, we need to put tools that can both detect fraud and authenticate identity into the hands of the public.

First, we need to adapt U.S. policy to achieve important authentication and integrity objectives. Plainly, this will mean significant modification to the Clinton administration's position on cryptography.

The U.S. government has taken the lead in encouraging the development of technologies that ensure authentication and integrity (most notably through the support of the work of the National Institute for Standards and Technology and the National Security Agency on the advancement of digital signature and hashing). It is critical that this support extend to encryption technologies as well. It is encouraging to note that the current policy has undergone several changes already, and a basis for some sort of compromise may exist.

Besides helping to reinforce the integrity and authenticity of services provided over the Internet, further shifts in export policy would be welcome to both the software industry and civil liberties advocates.

Next, the United States must take international positions in support of these objectives. Indeed, this may be easier said than done, considering many other nations may not share American cultural biases in favor of the right to privacy. Nevertheless, the U.S. government and its allies should vigorously pursue this goal.

Moreover, the government should encourage industry exploration of cryptographic techniques to achieve these objectives. Just as seed money from ARPA research led directly to the development of the Internet, I believe strong government support of research into advanced cryptographic methods for public use will yield benefits as well.

Finally, it is vital that every user act to help police his or her own digital neighborhood. One of the most wonderful aspects of the Internet is its resistance to regulation and censorship. It is clear that while we are perusing Internet content, we need to act as our own editors.

Don't believe everything you read, see, or hear on the Internet (or any other mass medium for that matter). Be constructively skeptical, and be sure to check facts and confirm sources. If we fail in this effort to "regulate" the Internet for ourselves, it is likely government authorities around the world will attempt to do it for us, using new laws and regulations in ways that ignore the Net's unique nature—like a blunt object, designed to bring it to heel. This would be an unwelcome development, as legislators with legitimate fears, but without first-hand expertise of the Internet, may design regulatory structures and laws that may retard its use, slow the proliferation of new services and, in the worst case, completely destroy its promise as a flexible new, global medium of communication.

NOTES

1. See http://www.dciexpo.com/news/9705/tame.htm for more details.
2. For a more detailed discussion of electronic cash, see Chap. 6, "Banking Without Boundaries," and Chap. 18, "You Can't Declare Cyberspace National Territory."
3. http://www.aiag.org.

CYBERSPACE

THE NEXT FRONTIER?

by Riel Miller[1]
OECD

Few dispute the likelihood that within 20 years the Internet will become as generalized, indispensable, and taken for granted as today's phone or electrical networks. Many commentators also expect this digital Web to become the host for cyberspace, the next frontier.

Remarkably, this new frontier is emerging, not out of the sea like a continent from the earth's crust, but from our collective imagination and technological capability. Mere discovery, however, will not provide a blueprint for future settlement. Cyberspace could turn into a place where people set up shop, build communities, share ideas, and shape the future democratically. Or it could remain a Wild West style outpost where anonymity, lack of privacy, and unsecured communications keep outlaws and high risk takers happy.

Which of these divergent paths will be taken? That will depend largely on what kind of infrastructure develops. Cyberspace will be shaped by a range of structures—physical, economic, legal, social, political, and cultural—that emerge to guide commerce and community building. But when it comes to infrastructure on this scale it will not, nor has it ever been, just a question of building something like the railroads and then waiting for prosperity. Argentina, Russia, and Canada all built railways but the results were hardly the same. Wealth creation and well-being both inside and out of virtual reality will depend on what kinds of infrastructure emerge. Cyberspace is there to be developed, the open question is how.

Two general infrastructure-related questions merit examination:

1. How will technological and institutional problems like network overcrowding, lost messages, and fraud be overcome?

2. How will political choices influence the way businesses, individuals, and governments respond to a world where the flow of information and commerce is seamless, inexpensive, and of high quality?

Making predictions is risky. Both the uses and advances of technology can develop in unforeseen ways. Many inventors—from Thomas Edison to Allan Turing—have been far off the mark when predicting how new technology would be used or what it might achieve.

Yet looking to the future is crucial to avoiding catastrophe and, perhaps more important, to steering a chosen course rather than being carried by the winds of chance. Fortunately, over the past few years there has been a deluge of analysis and debate regarding the Internet and the implications of information technology. This voluminous literature reveals a number of powerful trends and key choices that are likely to shape the answers to these questions. These trends and choices also form the basis for the speculations in this chapter.

BUILDING THE NET

The Net is expected to continue growing at an explosive rate well into the next century. Digital traffic over the telecommunication backbones, the number of connected users, and the range and depth of content will all increase dramatically.

Less certain is exactly how—with which products and institutions—the Net's basic infrastructure will be scaled up to provide:

- The physical capacity (bandwidth, switching, etc.) to handle the huge amounts of digital traffic

- The compatible, interoperable, and sophisticated software (applications, operating systems, and intelligent agents) necessary to link all users in a seamless, easy-to-use and useful Web

- The privacy, copyright, means of payment, and policing safeguards essential for reassuring both suppliers and consumers of information

- The ease-of-use that can integrate the Net into everyday life so that it becomes as natural as switching on a light, dialing a phone number, or driving a car

The many prospective solutions to these challenges can be divided into three categories of infrastructure: operational, functional, and public.

OPERATIONAL INFRASTRUCTURE

In basic components like fiber-optic cables and microprocessors, the technological direction is clear: products will become faster, smaller, less energy-intensive, and cheaper for a given level of performance. In short, large efficiency gains can be expected. But there is no telling what the exact mix of winning products will be. There is strong evidence that a variety of physical pathways will coexist in the realm of data transmission. Twisted-pair, fiber, and coaxial cables will all compete with a wide range of wireless, satellite, and infrared transmission methods. It seems likely that diversity and much greater efficiency will also reign in receiving and transmitting hardware. Our everyday activities will take place surrounded by a wide range of computing devices that are ultra-fast, energy-efficient, and interconnected. These will include wearable digital assistants integrated into our clothing (or perhaps even implanted into our skin); embedded systems that link the special-purpose microprocessors in our car, refrigerator, and briefcase; and convergence machines that combine and network business and household video, audio, and computing.

Similar advances can be expected in basic network protocols and operating software standards. Over the next decade there will be a stampede of companies and self-regulating consortia—from the benevolent Internet Engineering Task Force's supervision of protocols to Sun Microsystem's profit-motivated promotion of Java— attempting to stake claims at the frontier of the Net's operational infrastructure. There are huge incentives to reach agreements,[2] although this next phase will not be as easy to capitalize on as the initial, publicly funded breakthroughs like TCP/IP (U.S. Defense Department Advanced Research Projects Agency) and the World Wide Web's hypertext browser (European Laboratory for Particle Physics). Such standards are essential for a seamless, high-speed Web where everyone can connect easily, and information—from electronic mail and video to specialized applications and digital signatures—flows freely. Without this kind of interoperability the Net would disintegrate into a patchwork of sealed-off cells incapable of creating the network efficiencies central to continued growth and profitability.[3]

FUNCTIONAL INFRASTRUCTURE

A second set of challenges involves the development of the institutional and policy-derived standards, regulations, and conduct codes that will enable optimal use of the network. Three factors, all related to transaction costs, will determine whether the Net actually offers a breakthrough in the way we buy and sell information, goods, and services.

First, the digital world often shows little regard for property rights; others' work is reproduced on a whim, and frequently for profit. Methods for ensuring property protection and deriving revenue from the ownership of copyright material must therefore be made part of the Net's functional infrastructure.[4]

Second, the cost of sharing information or buying and selling depends considerably on the degree of trust among the traders. Without trust, both the risk and the enforcement costs of transactions skyrocket. On the Net, with its global reach and indifference to borders—be they national, cultural, or moral—establishing trust will require knitting together international legal frameworks that offer users a number of features. These include identity verification, secure payment, contract and liability enforcement, ease of delivery, clear tax rules, information transparency, and privacy.[5]

Lastly, unless operating rules, guide posts, and interface design are global, the costs of searching, screening, and navigating the Net will either remain or become (as content expands) too high for many current and potential users. This model of consistency must be comparable to that of driving a car.

All three of these impediments to a functional Net will be overcome within a decade, albeit with varying degrees of difficulty and important variations in the pace and scope of the solutions across countries.

Dependable mechanisms for protecting property and ensuring payment to copyright holders will be the most complex to implement. Here the obstacles are not primarily technological. The major problems will be legal, particularly with respect to the updating of copyright law and obtaining the necessary international agreements. One of the main challenges is to reconcile the interests of the creator/vendor and those of users and society at large in an economically efficient way. On the one hand, the free flow of information and intellectual property is expected to become even more important as we move away from an industrial economy and toward a knowledge economy. On the other hand, stringent copyright law and enforcement could erect so many proprietary roadblocks in cyberspace that the Net could end up hindering rather than helping the sharing of ideas and innovation. Lawmakers will need to devote time and considerable effort to negotiating and implementing both the local and global mechanisms that will reliably and universally signal copyrighted digital products, amend copyright laws in ways that balance competing interests (including those of fair use for public benefit), and fully integrate simple per-use payment systems into Net technology.[6]

The challenges of establishing trust and developing easy-to-use interfaces are both closer to being resolved than the handling of property rights. The Net's functional infrastructure is being swiftly driven forward by powerful commercial interests and advances in information technology. With millions of dollars and market share at stake, private sector initiatives will continue to pressure the sluggish responses and jurisdictional limitations of governments. There are many players, all intent on establishing—as soon as possible—the trust, security, ease-of-use, and dependability upon which everyday market transactions depend. They include banks, credit card issuers, and a wide array of vendors who provide goods and services ranging from merchandise (cars, clothes, books, pharmaceuticals, food) and digitized entertainment (music, video, multimedia, games) to professional (legal, medical, financial) and information services (magazines, newspapers, education, health care). Spurred by the prospect of establishing, conquering, or defending market share (and first-mover profits) in the rapidly expanding cybereconomy, firms are rushing to introduce a variety of functional improvements. These include secure payment and customer redress mechanisms, unassailable encryption, unique digital signatures, easy-to-learn interactive interfaces, privacy safeguards, and rating schemes that allow user standards rather than blanket censorship to regulate access to the Net's contents.

Unfortunately, establishing the rules of the market game may take longer than today's businesses and consumers might wish. For an Internet start-up or an Internet shopper, a wait of 5 years is the same as eternity. Still, getting to the point where Internet transactions are as trustworthy and substantively as risk-free as cash payment for an item at the corner store will probably take a few more years. It will also require close cooperation between the public and private sectors. Indeed, public infrastructure will play an indispensable role.

PUBLIC INFRASTRUCTURE

Tracing the future dividing line between public and private provision of infrastructure is difficult, given that countries differ and the requirements of a new frontier are as yet uncertain. In most cases, five factors will decide which side of that line a particular part of the infrastructure falls on.

1. *Government regulation of competition.* It remains to be seen how governments will establish and maintain competitive conditions in key markets such as telecommunications and computer hardware and software development. If government antitrust policies are effective in guarding against collusion or unfair market dominance, there will be less reason—and less political pressure—for other, more direct forms of public intervention. Strong competition is more than feasible, given the number and diversity of potential players in the private sector. These include phone companies, cable operators, Internet access providers, chip manufacturers, computer vendors, electronic appliance producers, software developers, and a vast range of content providers.[7] Assuming that governments will succeed in encouraging competition and preventing excessive market domination in these many areas, the private sector will undoubtedly provide the lion's share of the Net's operational and functional infrastructure. Everything from electronic mail and cryptographic security to computing appliances and network connections will be offered by a broad range of companies from all over the world.

2. *Ensuring access and trust.* Government will play an important role in determining how to provide universal, equitable and inexpensive access, trust, and interoperability in cyberspace. One country's definition of access can be close to another's conception of exclusion. But not everyone needs to share the same approach and competing models may even provide the opportunity for nations to learn

from one another. Some countries will want to ensure security and access to cyberspace using publicly owned and managed services. Others may trust private providers to ensure affordable connections protected by unbreakable cryptography. Considerable scope exists for mixed public-private consortia to set out the rules and standards and, in certain cases, even direct services such as the oversight, registration, and management of Internet domain names.

Public-private cooperation will also be essential at the international level in order to establish a global commercial code, as proposed by the Clinton administration in mid-1997 in its "Framework for Global Electronic Commerce." Over the next decade, agreements of this type—and the organizations that support them—will be fundamental in fostering trust among producers and consumers. They are vital if electronic commerce is to boom.

3. *Civil rights and responsibilities.*   Again, countries have diverse histories and traditions: some rely more on legal or constitutional frameworks (and the courts) to shape the way rights and responsibilities are exercised, while others depend more on direct, publicly provided services to ensure, for instance, that a citizen's right to privacy is not violated by computerized databases. In the future, as more civic and civil activity takes place in cyberspace the public sector will probably take on new roles. The right to vote, for example, and the right to have a verifiable identity in cyberspace are not yet on par, but there may come a time when expressing one's political views or learning about the views of others will require having a presence in virtual reality. When this comes to pass it is likely that electorates will insist on a strong role (indirect or direct) for government in areas such as cybercitizenship. After all, electoral lists and citizenship are universally the domain of public authorities and are likely to stay that way.

4. *Cyberspace and government activities.*   Cyberspace will greatly affect a number of areas where governments have traditionally played a major role, including taxation, supervision of currencies and financial markets, policing, and national defense. Governments will be forced to confront issues such as the potential erosion of the tax base, as individuals and firms seek cyberspace havens from sales and income taxes; the implications of Net-based credit and electronic-money for national and global financial systems; and the need to streamline customs clearance so as to reduce the transportation costs when ordering a physical good from some far-flung Internet address.[8]

Again, it will take time to work out the exact configuration of national, international, and even local laws and institutions that will effectively undertake tax collection, supervise financial markets, and guard against crime and warlike aggression. In these areas, limited jurisdictional authority and insufficient interest or skill in negotiating international agreements will probably make it difficult for public sector efforts to keep pace with the rapid advances of a seamless global Net.[9]

5. *Cyberspace and government services.* The last factor influencing the dividing line between public and private infrastructure in cyberspace concerns those services that remain, in many countries, outside the commercial sphere. These include health care, education, and social security. For now, the extension of this public infrastructure into cyberspace will consist mostly of traditional services. Governments will pursue Net-based delivery partly for efficiency reasons and partly because there will be a demand, particularly for educational programs and health information.

In the future a dual challenge exists: first, to make sure that the Net provides the privacy, respect for human rights, and universality that are required in these areas; and second, to explore the new models of governance (collective decision making) and social responsibility that are made feasible by a fully operational, functional Net.[10] More ambitious and innovative infrastructures—for example, new ways of organizing risk management funds like public pensions, and administering unemployment insurance and welfare—will only emerge as a result of political courage and foresight. How widespread these qualities will be is impossible to predict.

BEYOND THE NET: GRASPING THE NEW SOCIOECONOMIC POSSIBILITIES

As with any period of significant change it is difficult, yet of considerable importance, to examine how collective political and cultural aspirations might use the Net's potential to reshape society. The impact of technologies that have become intrinsic parts of everyday life (for example, the automobile) varies in societies with different traditions, values, and political preferences. The Net is no different; it opens up possibilities, from the ominous to the utopian, for both developing new social orders and consolidating the old ones.

For instance, the Net is clearly well suited to handling the output of a knowledge economy in which value is derived through exchanging many products and services that are not material. As such, it could play a major role in toppling the already disintegrating mass-production, mass-consumption society so characteristic of OECD countries in the postwar era. Certainly the Net has the capacity to encourage unique products, direct consumer-producer linkages, completely flexible working arrangements, and the easy entry of competitors from all over the globe into geographically dispersed markets. Such developments lead some commentators to envisage a society where the patterns of work and play move away from the fixed time slots and locations of offices and factories, suburbs and shopping centers, urban mass transit, and mass education.[11] Instead of being concentrated in firms, employment could diffuse to wherever wealth creation actually occurs. And wealth creation itself could extend in time and space to wherever and whenever the consumer-producer undertakes value-added activity.

Such reconfigurations of when, where, and how we work and live have already occurred earlier in this century, with the shift out of agriculture and, more recently, away from manufacturing. As befits a new frontier, a vast and creative range of scenarios, reflecting different aspirations and priorities, is emerging.

Some people see cyberspace as a means of developing a more tolerant, democratic, and community-oriented society. With concerted efforts to ensure access, confidence, and competition, cyberspace could enable a considerable transformation in economic and political decision making. Power could be shifted away from managers and political representatives and into the hands of individuals who are directly engaged in adding value and in shaping their community based on personal knowledge and tastes.[12] In such a future society, cyberspace will enable the artisan, the citizen, and the individual worker—rather than today's technocrat, bureaucrat, and employer—to control what they produce and the kind of community they live in.

Other visionaries see the potential of cyberspace to reduce environmental burdens, if "green" values and policies prevail. Cyberspace efficiencies could make possible, even affordably practical, forms of wealth creation that are less environmentally destructive. They could help slash private automobile use (no commuting to work, school, or shopping), cut waste in the delivery of goods and services (better scheduling and pooling for tangible goods, direct download for digital items), and improve energy generation and management.[13] Rendering space and time more pliable and markets more efficient will make it possible to live outside the crush of urban life and mass society without being cut off from the web of information and exchange that makes everyone so interdependent. Combining the global and the local might be doable.

There is also the possibility that participants across a wide range of different types of transactions will become much less anonymous to one another as vast databases, telepresence, and virtual reality unveil exchange relationships once shrouded by the limited availability (or inadequacy) of information on price, quality, and past buyer's experiences. Hidden behind the products on today's supermarket shelves are long chains of production, not to mention people. Consumers could begin to pierce this veil of mystery. Using the Net it may once again be possible to know the cow that produces the milk you drink (but this time without getting your boots dirty). With the proximity enabled by virtual reality it becomes feasible to know the highly skilled artisan that weaves your carpets, writes your software, builds your bicycle, cobbles your shoes, and composes the music you like. A new fabric for commerce and invention becomes possible.

Turning the possible into the probable will not occur without significant and, at times difficult, adaptation on the part of workers, managers, owners, and consumers. The requisite firm, household, and community infrastructure will emerge, in part, as people seek to achieve their political and social goals and, in part, from the pressure exerted by the competitive forces unleashed by the Net's transparency and global reach.

Should the Net succeed in surpassing the current traditional supplier and consumer relationships it may also profoundly alter two critical determinants of the competitive conditions of most markets. The first is the cost of developing a product and then entering a particular sector by becoming a producer. The second is the cost of becoming known or gaining access to buyers, i.e., being able to tap into large pools of potential consumers.

One perspective holds that tomorrow's Net-based knowledge economy may unleash a storm of competition as both the capital costs of entry into a market and the difficulty of establishing recognition and trust on the part of the consumer evaporate.[14] An opposing view argues that slashing information costs is just as likely to spawn massive firms that leverage the Net's capacity to enhance intrafirm coordination (via intranets), product branding and discriminatory distribution channels, in order to achieve unassailable market dominance in a world characterized by information overload.[15] In this latter scenario, producers will continue to band together, even more efficiently and with greater risk of collusion, and the role of experience in building trust and confidence will continue to give familiar employers and suppliers an advantage over the unfamiliar.[16]

Which of these two scenarios prevails will largely hinge on whether or not both suppliers and consumers manage to develop the organizational infrastructure (virtual or not) that can assure inexpensive and accurate sharing of information about quality and price in ways that encourage razor-sharp competition, without overreaching to become cartels. On balance it seems unlikely that the advantages accruing to large, long-standing suppliers due to a proven capacity to coordinate production and inspire consumer confidence will vanish. There may even be the risk that a new amorphous centralization or virtual exclusion (like the cyberspace shopping mall and single-firm intranet that can control entry conditions), enabled by the Net, will end up stifling competition and forestall the emergence of a new, artisanal value chain where the consumer is able to become a producer and enter the market. Once again, politics will make a difference in determining the outcome.

Political Vision and Rules for Radicals

When daily life was structured according to the cycle of the sun and seasons, it seemed inconceivable that other ways of organizing time might exist. But with the arrival of the factory whistle, things changed dramatically. Take the introduction of compulsory schooling, which radically changed both the supply of labor (by keeping children out of the workforce) and the competitive position of previous generations who hadn't been offered free upgrading of their human capital. Or consider the establishment of the Securities and Exchange Commission (SEC), which imposed radical requirements like common accounting and reporting conventions on a wide open stock market.

These radical rules of the industrial age tended to encourage standardization. For example, young people emerged from school with a basic set of cognitive and behavioral skills (reading, writing, arithmetic, punctuality, and obedience). Such uniformity benefited mass-production factories, armies, and centralized stock markets. But it is not the way to make the best use of cyberspace.

As new horizons beckon, it remains uncertain what lies ahead. It remains far from clear what political or social process will lead to the replacement of today's passive worker and consumer, who wait to be told what, when, where, and how to produce and consume, with another way of living and working. We know that fashioning a society of industrial workers from a world of farmers took policies that were radical for the time. Major upheavals were also involved, from wars and depressions to mass migrations and revolutions. It will take leadership, insight, and probably a bit of luck to successfully extend and then go beyond the traditional habits and policies that suited our industrial past. It will take new rules that break with the past and encourage developments as yet unforeseen.

Future public policies—especially those involving frameworks for financial or labor markets—must foster uniqueness and creativity. The new rules must not only loosen many old constraints but also reduce the risks of independence. Otherwise going it alone will remain the rare act of the frontier outlaw or desperate outcast, instead of the widespread way of adding value in a decentralized, artisan society. Tomorrow's radical rules will need to liberate as much as, if not more than, they constrain.

VALUING HUMAN CAPITAL

One area where such new rules are needed is in assessing what people know. In the past, a high school diploma was considered a good indicator of someone's knowledge: it guaranteed basic literacy and dependability. Employment records, gathered from familiar firms in recognized occupations, also told a generally intelligible story about what a person knew how to do. These vague indicators of productive capacity were adequate for old-fashioned white- and blue-collar jobs held for years on end.

They won't do for cyberspace, however, where one of the differences between a thriving settlement and a barren one will depend on reducing the high cost of employee searches, the length of probation periods, and the risk of regular failures in finding the right person for that one-off job. Realizing the full potential of cyberspace will hinge, in part, on establishing standards that provide universal, accessible, and dependable information about what people know and what they can do. Thus, when you need to hire someone to cook for your next dinner party, design and fabricate your wall paper, check the equations in a technical paper, or find the perfect vacation spot—you'll know their track record.

Rules for assessing and making publicly available a record of a person's accumulated achievements and abilities will help people find the producers (artisans) they need. And, such a flexible, tailored system will encourage knowledge investment and accumulation—by both consumers and producers—in its many, often radically innovative forms.[17] For example, with improved information about a person's competencies it becomes possible for the blacksmith-turned-factory-worker-(re)turned artisan to sell his/her skills in the cybermarketplace. Using the information provided by a neutral evaluation service that validates the artisan's competencies, the buyer of such services faces less risk and lower search costs. Spontaneous supply chains become more feasible as the dangers of fraud and failure are reduced.

Somewhat paradoxically, the policy challenge involves finding the conventions and rules that encourage the unfettered world of the imagination. The economic viability of continuous invention is enhanced by open and dependable standards that help to guide transactions and information sharing. Many new institutions, habits, and norms will need to emerge for the radical potential of cyberspace to be fully realized. One is cybercitizenship.

CYBERCITIZENSHIP

Encouraging the creativity made feasible by the Net will likely involve new rules for establishing a person's identity.

At the moment, as all good internauts know, anonymity on the Net can be almost complete. This keeps information costs on the Net to a minimum because there is no extra data attached to the slim profile of the anonymous cybersurfer. But such minimal information also limits both the economic and social development of cyberspace. What if people don't want to be anonymous? Even more important, what happens when a lack of verifiable identity undermines credibility and liability? This is where the information costs of the Net become, at least for the time being, greater than in the material world.

Consider a few everyday ways of using the Net: making a deposit in an Internet bank, purchasing a subscription to a virtual magazine, returning a faulty blender purchased via the Net, or submitting a report back to the home office. Does it matter that a bank has little capacity to verify that you actually are who you claim to be? Does it matter that you have little way of knowing if the bank or magazine really exists and isn't just a virtual scam? Is it an obstacle to buying an item via the Net if you don't know who to go back to if the product is faulty or what laws or jurisdiction apply to the virtual store? Will you think twice before submitting a crucial document via the Net when you know how easy it is for someone to impersonate you?

The answers to all of these questions is yes. In the virtual world of cyberspace, companies and people still need a verifiable identity. Banks don't want to deal with impostors and no one wants to deposit money into, or get their news from, a front operation that pretends to be an established company. People care about the claims made by the manufacturer of the blender they are thinking of buying, and they want clear, enforceable laws on warranty, liability, and false advertising. Everyone also needs to be sure that, when they e-mail the boss or mom, their identity can be easily and dependably established.

Cryptography is necessary but not enough on its own. Encrypted communication and personal keys ensure that identity is not violated once it has been established. But this still does not address the issue of universal access to an easily verifiable identity. This is an area where there is scope for new rules that go beyond business-as-usual to envision a different way of living and working. This is where cybercitizenship enters the picture.

Cybercitizenship must be universal, free, and protected by a strong legal framework that dissuades tampering, falsification, and unauthorized access. One possible approach is to set up cybercitizenship "accounts" (perhaps stored by a national "certification authority") that would contain only the information needed to establish your unique identity and national citizenship. Subsequently, information could be added and modified at your discretion. Except for the basic data and unique name that is set when the account is initiated, the information belongs to you, not the government.

In this way everyone would have access to an identity in cyberspace. Anonymity would still be widespread and easy to preserve, but cybercitizenship would offer an equally simple foundation for privacy and an inexpensive way of verifying that the name you are using is unique (based on a "public" key that is registered) and really exists. Impersonation would still be possible, of course, since "private" password keys could be stolen and unattended computers that have been logged-in on could be taken advantage of. But such impersonation would be made more difficult. Moreover, it would be much easier to verify the existence of other voters, debaters, and friends while in cyberspace. This kind of clear, secure identity is pivotal for the development of both electronic commerce and tomorrow's virtual communities.

Cybercitizenship is a good example of how realizing the economic, social, and political potential of the Net is likely to depend on developing new rules. Many civic rights and responsibilities were won long ago and are now widely accepted; the challenge is to find ways of extending these familiar aspects of citizenship into a new dimension.

GETTING FROM HERE TO THERE

Our political and social infrastructure must be radically transformed if we are to take full advantage of the possibilities opened up by the technologies underpinning cyberspace. But neither market forces nor individual initiative are likely to push through all the changes needed. The inertia of how we currently do things exerts a powerful pull. Consider the following everyday examples. Commuting by car pollutes, takes time, consumes energy, and is costly in terms of physical infrastructure, yet most people take their car to work, to shop, and to play. Even though many people suspect that dangerous pesticides or preservatives may have been added to their breakfast cereal, few have the time, money, or even desire to discover exactly who produced it or what methods they used. Nor do many people worry about how their community might change if the new zoning bylaw is passed.

Too often, given the current culture and incentive systems, the future of our quality of life is a secondary concern. Gathering the necessary information, sharing ideas, and learning enough to make informed decisions are costly pursuits that remain outside the realm of practical, everyday activity. In this context, it is not surprising that most citizens' democratic participation is limited to voting—if they bother to do that. Little wonder that discouragement and cynicism surround many of our political institutions.

New technologies like the Net will not magically cure these ills. At the moment it is uncertain whether cyberspace will actually become a new frontier—not just a new marketplace, but a space for the democratic realization of human aspirations. It may simply enhance the efficiency of existing society without truly transforming it. Will explicit, democratically posed choices shape the future direction of cyberspace? Or will the political process lag too far behind the practical changes and thus miss the opportunity to play a determining role?

Sadly, history has demonstrated that simply discovering new territory does not guarantee either prosperity or advancement of the human spirit. As the Net's operational-functional infrastructure pushes ahead in the next decades, collective choices and the aspirations underpinning them are what will make the difference.

NOTES

1. The opinions expressed here are those of the author and draw heavily from his prior work [see Organisation for Economic Co-operation and Development (OECD), Paris, International Futures Programme Highlight at *http://www.oecd.org/sge/au/highligh.htm* and a series of articles entitled "Rules for Radicals" at *http://www.intellectualcapital.com/*].

2. OECD International Futures Programme, CD-ROM *Future Trends* (www.oecd.org/sge/au/sifploase.htm) (Paris: Organisation for Economic Co-operation and Development), entry 7002 [Dertouzos, Michael, *What Will Be: How the New World of Information Will Change Our Lives* (New York: John Wiley & Sons), 1996, p. 336].

3. Ibid., entries 6863, 6889 [Leebaert, Derek, ed., *The Future of Software* (Cambridge, Mass.: MIT Press), 1995; and EUROBIT, *European Information Technology Observatory* (Frankfurt/Main, DE: European Information Technology Observatory), 1997].

4. Ibid., entries 6859, 6858 [Spar, Debora, and Jeffrey J. Bussgang, "Ruling the Net," *Harvard Business Review*, vol. 74, no. 3, 1996, pp. 125–141; and Bollier, David, *The Future of Electronic Commerce: Fifth Annual Roundtable on Information Technology* (Washington: The Aspen Institute), 1996].

5. Ibid., entry 2093 (Wooddall, Pam, "A Survey of the World Economy: The Hitchhiker's Guide to Cybernomics," *The Economist*, vol. 340, no. 7985, p. 24).

6. Ibid, entry 6858 (Bollier, David, *The Future of Electronic Commerce*).

7. Ibid., entries 2093, 6033 (Wooddall, Pam, "A Survey of the World Economy"; Patterson, David A., et al., "Information Technologies," *Scientific American*, vol. 273, no. 3, 1995, pp. 48–71).

8. Ibid., entry 7002 (Dertouzos, Michael, *What Will Be*).

9. Ibid., entry 6862 (Pyle, Raymond, "Electronic Commerce and the Internet").

10. Ibid., entries 6664, 6860 [Dyson, Esther, George Gilder, George Keyworth, and Alvin Toffler, "Cyberspace and the American Dream: A Magna Carta for

the Knowledge Age," *The Information Society,* vol. 12, no. 3, 1996, pp. 295–308; External Relations Division, OECD, *Labour Management Programme: Global Information Infrastructure,* Global Information Society (Paris: Organisation for Economic Co-operation and Development), 1996].

11. Ibid., entries 6567, 6917 [Hoppe, Maria-Therese, Arno Victor Nielsen, Lyngsø, and Axel Olesen, "Future Communication," (trans. "Fremtiden Kommunikation"), *Fremtidsorientering,* no. 4, 1996, pp. 7–34].

12. Ibid., entry 6093 (Cornish, Edward, "The Cyber Future").

13. Ibid., entry 5929 (Mitchell, William J., *Space, Place and the Infobahn*).

14. Ibid., entries 6862, 6859 (Pyle, Raymond, "Electronic Commerce and the Internet," *Communications of the ACM,* vol. 39, no. 6, 1996, pp. 23–99; Spar, Debora, and Jeffrey J. Bussgang, "Ruling the Net," *Harvard Business Review,* vol. 74, no. 3, 1996, pp. 125–141).

15. Ibid., entry 6625 (Griffith, Martin Wyn, and Bernard Taylor, "The Future for Multimedia—The Battle for World Dominance," *Long Range Planning,* vol. 29, no. 5, 1996, pp. 643–651).

16. Ibid., entries 2004, 2093 [Burstein, Daniel, and David Kline, *Road Warriors: Dreams and Nightmares along the Information Highway* (New York: Penguin Books), 1995; Wooddall, Pam, "A Survey of the World Economy: The Hitchhikers' Guide to Cybernomics," *The Economist,* vol. 340, no. 7985, 1996].

17. For a more in-depth analysis see Miller, Riel, *Measuring What People Know: Human Capital Accounting for the Knowledge Economy* (Paris: Organisation for Economic Co-operation and Development), 1996 (*http://www.oecd.org/sge/au/pubs/measure.htm*).

INDEX